The Egyptian Expeditionary Force
in World War I

LIBRARY OF CONGRESS CATALOGUING-IN-PUBLICATION DATA

Mortlock, Michael J., 1933–
　　The Egyptian Expeditionary Force in World War I : a history of the British-led campaigns in Egypt, Palestine and Syria / Michael J. Mortlock.
　　　　p.　　cm.
　　Includes bibliographical references and index.

　　ISBN 978-0-7864-4871-5
　　softcover : 50# alkaline paper ∞

　　1. Great Britain. Army. Suffolk Regiment — History — World War, 1914–1918. 2. Great Britain. Army. Egyptian Expeditionary Force — History. 3. World War, 1914–1918 — Regimental histories — Great Britain. 4. World War, 1914–1918 — Campaigns — Egypt. 5. World War, 1914–1918 — Campaigns — Palestine. 6. World War, 1914–1918 — Campaigns — Syria. 7. Mortlock, Jake — Correspondence. 8. Soldiers — England — Suffolk — Correspondence. 9. Great Britain. Army — History — World War, 1914–1918 — Sources. I. Title.
　　D547.S85M67　　2011
　　940.4'1241— dc22　　　　　　　　　　　　　　　　　　2010036387

British Library cataloguing data are available

©2011 Michael J. Mortlock. All rights reserved

No part of this book may be reproduced or transmitted in any form or by any means, electronic or mechanical, including photocopying or recording, or by any information storage and retrieval system, without permission in writing from the publisher.

Front cover: (right) Private Jake Mortlock, 1917 (photograph courtesy Mortlock family collection)

Manufactured in the United States of America

McFarland & Company, Inc., Publishers
　Box 611, Jefferson, North Carolina 28640
　www.mcfarlandpub.com

Dedicated to all British, Dominion, and
Imperial soldiers, sailors, airmen, and nurses
who truly served monarch and country.

Table of Contents

Acknowledgments	ix
Preface	1
Introduction: The Middle Eastern Theatre	3
One. Egypt and the Suez Canal	19
Two. The Sinai Peninsula and the Failures at Gaza — The Gateway to Palestine	55
Three. A Change at the Top, Then Success at Beersheba and Gaza	102
Four. Lloyd George's Christmas Present	149
Five. Advance, Delay, Advance: The Judean Hills and the Jordan	161
Six. The Final Stroke	184
Seven. Backlash	227
Postscript: Back Home	235
Appendix A: Participants in the Palestine Campaign	239
Appendix B: Basic British Army Structure	241
Appendix C: Casualties	242
Appendix D: Order of Battle of the Egyptian Expeditionary Force	244
Appendix E: General Allenby's Official Report	249
Appendix F: The Egyptian Government	250
Appendix G: Statement of Aims in Palestine	252
Appendix H: Norfolk Regiment Officers	253

Appendix I: Royal Army Service Corps Officers, 54th (East Anglian) Division	255
Appendix J: Equipment on Company Establishment	257
Appendix K: Field Marshal Lord Allenby's Letter	258
Chapter Notes	259
Bibliography	273
Index	291

Acknowledgments

I am indeed indebted to a veritable host of people — historians, scholars, technicians, inter-library loan librarians, archivists, secretaries, and proofreaders, together with almost innumerable long-deceased soldiers, sailors, airmen, doctors and nurses who created the story I am about to tell.

To begin with I must thank the director of collections management at Boatwright Memorial Library, University of Richmond, James E. Gwin, for his very great kindness in allowing me free access to his office and personal computer for nigh on ten years. To Mr. Gwin's name I wish to add my indebtedness to other kind friends, colleagues, relatives and acquaintances for their contributions. My brother, Richard Mortlock, furnished our father's wartime autograph album, which has proved invaluable. The late P.H. Field provided splendid photographs of the Maltese hospital wherein Private Mortlock was treated.

M. Juliannne Roman encouraged me at my many low points, insisting I not give up, and also contributed much invaluable assistance with the text and indices. My good friend Dr. Emory C. Bogle, a Middle Eastern scholar, provided me with much assistance and kindly counsel. Deborah Govoruhk, administrative secretary at the Department of History at the University of Richmond, gave a great deal of her own time to solving a pagination problem which had plagued this work for years, and her perpetual optimism in my eventual success encouraged me to soldier (no pun intended) on.

I owe a very great deal to the Inter-library Loan Office of the Boatwright Memorial Library at the University of Richmond in Virginia and the two ladies in charge, Nancy Vick and Noreen Cullen, who obtained all the primary source material requested — much of it obscure — with commendable patience and irrepressible good humor. Likewise, the invaluable assistance, advice, and technical expertise of faculty, staff, and student-assistants at the Technology Learning Center of the University of Richmond enabled me to well nigh perfect the layout, quality, and scale of the maps and illustrations. In particular I wish to pay tribute to Dr. Patricia Schoknecht, director of the Center for Teaching, Learning and Technology; Professor Frances White, coordinator of academic technology services; Susan McGinnis, academic technology consultant; and, in particular, Melissa Foster, technology learning center specialist. These women — together with student assistants Michael Frankson, Roberto Ritano, Robert Vigor, Miss Ethiopia (Sonya Anani), Miss Vietnam (Anh Chu), and Robin Haskins — all rendered sterling service in the field of technological expertise. Henrico County Library, Dumbarton Branch, has afforded me use of their facilities and reference research over a total period of a quarter of a century — and for all of this I wish to pay tribute. I am also indebted to Glenn and Thomas Walters for their invaluable contribution in personal computer expertise.

Last, but by no means least, I am deeply indebted to a trio of really good friends — Gene Payne, for reproducing, scanning, and improving the quality of old family photographs to be used in the illustrations; David L. Everette, of A Better Image, worked with great skill and good humor to improve some photographs appearing in this history; likewise, the highly professional cartography of Ernie Winters, of Action Graphics of Virginia, put the icing on the cake. I am also indebted to the last-named gentlemen for so kindly granting me office space within their walls.

Preface

This military history seeks to follow the fortunes—and misfortunes—of the soldiers of the 54th (East Anglian) Division during the Great War of 1914–1918 and deals with their period of service in Egypt, Palestine and Syria. These men eventually had the distinction of being the only white infantry division to remain in the Palestine theater of operations following the German breakthroughs on the Western Front in their spring and summer offensives of 1918, thereby earning for themselves the nickname "Allenby's pets."

All the units comprising the 54th Division ended the war as highly trained veterans—many with four or more years' service behind them. Most had seen action in Gallipoli, some in France; they had fought in all three of the battles for Gaza, the battles of Jaffa, Sharon, and Megiddo (Armageddon), and were largely instrumental in contributing to knocking the Turco-German forces out of the war. Their story has been overlooked. All too often the Australian Light Horsemen and Lawrence of Arabia monopolize the limelight to the exclusion of other crucial elements. The author's aim is to rectify this, while at the same time providing the reader with a history of the campaign as a whole. He makes no apology for extensively using primary source materials—a considerable amount of which was obtained firsthand from his father or his father's fellow combatants in the most horrific war in history.

Introduction

The Middle Eastern Theatre

Once the Great War erupted and the English Channel ports were placed in jeopardy, the waters around the British home islands became the Royal Navy's most urgent concern, but the safety of the Suez Canal was nearly as important, for various reasons. Obviously, the loss of this vital waterway would greatly lengthen Britain's sea communications with Australasia, India, Persia, and the Far Eastern possessions. The British likewise feared that the loss of the canal might lead to the loss of Egypt in its entirety. Although Egypt was far less important to the British Empire than the Indian sub-continent, the British government understood that an Ottoman reconquest of Egypt would amount to a major propaganda coup in the Sublime Porte's attempts to define the war as a pan–Islamic struggle against a Christian coalition. The specter of another Indian mutiny haunted the British and gave the kaiser added motivation for supporting the Ottoman Empire.

The link between Egypt and India became even closer when the British government decided to employ Indian troops to safeguard the Suez Canal. Sir Henry McMahon, who replaced Lord Herbert Kitchener as high commissioner for Egypt when the latter was appointed secretary of state for war, decided against using Egyptian soldiers for canal defense owing to their presumed pro–Ottoman partialities. Two Indian infantry divisions thus constituted the backbone of Great Britain's Egyptian strategy, which established the canal itself as the main bulwark of defense while surrendering the Sinai Peninsula to the Turks.[1]

In the war's infancy the Canal Zone garrison was soon significantly swelled by large numbers of frequently boisterous Antipodean troops—most of whom were fresh from voluntary enlistment, and largely deficient in the barest concept of discipline.

Following the Dardanelles debacle and the evacuation of the Gallipoli Peninsula, the number of troops stationed in Egypt skyrocketed, as will be detailed below. Although for many soldiers this posting was short-lived, the garrison defending the canal was never to revert to its earlier nominal roll and ration strength.

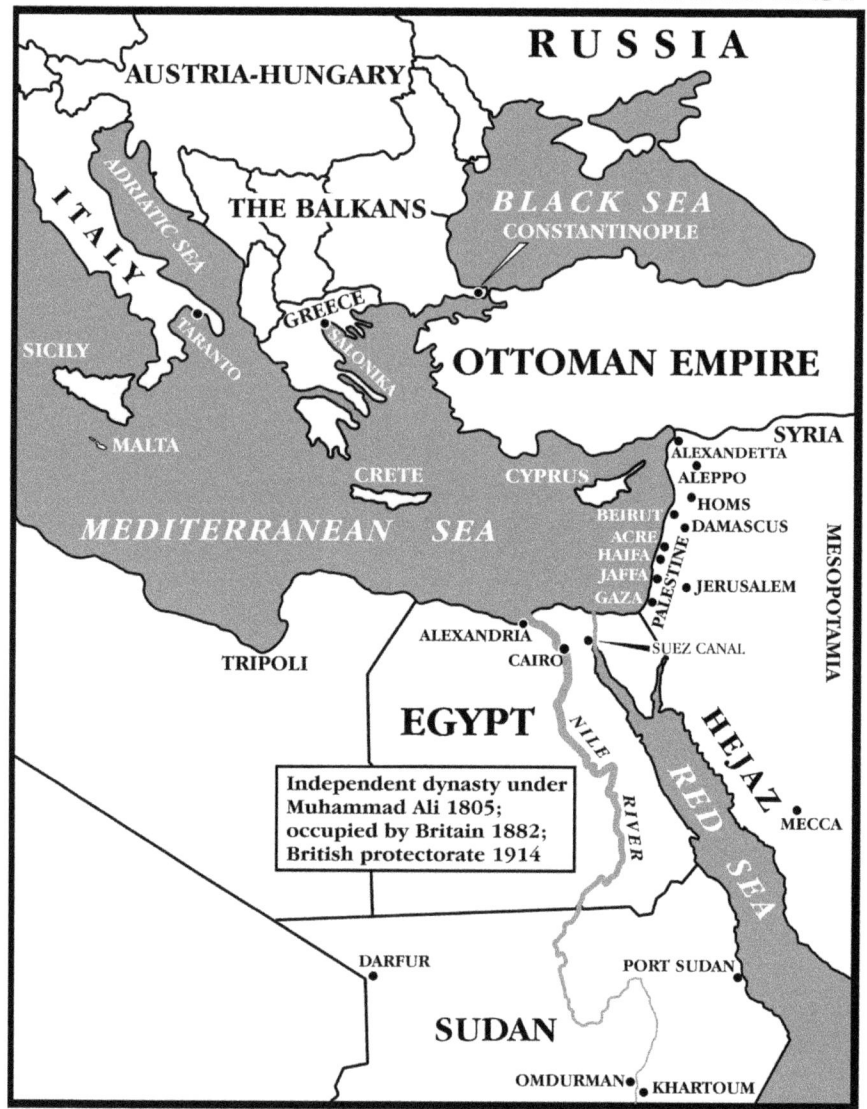

MAP A
EASTERN MEDITERRANEAN & THE MIDDLE EAST

The Reorganization of Commands in the Mediterranean

The Cabinet had waited only for the evacuation of Suvla and Anzac (19–20 December, 1915) to include the Mediterranean in a reorganization of command, which had begun in the Western Theater. Next day, 21 December, General Sir Charles Monro was informed of its scope. He himself, having accomplished the work for which he was appointed — to assess and pronounce a verdict upon the situation on the Gallipoli Peninsula — took command of the First Army in France, vacant owing to the promotion of General Sir Douglas Haig to the chief command. General William Birdwood was to remain in command of the force left on Gallipoli, and General Sir Brian Mahon was to command the Salonika Army, which had now grown to five divisions.

The headquarters of the Mediterranean Expeditionary Force (M.E.F.) had moved to Lemnos from Imbros, a new headquarters being formed on the latter for General Birdwood. Headquarters M.E.F. was now to move to Egypt, from which it was to control and supervise the operations at Salonika. Its most important function was, however, to be in Egypt itself. The War Office considered that General Sir John Maxwell was so fully occupied with the internal military affairs of Egypt and the defense of the Western Frontier that he had no time for the control and reorganization of the large forces which were now assembling in the Canal Zone. For this purpose it was thought necessary to have a separate command, and since the M.E.F. headquarters staff was in existence, it was convenient to employ it. Lt. General Sir Archibald Murray, who had been succeeded by General Sir William Robertson as chief of the imperial staff, was appointed to succeed General Monro.[2]

Lt. General Sir Archibald Murray. Like many of his Western Front contemporaries, he distanced himself from the actual fighting.

Sir Archibald Murray brought with him special instructions from Lord Kitchener, secretary of state for war, regarding the new system of command in the Mediterranean. He was to have his headquarters in Egypt, to command the troops assembling and refitting in that country — plus being responsible for the defense of the Suez Canal; while the force at Salonika was to be under his "general supervision."* He was to make his own arrangements with General Sir J. Maxwell as to what troops were to be under the latter's command for the protection of the Western Frontier and the maintenance of order in Egypt. As to the line of demarcation between the M.E.F. and the Force in Egypt; the general principle was that he should, so far as possible, keep all formed divisions directly under his own orders, while unattached brigades and units should be under Sir John Maxwell's.

---

*It was not explained whether this phrase implied command, administration or training. It actually comprised all these.

During the Gallipoli Campaign and the landing at Salonika, the influx of the sick and wounded rose alarmingly. Hospital bed requirements escalated from 3,500 to 36,000, and 104,000 cases passed through Egypt. While awaiting the arrival of proper establishments from the United Kingdom, Australia and New Zealand, improvised nursing personnel were mobilized to supplement the scanty medical assistance available. The *hôtels de luxe* of the Nile, down to Assouan, were organized as convalescent hospitals in order to avoid the evacuation of the lighter cases to Great Britain and ensure that they should be sent as early as possible after recovery to the reinforcement depots.[3]

A small headquarters, still organized upon the system which prevailed in times of peace, was also burdened with embarkation duties upon a great scale, with the movement of large bodies of troops by rail, with the provision of supplies and stores, and with many other duties for which it had not been devised.[4]

Such were the first arrangements made to meet the new conditions. As early as 9 January they were modified owing to a change of plan at Salonika. Sir Archibald Murray was now informed that the British force there was to come under the orders of the French commander, General Sarrail, for operations, and that his responsibility would be limited to the supervision of administration. Even that function he was to exercise only until the following September, when the Salonika Army became completely independent.

On 9 January 1916 General Murray arrived and took over command from General Monro the following day. He found the Suez Canal a scene of great activity. Fleets of *dahabiehs* had been brought from the Nile to the canal and were carrying stone and railway material to the termini of the roads and railways on the east bank and pipes for the pipe-lines which were run out into the desert at right angles to the line of the canal. Light railways in the delta had been picked up and transferred to the Canal Zone. Hundreds of *dahabiehs* sailed each day from Port Said with impressive tonnages of the aforementioned materials.[5]

The 53rd and 54th Divisions, very weak and without artillery, arrived in Egypt from Gallipoli over a period of days in mid December 1915.[6] The men were so debilitated that "rest, reorganization, training and complete re-equipment were necessary before any campaign that involved marching could be undertaken. For the purpose no better situation than Egypt could have been found. Its climate from November to March is as healthy and invigorating as any in the world."[7]

The formations that left the Gallipoli Peninsula, or the adjacent Aegean Islands, were extremely debilitated, and thousands of men who had been manning the trenches there would, in any other campaign, have been committed to hospitals.[8] The 54th (East Anglian) Territorial Division was no exception, as it left the Gallipoli theater severely depleted by casualties and sickness. "The infantry of the Division left the peninsula nearly 60 percent below stablishment."[9] During their four months' stay on the peninsula the troops had experienced the climatic contrasts of a merciless burning sun and arctic blizzards with some of the attendant afflictions, sunstroke and frostbite. Initially units went to the offshore island base of Lemnos. In the case of the 1/5th Battalion, the Essex Regiment, the soldiers "reached Mudros at noon on December 4th in lovely weather." Then they "had a three mile march to camp, and it was a very weary crowd that toiled so slowly up the hill. The men were as weak as rats and could barely struggle on under the load of their equipment, but they were as cheery as ever." Upon arrival at the camp "they were told off to bell tents, a luxury they had not enjoyed for many a long day. In peace time a bell tent would be considered hardly adequate accommodation for 15 men; but twice that number got into each of those tents and slept the sleep of the just."[10] Their historian also recorded:

> We spent a pleasant week at Mudros playing football [soccer], donkey-riding, and indulging in other rural delights. In the evenings we had sing-songs, organized by that indefatigable padré, Bond. The latter and I rode out about six miles on donkeys to a place called "Therma" where there were some natural hot springs, and enjoyed the indescribable luxury of a hot bath. The natural temperature was just the correct one, and there was quite a decent bathhouse with soap and clean towels provided. It was evidently a very ancient establishment but I could not find out the history of it. The inhabitants, who were mostly Greeks, charged exorbitant prices for everything, except the aforesaid baths, for which there was not apparently much demand.[11]

An Australian soldier, Lance Corporal Thomas Part, and his cobbers also patronized this establishment — let his own words speak:

> *Dec. 25th.* Christmas Day, all happy & contented, visited CONDIAP & PORTHIANOS (our camp was at SARPI). We had an excursion under the leadership of "BILL" to THERMOS, on our way there we climed [sic] over rocky hills. It was a glorious day — a little on the hot side but we were recompensed by having a wash at the ancient hot springs hundreds of years old where the famous HELEN OF TROY bathed. How we enjoyed that wash, words can't express the gratitude we felt for that wash. On this island, run by the GREEKS, a good many slap-dash shops sold oranges, nuts, chocolates, and biscuits, which constituted the main things we could buy, sickly cream and coffee was sold at 2d. [two pence or "tuppence"] a time in condensed milk tins. While on the island we had bayonet drill & schirmishing [sic] & they rocked it hot & strong.[12]

Lt. Colonel Gibbons goes on to relate that "there were nursing sisters at the hospitals and we often walked out of our way to have a look at one. I hope they didn't think us rude, but it was good to see a woman again — and an English one too."[13] On the 13th the Essex boarded HMT *Marathon* and sailed for Egypt.

The 1/4th Battalion of the Northamptonshire Regiment "was withdrawn from Gallipoli, and on 8th December proceeded to Mudros and thence to Egypt."[14] The two battalions of the Norfolk Regiment left Mudros for Alexandria on HMT *Victorian*, where they arrived on 19 December. They were accommodated at Sidi Bishr camp until the beginning of February 1916, when they were transferred to Mena Camp near Cairo.[15]

This, almost certainly, depicts a hospital ship — possibly leaving Gallipoli, or else some kind of deck drill, as all personnel are wearing Red Cross armbands (Mortlock family photograph).

On disembarkation at Alexandria during December 1915 the soldiers' condition fell well short of A1, as the 1st/5th Suffolk's officer-historians put it: "We were all run down and in poor physical shape."[16] Another source stated that of those of that particular battalion who sailed for Alexandria on December 15 aboard HMT *Victorian*, only forty-three were pronounced fit.[17] But at least they "had reached a land of peace and plenty at last!"[18]

The 8th Battalion of the Hampshire Regiment reached Alexandria on 19 December and went to Sidi Bisr Camp. Their historian notes that when the battalion transferred to Mena Camp, Cairo, early in February, "where the Division was collecting, its own artillery now coming out from England with other details, including transport men, whom the battalions had left behind [when sailing for Gallipoli],"[19] as "contrary to general expectation the Divisional Artillery was not detailed to accompany them."[20]

Lieutenant Edward William Bell of the machine gun corps described, in a diary type letter to his family, the arrival at Alexandria.

> *Monday, June 11th, 1 P.M.* ... A thin grey streak due south, resting on the surface of the sea. Some say it's Africa, so does everybody else. Alexandria it is! The noise on board is deafening. But we've miles yet.

Mena Camp. Many of the units of the 54th (East Anglian) Division — including the Suffolks — spent time quartered here.

Blissfully tranquil scene on the Mena Road (both images from Fair and Wolton, *The History of the 1/5th Battalion: "The Suffolk Regiment"*).

2 P.M. ... The houses are clearly seen, the docks, the streets, the well-known lighthouse.

3 P.M. ... We stop outside the harbour, and run little flags up and down a piece of string tied to a pole at the front end of the ship. A pilot comes out to us in a tiny steamer. He takes months to reach us, and we hope he is seasick with the tossing about. But he isn't. He wears a fez, therefore he must be a Turk. He guides us between the mines — at least we are told so — safely into dock. The inhabitants come out in thousands to greet us — I do *not* think. The Pilgrims no longer need their burdens, so life-belts are not only discarded, they are hurled across cabins, and at friends of

long standing. Little motor boats run around us with staff officers in, and ladies in summer white. Pleasure boats, nurses and parasols are abundant. Important Persons board the ship and examine the papers.

4.30 P.M. ... With an effort, for it is very hot, we breathe again, we live, we are on land. We look back from the Quay where we stand surrounded by only too obliging Arabs, and bid a last, long Farewell to the old ship, and wish her many another safe arrival. We are sorry, in a way, to say good-bye. She is a dear old ship, the *Kashmir*. Now we are safe — safe to settle down to peaceful fighting, after having risked the Horrors of War for eight days. In our different ways, we offer up thanks, for "We're all together agen we're here!"[21]

At the turn of the century, American traveler John Stoddard said of Alexandria:

The European quarter of Alexandria is well lighted and possesses many handsome residences. Much capital is invested here and evidences of wealth abound. The future prosperity of the city seems assured. Within its sheltered harbor is abundant sea-room for the largest fleets, and from this ocean gateway railroads now extend to Cairo, Port Saïd, Suez, and the Upper Nile; while at this point the Mediterranean cable joins the telegraph wire along whose metal thread the messages of war and commerce, or tender words of love to distant friends, may be conveyed at lightning speed from Europe, Asia, or America, to the heart of Africa.[22]

The officers and men of the 54th (East Anglian) Division were not without company upon their arrival in North Africa. Egypt already contained a garrison of some 100,000 troops, and all of the British, Imperial, and Dominion components of the Mediterranean Expeditionary Force evacuated from the Dardanelles debacle went to Egypt initially. Many staff officers frequented the best hotels in Cairo — indeed, general headquarters was housed in one. Lt. Colonel T. E. Lawrence, working at military intelligence at the time, related the reaction of a friend and colleague: "More like a carnival," was Deedes's description of Shepheard's Hotel in January 1916.' Even the allegedly easy going Lt. General Sir John Maxwell, general officer commanding Egypt, saw red and officially rebuked those responsible for "the very undesirable state of affairs now existing in Cairo when crowds of idlers in military uniforms throng the streets from morning till night."[23]

Some of the sudden influxes of units were shuffled around to form hybrid organizations. The 54th (East Anglian) Division was allocated to what was known as the "Force in Egypt." General Sir Archibald Murray details this body's components as of 27 January, 1916:

The chief troops then composing the Force in Egypt were as follows: 2nd (now 6th) Mounted Brigade.

> 1/1st North Midland (now 22nd) Mounted Brigade.
> Imperial Yeomanry Brigade (2 regiments).
> 53rd Division.
> 54th Division.
> 2/1st London Infantry Brigade.

Composite Territorial Infantry Brigade.
South African Infantry Brigade (subsequently).
15th (Ludhiana) Sikhs.
'A' Battery, Honourable Artillery Company.
Nottinghamshire and Berkshire Batteries, Royal Horse Artillery, Coast Defence Artillery.
Hong Kong and Singapore Mountain Battery (6, 10-pounders).
2 Armoured Trains.
Garrison Battalions
Motor Machine-Gun Battery.
Naval Armoured Cars.[24]

As Sir Archibald Murray pointed out, eventually most of the Gallipoli army divisions were shipped to other theaters of war, such as Mesopotamia, Salonika, or parts of the empire — Aden and India. Most were posted to the charnel house of the Western Front "the Incomparable 29th Division" — which suffered so heavily in the April landings at Cape Helles, in subsequent battles there, and at Suvla Bay — was one of those decimated on the first day of the Somme, and it went on to lose even more personnel in the Third Battle of Ypres the following year). Those which remained in Egypt later became part of a new creation of 19 March 1916: The Egyptian Expeditionary Force (E.E.F.).

Garrison Life in Egypt

The troops stationed in Egypt had greater opportunities of corresponding with their friends, family and loved ones than had been the case on the Gallipoli Peninsula. Writing to his mother from Egypt in early 1916, Lieutenant Horace William Fletcher, of the Royal Welch Fusiliers, vented a religious vein of perspective.

> I wonder how the thoughts of people are tending in England now. Not so much about the course of the present war as about the world's future afterwards. Do you think that the experience of this war has made the general public realize that there must be other ways of settling points of dispute which are as satisfactory as the way of bloodshed? Ought we not to be praying that the mind of the Church — that great intangible authority — may be led by the Holy Spirit and guided by His power, to stop war henceforward? We know God can do it, that He waits for our co-operation. If man were to make a venture of faith, and believe that there *is* a way (if demanding more patience), such a way would be found. We must believe that our Lord's kingdom on earth is a kingdom of *love*, and also that it is *here*, waiting to be established if mankind will reach up for it. And in this kingdom of love, war and hatred of nation for nation, and man for man, can have *no place whatsoever*. Don't you feel how far this shows us to be from the coming of the kingdom?[25]

The IXth Army Corps, to which the 54th (East Anglian) Division was attached for some of the Suvla disaster, continued, and the 54th was transferred back to its ranks, after serving under General Birdwood of ANZAC fame. Previously it lost the 10th (Irish) Division to the Salonika Expeditionary Force in October 1915, and the spring of 1916 saw the 13th (New Army) Division posted to "Messpot." The 54th now rejoined the force called the IXth Army Corps with Major General (temporary Lt. General) Sir F. J. Davies as corps commander. Major General S. W. Hare commanded the 54th Division.

The early days of their service in the Egypt Force and E.E.F. were ones of comparative bliss in contrast to the horrors and deprivations of the Gallipoli Peninsula. Alexandria, Mesa, Ismailia,[26] and El Kantara were camps where even impecunious infantrymen could indulge themselves, sampling the wares of the bazaar merchants and souvenir-sellers, and be flirted with, tempted, or seduced by delightful *demimondaines* in Cairo or Alexandria. Lieutenant Siegfried Sassoon, M.C., who arrived in the same vicinity a couple of years later, recorded his impressions in his diary: "*February 28* [1918]. Arrived Alexandria after exactly three days' voyage. A clear, gentle-clouded afternoon; blue sea; creamy red-brick terra-cotta, and grey city; wharves and docks with drifting smoke and thickets of masts and funnels. Sunshine, not glaring. Everything breezy, cheerful, and busy. British officers watch it all for a while, nonchalantly — then go below for tea. I also; no more excited than the rest of them."[27]

Following his transfer to No. 1 Base Depot at Kantara, "where the majority of his fellow-officers continued to irritate him, making the camp seem an arid waste of officer mentality," it quickly became for Sassoon the absolute visible expression of time wasted in the war. "The sand and the huts and the tents and the faces, all are meaningless. Just a crowd of people killing time. Time wasted in waste places."[28] Kantara, incidentally, was a small place of only local significance before the outbreak of war. Then, "in due course Kantara was transformed from a small canal village into an important railway and water terminus, with wharves, cranes, and a railway ferry." Also in that location were the vital water filtration plant and main pumping station "capable of supplying 1,500,000 gallons of water daily; reservoirs were installed, tons of stone being transported from distant quarries."[29]

There were indeed many problems that had to be met in that eventual advance across Sinai via Romani, El Arish, El Burg, Sheikh Zowaid, and Khan Yunis, and of them all perhaps the most vital was the water supply. Until discovering the wells at Khan Yunis, Beni Selah, Deir el Belah, and Shellal, the men depended on water from the Port Said branch of the Sweet Water Canal at Kantara for drinking. A plant to filter some 600,000 gallons of water a day was installed at Kantara. The filtered water was pumped through siphons under the Suez Canal into reservoirs on the east bank, then conveyed by 12 inch, 10 inch and 8 inch steel pipes laid in the sand of the desert divided in four sections of about twenty-five miles each, to El Arish and later to Rafa, where smaller lines radiated to the front line south of Gaza-Beersheba.[30]

Lieutenant Sassoon also preserved for posterity his impression of a concert

Ordinary Telegrapher Albert Joseph Brown, Royal Navy, was mentioned in dispatches for his role during the sinking of H.M.S. *Irresistible* in the Dardanelles in March 1915. Although the majority of its complement was rescued, one seaman perished trying to save the ship's cat. Later in life Brown married a French girl in Cairo and did not return to England to live (Mortlock family photograph).

HMS *Irresistible*, Albert Brown's ill-fated battleship (Mortlock family photograph).

party at Kantara, in verse and prose. "One of the most poignant reflections in *Sherston's Progress* comes during the account of a concert party given at Kantara base camp in Egypt just before Sassoon and his men embarked for France in late April 1918. In the lightly fictionalized account, Sherston reflects on how little the brave soldiers expect out of life, huddled around their makeshift stage."[31] Sassoon rather than "Sherston" penned the poem which so very closely echoes the prose version. "The 'Concert Party,' one of the earliest poems included in his next volume of verse, *Picture Show* [1920], was Sassoon's attempt to display a growing attachment to and identification with his men."[32]

Concert Party (Egyptian Base Camp)

They are gathering round...
Out of the twilight; over the grey-blue sand,
Shoals of low-jargoning men drift inward to the sound —
The jangle and throb of a piano ... tum-ti-tum....
Drawn by a lamp they come
Out of the glimmering lines of their tents they come,
Over the shuffling sand.

O Sing us the songs, the songs of our own land,
You warbling ladies in white.
Dimness conceals the hunger in our faces,
This wall of faces risen out of the night,
These eyes that keep their memories of the places
So long beyond their sight.

> Jaded and gay, the ladies sing; and the chap in brown
> Tilts his grey hat; jaunty and lean and pale,
> He rattles the keys ... some actor-bloke from town....
> *God send you home;* and then *A long, long trail;*
> *I hear you calling me;* and *Dixieland*....
> Sing slowly ... now the chorus ... one by one
> We hear them, drink them; till the concert's done.
>
> Silent, I watch the shadowy mass of soldiers stand.
> Silent, they drift away, over the glimmering sand.[33]

The same event is described using an alternative literary vehicle of expression:

> It wasn't much; a canvas awning; a few footlights; two blue-chinned actors in soft felt hats—one of them jangling rag-time tunes on a worn out upright; three women in short silk skirts singing the old, old, soppy popular songs; and all five of them doing their best with their little repertoire. They were unconscious, it seemed to me, of the intense impact of their audience—that dim brown moonlit mass of men. Row beyond row, I watched those soldiers, listening so quietly, chins propped on hands, to the songs which epitomized their "Blighty hunger," their longing for the gaiety and sentiment of life.
> In the front rows were half-lit ruddy faces and glittering eyes; those behind loped into dusk and indistinctness, with here and there the glowing spark of a cigarette. And at the back, high above the rest, a few figures were silhouetted against the receding glimmer of the desert. And beyond that was the starry sky. It was as though these civilians were playing to an audience of the dead and the living—men and ghosts who had crowded in like moths to a lamp. One by one they had stolen back, till the crowd seemed limitlessly extended. And there, in that half-lit oasis of Time, they listened to "Dixieland," and "It's a long, long trail," and "I hear you calling me." But it was the voice of life that "joined in the chorus, boys"; and very powerful and impressive it sounded.[34]

The concert-party concerned "was given by Lena Ashwell[35] (1872–1957), an actress-impresario who had been organizing concert-parties for soldiers since 1914—after initial rejection by the authorities. She and her group struck Sassoon as particularly good and he was deeply moved by their effect on the men."[36] Just after Christmas 1916 part of the 54th (East Anglian) Divisional Artillery, "B" Battery, 271st Brigade, R.F.A. (Royal Field Artillery), on outpost duty at El Shatt Railhead and Gebel Mur, experienced a freak flood, and their historians recorded that: "an enjoyable incident during the flood was caused by the arrival of a Lena Ashwell Concert Party, the lady members of which had to be carried between the marquee and their cars by willing troops."[37] Also with the 54th Division, Lt. Colonel Gibbons, of the 1/5th Battalion of the Essex Regiment, relates that he and his men enjoyed one of Ashwell's concerts.[38] Likewise, Sapper Frederick T. Mills, a Royal Engineer at Kantara Base Camp, wrote on 2 April 1918:

> Was lucky enough to draw a ticket for Miss Lena Ashwell's concert party at the Y.M. [Young Men's Christian Association]. So many wanted to get in besides the lucky ones that the doors and windows were burst in, chairs were smashed in the rush and

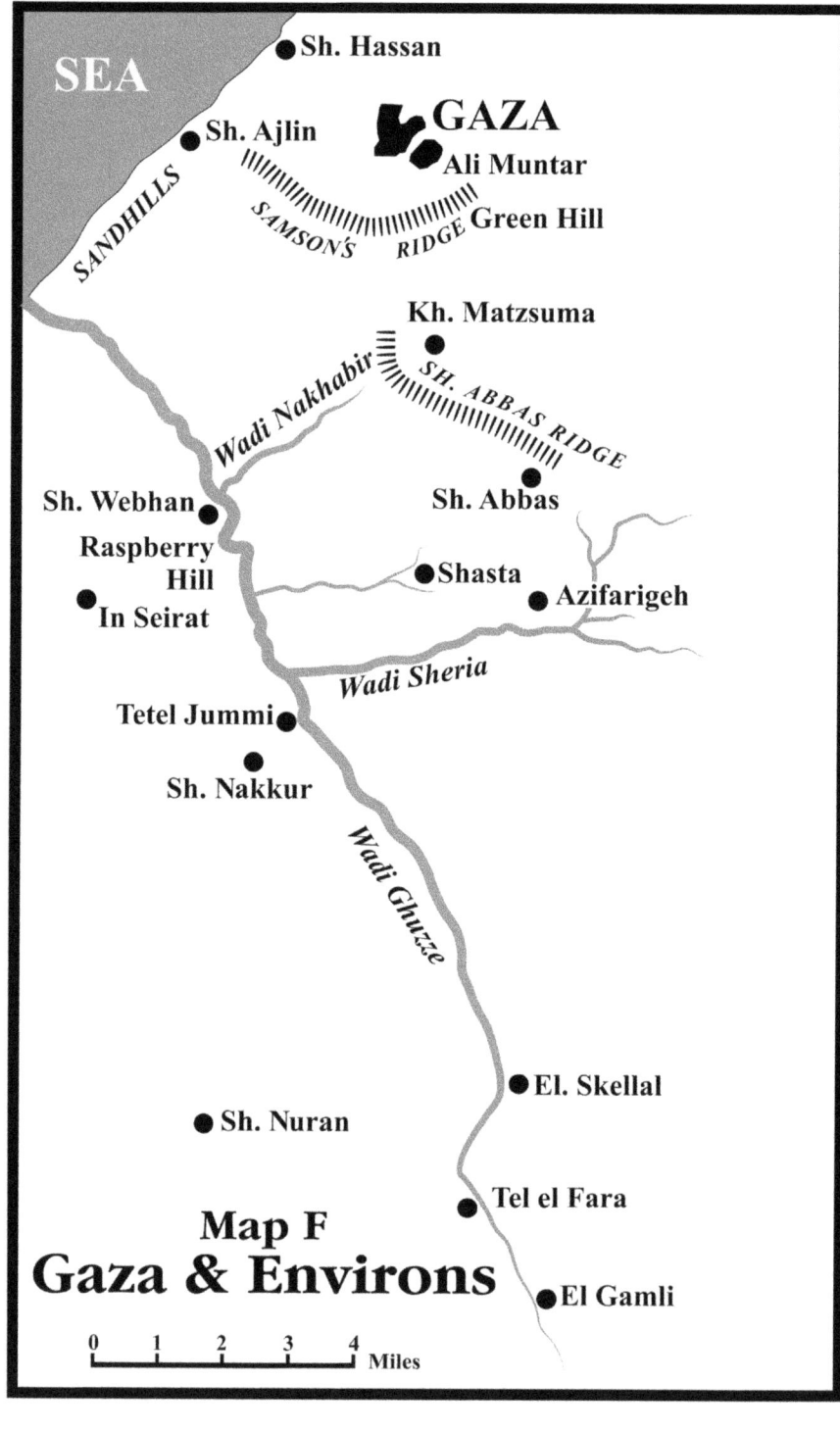

A rural scene in the Nile Delta; note the telegraph poles (Mortlock family papers).

crush inside. I quite expected to see the whole building collapse — and it is not exactly a castle — but all quietened down and the concert was fine.³⁹

Field Marshal Sir Douglas Haig, General Headquarters, British Army in France, writes of his appreciation: "June 1917. The Concerts at the Front, organised by Miss Lena Ashwell, have been a source of endless pleasure and relaxation for many thousands of soldiers. I am personally very grateful for the untiring efforts of those who have contributed to make them such a success, and I know that I am only voicing the opinion of all ranks of the army in France in wishing that your scheme may not collapse through lack of funds."⁴⁰ Lt. Colonel Badcock, of the Camel Transport Corps, related, "The 60th Division had a first-rate concert party — 'The Barnstormers' — and they were very much in request in 1918. I believe many of them were London artistes; certain it is they were extremely good."⁴¹

These pleasant times, however, were numbered, as General Sir Archibald Murray planned a thrust into the Sinai to give greater security to his eastern flank, and successes at Rafa and Magdhaba caused the Turko-German forces to abandon the town of El Arish, bringing the Egyptian Expeditionary Force to the very gates of Gaza.

So, the stage was now set for the first of the battles to capture the ancient city of Gaza — indeed, one of antiquity's earliest known habitations, which had seen conquerors down through the ages seek passage via its time-hallowed portals — Pharaoh Thutmose III, Alexander the Great, and much more recently, Napoleon Bonaparte.

Chapter One

Egypt and the Suez Canal

The history of the 54th (East Anglian) Territorial Division after their arrival in North Africa forms a very vivid to contrast to that of the preceding four months of almost unrelieved misery. Their first camp was also by the sea — but with what a difference. Instead of a beach busy with all the hectic life and bustle of a major sea port; instead of all the urgent haste and frequent interruptions due to enemy shellfire, there was peace! No wharves, no shipping, no communication trenches, and last, but by no means least, no seemingly never-ending carrying or working parties. Instead of stinking dug-outs, the men had tents, open ground, and rolling countryside. Exchanged for the chatter of machine-guns, the continuous crackle of rifle fire, or the boom of the arrival of a shell was a blissful silence. Many-sailed windmills moved gently in the breeze, which added a quaint touch to the novelty of the division's sojourn in the Nile Delta. So placid and peaceful was this new situation, it almost warranted the term "idyllic." The soldiers found many beaches, varied by rocks and coves, ideal for bathing — and free from the constant fear of a shrapnel burst, or the sniper's bullet. Lieutenant Robert Wilson of the Royal Gloucester Hussars, who arrived at Sidi Bisri Camp (where 1/8th Hampshire went after Gallipoli) on June 18, 1916, wrote his mother:

> Just a line to say I have arrived safely after a delightful voyage — we got into harbour last night about 7.30. We hope to stay here for a fortnight, before joining the regiment, in order to acclimatise. The heat isn't half bad — people say that today was as hot as they ever get it and none of us was the slightest bit knocked up, although we disembarked and marched up here in the heat of the day. The nights are lovely — just like a May night at home, there is practically no twilight and the sun sets about 6.45....
> This is a lovely camp, 7 miles from town, on the sands. My tent is farthest from the sea and is not more than 20 yards from it at high tide; we bathe nearly every day.[1]

The large cosmopolitan metropolis of "Alex" was only a *piastre*[2] for the round trip away — although the vast numbers of service personnel standing in line to avail themselves of this form of transport was daunting. Few walked to the tramlines as innumerable donkeys with their "boy" owner-drivers plied and vied for hire. Once the fare mounted, the "boy" ran behind urging or chastising his beast from the rear. In the mile and a half to the tram, many other army camps were passed as well as countless donkeys, camel-mounted Egyptian coastguards, Arabs on horseback, six-horse teams in double tandem hauling service wagons, various motors, and many other sights—all interesting and all for the sum one big *piastre*.[3]

The demand for the tram ride was extremely high, however, and upwards of two hundred soldiers generally formed a queue waiting their turn to board the next one. Once in the city the men saw streets with shops and restaurants all looking very cheery and wonderful, particularly at night.[4] There, too, were women,[5] and men of all kinds and many nationalities, whose diverse costumes made a pleasant change after the universal khaki of Gallipoli. The visiting troops found the possibilities practically inexhaustible, and the ubiquitous boot-blacks, who formed a greater part of the population, unavoidable. Lieutenant Siegfried Sassoon bought a watch in Alexandria to replace the one stolen from him on the train spent overnight on the platform at Taranto station. "It is hexagonal and was very expensive. If anything like the face of the dago who sold it to me, it will let me down badly as regards timekeeping."[6]

The Essex Artillery Brigade's historians, Blackwell and Axe, record the unit's arrival at Alexandria thus:

> Alexandria was sighted low down on the horizon, the white buildings and mosque minarets of Ras-el-Tin appearing to rise out of the turquoise surface of the sea. The steamer arrived just in time to pass into the splendid harbour before the narrow entrance through the protective minefield was closed, thus effectually sealing it against enemy warships or submarines during the hours of darkness. Journey from thence to Cairo:
> The disembarking commenced at half-past 9 in the evening of February 14, and was immediately followed by entraining about midnight, which was quickly carried out: at about 3 o'clock in the morning following our arrival in Egypt our train pulled into Cairo station.

On the morning of February 16, the admirable pair relate: "When all ranks line up for an hour or so for one of the doubly-blessed ceremonial inflictions. On this day, the Divisional Artillery was inspected by General Maxwell, and quite a large number of the troops collapsed with the heat and had to be carried away."[7]

Australian Lance Corporal Thomas Part recorded in his diary:

> *Jan. 9:* Left LEMNOS for EGYPT by the "MINNEWASKA" landed safe and sound
> *Jan. 11:* at ALEXANDRIA.
> *Jan. 12:* Travelled at midnight by open air truck [rail car] cold as— & arrived early this morning at TEL-EL-KEBIR, where our two divisions were to camp. All tents were erected by this afternoon, everyone merry. This place is a sandy desert—a railway runs alongside the camp, also a channel. The train runs to CAIRO and ISMAILIA & the channel water is from the NILE river.[8]

Frank Apperly, a young Australian Rhodes scholar who had recently graduated from Oxford University and enlisted as a medical officer in the British army, described in a medical journal article fascinating detail the work, the climate, the clothing, the conditions, the afflictions, and the temptations appertaining to Egypt: "Owing to the urgency for reinforcements for Gallipoli in July 1915, many green troops had arrived in Egypt unvaccinated, uninoculated and still wearing heavy English uniforms. These men were sent to desert camps for hardening. Here the troops suffered from heat, were bored, and found themselves too close to these large Eastern cities with all their evils."

Medical officers, he goes on to say, soon realized that they required all their ingenuity and all their experience of men to deal with difficulties in a world with which they themselves were unfamiliar. Light cool uniforms had to be obtained (later even these were discarded) though no general order had been given for that purpose, so that much personal work and interviews with minor officials and officers had to be done. Lieutenant Apperly made an early discovery that the higher the rank of the officer, the easier he was to deal with, when that gentleman realized that one was also trying to do his best. Nearly all the loose talk about "brass hats" he found to be "nonsense." He found the only people who created difficulties were the newly joined junior officers still full of self-importance, or perhaps trying to cover up a lack of confidence and experience. Medical officers had to see that troops were vaccinated, which led to trouble with battalion commanders intent on men continuing their training and practicing bayonet fighting on the eighth and ninth days following, when the men's arms were sore and tempers short. This often required much diplomacy.[9]

Although still a long way from home, the men of the 54th (East Anglian) Division managed to celebrate Christmas as far as possible in keeping with tradition. The historian of the 1/5th Battalion of the Essex Regiment related, "On Christmas Day we had football, officers' and sergeants' messes exchanged calls, etc., and Alexandria produced a very respectable bill of fare for the Battalion Christmas dinner."[10] Two days later they came under detail. Shortly after Christmas 1915, because of the activities of the Senussi Arabs to the west, the 161st Brigade of the 54th East Anglian Territorial Force Division was detached from it and detailed to guard the Khedivial Railway line, running west from Alexandria to Dabaa, to prevent communication between the desert and the coast.[11] Some personnel of the 161st Brigade, the 1/5th Battalion of the Essex Regiment, was told off for the village and station of El Hammam, some forty miles from Alexandria, where it also provided a garrison for the armored train which patrolled the track.

The 1/5th Essex historian, Lt. Colonel Gibbons, writes: "The train garrison consisted of Colvin and Scragg with 80 men; also some Egyptian gunners with two old Krupp guns in which they took a great pride. Detached duties are always popular with the men, and the armoured train 'stunt' was no exception. The garrison lived on the train and made themselves very comfortable."[12] He con-

Lieutenant Frank Apperly was an Australian Rhodes Scholar and teaching hospital intern in Dublin who volunteered to serve in the war. He saw service in Egypt, Gallipoli, and London. After the war he resumed his medical career in Dublin, where he met and married the Irish actress Elizabeth Foley. The couple eventually moved to America, where she continued acting for a time and he rose to become professor of pathology at the Medical College of Virginia in Richmond, where his portrait still graces a wall (Lane family photograph).

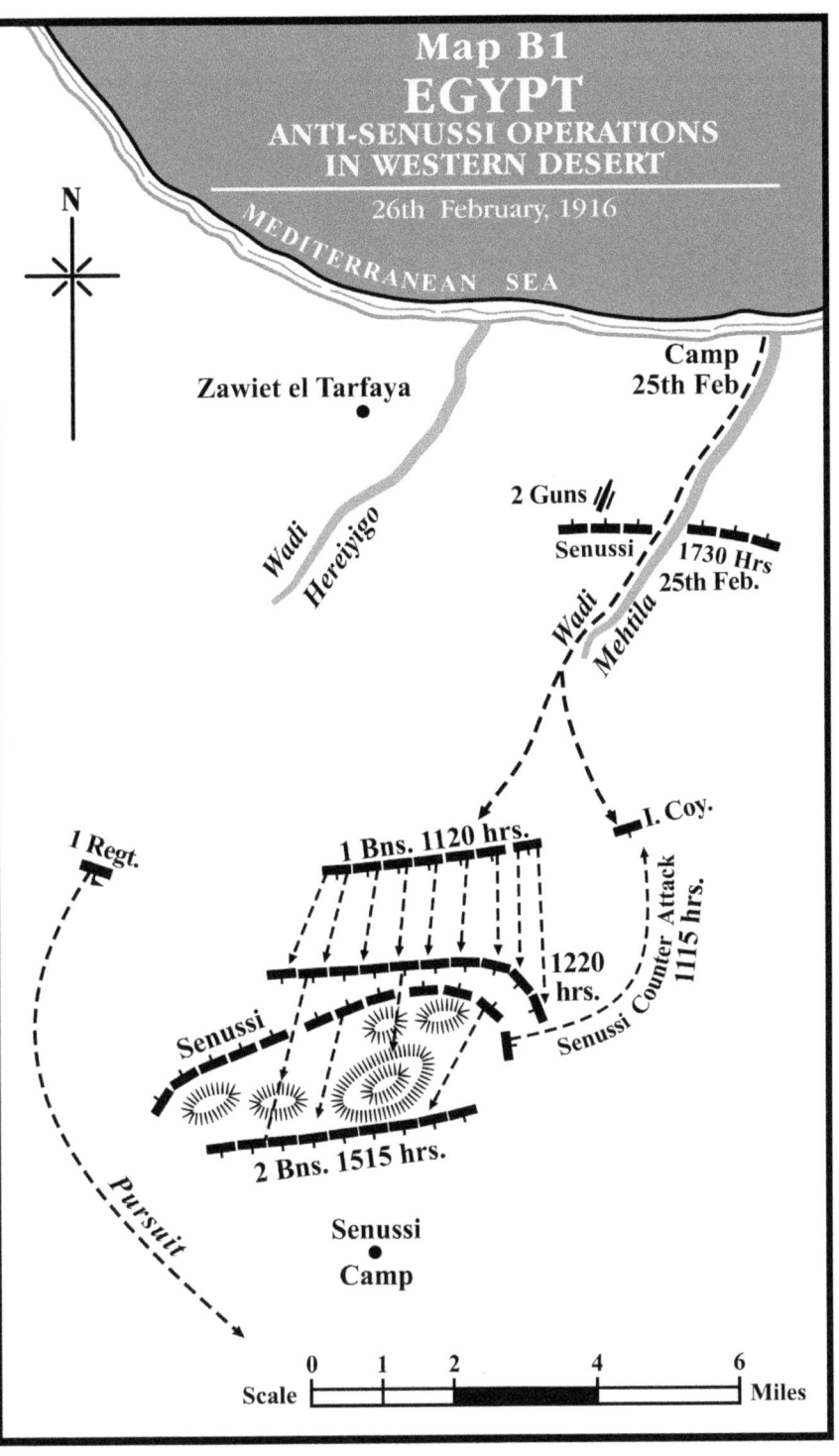

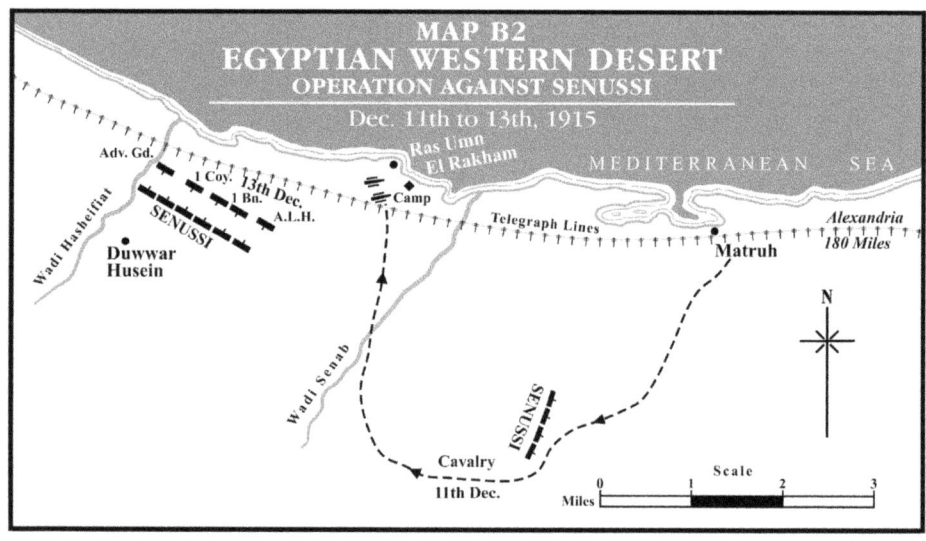

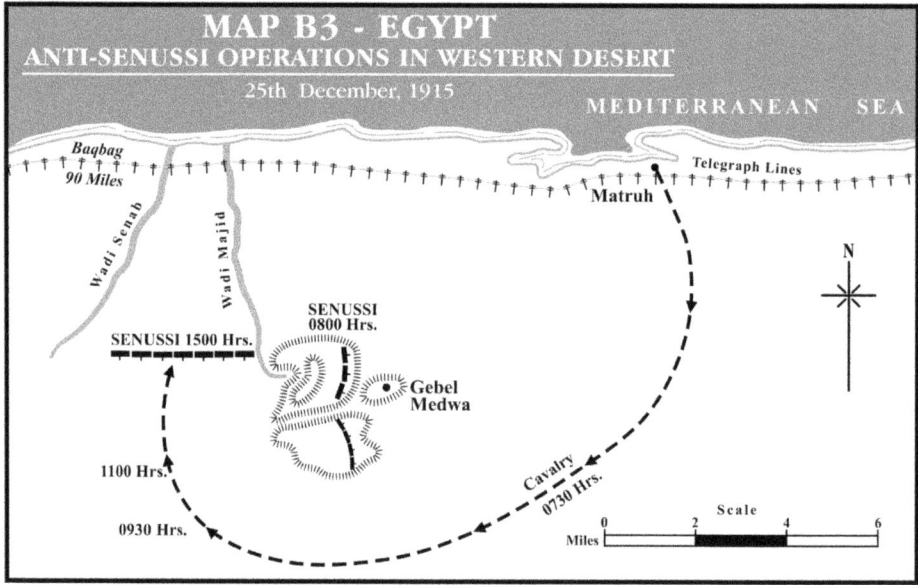

tinues his delightfully descriptive prose: "El Hammam was an important place, with several good wells, a large market, and a railway pumping station. In addition to the armoured train there were two aircraft, an airfield with hangars, thirty-five fast-trotting camels, and a squadron of yeomanry. Plus within a few days some armoured cars joined the garrison which busied itself constructing, and strengthening defences, as well as day and night patrolling."[13]

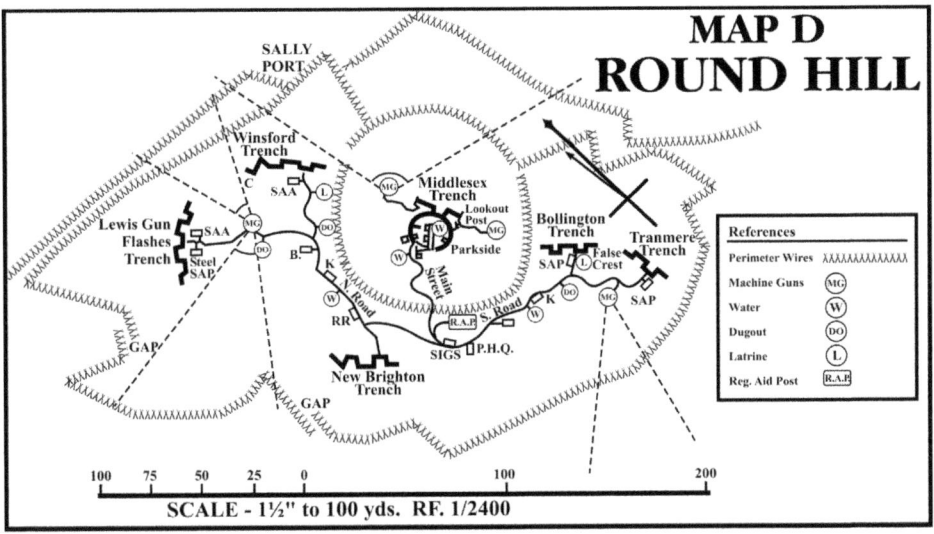

It seems that Captain Walker, of the Brigade Machine Gun Company, had occasion to earn the gratitude of one of the Arabs in the "town," who thereupon invited him to his tent. Captain Walker graciously accepted the invitation, and the Arab, after thanking him for the service he had rendered him (probably gave him firewood or old clothes) offered to give him his daughter as a slight token of his esteem. Walker was taken aback, but thought the proper thing to do was to hand the simpering damsel back to papa, which he did. But Colonel Gibbons heard afterwards that the gift was seriously meant and the family felt slighted, besides being annoyed at the failure to get their daughter off their hands.[14]

Colonel Gibbons changes to another fascinating facet of life out there in El Hammam to the west of the metropolis of Alexandria:

> There is probably more rain in this district than at any other place in Egypt, and storms were fairly frequent, but didn't last long. They were often accompanied by thunder and very vivid lightning. Meteors were common, and some of them were very brilliant. Sentries at night more than once reported "Star shells" in the distance and there was every excuse for that mistake. "A bright light in the desert" was also frequently reported, but generally turned out to be Sirius or perhaps Jupiter rising out of the sand. In England the heavenly bodies are seldom seen until well above the horizon, owing to the vapours in the atmosphere. In Egypt they can be seen actually to appear from the skyline itself.
>
> Sandstorms were much more unpleasant than the rain storms. The sand reached an enormous height and blotted out the sun. Those of us who lived within stone walls had a great advantage over tent dwellers on these occasions.[15]

On January 25 a gale demolished the camp at Sidi Bisr in spite of all the efforts to thwart it. "The gorgeous cinema marquee just erected near the tramway was a mass of shapeless ruin."[16] A week later the division entrained for "somewhere else" in Egypt, and the journey through the emerald green of the Nile Delta gave the many former farm lads composing its ranks an opportunity to study the farm life of that part of Egypt: water-wheels turned by a patient, endlessly plodding buffalo; primitive wooden ploughs sometimes drawn by a ludicrous pair of draught animals, a camel and a donkey; and the swarming life of the native villages.

Although the 54th (East Anglian) Division was now enjoying a healthier environment of Northeastern Africa, one of its personnel, Private Jake Mortlock, of "D" Company, 1st/5th Suffolks, was languishing at No. 1674, Isolation Block, of Imtarfa Hospital, Malta, in the company of other casualties of the Gallipoli disaster — Private Horsford of the 6th Lincolns, and Private Musk of the 5th Suffolks, to name but two, both of whom would contribute to his unique autograph album. Subsequently they went on St. Bartholomew's Hospital, London, and afterwards to its convalescent companion building.

On February 2, 1916, Lt. Colonel Sir Victor Horsley of the Army Medical Services[17] wrote from Egypt to a friend: "As to what we are doing, I can only say that my whole life is spent trying to get order out of chaos, trying to make the aged and incompetent realize that the British soldier *is* a human being."[18]

Writing to his wife from Alexandria on June 20 of the previous year, Sir

Panoramic view of Imtarfa, Malta, with the former Isolation Hospital marked by an arrow. This is where Private Mortlock spent some months beginning in November 1915 (Mortlock family photograph).

One of the entrances to the former Imtarfa Isolation Hospital.

Entrance gateway to St. Bartholomew's Convalescent Hospital, where Private Jake Mortlock and Private William Horsford were nursed back to good health (both images Mortlock family photographs).

Private William Horsford, 6th Lincolns and Reconnaissance (Mortlock family photograph).

Sketch drawn in Mortlock's autograph album by Horsford (Mortlock family papers).

Victor described the deplorable state of affairs faced by the military hospitals in Egypt.

> I had to go into Alexandria to hunt up some X-ray help, since the creators of chaos have poured 160 wounded upon us while we are getting in, and while our X-ray apparatus cannot be fixed up, as they know, till Thursday. This is the history of all the hospitals here; and some have none at all. The public-house loafer at home is far better treated by the nation medically than the soldier who has sacrificed his life. Of course, the usual lie is uttered, "Oh, but this is war." The net result is that the shirker and drinker benefit enormously and the unfortunate wounded are practically told to shut-up. The work as you can understand is depressing beyond words, and the more so as every effort to get better drugs and conditions is criticized and thwarted as if something unreasonable was being asked, instead of the bare essentials of medical treatment.... All my energies are devoted to trying to get our unfortunate men the merest elements of medical care.[19]

At this point it should be noted that on February 14 the 54th's Divisional Artillery arrived at Alexandria from Marseilles after a spell on the Western Front. That this arm had not gone out to Gallipoli with the infantry brigades, but stayed behind in England until November 17, 1915, when it sailed for France.[20] One historian wrote,

> Egypt roused them from their nostalgia, for a little while at least, as they absorbed its strangeness, inspected it critically, enjoyed some of its exotic attractions, and measured everything against the familiar objects at home. They weren't much impressed by the train on which they travelled from Alexandria to Cairo, which was a bit like riding in a cattle van compared with the carriages provided by the London and North Western Railway Company. The rolling stock here was open-ended, to

allow air to cool things down inside, and it looked dangerous to the Englishmen, as indeed it could be if the passengers did not take care: two soldiers were to be killed before long, after falling out when trains were travelling at speed.[21]

The troops arrived at Cairo at dusk, and the Suffolk lads soon found themselves marching towards the "pyramids silhouetted against the sky in the light of the moon."[22] A little later, Lt. Col. Gibbons, of the 1st/5th Battalion, the Essex Regiment, wrote regarding an identical redeployment:

> On the 5th [March 1916] the battalion left by train for Mena Camp near Cairo, where the division, less the 161st Brigade, had been quartered for some time. The journey through the Delta to Cairo was full of interest. The fertile country, crowded with industrious *fellaheen*, was a great contrast to the aridity of Hamman and fully explained the veneration in which all Egyptians hold that most wonderful of all rivers, the Nile. Detraining at 8.30 we were able, through the kindness of some of the English residents, to obtain good refreshment at Abu Ela Station, and marched about ten miles by moonlight through Cairo and by the wonderful Gizeh causeway, to the camp, which was practically overshadowed by the Pyramids. The huge bulk of these most ancient of the world's buildings was immensely impressive. We got in at 1.30 A.M. and put the men into large rush huts, where they slept comfortably. The officers had tents.[23]

The artillerymen of the 54th Division arrived at the main Cairo station in the wee hours of February 15. They detrained, fell in, hitched up, and set off for distant Mena Camp. The column crossed the Nile by the Kasr-el-Nil Bridge, turned around the Ghizeh corner, and entered the four-mile straight road leading to Mena Camp, under the shadow of Cheops' masterpiece and the minor pyramids, the Sphinx and the Valley Temple of Khephren (or the "Granite Temple"), and all the ancient and historical monumental relics of Ghizeh.[24]

It proved to be a twelve-mile march to reach Mena Camp. The following morning the soldiers could admire the pyramids which towered up on a ridge about a mile to the south, as well as enjoy a fine view of Cairo and its citadel in the opposite direction. But as the 1/5th Suffolk's officer-historians observed,

The Sphinx. This and the pyramids were almost in Mena Camp grounds (Fair and Wolton, *The History of the 1/5th Battalion: "The Suffolk Regiment"*).

We sadly missed the sea. Still we found the tram[25] carried us the eight miles to Cairo for half a *piastre*, and on the way were the zoo and the museum. The streets of Cairo were themselves a continual show, with pedlars innumerable, selling carpets, oranges, cigarettes, roses, rabbits, tables, statuettes, walking sticks, cakes, beads, and so on. Uniforms of every kind could be seen, the Mousky and the Mosques provided endless entertainment, and in our two months' stay we did not nearly exhaust the possibilities of Cairo. The zoo was probably the most popular place, and "Said," the hippo, who answered his keeper's call, the most popular personage in it. Next came the bazaar with all its wonders.[26]

Where, in all probability, Private Tim Burlham, and his fellow Black Ace Gang members of "D" Company, 1/5th Suffolks, were already getting their hands in — quite literally.

An itinerant American missionary from Virginia, Dr. W. H.T. Squires, observed:

> It should be said, however, that by the side of the medieval, Moslem, Arabian Cairo, a modern European Christian city is building. The broad boulevardes, ornate private homes of wealth and luxury, the cool green parks and garden spots, the palm-girt avenues with elegant administrative buildings suggest Paris, Lisbon and other handsome capitals.
>
> It is a unique experience to step from one age and civilization into another. Cross a street, walk not an hundred feet, and you pass from the twentieth century to the ninth. It is as though an expert magician had hypnotized you with his wand. Look about! Gone are all the evidences of cleanliness, order, wealth and civilization. About you are squalour, filth, dirt, desolation, ruin and decay. Naked children and mal-

Some of "the Boys of the Old Brigade," members of "D" Company, 1/5th Battalion, the Suffolk Regiment (Mortlock family photograph).

odorous goats fight in the reeking streets for the garbage flung carelessly from windows or doors. From some minaret nearby the be-whiskered, wild-eyed, dirty-skinned muessin (holy man!) calls the faithful to prayer.[27]

For the soldiers this leisurely state of affairs was not to last indefinitely. The red-tabbed deities soon began to take an active interest in the division.

On 8 February, General Maxwell, general officer commanding in Egypt, inspected the 54th (East Anglian) Division, which thereafter commenced training. The weather was not unpleasantly hot, so the soldiers marched, worked, and trained until they felt quite fit again. During this month (February), however, they had their first experience of the *khamsin*—a wind that blows from the south as from a furnace for three days. Fine sand fills the air and darkens the sun. It penetrates everywhere and is the cause of a thirst that is priceless when there are satisfactory ways of quenching it.

Cairo itself was literally "overflowing" with generals at this time — they were as common as the proverbial blackberry in England in a warm September; and in addition the ancient land of Egypt was "split up," so far as military command went, into three. "Split up" really explains the situation, for no one rightly knew the lines of demarcations.[28] The city housed the general head quarters (G.H.Q.) of the Mediterranean Expeditionary Force (M.E.F.), late of Gallipoli — which was then also responsible for the expeditionary force at Salonika. General Sir Archibald Murray was its general officer commander-in-chief (G.O.C.-in-C.). Lieutenant-General Sir John Maxwell as G.O.C. Egypt likewise resided in that city. To carry this lunacy a step further, G.H.Q. the Levant Base, with Major General Edward Altham as G.O.C., was also lodged in Egypt at Alexandria.[29] As one wag, rather irreverently paraphrasing the Athanasian Creed, put it: "The first is incompetent; the second is incompetent; and the third is incompetent. They are not three incompetents but one incompetent, and yet there is not one commander-in-chief, but three commanders-in-chief—the first is incompetent, etc."[30] The immortal T. E. Lawrence, who was still based "in Cairo at this time, working from 9 A.M. to 10 P.M. in the Military Intelligence Office and

Private Maurice Williams, later Captain Williams of the South Staffordshire Regiment (Mortlock family photograph).

One. Egypt and the Suez Canal 33

Hauntingly beautiful timeless street scene of Cairo (Crutchfield family photograph).

sleeping at the Grand Continental Hotel,"[31] would almost certainly have agreed with the above assessment. Indeed:

> One of the most intimate glimpses we get of Lawrence in 1915 is of a grinning second-lieutenant, with hair of unmilitary length and no belt, hiding behind a screen at the Savoy Hotel with another equally unmilitary colleague, softly counting "One, two, three, four!" ... through a hole in the screen. They were counting generals. An important conference was going on in the room, for generals only. His colleague swears to me that Lawrence counted to sixty-five. He himself only made it sixty-four, but one of the brigadier generals may have moved.[32]

Lawrence came to Cairo in 1915 as a young and unconventional second lieutenant in the British Army's Department of Intelligence. Two of his brothers had already perished in the war. Already a leading authority on Crusader castles, and freshly returned from an expedition to unearth Hittite settlements on the Euphrates, he conjured up the idea of enlisting Arabs in Mesopotamia (now Iraq) to undermine Turkish authority in the Damascus region, and broadcast such ideas in the newly-formed Arab Bureau. This group was dedicated to working with Arabs resisting Turkish rule. "If these rudimentary activities could be coordinated," he wrote to his mother, the ensuing Arab revolt would be the biggest thing in the Near East since 1550.[33]

"Later in the war, a *havildar* [sergeant-major] with sixteen men of the 2/3rd Gurkhas and thirteen men of the 3/3rd Gurkhas served under the famed Lawrence of Arabia when they volunteered for a secret mission on camel-back into the Hedjaz with *Bimbashi* [Major] F. G. Peake of the Egyptian Army,"[34] wrote Farwell.

Lt. General Sir Archibald Wavell, in his admirable military history, *The Campaigns in Palestine*, summed up the confused command structure in Egypt thus:

> A preliminary problem to be solved in Egypt was that of command. At the beginning of 1916 there were three separate commands in the country. Lieut. General Sir Archibald Murray had arrived in January to command the Mediterranean Expeditionary Force, lately evacuated from Gallipoli, and now holding the Canal Zone. Sir John Maxwell's sphere of responsibility was then confined to the troops in the Egyptian Delta, the Western Desert, and the Sudan; but he continued to administer martial law over the whole country including the Canal Zone. Major General Altham was in charge of an organization known as the Levant Base, which had been formed by the War Office towards the end of 1915 as a pool of stores of all kinds for the Gallipoli, Salonika, and Egyptian theaters. Obviously this system of three independent commands in a comparatively small area was impracticable, and early in March Sir Archibald Murray succeeded to a united command. At the same time the title of the Mediterranean Expeditionary Force was changed to that of the Egyptian Expeditionary Force (colloquially "the E.E.F."), by which name it was known for the remainder of the war.[35]

The men of the 54th (East Anglian) Territorial Force Division found that Cairo was, if anything, more accessible than Alexandria. Soon they sampled the city's many fascinations, and many — like peacetime actor Major Vivian

Soldiers, camels, and the pyramids. Privates Turner (left) and Mortlock (right) pose on "ships of the desert" (Mortlock family photograph).

Gilbert of the 60th (London) Division, who spent three days leave in Cairo—were photographed on a camel with the pyramids as a background.

Major Gilbert stayed at Shepheard's Hotel[36] and related his impressions:

> After dinner I sat on the veranda of my hotel, sipping strong black coffee and gazing at the ever-changing panorama of the streets. In the distance I could see the lighted lanterns twinkling in the trees of the Ezbekia Gardens.[37] Carriages drawn by fast-stepping Desert ponies with glistening silvered harness, flashed by with a jingling of bells and a cracking of whips. Now and then a luxurious limousine, bearing some beauty of the hareem but faintly seen, veiled and mysterious, would glide through the traffic, silently. Native guides, water-sellers, and vendors of Oriental merchandise, mingled with soldiers in smart summer khaki drill uniforms, their shorts exposing bare knees burnt brown by the sun. From the Mouski came the weird chanting of some endless Arab song. The air was heavy with the penetrating, aromatic odour of the East. I drew a deep breath of contentment and sank back amongst the embroidered cushions in my chair."[38]

In the summer of 1918 Sapper Fred Mills, Royal Engineers, working at the Base Camp, Kantara, wrote in his diary: "*Sunday, July 7th.* Proceeded to Cairo for seven days' leave. Have put up at a very fine hotel, the Eden Place facing Ezbekiah Gardens. A good bed with mosquito net and proper bedroom furniture. Dining room and lounge are very nice. Plenty of palms so pleasant to the eyes after so much sand. We went to Luna Park at Heliopolis, a White City on a small scale, and listened to a band in the Ezbekiah Gardens in the evening."[39]

A young Australian Intelligence Officer, Lieutenant R. Hugh Knyvett, of the 15th Australian Infantry, wrote of his sojourn in Egypt:

> A favourite rendezvous in Cairo was the Ezbekiah Gardens[40] of a Sunday afternoon. There were beauties there from many nations, dressed in the *dernier cri* of fashion, who were tickled to death to be escorted by the bronzed giants from "down-under," and though one failed sometimes to find words that were understood, yet sufficient was said in glance and shrug to make a very interesting conversation. And the Sultan's band was always there to fill in pauses and, in fact, played so well as to be an encouragement to flirtations that were delightful in spite of differences of nationality.[41]

Lieutenant Hugh Knyvett of the Australian Imperial Force, author of *"Over There" With the Australians* (Knyvett, *"Over There" With the Australians*).

Lt. Knyvett also mentioned that a Y.M.C.A.[42] building was located in this pleasure park and that he enjoyed "the best meals I had since leaving home" there, "so here's a thank-you to those ladies and the management."[43]

Early in the war the bulk of the troops that passed through the port of Alexandria were quartered in and about Cairo, one of the most vicious cities in the Orient. The majority of the men were Australians or New Zealanders, vigorous, undisciplined men of the frontier, for the first time in contact with an Oriental civilization. The venereal problem developed at an alarming rate. At a conference of military officers, Y.M.C.A. workers, and Australian Red Cross representatives, it was decided on the establishment of soldiers' clubs. The management was entrusted to the Y.M.C.A., whose funds were to be supplemented from the government and British and Australian Red Cross. A soldiers' club was built on the quay at Alexandria, and the beautiful Ezbekieh Gardens, a park in the very center of Cairo, were leased. Here were an open air theater, a restaurant, and later, an outdoor swimming pool, a gift from America. A cinema, concerts, plays, billiards, roller skating, and a variety of games made this spot the gathering place of soldiers in Cairo. English women presided at the tea counter, and the Ezbekieh became famous throughout the East.

The other great Y institution of Cairo was the Anzac Hostel, which opened in March 1916. This house could normally accommodate three or four hundred men a night, but as many as seven hundred were taken care of on occasions. It was formerly the building of the Cairo Bourse. Its use as a hotel where men on leave could get a clean bed and good food in wholesome surroundings was a great success. The Anzac Hostel was open day and night for three and a half years, not closing until late in 1919. Beside work in training and rest camps of the character indicated above in the vicinity of Cairo and Alexandria and later in the Suez region, the Y undertook a great deal of hospital work at the Citadel, Bulac Dacrour, the hospitals, and other centers where the wounded and convalescents were gathered. Y work in Egypt increased by leaps and bounds. At Alexandria there were nine centers when the war ended, at Kantara on the Suez Canal, and at every point where large numbers of troops were concentrated for training, rest and reorganization.[44]

In its own account of the objectives which developed to meet wartime needs, the Young Men's Christian Association's *Service With the Fighting Men* relates:

> One point of emphasis should be particularly noted. The "homing instinct" of the Association has been almost universally noted by observers. If it began as an instinct, it was developed deliberately. The camp "sing-songs," the entertainments, the canteens, the writing-rooms, the religious services, were all directed definitely to draw men's thoughts away from the hard business of fighting and remind them of home. For those who responded to the appeal, the "hut" presented a golden opportunity to leave behind the hardships and brutalities and meannesses of war and become again a part of the collective conscience of the nation.[45]

However, in spite of the most commendable objectives of the Y.M.C.A. and allied organizations, there were still many who sought out the seedier side of life. This included those from "Down Under," although one Antipodean, New Zealand infantryman Private Alexander Aitken, betrayed a certain sanctimonious apprehension of venturing into the big foreign city:

> I have nothing to say of certain demoralizing, and in some cases permanently ruinous, effects of the night-life of Cairo. For completeness and full understanding something should be said of this, but not by me, incompetent to deal with an aspect of life in barracks more adequately described by others. Cairo at night held no attraction for me. I preferred to practise on the violin in the almost empty hut, the few who might otherwise have been attentive listeners being engaged on other things.[46]

Likewise, the historian of an Australian infantry unit described Cairo's less seemly side as "the loathsomeness of the native quarter, where humanity is to be seen in its grossest debasement."[47] A native son of "the Outback," twenty-year-old Australian Private A. B. Facey of the 11th Battalion, related:

> A lot of lads from our unit used to visit Cairo every chance they got. I would get a mate and go around sightseeing. Cairo wasn't very interesting to me. I was shy where women were concerned, and we had been lectured several times about the bad women who had come to Cairo when it was known that the A.I.F. was there. One lecturer told us that it was estimated that there were some thirty thousand women doing a roaring trade as prostitutes, and the authorities were trying to make them submit themselves for examination for venereal disease. Many soldiers had contracted this dreadful disease venereal disease. The lecturers didn't pull their punches when describing what could happen if you got a dose of venereal disease. So I completely refused to have anything to do with these women.[48]

A great many of the service personnel, however, by way of a contrast to the above, patronized the photographers' studios to leave pleasantly refreshing evidence of their sojourn in foreign parts. These portraits would come to grace many an album, but often were to occasion future frustration due to absence of identity—as in the ones shown.

The Egyptians were soon aware that their country was not occupied by a small British garrison but an immense foreign army engaged in war. The towns were invaded by tens of thousands of servicemen, and while their spending brought great wealth to some it only meant a crippling rise in prices for most of the inhabitants. On the other hand, the uninhibited behavior of the soldiers caused less offense than might have been expected to the urban Egyptians, who are rarely sullen and respond easily to cheerful friendliness. Ronald Storrs records that the Australians were "terrifying but popular." Colonel Elgood remarked that their magnificent physique made them "supermen from another world" but added, rather primly, "Unfortunately the self-control of some of these giants was in inverse ratio to their bodily proportions.... There seemed sometimes no form of temptation, however repulsive, which one type of Australian could resist." However, "the fault was not wholly his: for Egypt pandered gladly to his grosser appetites."

A well-turned-out 5th Suffolk soldier (Mortlock family photograph).

Three 5th Suffolk soldiers (Mortlock family photograph).

Whereas Wellington's armies had been decimated by dysentery, improved sanitation ensured that this was not a threat to the Egyptian Expeditionary Force; its place was taken by venereal disease. As we have seen the sale of alcohol could be restricted and controlled under martial law, but the Capitulations' Treaties imposed upon the Ottoman Empire by the stronger European powers along with contemporary prejudice combined to prevent the same being done for prostitution. In 1916 the average annual incidence of venereal disease was twelve percent for the Expeditionary Force and as high as 25 percent in some units. The failure to deal sensibly with the problem was vividly illustrated by the authorities' inaction in Cairo.[49]

Australian soldiers received quite generous pay—"six shillings a day for privates," which led to them being dubbed "'six-bob-a-day tourists.'" Many preferred the city's flesh-pots to its intellectual delights, and on the eve of "their departure from Egypt—for Gallipoli—a brothel brawl over money became the 'battle of the Wadir,' and the Anzacs burned the place down."[50]

An Australian signaller, L/Corporal Thomas Part, wrote in his diary: "Aug. 1: On Saturday a riot occurred at the 'Wazza' by Aust. soldiers several houses of questionable reputation were burnt down. In consequence of this we were confined to camp thence Heliopolis was fixed as the boundary. On Monday orders were issued that not even officers were allowed out of camp until further notice."[51]

Some six weeks after the Second Battle of Gaza (April 19, 1917) Sapper Harry Bonser of the Royal Engineers (Signals), 74th Divisional Signal Company, was posted back to Cairo (Abbassia Barracks) on "temporary base duty." He recounted his impressions of Cairo thus:

> In my new unit, U.U. Cable Section, I found a couple of enquiringly minded fellows, and we spent many evenings exploring native Cairo. We met with far more courtesy than hostility.
>
> One evening we found ourselves in a kind of courtyard where men were sitting smoking, and where children were playing. In a corner were three or four not-too-fat cats. Dusty—so called because his name was Miller—bought a piastre worth of meat at a little shop and we cut this up with jack-knives and fed the cats. This caused quite a stir. The men made friendly noises, and a number of them offered us sweetmeats. Afterwards in that quarter we were always greeted as, "The *askaris* who fed *pussini*."
>
> There were quarters in Cairo and Alexandria that one doesn't talk much about in decent society. Places where girls sat on chairs outside a door, waiting for hire. I think most of our chaps went to look at them for curiosity. One of their tricks was to snatch a soldier's hat and run into their room with it, in the hope that he would follow.
>
> I knew one man who used to go to see one of these girls every week; if he hadn't a shilling he would take a vest [singlet] or shirt. And she would hold it in pawn until he was in funds.[52]

The gunners of the 54th Divisional Artillery, also in Cairo for the first time, found that "it was only necessary to invest a *piastre* apiece in the Cairo

City tramways, and this magic carpet deposited us at Esbekiyeh, the centre of the fashionable and European quarter of the city of Caliphs, contrasts, exorbitant prices and rare smells."[53] Captain C. E. W. Bean, the official war correspondent for the Australian Imperial Forces, writing in January 1915, gave a more hesitant view of Cairo's attractions. "Cairo with its bright, teeming streets, and amusements descending to any degree of filth, beckoned to the troops in their short leisure hours."[54]

Prior to the evacuation of Gallipoli, the garrison in Egypt was around 100,000.[55] Thereafter the figure shot up. "After the evacuation of Gallipoli there were constant rumours of another attack being contemplated [of another attempt by the Turks to threaten the Suez Canal] and for several months the Australians and New Zealanders were kept in Egypt for the defence of the Canal."[56]

Aussie signaler Tom Part's diary gives a little humorous digression as he and his comrades killed time. "*March 3*. Doing night shift, messages in galore. Billy Watson wanted to know if the time had come for a trip.... Hot. Capt. Fawley slept outside sig.[nals] office. *March 4*. Had to dig the Capt. out of the sand. 'Gott Straffe' these dust storms."[57]

It was said thirteen divisions (approximately 400,000 men)[58] were now available in Egypt, and an advanced line east of the canal was being constructed. There were ample numbers available, so that a large part of the force could be rested and trained, while the remainder was engaged in digging and fortifying the new defences. There were three sections, in each of which was one corps. In the southern sector, front, it was the IX Corps. Each was able to arrange its own reliefs, and periods of rest and of training for its units, so that the tired divisions from Gallipoli were soon in a fit condition to take the field.[59]

During March ten divisions were shipped out of Egypt. Most of these were bound for Marseilles and destined for the Western Front.[60] It also should be pointed out that on "March 19th — Sir John Maxwell handed over his command to Sir Archibald Murray. The Mediterranean Expeditionary Force and the force in Egypt became now the Egyptian Expeditionary Force."[61]

The newly appointed "commander of the British Egyptian army, Sir Archibald Murray, was a capable but unlucky general. For a very short time in the autumn of 1915 he had been C.I.G.S. [Chief of the Imperial General Staff], but at the end of the year he had to make way for Robertson and was sent to Egypt. Accepting his diminished role with a good grace, he made an excellent start in it throughout 1916. After defeating a Turkish force within a few miles of the Suez Canal he pushed forward to the Palestine border, laying a railway line and a water main to sustain the position thus gained."[62]

Lt. Colonel J. W. Wintringham of the Lincolnshire Yeomanry related:

> For months on end we had a monotonous diet of tinned [canned] "bully" beef and hard army biscuit.... Our drinking water had to be heavily laced with chloride of lime to combat the microscopic animal life which it carried. The worst of these was

Bilharzia[63] — a minute liver fluke always present in the waters of the Nile — and the Bahr Jusef which could enter a man's blood stream through the skin of his hands while he was watering his horse and could prove fatal if not treated in time. The bell tents with which we were equipped were no doubt the best that could be obtained in sufficient numbers, but the single sheet of canvas allowed the sun's heat to come through and that heat was sometimes as much as 120 degrees F — twice the normal room temperature in England.[64]

Colonel Wintringham goes on to describe crops grown in the Nile delta and other areas, including sugar cane, cotton, millet, lucerne, some barley; and chicken farmers with their beehive-like incubators. He details forage used for the yeomanry horses — "small quantities of wheat and barley. A large proportion of feed had to be chop — mostly chopped straw [chaff] which was known locally as 'tibn' and was not very nourishing. Our horses lost a good deal of weight and condition. We were very lucky that they kept as fit as they did."[65]

The 1/5th Suffolks did a night march to Cairo on 30–31 March 1916, and entrained at 0200 hours, to arrive at Shalufa on the banks of the Suez Canal after a dismal nine-hour journey in cattle trucks.[66] "The rail journey from Cairo to Suez via Ismailia is no joy ride.... The country in the neighbourhood of the canal and railway is sandy, scrubby desert, with frequent groups of sandhills, and in places quite dense scrub."[67] It was here at Shalufa that they first viewed a desert proper, a limitless expanse of sand, the desert of Sin [the Biblical Wilderness of Sin] that was to be their home for the next nine months.

In April 1916, the 4th Battalion of the Northamptonshire Regiment also moved to positions along the Suez Canal. "And while here Lieutenant Colonel John Brown assumed command, Colonel Curtis being evacuated to hospital."[68]

"In Egypt, scattered outposts in the desert suffered the last indignity;

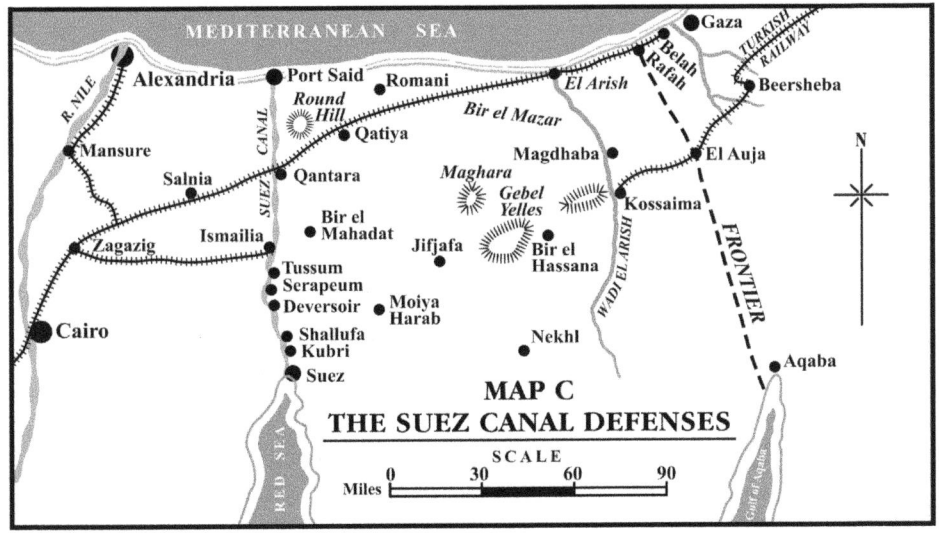

marooned in sand with nothing to do," whereas the men at the bases and in the training camps were brought into touch with Oriental vice among one of the most complex populations on the face of the earth.[69]

There was a permanent pontoon bridge about every ten miles or so along the canal. A light railway ran west to east seven miles to the rail-head; parallel with this was a macadamized road. Australian Intelligence Officer Lieutenant Knyvett wrote:

> From the rail-head, which was also the end of the pipe-line, food and water were loaded onto camels; as I had seen something of camel transport in western Queensland, I was for a few weeks put in charge of camel-loading. Camels[70] are curious beasts and know to an ounce the weight they carried yesterday, and if you attempt to put on them one jam-tin [can] more they will curse you long and loud, end up with some very sarcastic and personal remarks, and then submit to the injustice under protest.... A camel has never really been tamed and they protest against everything they are asked to do. They growl and swear when made to kneel, and make as much fuss again when urged to get up. Their skin never heals from a cut or a sore, but they can have no feeling in it, for the Arabs simply stitch a piece of leather over the place. An old camel is all shreds and patches. They have to be provided with separate drinking-places from the horses, for they put germs in the water that give the horses some kind of disease.[71]

Captains Fair and Wolton, the 5th Suffolk's historians, elaborate on the arrangements pertaining:

> At the rail-head the road split into two, one travelling north, the other south. Each ten-mile sector was, at that time, normally manned by a brigade; one battalion being at the bridgehead and on the banks of the canal; one at the rail-head; and two in the front line about a mile to the east of the road. The battalion at the bridge-head garrisoned the canal posts and provided frequent patrols along the banks. These deployments were to prevent a repetition of the successful exploits of the enemy in laying mines in the canal, and also check enemy agents or unauthorized traffic on the canal. The previous year the canal was blocked for fourteen hours as a result of enemy mine-laying.[72]

The same source states, "Later on, 25th April, while stationed at Geneffe just south of the Bitter Lakes the Prince of Wales [later to become Edward the Eighth for a short time and thereafter the Duke of Windsor for the rest of his life] on a visit to the front embarked from thence."[73]

Lt. Colonel Badcock, in his "Personal Reminiscences" section of his history, also witnessed this event: "His Royal Highness the Prince of Wales was at G.H.Q. for several weeks about this time [March 1916].... I have met but few people who possessed to a greater degree that power of personal attraction which his Royal Highness is so pre-eminently gifted with; no matter who you were or what you were, or however slight the service anyone rendered, his thanks were as sincere as they were gracious."[74]

The Australian signals N.C.O., Thomas Part, also witnessed the royal presence: "March 17. Review of 6th Bde. By HRH PRINCE ALBERT EDWARD (19 yrs. of age). He is the 1st son of HM KING GEORGE. We are the 1st Bde. to be inspected by him & the 2nd Div. leave for FRANCE first. Our old pal LT. GENERAL BIRDWOOD accompanied the Prince of Wales."[75]

It was around this time that Colonel Badcock extolled the virtues of the caterpillar tractor:

> In looking back from 1924 as I write these notes I cannot refrain from recording the persistency with which my then director (Major General F. W. Koe) used in 1916 to advocate the use of caterpillar tractor for tackling the problems of desert transport. Undoubtedly he was on the right "track." We tried many experiments with cars and caterpillar tractors to tackle the question of how best to get over sand; and had we had or been able to obtain sufficient caterpillar tractors and trucks, it certainly would have been an asset of great value. The United States formed the source of supply for our Holt caterpillar tractors, and such few as we had had of necessity to be pooled for heavy guns, the laying of the water-pipe line across Sinai, and a few for supply purposes. Meanwhile our friends the French appear to have tackled the sands of the Western Sahara successfully with Citroën cars fitted with tracks of a somewhat similar principle to the Holt tractor.[76]

Returning to the subject of the Suez Canal, it should be should be borne in mind that — as previously stated — German-led Turkish units under the overall command of German General Kress von Kressenstein had on previous occasions attacked it, even to the extent of crossing it once[77] and placing mines in its waters on another occasion, so it was in reality a front line situation that the 54th Division found themselves in again. Lieutenant Siegfried Sassoon, in the same locality two years later, describes his impressions of the area.

> Here I sit, in a flapping tent close to the main road through the camp. Strong wind and sand blowing everywhere. Nearest tree God knows where! Remainder of battalion arrives tomorrow morning. Our party was getting up tents this morning. After one o'clock I escaped to a lake, about a mile away in the salt marshes where nothing grows. It was quite solitary except for an aeroplane overhead and a flock of flamingoes. Kantara's tents and huts were a sand-coloured blur on the edge of the afternoon.[78]

Digging defensive works in sand is not a simple task. Captain Knyvett wrote in his fascinating account of the Great War, *"Over There" with the Australians*: "In the desert, also, did we dig trenches. No, not the same thing as digging trenches anywhere! For it is really nearly as easy to dig trenches in the ocean. For every spadeful you throw out two fall in, and if, by the use of much cunning, you *do* manage to get a hole dug, then you must not leave it for a single instant, it is only waiting until your back is turned to disappear."[79]

At the beginning of May 1916 the officer-historians of the Suffolks narrated:

> We moved to the front line, eight miles east of the canal; and the Battalion occupied the two posts of Salford and Oldham. Here we experienced our worst *khamsin*. For three days it blew, the temperature in the shade being 122 [degrees F.] and water being short! As the water came by barge, train and camel combined it was surprising it was so regular.
>
> Entrenching was no light task. The sand was so fine that in order to reach a depth

of 6 ft. the sand taken out had to be thrown 12 ft. from the trench. Each trench had to be revetted with boards and matting, and each revetment well anchored and braced. Nature was continually fighting against our work. Even the barbed wire entanglement served to collect sand which gradually rose and threatened to submerge the wire. The trenches were covered with matting while unoccupied, but, in spite of this, required constant cleaning out. The flies increased in spite of all precautions, and the fact that "stand-to" was now at 3.45 A.M. curtailed the hours of rest.... At the end of May the battalion moved, with much baggage, and by a very indirect and badly-timed [route?] to Serapeum rail-head — about twenty miles north. From here it went to the front line, splitting up into company posts at Peter's Peak and Habieta. This was the scene of the Turkish attack on the canal in February 1915. Some cartridge shells and iron-shod hooves of oxen were all the relics that now remained to mark their camps.

Six hours' work per day was steadily carried out on the defences. But the heavy dew quickly rotted the sandbags, and a continual effort to reduce the garrisons and the number of posts to release a mobile force involved constant reorganization and fresh work.[80]

An enemy aircraft dropped some bombs in the locality in mid–June, and the possibility of a further thrust at the canal kept the troops on the alert. This thrust came "in mid–July 1916, [when] the Turks actually launched an attack against the Suez Canal and Egypt. The attack was repulsed without very much difficulty, but it emphasised the disadvantages of a purely defensive attitude in these regions."[81]

About the same time in a more southerly sector, the 54th Division's gunners suffered an air attack. "Early on the morning of July 20 two enemy aeroplanes arrived over the camp, flying at a good height, and proceeded to drop bombs both on the camp [El Shatt] and Port Tewfik opposite. One bomb fell close to our guard tent, severely wounding the N.C.O., Bombardier Warren, and four gunners on duty.... An infantryman, in the custody of the guard alone escaped injury. Two or three bombs also fell in the camel lines close to the camp, thirty-two camels being killed or so badly injured that they had to be destroyed. In addition, seven men were wounded in other batteries (including three natives), one man killed, and ten horses destroyed."[82]

Speaking of airplanes, Lieutenant Robert Wilson, of the Royal Gloucester Hussars, related what the Royal Flying Corps' pilot who was shot down by Australians said: "I would much rather fly over Turkish lines than those of the 'colonials'!"[83]

Lt. Colonel Gibbons, in a paraphrased version, also described the difficulties faced: The routine at the forward posts during the summer varied very little and the revised 'stand-to' time was now the highly unpopular 3:30 A.M. Following breakfast a further two hours were worked by the men, and then they endeavored to rest until 4 P.M., when work was resumed. Generally the nights were cool with very heavy dew.

Private Jake Mortlock said the contrasts between day and night temperatures in the desert were unbelievable.[84] The mornings often dawned with a

Entrenching, showing revetments to prevent sand collapses (Fair and Wolton, *The History of the 1/5th Battalion: "The Suffolk Regiment"*).

thick fog reducing visibility to fifty yards. Frequently it lifted and vanished entirely, only to return about a quarter of an hour later. "This element was never a welcome visitor."[85] Several sources refer to the heavy dews and thick fogs that sometimes actually rotted the sandbags, creating extra difficulty for the troops.[86]

Lt. Col. Thomas Gibbons' *History of the1st/5th Essex in the East* also sets out the vast amount of physical effort needed to maintain the status quo, let alone the expansions, extensions, and improvements the soldiers were called upon to make: "In addition to the fire-trenches huge excavations had to be made for water storage, command posts, dressing stations, etc. Communication trenches six feet deep, with overhead cover had to be provided. Without overhead cover it would have taken the whole garrison all their time to prevent these trenches from getting filled up."[87]

Plans by officers of the 1/5th Battalion of the Suffolk Regiment to suitably mark the Battle of Minden Day — including granting a half day's holiday and obtaining a supply of beer — were thwarted by the higher powers.

> On the 1st of August a great celebration of Minden Day was arranged. The desert blossomed with roses and the camels groaned under their precious loads of cases of bottled beer. But "man proposes and the staff disposes," and we spent the afternoon moving to the rail-head, Serapeum, where Lieut. Col. H. A. Wollaston, D.S.O., Rifle Brigade, assumed command of the battalion, and 2nd Lieut. G. G. Oliver rejoined, and 2nd Lieuts. H. B. Jillings, A. H. Godfrey, and D. Green joined us.[88]

The 54th Division was redeployed in the forward posts screening the Ismailia sector of the canal east of Lake Timsah, moving thence on 4 August

The Battle of Minden on 1 August 1759 was an overwhelming victory by a combined British and Hanoverian army under Prince Ferdinand of Brunswick over the French under the Duc de Contades. The French suffered 10,000 casualties to the Allies' 2,200. The British foot regiments (the 12th of Foot was later to become the Suffolk Regiment) wore roses in their headgear that they had plucked on the way into battle — and still to this day the regiments which took part wear roses on Minden Day. In Bury St. Edmunds, Suffolk, there is a public house called the Minden Rose (Murphy, *The History of the Suffolk Regiment, 1914–1927*).

1916. All the camp's tents were struck, all baggage loaded, and the division marched out of camp at 5 A.M. to the bridgehead, where it entrained for Moascar. From there the troops marched through Ismailia to Ferry Post. The local French band headed the column, and as the soldiers had been exiled on the sands for over four months, it was with keen appreciation that they marched through the beautiful avenues of trees and passed the cool and pleasant houses that bordered them. From the bridge head the contingents went by train or lorry to the rail head, and thence across the sand to posts, where the 1/5th Battalion of the Suffolk Regiment relieved the 2/10th Middlesex and the 2/4th Queens. The relief took place at most posts about midnight, and the battalion, which had had practically no rest or sleep and only scanty haversack rations, felt it had done quite enough by that time. They settled down to occupy the Sphinx, Round Hill, Plateau, and Katoomba posts. The unsuccessful attack by the enemy on Romani was taking place at this time, and this was the cause of the hurried move.[89]

Lt. Colonel Wollaston, Rifle Brigade, was commanding officer of the 1/5th Suffolks from August 1 (Minden Day) 1916 until tragically killed in an air raid on London while on leave in mid–March of 1918 (Fair and Wolton, *The History of the 1/5th Battalion: "The Suffolk Regiment"*).

These Turkish forces, stiffened with strong German elements, made what was to be their last attempt to attack the Suez Canal. Although the enemy assault was eventually routed at Romani in its early stages, the maneuvers met with some considerable success. These serious incursions into Egypt during this period by the enemy to try to sever the British Empire's metaphoric jugular vein are seldom accorded the importance they warrant; for, had Dame Fortune smiled upon these ventures, the outcome of the entire war might well have been much different.

In some interesting asides, Lt. Colonel Gibbons related:

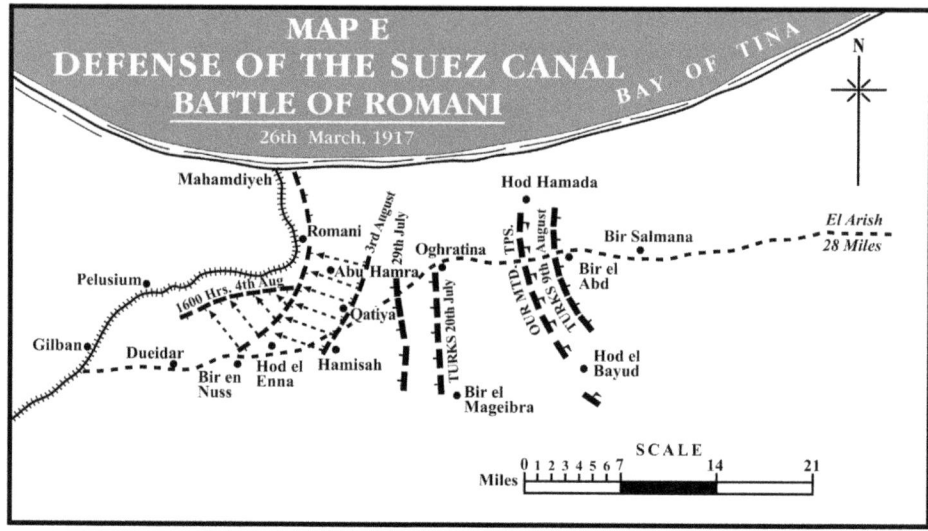

A welcome addition to the amenities of life was received on August 7th in the shape of a gramophone, presented and sent out by the inhabitants of Little Waltham, and accompanied by a very kind letter from our good friend and former C.O., Col. W. Neville Tufnell, D.L.

On the 9th the name of Sergt. W. Chapman (of Thaxted), appeared in orders as having been mentioned in despatches. The 14th was the anniversary of the advance at Suvla and was observed as a holiday. A capital day's sports were arranged, including aquatic sports in the Canal. Route marches in the desert were dull affairs, but excellent training, both in march and water discipline, which afterwards stood us in good stead. Falling out on a route march was looked upon as an indication that the stragglers required further training, and they were sent on an extra trip to Oldham [Post] and back the next day. The party, which was never a large one, was known as "Oldham Athletic" and came in for a good deal of chaff, which probably did as much as anything to reduce casualties on route marches.[90]

It should be noted that on "October 18th.—the troops on the Canal and in the Sinai were now under one commander, as Eastern Force, with headquarters in Ismailia."[91] Shortly thereafter, in October 1916, Sir Archibald Murray moved his headquarters from Ismailia to Cairo. The western frontier of Egypt still lay under the threat of the Senussi force in the western oases; in the Sudan the revolt of Ali Dinar, Sultan of Darfur, had been defeated but not finally liquidated; the fate of the Arab rising in the Hejaz hung in the balance; the functioning of martial law and the internal situation in Egypt required careful watching; finally, General Murray still had some responsibility for the administration of the British force at Salonika.

All these commitments could be more expeditiously handled from Cairo, and the move was perhaps at the time inevitable. But at Cairo Murray and his staff lost touch with the fighting troops. He was henceforward an administrator rather than the commander of an army in the field. He entrusted the conduct of the advance of the in Sinai to Lt. General Sir Charles Dobell, under whom were placed all troops east of the canal, to be known as Eastern Force.[92]

Regarding what Brevét-Colonel Badcock placed under the heading of "Comfort" in his "Personal Reminiscences," read on.

> It may well be urged by some who chance to read these random reminiscences that life at G.H.Q. in the E.E.F., Ismailia (1916), Cairo (1916–1917), Kil-Abd (near Rafa) (1917), and Bir Salem (1918), represented the acme of comfort; and I for one would not contradict them. Certainly we were comfortable, and conversations I've had since those days with others who served in France, Macedonia, Mesopotamia, and East Africa leave me in no doubt that of all the theatres of war during 1914–1918, we in Palestine had the pick of them. We had our share of heat and cold, dust and rain, mosquitoes and sand-fly, but even so we must have been "better off."
> One day in the summer of 1918 I was out at XXth Corps Headquarters at a place called El Fukari, not far from Shellal [Gaza area]. The corps commander's [Lt. General Sir P. Chetwode] mess hut, though simply constructed, might well have been a summer-house on a riverside lawn on the Thames at Maidenhead. I couldn't refrain from comment; then came the corps commander's reply: "A lot of people think that because you are on service you must therefore make your surroundings and all as Spartan as possible. There was never a greater mistake. Take General—; he came up to fight the Battle of—, accompanied by an A.D.C. [Aide de Camp], one blanket, and a tin [can] of sardines. I offered him a tent, which he refused, and he just lay out on the sand with his ear to the telephone. He deserved to lose; no man can win battles when he is directing them under such conditions.[93]

With regard to Ismailia, Captain Oskar Teichman, Royal Army Medical Corps attached to the 1st Worcestershire Yeomanry, wrote in January, 1918: "A two weeks' course for the M.O.s [medical officers] of the Desert Mounted Corps was held at Moascar, near Ismailia, which many of us attended. The pleasant little town of Ismailia was only a couple of miles distant, with its excellent French Club, whose cooking was very much appreciated after the somewhat crude fare we had been accustomed to."[94]

Between August and the end of 1916, the 54th East Anglian Territorial Force Division was deployed at different sectors of the actual canal or in forward outposts in front of it: Serapeum, Toussum, Kantara, Round Hill, Moascar, Deversoir, Gazelle Heights, the Sphinx post, Mount Lofty, and Habieta. It was while garrisoning the four last-named that the 1/5th Suffolk's officer-historians recorded that conditions were now reasonably comfortable, and the desert was wonderfully exhilarating. Christmas 1916 will be remembered by all as one of the happiest that they spent during the War.[95]

> A short service was held at 7 A.M. The cooks provided an excellent breakfast at 8 A.M., and during the morning inter-platoon football matches were played, concluding with the issue of a pint of beer per head. A real Christmas dinner of ham, sausages, green peas, and plum pudding, with another precious pint, made us forget our surroundings for a time. The afternoon saw boxing contests and various sports. Tea produced the luxury of Egyptian eggs, cakes, and oranges, and a whist drive concluded a really enjoyable day. The brigadier concluded his Christmas wishes with

the hope that next year we would be nearer the enemy — a hope that was abundantly fulfilled. Even the weather lent a Christmas touch; a sharp wind, thunder, and heavy hail accounting for a good many tents.[96]

Private Jake Mortlock and a comrade borrowed or hired a couple of bicycles and went AWOL (absent without leave) at Christmastime in 1914. On their return they were charged, brought before the commanding officer, and sentenced to 7 days of confinement to barracks ("jankers" in service parlance) which also entailed mounting nightly with the guard in full battle order. Upon pronouncing the sentence, their commanding officer observed that their conduct was all the more reprehensible because the two men had consumed their Army Christmas dinner at His Majesty's expense prior to going A.W.O.L.[97] The punishment did not, apparently have the desired deterrent effect, as Mortlock absconded on a weekend to attend a party which included his great friend, 2nd Lieutenant Bernard Alexander Powers of the Middlesex Regiment. On this occasion his absence went undetected.

As for "B" Battery, 271st Brigade, Royal Field Artillery of the 54th's Divisional Artillery, its historians related: "At the approach of Christmas, 1916, as on previous occasions, every effort was made to ensure that the festive occasion should be celebrated in accordance with established custom, as far as was possible under the conditions of active service. The battery quartermaster sergeant was charged to procure turkeys and other stores from Suez."[98] The good fellow did his best but the condition of the birds he brought back to camp left a lot to be desired. Not only that, but one perished *en route*— killed by a crate descending on its head, which it had poked out in curiosity. Another died unaccountably, and thereafter the casualties amounted to roughly one a day. Only a few remained with still a week to go so the sergeant was dispatched back to Suez with the remnants,

Private Jake Mortlock's postcard from Colchester (front). The photograph was taken at Colchester — a garrison town since Roman times — when he was 19 (Mortlock family photograph).

The back of Private Mortlock's postcard. The writing refers to the second time he went AWOL (Mortlock family papers).

Lieutenant Bernard Alexander Powers, Middlesex Regiment and the Royal Flying Corps, age nineteen. The photograph was taken just prior to his being posted to France, according to a note on back dated May 1917. Lt. Powers and his aircraft disappeared on Tuesday, 25 September 1917, and no trace of either was ever found. He was officially posted as "Missing" and his poor mother kept his room ready for his eventual return well into the 1920s. Powers was one of Jake Mortlock's best friends, and in Mortlock's own words: "This war has something to answer for." Lieutenant Powers' name is inscribed on the Arras Flying Services Memorial, Pas de Calais, France. It commemorates almost 35,000 aviators from New Zealand, South Africa, and the United Kingdom who died in the Arras sector and have no known graves (Mortlock family photograph).

both dead and alive, instructed to procure birds of a stronger constitution in exchange. He returned in the evening with a number of ducks and small geese, which, by some mysterious methods of persuasion, he had induced the wily poulterer to part with in exchange for the turkeys.[99]

So, when the day finally arrived, these domestic waterfowls were duly cooked. Supplemented with a liberal supply of Japanese beer, the two combined to make the Christmas dinner a great success.[100]

Chapter Two

The Sinai Peninsula and the Failures at Gaza — The Gateway to Palestine

The year 1916 was a fairly peaceful one for the 54th (East Anglian) Division after the rigors of Gallipoli, and it spent it in Egypt proper or along the line of the Suez Canal. The year 1917 would prove somewhat different for the troops literally "On Active Service"—if not for the General Headquarters staff. Rather like the Civil Service, they tended to proliferate. "Even so the size of Murray's staff (662 in early 1917) at Cairo was a byword among all who were who were not members of it."[1]

Kearsey outlines the situation.

1. OBJECT. Our object was still the active defence of Egypt.
2. FACTORS affecting its attainment.

(*a*) *Strength and location of opposing forces.* The enemy in the vicinity of Southern Palestine might be estimated at approximately 1,000 sabres, three weak divisions, providing a total of approximately 12,000 to 16,000 rifles and 74 guns.

Our own troops available for further offensive action would be the 52nd, 53rd, and 54th Divisions, and the Australian and New Zealand Mounted Division, the Imperial Mounted Division, a light-car patrol, and two light-armoured motor batteries, making a total of 8,500 sabres, 92 guns, and 25,000 rifles.

In addition to the Eastern Force just enumerated, there would be the 74th Division, which was being formed in Egypt from Yeomanry units.

Our position at El Arish would enable us to advance on Beersheba via Auja or via Rafah on Gaza. The Turks' main body was disposed about the area Huj-Nejile, with detachments at Gaza, Hureira, Sheria and Beersheba and, as already noted, in the Wadi Arish at Auja and Kossaima to cover their base at Beesheba. Large reinforcements would not be expected, as General Maude was pressing them on the Tigris. Their forces were dissipated in detachments.

(*b*) *Topography.* The area most suited for mobile warfare and for operations of our mounted arm, in which we had a large preponderance, was the coastal Plain of Philistia, about twenty miles wide.

East of this plain are the Judean Hills, which are passable only for a body of troops by the road running from south to north from Beersheba via Hebron to Jerusalem. Through Jerusalem a road runs north-east to Jericho and west to Jaffa. From Gaza, partially metalled roads run by the coast of Jaffa and for thirty-five miles in an easterly direction to Beersheba.

The most important features in this area are the Wadis, which are transverse obstacles, at right angles to our line of advance in a northerly direction. Half-way between Gaza and Belah is the Wadi Ghazze. One of its main branches runs past Sheria and Hureira, and another branch from Esani north-east past Beersheba and south-east to Khalasa and Asluj. It is a formidable obstacle, as its sides are very steep, and its bed is stony in places. It is 300 yards wide. Water can be found by digging near the coast, and there are springs at Jemmi, Khalasa, Asluj, and Esani. These water supplies, when developed, are invaluable for a mounted force advancing on Beersheba.

An important point to be noted for the use of cavalry is the nature of the country between Sheria and Beersheba, where, owing to the Judean foothills, it is rocky, and is consequently not so suitable for mounted action as it is in the downs west of Sheria.

South of the Wadi Ghazze there is excellent cover for troops advancing in a northerly direction. At In Seirat Hill, four miles east of the coast, there is a dominating position commanding a view over the Wadi Ghazze, and over the ground north of it. Gaza stands on an irrigated plateau, with a series of ridges surrounded by high cactus hedges, which make a very strong natural obstacle against advancing infantry, and in which were valuable machine-gun nests for the Turks.

The centre of this town is about 4,000 yards from the sea. West of the road from Gaza to Belah there is a long sandy ridge running south-west. This we named Samson Ridge. The highest point on it, 4,000 yards from the centre of Gaza, is a hill which we called Umbrella Hill. About a mile south-east of Gaza is Ali Muntar, 270 feet high. This hill dominates the town, and its occupation by our troops should make Gaza untenable for the Turks. From Ali Muntar are two ridges running south to the Wadi Ghazze.

The western one is called Sire, and the eastern one is Burjabye. From Ali Muntar we named the points on Sire Ridge, Outpost, Lees, and Kurd Hills respectively from north to south in this order. Six thousand yards south-east of Ali Muntar is Sheikh Abbas, which forms a salient running west along Mansura to Kurd Hill, and south to the Wadi Ghazze.[2]

About this time Private Mortlock (who spent most of 1916 recovering and convalescing from his near-death experiences) received a second parcel of disappointment (the first was on Gallipoli) from his Aunt Kate containing not tinned cake, jars of preserves, cigarettes, or even local newspapers—but another batch of the highly moral, decidedly innocuous, and definitely juvenile periodical, *The Little Gleaner*.* Mortlock related how, in spite of everyone's initial reaction, his comrades-in-arms each accepted an issue of this publication: "They were glad of something to read."[3]

On January 26, 54th Divisional maneuvers were held on the desert, and the 54th Division's artillery deployed at the site of the Battle of Tel el Kebir—an occasion which afforded an opportunity of testing the efficiency of both bars and pedrails (employed to assist the movement of guns and limbers through the areas of deep sand). The latter proved to be a continual source of annoyance owing to the breakage of chains, with the result that the whole contrivance fell

---

*The timing is uncertain, as it is now thought that Mortlock returned to the theater of war after extensive convalescence possibly as late as 16 February 1917. His autograph book has an entry dated 20 February 1917; another March 1917, and he fought in the First Battle of Gaza, 26–27 March 1917. His first, still extant, letter bears the date Thursday, 10 May 1917.

Two. The Sinai Peninsula and the Failures at Gaza 57

Captains Rowley and Warnes at IN SEIRAT (Fair and Wolton, *The History of the 1/5th Battalion: "The Suffolk Regiment"*).

off the iron-shod spoked wooden wheels. A stronger pattern which was subsequently issued was completely satisfactory, being indispensable on the long march over the desert to Palestine.[4]

Thus commenced what was to prove a lengthy trek from "fleshpots of Egypt" and the banks of the Suez Canal to the frontier of Palestine, "The Promised Land." The joint-historians of one of the 54th divisional artillery batteries related: "After five quiet days spent at Romani, the march was continued on February 10, with seventeen camels attached to the battery for water and food.[5] Leaving camp about 2 o'clock in the afternoon, we marched to a post called Rabat, which was encircled by groves of date palms, and possessed an abundant supply of water, although of the usual brackish nature."[6]

The 54th Divisional infantry, whom the brigade (271st, R.F.A.) was accompanying, had had a very strenuous time since leaving Kantara. Although the stages were generally short, the difficulty and fatigue of marching over the desert under a hot sun, and carrying packs, kit, rifle and ammunition, made the day's journey equivalent to at least treble the distance, augmented by the scanty supply of drinking water. Over the worst part of the route, however, miles of wire netting had been laid down so as to form roads or tracks wide enough to take a column of infantry in fours. This device, which was one of the discoveries of the war, considerably lessened the strenuous labor of marching.[7]

Blackwell and Axe describe their arrival:

> At the end of a ten mile march, on the 24th [February], we finally reached El Arish in the afternoon — within measurable distance of Gaza. Above the column a German

Suffolks rest on a wire netting road. These thoroughfares, when laid over fine sand, made marching much less strenuous (Fair and Wolton, *The History of the 1/5th Battalion: "The Suffolk Regiment"*).

aeroplane circled, the observer apparently taking a keen interest in the proceedings. The route during the last few miles lay close to the beach, and later the troops were able to indulge in a very acceptable bathe. The Battery had been twenty-five days on the desert since leaving Moascar, and the supply of water had been somewhat limited. El Arish had been captured on December 21, 1916, a large camp had already sprung up along the coast and the Battery was able to secure tents[8] for the first time since the commencement of the march.

El Arish, a picturesque Egyptian town with its flat-roofed mud houses grouped around its one substantial stone mosque, had been completely denuded by the Turks of all men of military age, so that only old men, women and children remained. From the minaret of the mosque the voice of a *muezzin* would be heard thrice daily calling the faithful to prayer, as it calls from thousands of minarets in various parts of the Old World:

Allah is most great! I witness that there is no God but Allah!
And Mohammed is the apostle of Allah! Come to prayer!
Prayer is better than work! Come to salvation! God is most great!
There is no God but Allah!

A magnificent voice had the *muezzin* of the mosque of El Arish. Sonorous and clear, it echoed and re-echoed among the houses, penetrating to every part of town, and fading to silence in the sand-hills of the desert. On the north side of the town there were extensive groves of date palms and fig-trees, with here and there fields of mealies [Indian corn, maize].[9]

The 1/5th Suffolk historians described the first sight of the town of El Arish from afar—"From Maadan we saw with interest the minaret of the Mosque of

Two. The Sinai Peninsula and the Failures at Gaza   59

El Arish against the distant sky." However, upon arrival it took on a less appealing aspect:

> El Arish looked well from a distance and, as the first town we had seen on the desert, aroused great interest. The fort showed signs of the shelling the Navy had administered, but the town itself, with its blind mud-bricked walls facing its narrow streets had little to attract. The Mosque was a very modest one, and the administrator's building was solid but plain. The few inhabitants, fair-skinned, and looking cheerful and fit enough, were unlike the Egyptian type and recalled memories of the last European army that had marched over this route, led by Napoleon. There was a fair amount of cultivation round the village. Small melon plantations followed the course of the Wadi; fig trees grew along its banks, and lovely date palms studded the sands and clustered near its mouth. The chief interest was the new part near the coast, where the railway station was a scene of busy life, and dumps of forage, rations, and R.E. material were being steadily accumulated. There were large camps scattered over the hills and numerous canteens to supplement our rations, while delightful sea bathing added greatly to the *joie de vivre*.[10]

Private Jake Mortlock said that most, if not all, of the humbler dwellings he saw "were just mud huts."[11] One of his best friends, L/Corporal Charlie

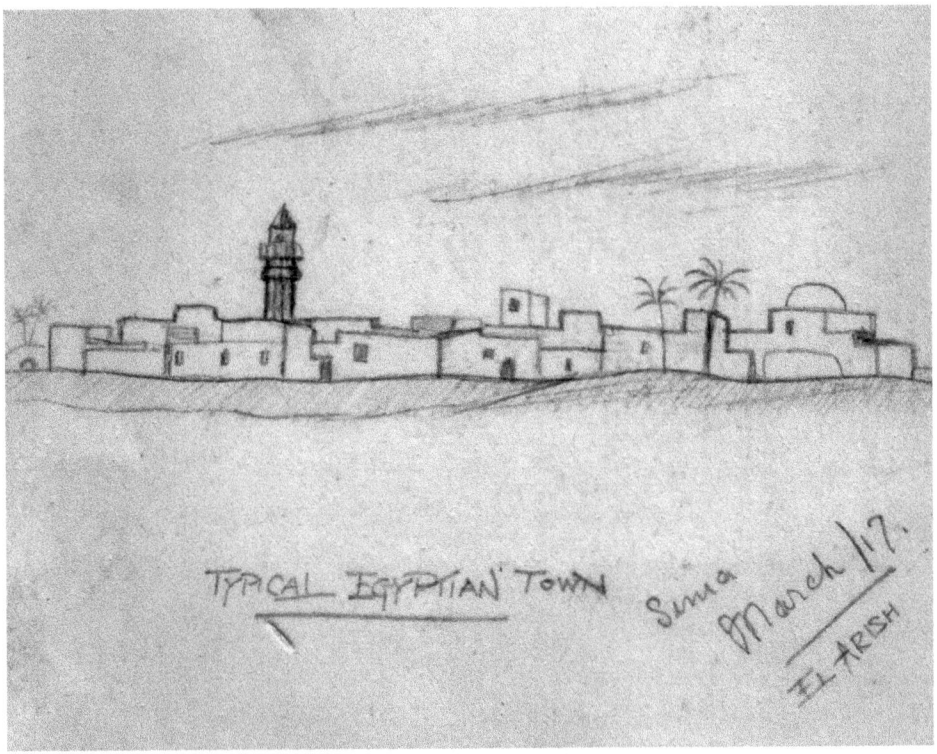

Sketch by Lance Corporal Charlie Bolton of the Sinai town El Arish; most of the dwellings were mud huts (Mortlock family papers).

Another — more humorous — sketch by Charlie Bolton. Both drawings are in Private Jake Mortlock's autograph album (Mortlock family photograph).

Bolton — with whom he sometimes bivouacked — sketched the town of El Arish (dated March 1917) in Jake's autograph album.

The Essex gunners' historians recorded: "On March 3, Major H. S. Martin, posted from the Norfolk Brigade of our 54th Divisional Artillery, arrived to take over command of the battery,"[12] which was Battery "B," 271st Brigade (1/2nd Essex Battery), R.F.A.

Boundary pillar, Rafa (Fair and Wolton, *The History of the 1/5th Battalion: "The Suffolk Regiment"*).

In early March 1917 General Sir Archibald Murray mobilized a massive army in the Sinai Peninsula and prepared to assault the enemy defensive line Beersheba to Gaza. As part of this, the 54th (East Anglian) Division deployed in Sinai and moved eastwards towards Gaza as part of General Murray's invasion force. "On the 24th the advance was resumed, the 53rd Division moving from Rafah to Khan Yunis and the 54th from Sheikh Zowaiid to Rafah. By midnight on the 25th the force was concentrated close to the Wadi Ghazze (Ghuzzie) as follows: the two mounted divisions and the 53rd at Deir el Balah[13]; the 54th Division at In Seirat, 2 miles east of Deir el Balah; the 52nd Division at Khan Yunis; the Camel Brigade at Abasan el Kebir, 5 miles south-east of Khan Yunis.[14]

Lt. General Walter Campbell described the transport problems created by such huge concentrations of military personnel in what was largely an inhospitable environment:

> A clear understanding of the enormous difficulties to be overcome is therefore necessary to an adequate comprehension of the methods whereby they were surmounted. In the history of that ancient land it is probable that no greater demand was ever made on the "ship of the desert" to carry freight across its native element, and the management of 40,000 burden camels alone was a gigantic undertaking. Side by side with this archaic form of transport there were introduced the most modern types of mechanically propelled vehicles; and so, with this strange blending of the Oriental and the Occidental, the demands of the forces were unfailingly supplied.[15]

Under the heading "Allotment of Camels and Donkeys to Corps During 1918 Operations," Colonel Badcock gives some interesting statistics—for instance the 21st Corps had 13, 206 camels and 1,984 donkeys; the 54th (East Anglian) Division alone had 1,166 camels and an unspecified number of donkeys.[16]

"During the past year [1916]," writes Lt. Colonel Kearsey, "our advance had depended on the construction of the railway and pipe line, which had accompanied our advance through Sinai. The railway line was standard gauge, and was constructed at the rate of twenty miles a month."[17]

The question of water was a good deal more complex because a staggering numbers of men and animals depended upon it. Colonel Kearsey continues: "The water for the troops was brought through pipe lines, 6 inches, 8 inches and 12 inches in diameter, which followed the railway and was pumped by a series of pumps from the Nile. From railhead, the water was carried to the troops by camels. Each could carry two $12^1/_2$-gallon tanks ... in the following year, a Camel Transport Corps of 35,000 camels was formed, and also four companies each of 2,000 donkeys. The Egyptian Labour Corps for work on the railway was increased to 55,000 labourers."[18]

In a chapter titled "Personnel of the C.T.C." (Camel Transport Corps) of his work, *A History of the Transport Services of the Egyptian Expeditionary Force, 1916-1917-1918*, Colonel Badcock—with tongue firmly in cheek—enumerates the "several classifications of Egyptians as known in the C.T.C.":

You may divide them into men who can and cannot see at night; or you may grade them by colour from yellow to black; officially they are classed as medical officers, medical orderlies, native batmen, veterinary orderlies, sanitary squads, clippers, saddlers, bash raises, raises, and drivers, attested and unattested.

Storemen live lives of temptation and invariably succumb. They must have sound knowledge of English, for Q.M.s have not the gift of tongues. They must issue nothing except on written order; hence the following correspondence between a well-known Q.M. of the corps and his storeman:

"Give it two drums Mange Dressing.
(signed) — , 2/Lieut. and Q.M."

Back came the answer in a shaky hand:

"To Mister — , Finish Mange Dressing.
Wassif — ."

Admit a general failure of *morale*, and there stand out the few who carried on, confessed to no discomfort, shirked no work, answered every call; in short, kept clean the record of a corps that never failed.[19]

In another part of his extensive account of the Camel Transport Services, Colonel Badcock enumerates the camel-borne devices for the transportation of the sick and wounded:

Cacolets.— Work done by the Camel Transport Corps included the transport of the sick and wounded. The Egyptian Army pattern cacolets held the field in 1915-16. The type later in use with satisfactory results was a development of the Turkish cacolet. The saddle was the ordinary heavy-burden pack saddle adapted to cacolet work by iron frameworks, one near and one off, interchangeable, each clamped to the side of the saddle near the arches and provided with brackets into which iron arms of the bed frame or chair fit. The bed frames in the lying-down cacolets were steadied by "girths steadying" passing beneath the camel's belly from outside to outside the bed frame. This pattern has the extra advantage of being available for ordinary transport work when not required for medical services, and of bringing the work of transporting casualties within the compass of the heaviest camels.[20]

British Prime Minister Lloyd George wrote: "Sir Archibald Murray, who was running a railway line across the desert of Sinai and bringing a pipe for water, wished to defeat the enemy forces in front of him, to ensure the safety of his railhead from an attack by them. So, in the latter part of March, he pressed forward towards Gaza, and on March 26th he launched an attack on the Turkish forces in that town."[21]

Halsey, in his history of the war, gives this description:

Gaza — Samson's Gaza — lies forty-eight miles southwest of Jerusalem. In the *Book of Judges* it is recorded how Samson, escaping from Gaza, "took the doors of the gate of the city, and the two posts, and went away with them, bar and all, and put them on his shoulders and carried them to the top of an hill that is before Hebron."[22,23] Thus, once more the war in the East put an old and sacred city again on the map, giving a military importance to historic localities of which little more had been left in modern memories than a name and a tradition. The Dardanelles expedition had reanimated the Plain of Troy. Mecca and Medina, the old shrines of Muslim pilgrims, had become modern strategic points. Baghdad, city of the Caliph, came again into chronicles of great deeds. The campaign of Xenophon's "Ten Thousand," after twenty centuries had acquired a new parallel at Trebizond. A battle for mastery in Mesopotamia and Asia Minor was fought in the "Garden of Eden." Much that happened read like chapters from Rawlinson. While the Western Front had been a great theatre of war since the time of Cæsar, it was the Far Eastern Front—the Holy Land and the Tigris and Euphrates—that revived the oldest of war's romances. That the cradle of the human race should have become in our century a great battle-ground, stirred romantic recollections as no other of the war's campaigns could do.[24]

The Plan of Attack

Lt. General Sir Charles Dobell proposed that the Desert Column, under the command of General Chetwode, should carry out the attack, while the remainder of the Eastern Force moved up so as to be ready to give support if required.

Eastern Force was rearranged for the operations, the Desert Column now comprising the A. (Australian) and N.Z. (New Zealand) Mounted Division (less the 1st Light Horse Brigade), the Imperial Mounted Division (less the 4th Light Horse), and the 53rd Division. The remaining troops, directly under the command of the general officer commanding (G.O.C.) Eastern Force, were the Imperial Camel Brigade, the 52nd and 54th Divisions, and the 229th Brigade, the only formation of the 74th Division as yet available.

The plan of operations drawn up by G.O.C. Eastern Command received the approval of General Headquarters on 19 March. Its essence was that, after making good the line of the Wadi Ghazze, the Desert Column should carry out the *coup de main* against Gaza, while the 54th Division moved out and stood by to protect it against a Turkish counter-stroke from the east, of which General Dobell was apprehensive.[25]

"The development of a supply of water from the Wadi Ghazze (which, though nearly dry, had numerous springs in its bed) by divisional engineers was begun.... A supply sufficient for all the troops engaged was obtained, long rows of canvas troughs being put up for watering the horses."[26]

The Fog at Dawn on the 26th March

"The occupation of the line of the Wadi Ghazze, unopposed by the enemy, was to be interrupted by the weather. About 4 A.M., after a still, cold and very dark night, fog rolled up from the sea, gradually thickening till by 5 A.M., just before dawn, objects could not be distinguished at 20 yards distance."[27]

Captain M. B. Buxton, 163rd Brigade intelligence officer, gives his account of this phenomenon to Brig. General Ward:

> It was most unfortunate that there was a very thick fog on the morning of the 27th, for no one had any idea of the country between In Seirat and Gaza. There were several "wadis" to be crossed and the R.E. [Royal Engineers] had only made one or two crossings which were very difficult to find, and were usually crowded with columns of troops crossing. For this reason we must have lost about three hours, and it was not until 8 o'clock that we crossed the Wadi Ghuzze at Shekh Nebhan. The 53rd Division was advancing along the coast, while the 54th was detailed to capture Sheikh Abbas Ridge, which was ground about 300 feet high overlooking Gaza. On our right was the Australian Mounted Infantry and the New Zealand Light Horse [sic]. The 161st brigade was ordered to attack Ali-el-Muntar, a very steep hill at the S.E. corner of Gaza. The 162nd brigade were between them and our brigade.[28]

The 54th Division, commanded by Major General S. W. Hare, less the 161st Brigade and the 271st Brigade Royal Field Artillery in Eastern Force reserve, crossed according to orders behind the mounted troops, taking up positions of observation on the Sheikh Abbas Ridge, and began the digging of a line of entrenchments facing east. The 161st Brigade, which had halted at Sheikh Nebhan, on the bank of the Wadi Ghazze, received orders at 8:45 to cross and advance to El Burjabye, west of Sheikh Abbas and south of Mansura, where it would be in a position to support either the 53rd or 54th Divisions.

By 10:30 A.M., therefore, the mounted troops had accomplished their first mission of enveloping Gaza and interposing their main force between the town and the Turkish encampments to the east, thus creating a corridor for the main attack. At Sheikh Abbas the 54th Division covered the right rear of that attack. "It now remained for the 53rd Division to carry out its more difficult tasks: the capture of the Ali Muntar position, which dominated Gaza, and then the town itself."[29] An eye witness, Captain O. Teichman, R.A.M.C., observed:

> The early morning fog was followed at midday by a "Khampsine," and the heat became very great. The action now became general, the Fifty-third and Fifty-fourth Divisions making great progress south of Gaza, while the two cavalry divisions, being in action with the enemy reinforcements, completed the investment east and north. We heard afterwards that the Anzac Mounted Division had actually got into Gaza from behind and had captured the G.O.C. and staff of the Turkish Fifty-third Division, who were leaving the town in cabs.[30]

The 53rd Division pressed its assault with grim determination on the part of all units. The left battalion of the 158th Brigade, the 5th Welch Fusiliers, reached the "cactus garden" south of Ali Muntar, and there halted to allow the other battalions, which had more ground to cover, to come up on its right. The 1st Hereford, from brigade reserve, was brought up to attack Green Hill on the left front, since it enfiladed the advance of both the 158th and the 160th Brigades. The 159th Brigade had now come up on the right of the 158th and was directing its advance on Clay Hill. Heavy machine-gun fire met the troops as they approached the position, and the advance slowed down. By 3:30 P.M. the 161st (Essex) Brigade, 54th Division, had reached Mansura. Assured of a new divisional reserve, General Dallas at once sent the 7th Cheshire to rejoin the 159th

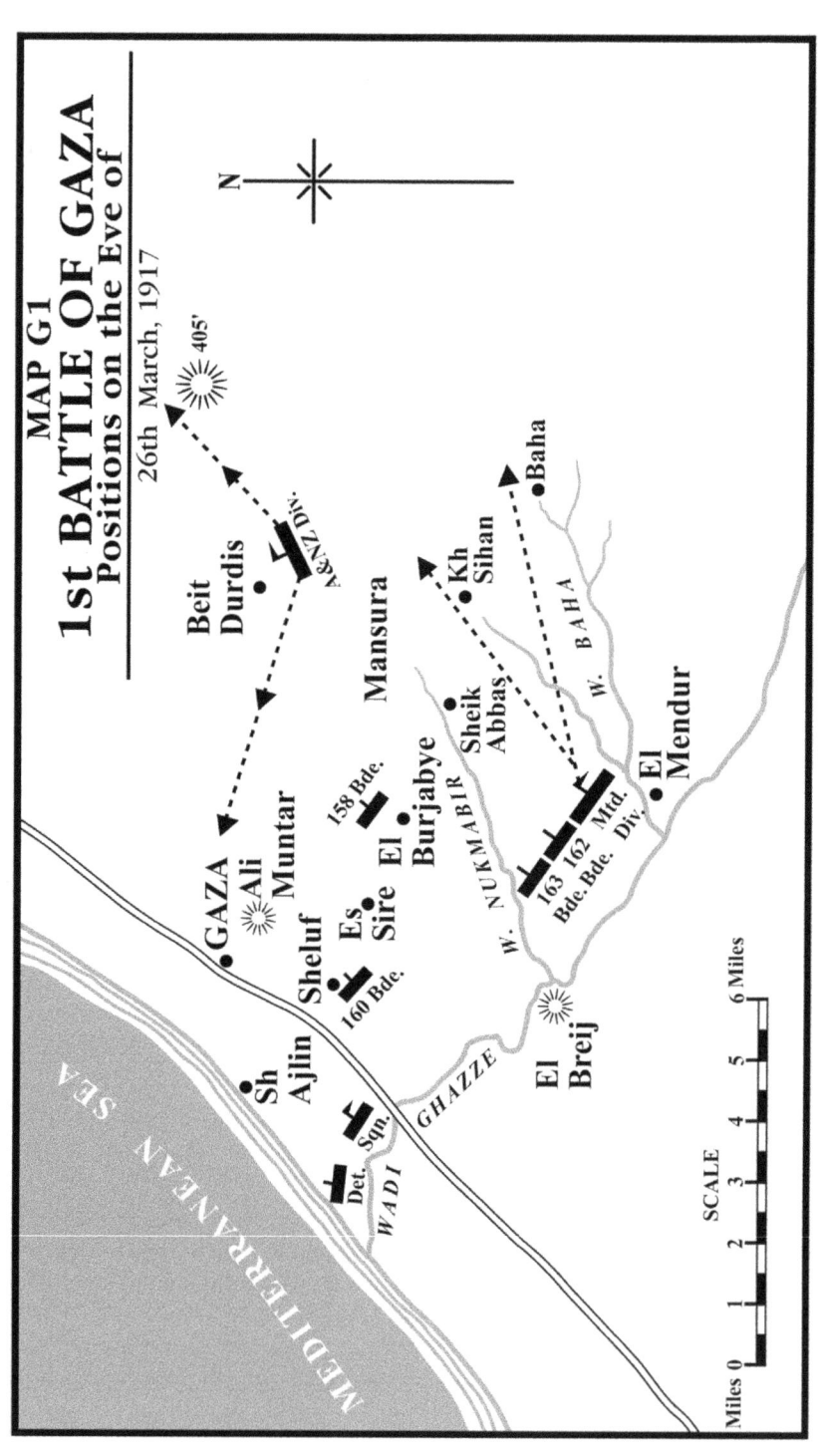

Brigade. The Cheshire was moved up in support of the 5th Welch on the left, which appeared to Brig. General Travers to be meeting the stiffest resistance and to have come to a standstill. "The support of the artillery had not been very effective in the early stages, partly owing to its unavoidably hurried entry into the attack. The arrival of the 271st Brigade, R.F.A. [54th Division] with the 161st Brigade Group produced a marked effect in diminishing the fire of the machine-guns on Clay Hill."[31]

Thus the British, Dominion, and Imperial forces, in the third week of March, surprised the enemy on a foggy morning. Defending the earthworks were seven Turkish infantry battalions with artillery of Austrian gunners.[32]

> During the afternoon [of the 26th] the battle developed, the infantry attacking repeatedly, and for the most part gaining their objectives. In several places they penetrated into the town, but losses had been heavy, and by half-past two in the afternoon the reserves had been drawn into the fight. The 271st Brigade [54th Divisional Artillery] was consequently ordered into action in support.[33]

The 161st (Essex) Brigade mounted Mansura Ridge at a point about a mile from the position of readiness, while the Essex Royal Field Artillery Brigade formed a line and came into action in the open, at short range from the enemy's positions on the Green Mound and Ali el Muntar, and at once opened fire in support of their fellow infantry's attack on a strongly entrenched hill just southeast of Gaza. The infantry stormed the hill aided by the effective fire of the brigade. Fire was then directed on Ali el Muntar and in support of the infantry attack on the Green Mound positions, which had so far been held up by machine-gun fire. Enemy machine-gunners concealed at the foot of Ali el Muntar (the mountain) were causing severe losses and holding up the advance. It fell to the lot of the artillery brigade to clear them out of their position. Several other objectives were engaged, principally enemy trenches among thick cactus hedges, which the infantry were finding very difficult to deal with. Every effort was made to break down enemy opposition. Owing to the gathering darkness and lack of information as to the exact whereabouts of the infantry, firing ceased soon after sunset.[34]

Lt. Col. Thomas Gibbons, of the 1/5th Battalion, the Essex Regiment, contributed his perspective:

A 1st Battalion, Herefordshire Regiment infantryman (Mortlock family photograph).

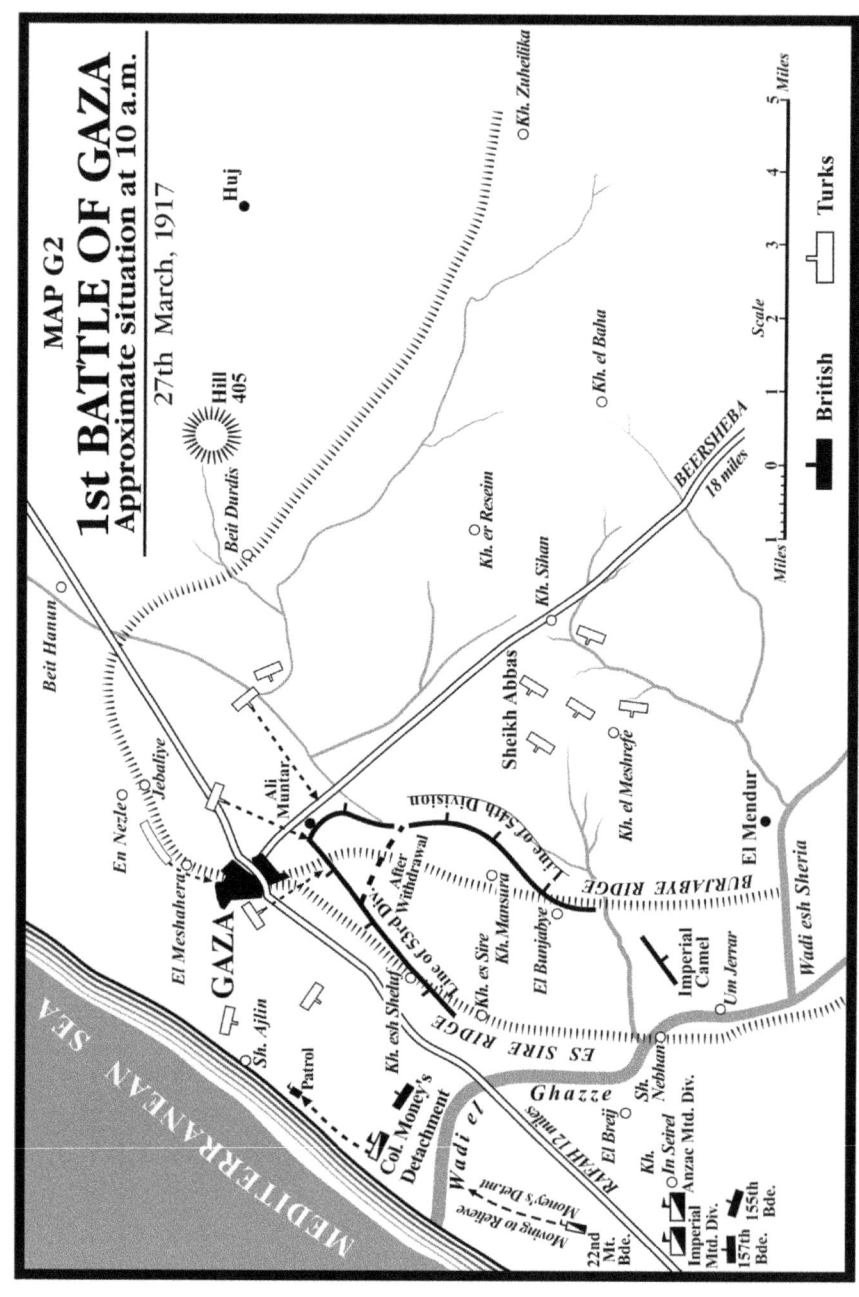

In the darkness of the early hours of the morning of March 26th, we were awakened by the cavalry making their way, accompanied by their batteries, down the slope towards the Wadi [Ghuzzi]. There was a thick fog, which made their role a very difficult one in country with no roads and broken by deep gullies and rocky hills. After an hour or more the sound of the last hoof and the crunch of the last wheel died away in the fog. Still no sound. Day broke, and it was thicker than ever. We knew that the infantry had started, but it was evident that they had not yet become engaged. We followed the tracks of the cavalry through the green corn and halted in the Wadi near Sheikh Nebhan. The mules enjoyed themselves on the green barley, we on that famous thirst producer, bully beef. Several armoured cars arrived and required some help in getting across the deep sand in the bed of the Wadi, but all were got across and disappeared to the N.E. After a short halt — too short for breakfast — we crossed and followed the Wadi Nukhabir (a branch of the Ghuzzi) in the same direction. It looked like the main attack being from the right, with the Essex Brigade to finish off the job — if the Turks from Beersheba didn't get there first. There was still no sound of a battle. We left the Wadi, turned north and halted on the south side of the El Burjali Ridge.[35]

General Dallas realized that more driving force was necessary if the whole position was to be carried. Machine-guns on Green Hill had delayed the 158th Brigade's advance all the afternoon, and that brigade's reserve battalion, the Herefordshire, which had been put in to attack the hill, had swung to the right, as so often happens in attacks of this nature. General Dallas ordered the 161st Brigade (Essex), leaving one battalion in divisional reserve, to carry Green Hill and fill the gap between the 158th and 160th Brigades. The brigade began its attack at 4 P.M., 1/4th Essex on the right, 1/5th on the left, 1/6th in brigade reserve, and, despite heavy fire, captured its objective at 5:30 P.M. By 6:30 P.M. the whole position was won; the Turks everywhere were running back into Gaza. So far, then, as the troops were concerned, all seemed over. By nightfall Gaza was surrounded completely, except for its southwestern side. Everywhere save among the sand-dunes, where a comparatively small body held its position in front of Money's Detachment (on the extreme left, close to the sea), the Turks had fallen back to the town. The British troops, weary but exultant, looked forward with confidence to the surrender of the whole garrison at dawn. Meanwhile, they were consolidating the positions won and pushing forward patrols, which felt their way among the houses till in the course of the night men of the Australian and New Zealand Mounted Division from the north and east met infantry of the 53rd Division in the eastern streets. Yet, while to them a brilliant victory seemed to reward their labors and sacrifices, Generals Dobell and Chetwode at In Seirat — some 8 to 10 miles back — found cause for anxiety. Although the town was enveloped, the advance of the enemy from the north and east boded ill for the morrow.[36]

The capture of Ali Muntar Ridge by the 53rd Division and the 161st Brigade of the 54th Division will bear comparison with the classic exploits of British infantry. The approach was over bare ground against an enemy strongly posted and entrenched, with numerous machine guns and a powerful artillery. All the advantages of observation and concealment lay with the enemy. The guns supporting the attack were few—twenty-four 18-pounders, twelve 4.5 inch howitzers, and six 60-pounders—and the narrow ridge on which lay the enemy's main position was a difficult target; the hostile trenches were hard to detect. The last part of the assault was blind fighting uphill through cactus hedges against unseen machine guns and riflemen. A pitiless Eastern sun beat down on men who had already marched far before deploying for attack. There was no shade and no water.

Yet these four brigades pressed quietly and steadily on over that exposed plain, up that steep ridge, and through that maze of cactus hedges, till an enemy whose skill and stoutness in defense are universally admitted gave way to them and yielded up his position. Little finesse was possible in this assault. Its success was a triumph for cool, practiced platoon leading and for straightforward disciplined valour. It is an action worth remembering when one is tempted to believe that infantry today are powerless against a prepared position unless they are convoyed by tanks or supported by an overwhelming mass of artillery.[37]

General Murray, "when ordered to invade Palestine the following March could not get beyond Gaza. Indeed, after capturing the town at the first attempt he soon had to withdraw from it."[38]

Private Jake Mortlock said that there was much cursing among the troops he served with. There was considerable bitterness among the frontline soldiers over what had transpired. Private Frank Cooke, of "D" Company, 1/5th Battalion of the Suffolk Regiment, by all accounts forcibly voiced the feelings of himself and his comrades-in-arms by giving vent to a stream of expletive-embroidered invective.[39] Fellow soldier Corporal Reg Lane elaborated, referring to the man in their platoon of "D" Company, 1/5th Suffolk, and identifying him. "Didn't Frank curse, Jake? Never heard cursing like it."[40] Mortlock said everyone was furious because "we'd taken it [Gaza]" and the commander-in-chief was way back "in Cairo."[41] Although he admitted they suffered a severe shortage of water, he was of the opinion that their advance would have taken care of that. At any rate, to give up all they fought so tena-

Private Reg Lane (Mortlock family photograph).

ciously for, which cost so many casualties, seemed tantamount to an act of betrayal.[42] Almost a year later Private Mortlock wrote: "March 18th, 1918.... Glad to say I am keeping quite fit and not having such a bad time — a lot better than this day a year ago in the first attack on Gaza when we were nearly dead for a want of a drink[43] and so knocked up with marching that whenever we stopped for a minute the chaps fell down like logs sound asleep."[44]

Blackwell and Axe observed, "The British forces had retired a distance of approximately five miles from the Gaza defences during the night of March 27/28, and, as it afterwards transpired, the Turks also were busy withdrawing from their positions, which fact would account for their failure to follow up or even harass the retirement."[45]

Sir Archibald Murray was not the only one who viewed the First Battle of Gaza through rose-colored spectacles. Someone who actually did view the battle, *The Times*' war correspondent, W. T. Massey, expatiated as follows:

Private Frank Cooke — a soldier who said what he meant in colorful terms (Mortlock family photograph).

THE DASH FOR GAZA
*****
AN EYE-WITNESS ACCOUNT
****
TURKS SAVED BY FOG
(FROM W.T. MASSEY.)

WITH THE DESERT COLUMN NEAR GAZA, MARCH 27.

For two days the troops of the Egyptian Expeditionary Force have been engaging the Turks in the neighbourhood of the ancient Biblical city of Gaza. By one of those swift movements which are the strong points of the Egyptian Force we surprised the enemy on a foggy dawn when he could have known nothing of the danger unless a German airman, soaring in the filmy clouds before sunset on the previous evening, was able to detect the columns of dust rising from the western fringe of the great plain of Gaza. Even if he saw this evidence of our advance the enemy probably never realized that his position would be attacked immediately after the heavy sea fog was dispersed by the fierce sun.

The fog was very unfortunate. It prevented the opening and development of the attack till ten o'clock. Time was the essence of the day's business, as the Turkish reinforcements were within 15 miles. A delay, however short, was of infinite value to the enemy. Another two hours of daylight yesterday and the whole town would have been ours. That we were able to do so much in a period of shortened daylight is an eloquent tribute to our troops, who worked so earnestly and thoroughly.

The position is separated from the sea by two miles of golden sand hills, which were entrenched. The trenches ran south-west, then bent towards the east, the position consisting of two main hills, one to the north of the other, with a subsidiary sandhill between. The southern hill nearest us was a perfect labyrinth of deeply-cut trenches and redoubts, skillfully sited. There was no barbed-wire framework to disclose the position. The position was one of formidable strength. There were seven Turkish infantry battalions, with artillery mostly served by Austrian gunners. We knew our attack would be hotly resisted.

A Picturesque Battlefield.

The preliminaries to the battle were most picturesque. On the evening of Lady Day [March 25], while the western skies were aglow with an exceptionally beautiful sunset, the vast plain was alive with troops. Imagine Laffan's Plain magnified twentyfold. Picture to yourself the troops, arrayed for battle, assembling for a review, and you get the idea of the scene. Enormously long lines trailed across the plain, lifting low clouds of dust. Equally long serpentine lines of cavalry raised higher dust clouds, while the artillery and ammunition columns made their own paths. Camels bearing troops and war material wound their way over the plain long after the crescent moon had ceased to cast its wan light on the country.

The troops had a pleasant bivouac in Palestine. They were on the move again before the sea fog had enveloped everything. The country fought over is difficult. It is intersected by ravines and nullahs, some of them big cracks in the ground, others wider with precipitous banks. The Wadi Ghuzzeh, which had to be crossed for an enveloping cavalry movement, has a soft, sandy bed and perpendicular banks, often 40ft. high.

Anzac [Australian–New Zealand Army Corps] mounted troops and British Yeomanry, with horse artillery batteries, got over this wadi in the dark, having cut down the banks and built ramps to get the guns across. Then the fog came on, and all marching was done by compass bearing. The troops were all disposed by 10 o'clock, so as to delay any columns of enemy marching in relief.

News that these columns were on the move soon came. They were marching down the coast road from the north, from the Huj area to the north-east, and from Nejeila, Sharia, and Harreira to the east. A long way off I could see a tremendous cloud of dust at the base of the Judean Hills, indicating the Turkish cavalry moving out of Beer Sheba. From a most favoured point of observation I had a splendid view of the battle. The town was visible in the background. The red-roofed and white-walled houses were enclosed by lemon and olive groves, and towering above all was the minaret of the mosque, formerly the old church of St. John, founded by the Knight Templars in the twelfth century, and taken from them by Saladin. I could also see Ali Muntar, the high mound up which Samson carried the gates of Gaza.

The artillery preparation was an inspiring sight. Bursts of shrapnel smudged the cerulean blue, and high explosive shell raised clouds and lifted vast quantities of earth from the enemy's entrenchments. I could see the infantry march to the attack, taking advantage of every bit of dead ground, rushing across the open, dropping to whatever cover mother earth afforded when faced with bursts of machine-gun fire, and pushing forward valiantly whenever opportunity offered. But I regret that I could not see and describe how these gallant Welsh Territorials engaged the enemy in hand-to-hand grips in a bewildering maze of zigzags. But as they conquered a crafty foe, famed for his powers of defence, we know that they behaved worthy of their race. These Welshmen moved from the south-east and east, and met with very strong opposition. About 1 o'clock a portion of the Anzacs and Yeomanry were ordered to close in from the north-east to assist the infantry attack. They began to take trenches at half-past 4. The infantry took their objective in the evening. The New Zealanders, who got to close quarters towards sunset, had a desperate fight till the close approach of reinforcements for the enemy necessitated the withdrawal of the cavalry, who were between two fires. This was accomplished without casualties before morning.

Turks' Desperate Final Effort.

During this afternoon the Turks made a tremendous effort to break through our line to the east. For two hours I witnessed a magnificent effort by our men to resist the enemy. The shrapnel of our artillery ranged perfectly and smashed the line of the attackers, and with the machine-guns of the infantry must have caused heavy losses to the enemy.

Where all the troops did well it is difficult to mention particular instances. The Anzacs, Yeomanry, and infantry all did magnificently. Of many deeds which will stir the blood of Britons I will describe two, though they are not the only gallant efforts worthy of record during these days.

One concerns the New Zealanders. The brigade got to the sea, north of the position, and were ordered to assist the infantry attack. At half-past 4, with the Yeomanry, they took an important ridge, and proceeded to cross the flats strongly opposed by the enemy in pits behind dense cactus hedges—very deadly obstacles, but they quickly carried them. The New Zealanders went on, got into the position, rushed the enemy battery, and captured 200 men, and howitzers, which the enemy made frequent and desperate attempts to regain. Finally, enemy gunners and some infantry got into a country house a hundred yards off and endeavoured to prevent the removal of the guns. The New Zealanders refused to leave the guns. They loaded them and used them against the house until they had demolished it and killed the occupants. Then the Turkish infantry tried to rush the guns, but were driven off with the bayonet. Darkness now set in. The New Zealanders were ordered to retire, but would not come away without the guns. They brought them back to our lines this morning. The New Zealanders' casualties during the day were two killed and 29 wounded. They took 225 prisoners, and probably killed and wounded as many more.

Another instance of dashing bravery is told of the armoured cars. The cars went out yesterday afternoon to assist to keep off 5,000 reinforcements from the Huj area. They cooperated so well that the whole of the enemy were held up at a critical period. When it became dark the cars retired, with an officer walking in front to find a practicable path over much broken country. They proceeded [walking] for four hours when the crews were given sleep till 4 o'clock this morning. Then they made ready to proceed to our lines through a waterless country. An officer went ahead in an unarmoured car to reconnoitre, and saw at once that he was confronted by a large body of the enemy. The outposts, only a hundred yards ahead, immediately opened fire. He abandoned the staff car and ran to the armoured cars and ordered an attack. It proved to be an amazing fight of eight cars against 5,000 infantry and artillery. The cars pushed forward, having to find paths over rough ground full of deep holes. The enemy tried with all their might to stop the armoured cars but the latter fought sometimes in line, sometimes in column, and mowed down the Turks at ranges of between 25 and 300 yards, and got through the whole of the 5,000 Turks in two hours, with one killed and four wounded, inflicting at a conservative estimate, 350 casualties. After the cars had got within our lines the bullet marks on the turrets showed that the Turkish musketry is not always bad. It is marvellous that the crews suffered so little.[46]

The New York Times reported that on Monday, April 2, the Right Honorable Andrew Bonar Law, a member of the War Council, told the House of Commons that "the total casualties suffered by the Turks in the battle of Gaza, in Palestine, were 8,000. The total number of British killed was less than 400. The operations against Gaza were most successful," said Law, "and had it not been for a fog, which delayed the attack, and a shortage of water, complete disaster would have overtaken the Turks." He denied categorically the Turkish report that 3,000 British had been killed in the attack.[47] On the same page of the paper reporting Bonar Law's Commons' statement — and perhaps explaining his optimism — is the reported announcement of General Sir Archibald Murray's assessment of the battle: "The operation was most successful, and owing to the fog and waterless nature of the country round Gaza just fell short of complete disaster to the enemy. Our troops are exceedingly proud of themselves, and I am delighted with their enterprise, endurance, skill and leading. None of our troops were at any time harassed or hard pressed."[48]

The New York Times coverage continued: "Official announcement was made here today that the French Commander, General Nivelle, had wired congratulations on the success won by the British against the Turks to Lt. General Sir Archibald Murray, commander of the British troops in Egypt, saying that the achievements of the British meant the opening under favorable conditions of the campaign in Palestine and Syria. An official statement dealing with the battle of Gaza, issued today [April 3, 1917], says":

> The primary object was to seize the Wadi Ghuzzeh to cover the advance of our railway. The Wadi was occupied without a fight, and advanced troops pushed forward in the direction of Gaza. It appeared to Lt. General Sir Charles Dobell, in command, that the enemy might retire without fighting, and to force them to stand he decided to attempt to capture Gaza by a *coup de main*.
>
> On the morning of the 26th a dense fog delayed operations, and it was not possible to attack the Gaza position until later in the afternoon, when the enemy first line trenches were captured, and more than 700 prisoners were taken. The German commander, von Kress, meanwhile moved up three columns toward Gaza to support his troops. These columns were admirably delayed by our mounted troops and armoured cars, and heavy losses were inflicted upon the enemy at slight cost to ourselves. The commander and staff of the Fifty-third Division were captured during this fighting.
>
> The time during which this operation could be carried out was limited by the supply of water available to the troops, the infantry being dependent upon what they could carry with them. Owing to delay by the morning fog, the supply of water with the troops proved insufficient to allow the attack to be continued, and our troops took up a defensive position from a point just south of Gaza toward Wadi Ghuzzeh. This position was attacked on the 27th by the Turks, who were repulsed everywhere with heavy losses, our camel corps completely defeating the Turkish cavalry divisions.
>
> On the next day our infantry were withdrawn to Wadi Ghuzzeh, our cavalry remaining in contact with the enemy's main position. The enemy showing no desire to resume the offensive, our troops remained in occupation of Wadi Ghuzzeh.
>
> The enemy's total casualties are estimated by the general officer commanding in chief to be 8,000. We captured 950 prisoners and two Austrian howitzers. Our total

killed amounted to less than 400. Some small parties of our men, totaling less than 200, who are believed to have fought their way into Gaza and been cut off, are missing.[49]

Many who had firsthand experience of the operations did not share Murray's complacency. For instance, a Royal Army Medical Corps officer, Captain Oskar Teichmann, summarized the affair as "a ghastly fiasco" which bore precious little resemblance to "the most successful operation" described by General Murray.[50] Captain Teichmann also quoted the enemy's version of what really happened: "The fight developed in the neighbourhood of Gaza on the afternoon of March 27th, and terminated in a brilliant victory ... the enemy suffered heavy losses, leaving numbers of dead on the ground ... the enemy retired in a south-westerly direction, pursued by our troops ... in spite of the extreme violence with which the fight was contested, our losses were quite small."[51]

Turkish reports present a somewhat less rosy picture. Headed "The Battle of Gaza" and dated March 30, Sinai Front, they read:

> The British rearguards are now entrenching themselves. Our airmen report that numerous British transport columns are retreating towards the south-west.
> According to the latest reports of the Battle of Gaza, besides the 125th Regiment, the 79th Regiment distinguished itself. Over three thousand British dead were found on the field by our clearing parties. One hundred and fifty British [are] wounded and are in one hospital, and others are being brought in. Twelve machine-guns and 20 automatic guns have been captured.
> Prisoners state that the British have met with great difficulties in supplying food and finding water.
> March 30.— In the Sinai Peninsula our troops drove back the British rearguard to the south of Wadi Gaza, 4 miles south of Gaza. The principal forces of the enemy withdrew more to the rear.
> March 31.— The situation is unchanged.[52]

British Prime Minister David Lloyd George pronounced his verdict in the following words:

> The story is told by a vivid pen in the *Official History* of the campaign. When Allenby arrived the Army was depressed by a sense of futility. The attack of Dobell and Chetwode on Gaza had been the most perfect sample exhibited on either side in any theatre during this Great War of that combination of muddle-headedness, misunderstanding and sheer funk which converts an assured victory into a humiliating defeat. Gaza was "virtually captured" when the order came to withdraw. We had in our possession at the moment of withdrawal intercepted wireless messages [from Major Tiller to General Kress von Kressenstein] which showed the German Commander considered the position hopeless. Dobell alleged that these messages only reached him after the withdrawal had commenced![53]

Lloyd George goes on to make the very valid point that "the defences of Gaza when Chetwode attacked were merely skeleton entrenchments and its garrison was heavily out-numbered by our Army in men and artillery."[54]

The same source, in a different volume, summed up thus: "The attack, which was directed by Sir Archibald Murray from his headquarters at Cairo, was badly fumbled so that the troops were withdrawn without capturing the town, though it was practically within their grasp."[55] He then went on to observe:

> But the operation showed that definite successes were possible for us on this front, on a scale which we could hardly hope for anywhere else. More resolute and skilful leadership would undoubtedly have realised a success, which might have had a decisive influence on the Palestine campaign, and in conjunction with Maude's victory might have ended in the collapse of Turkey in 1917. With an unimaginative and stubborn soldier at the centre and a nervous and overcautious soldier in Egypt, the opportunity was lost. Had Maude been in Egypt, he would have broken the Turkish lines and captured Jerusalem by Easter, 1917.[56]

General Kress von Kressenstein, in his account of the battle, says that the first reports of attack were received at 8 A.M. He at once ordered towards the battlefield all Turkish troops within reach. The leading regiment of the 53rd Division (which was marching down from Jaffa to Gaza) was due to reach El Medjel on the morning of the 26th; it was ordered to hasten its march on to Gaza. The 3rd Division (about 5,000 rifles and thirty guns) at Huj was directed on Ali Muntar, the 16th Division (5,000 to 6,000 rifles, twenty guns) to Sheikh Abbas and to the south of Gaza, and the Beersheba group (about 2,000 rifles and sabres) by Shellal to Khan Yunus. It took some time, however, to get these bodies on the move, owing to what Kress calls "typically Turkish" delays. When darkness came they were hardly halfway to Gaza. Kress had not sufficient confidence in the ability of his subordinate commanders or in the training of the troops to commit them to night operations. He acquiesced, therefore, in the cessation of action at nightfall, at which time he had every reason to believe that Gaza was in British hands. Next day, when he discovered the position of affairs, Kress wished to initiate a general attack with all available troops against the British, but Djemal Pasha, the commander-in-chief, refused to countenance the proposal.[57]

A German, Dr. Gaston Bodart, gives a general assessment of the campaign from the other side's perspective: "An attempt on the part of General Dobell to take Gaza by a *coup-de-main* failed, the English suffering heavy losses. An attack made by the Turks the following day against the English position (first battle of Gaza, March 27th and 28th, 1917) likewise met with no success."[58]

General Sir Archibald Wavell gave a penetrating assessment of the outcome of the First Battle of Gaza. This eminent soldier opined:

> The decision to withdraw the mounted troops has naturally been much criticized; but on the information available at the time it was fully justified. The issue of the fight at Ali Muntar was not known, the enemy was represented as pressing in the mounted screen, and the horses were reported as suffering from lack of water. It is curious that all three protagonists in this struggle accepted failure at almost the same moment: General Dobell issued the recall to his mounted force, Kress von Kressenstein halted the relieving columns, and Major Tiller, the German commandant of Gaza, blew up his wireless station and resigned himself to the prospect of captivity. In war a last ounce of optimism is sometimes a better reserve than many men.[59]

Captain Teichman relates that:

> As we crossed the Beersheba road in darkness, a motor dispatch rider rode by, saying that Gaza had fallen and that he was taking in dispatches. About 11.30 P.M., when the squadron horses were getting exhausted, by the greatest luck we fell in with our regiment, which we found resting by the roadside between Khirbit Sihan and Ali Muntar. Here we rested for about an hour, our C.O. receiving no orders; various units rode by, last of all the Imperial Camel Corps. "Who is following behind you?" called our C.O. "The Turks," was the laconic answer, which it appeared was perfectly true! And now we began to realize the ghastly fiasco that had been enacted. We knew that we had surrounded Gaza, and that our division had not been heavily engaged (our own brigade had had few casualties), that the infantry divisions had got into Gaza and had captured Ali Muntar, and that the Anzacs had entered the town from behind — and in spite of this we were retiring!
>
> *March 27th.* At 1 A.M. our own regiment commenced to retire, and riding through the night over very broken ground, often held up by retreating transport columns and guns and by precipitous ravines, we reached a crossing of the Wadi Ghuzze near Sheikh Nebhan at dawn. Just before descending from the higher ground into the valley, we had a last view of Gaza with its stately minarets, which we thought the day before was already ours.[60]

A contemporary military historian and strategist, Captain Basil Liddell Hart, succinctly summed up the Gaza debacle thus:

> Murray attacked Gaza on March 26, but the attempt fell short when on the brink of success. By nightfall Gaza was practically surrounded, but the victorious position was given up bit by bit, not under enemy pressure, but on the orders of the executive British commanders, through faulty information, misunderstandings, and over-anxiety. Nor did the harm end there, for Murray reported the action to the government in terms of a victory, and without hint of the subsequent withdrawal, so that he was encouraged to attempt, without adequate reconnaissance or fire support, a further attack on April 17–19, which proved a costlier failure against defences now strengthened.[61]

General Murray had missed success at Gaza by a narrow margin and could claim that the bad luck of the fog had been a major factor in turning the scales against him. Unfortunately his dispatches rather over-emphasized what had been achieved, greatly exaggerating the Turkish losses and leading the Home authorities to urge him to renew the attempt at once, when another effort should have been postponed until substantial reinforcements and above all much more artillery could be provided.[62]

After the frustrated triumph of March 26, Sir Archibald Murray dispatched an ambiguous telegram to London. In it he gave the impression that the operations had achieved a much greater degree of success than facts bore out. Or as another primary source put it: "Murray's strangely optimistic account of this battle led the Cabinet at home to believe that an easy success would attend a renewed effort, and he was ordered to advance into Palestine, with the capture of Jerusalem as his objective."[63]

Here is General Murray's own assessment of the action at Gaza:

The total of the first battle of Gaza, which gave us 950 Turkish and German prisoners and two Austrian field guns, caused the enemy losses which I estimate at 8,000, and cost us under 4,000 casualties, of which a large proportion were only slightly wounded, was that my primary and secondary objects were completely attained, but that the failure to attain the third object — the capture of Gaza — owing to the delay caused by fog on the 26th, and the waterless nature of the country round Gaza, prevented a most successful operation from being a complete disaster to the enemy. The troops engaged, both cavalry, camelry, and infantry, especially the 53rd Division and the 161st Brigade of the 54th, which had not been seriously in action since the evacuation of Suvla Bay at the end of 1915, fought with the utmost gallantry and endurance, and showed to the full the splendid fighting qualities which they possess.[64]

An even more fanciful assessment of the strategic position run in *The New York Times* probably reflects the misapprehension under which the War Cabinet and War Office labored as a direct result of the distorted picture given them by General Murray. Shrewd politicians such as Lloyd George would have hardly ordered an immediate second attempt had they known the true outcome of the first. The *Times*' assessment said:

After six centuries another crusade — the eighth — is advancing on Jerusalem. In the army of Sir Archibald Murray, however, unlike those of its seven predecessors, many are Moslems — Egyptians and Arabs — who are more concerned in vanquishing the Ottoman Turks than they are in restoring the Holy City to Christendom.

London papers of the last fortnight of March contain stories from their correspondents in Egypt who are permitted to tell something of Sir Archibald's aspirations, his military methods, and the objects of his campaign. It appears to be the belief in his army that all Judea is destined to fall into British hands within the next few weeks.[65]

As a direct consequence of Murray's report, "on March 30th a telegram was sent to General Murray indicating Jerusalem as an immediate objective of his army. He was undoubtedly taken aback at this unexpected extension of his role. In his reply he expressed his doubts on the feasibility on any rapid advance on Jerusalem, and drew attention once again to his unvarying estimate of the troops required — five full infantry divisions."[66]

The War Cabinet was set on a vigorous effort to eliminate Turkey, and the members of that body had some grounds for believing that Murray already possessed the necessary numerical superiority to justify their instructions for a rapid and determined push. Although Sir Archibald Murray loyally acceded to the role he was given, he did so with some serious misgivings; whereas he expressed himself hopeful of taking Gaza, and, subsequently of conducting a successful campaign in Palestine, he did not think the timetable envisaged to be realistic. "The truth is that, with his headquarters at Cairo, he was not properly in touch with the situation at the front, and that his reports in turn misled the War Office."[67]

So as a direct result of the foregoing, General Murray gave the orders for preparations to be made to launch an almost immediate second assault on the

Gaza defenses. However, the German-led Turkish army had received heavy reinforcements, and had immensely strengthened its positions, especially to the southeast, in which direction a strong series of works covered the Gaza-Beersheba Road. If the cavalry were to envelope Gaza as they had done on March 26, the infantry would have to break through that line first.

Captain Teichman's diary entry for April 3, 1917, includes a rather interesting anecdote:

> Owing to native spies having cut the air line between Belah and Khan Yunus, we were ordered to send out a patrol every night between these places. In the evening an Armenian M.O., who had deserted from the Turkish battalion to which he was attached, crossed the Wadi and joined us. He had taken a degree at Harvard, and told us in good English that the Turks had a large force at Jaffa, where they feared a landing with a view to an attack on Jerusalem; he also told us that the enemy had 50 guns around Gaza, two of which were 15-inch, but that at present they feared to take the latter off the railway.[68]

During the intervening two weeks between Gaza I and Gaza II the newly dug British entrenchments were largely left alone by the enemy — apart from spasmodic firing of "Jack Johnsons or coal-boxes" (5.9 inch howitzer shells).

On 16 April 1917, the commander-in-chief of Eastern Force issued the following:

Secret

EASTERN FORCE ORDER NO. 41
BY
LIEUTENANT-GENERAL SIR CHARLES DOBELL, K.G.B., C.M.G.,
D.S.O., Commanding Eastern Force

Headquarters,
Eastern Force.
16th April 1917.

Reference Maps: Palestine, 1/63,360; Gaza (X)a, 1/40,000

1. The latest information regarding the enemy will be notified separately before the second phase of the operations.

2. In accordance with Secret Instructions E.S. 163 of the 15th April, the G.O.C. intends to attack the enemy on....

3. The attack will be preceded by a bombardment of the enemy's position which will begin at Zero hour and will continue for two hours. The Royal Navy and the Heavy Artillery will engage the following objectives: —

(a) Royal Navy —	
H.M.S. *Requin*[69]	Ali Muntar Ridge
One Monitor	The Warren
One Monitor	The Labyrinth
(b) Heavy Artillery Group —	
15th Heavy Battery	Guns and trenches W.10 and W.5
10th Heavy Battery	The Quarry and the Ridge up to Fryer Hill — guns and trenches
91st Heavy Battery	El Arish Redoubt and Magdaba trench

201st Siege Battery, 6-inch Howitzers	Outpost Hill and Middlesex Hill
201st Siege Battery, 8-inch Howitzers	Labyrinth and Green Hill

After Zero plus two hours the ships and heavy artillery will lift their fire on targets in the area north and north-east of Ali el Muntar and north and north-west of Gaza.

Zero hour will be determined according to visibility, under arrangements made by B.G.R.A., Eastern Force, and will be notified to G.O.C. Desert Column and Divisional Commanders as soon as determined.[70]

4. The attack of the 52nd, 53rd, and 54th Divisions will be launched at Zero plus two hours.

5. The objective will be the enemy's positions between the Wadi running from Kh. Sihan to El Aseiferiye on the south-east, and the coast on the north-west.

The objective assigned to the 54th and 53rd Divisions, acting under the orders of G.O.C. 52nd Division, will be the enemy's positions between the Wadi above mentioned (exclusive) and the Ali Muntar group of works (inclusive). G.O.C. 52nd Division will allot their definite objectives to the 52nd and 54th Divisions.

The objective allotted to the 53rd Division will be the enemy trenches in the sand dunes south-west and west of Gaza as far as the line of the Mazar-Magdhaba-Rafah trenches.

6. *(a)* The Desert Column, less the division operating against Hureira from Shellal, will push forward on the right of the 54th Division up the Atawine ridge, against the group of works which have been located there. G.O.C. Desert Column will make every effort to clear this ridge — if necessary leaving his horses and camels behind and operating dismounted. The remaining Mounted Division of the Desert Column will be brought from Shellal to the neighbourhood of El Mendur under instructions issued separately.

(b) The 54th and 53rd Divisions will advance to drive the enemy out of the Kh. El Bir series of works and trenches, and to clear the Es Sire–Ali Muntar ridge as far north as the line Kh. El Bir-Australia Hill.

(c) The 53rd Division will first attack and make good the line Samson Ridge–Sheikh Ajlin. Special arrangements for co-ordination of the attacks of the 52nd and 53rd Divisions have been made between general officers commanding concerned, so that the final stage of the attack of the 52nd Division on Middlesex Hill may be as nearly as possible simultaneous with the final stage of the 53rd Division's attack on Samson Ridge–Sheikh Ajlin. When these preliminary objectives have been gained, the 52nd Division will move forward to the attack of the Ali Muntar group of works simultaneously with the advance of the 53rd Division to the attack of the Mazar-Magdhaba-Rafah trenches and the enemy's works in front (west) of them.

Direct communications by wire and visual will be established between G.O.C's. 52nd and 53rd Divisions, in addition to their communication through Eastern Force Headquarters.

(d) The 74th Division will move across the Wadi Ghazze by crossings C.8 to C.13 and C.20, so as to be assembled between Sharta and the Wadi Nukhabir not later than 5 A.M. The division will move forward thence to the Sheikh Abbas ridge so as to take up a position of readiness behind it by Zero plus one hour, with outposts on the Sheikh Abbas ridge from Hill 300 (Y.1 and 2) to the Sheikh Abbas ridge at W.20. The 263rd Field Artillery Brigade will be transferred from the 54th Division so as to come under the orders of G.O.C. 74th Division at Zero plus two hours.... G.O.C.

54th Division will inform G.O.C. 74th Division of the exact position of this brigade. The 272nd Field Artillery Brigade will come under the orders of the G.O.C. 74th Division from 6.30 on the previous evening, and will then cease to form part of the Eastern Force Artillery.

7. The attack will be pressed home in accordance with instructions already issued in Secret Memorandum E.S. 163 of the 15th April. When the right of the Eastern Attack has made good its objective, immediate steps will be taken to establish and consolidate a strong flank on a line running approximately north and south through Kh. El Bir.

As soon as it is clear that the Ali Muntar group of works has been taken, the 52nd and 54th Divisions, less such troops as are found to be required for the flank about Kh. El Bir, will go forward to clear the northern portion of the Ali Muntar ridge (Anzac Ridge). Simultaneously with this movement the 53rd Division will push forward between Gaza and the sea from the Mazar-El Arish-Magdhaba-Zowaiid-Rafah line of trenches, to make good the area west of the town, but keeping clear of the town itself so far as possible. G.O.C.'s. 52nd and 53rd Divisions will keep each other informed of their progress direct as well as through Eastern Force Headquarters, so that the commencement of their respective movements towards their final destination may be synchronized.

8. G.O.C. 74th Division will establish communication by cable and visual with G.O.C. 52nd Division, as soon as the 74th Division reaches Sheikh Abbas. In the event of serious difficulty in communication between the 52nd Division and Eastern Force Headquarters, G.O.C. 52nd Division is empowered in emergency, or in case of immediate decision being required in order to exploit success, to call upon the 74th Division to act as he may consider necessary in either contingency. Unless, however, he is satisfied that the situation on the right flank has been cleared up, either by the complete success of the 54th Division or by the definite location of the Turkish 16th Division, he will not move more than two infantry brigades and one field artillery brigade under this authority without first having received sanction from Eastern Force Headquarters. In any case, should the occasion arise for the exercise of this authority, G.O.C. 52nd Division will be responsible for ensuring that a report notifying his action shall reach Eastern Force headquarters at the earliest possible moment.

9. G.O.C. Desert Column will, after the initial movements of the operation, act on the instructions already given in Secret Memorandum E.S. 163 of the 15th April.

10. Special instructions regarding the Royal Flying Corps will be issued in due course, if the arrangements are varied from those made for the first phase of the operations.

11. If all the objectives are gained before nightfall, the 54th and 74th Divisions will take up defensive line facing approximately east, on the ridge running from the west of Kh. Kufiye, between Kh. El Bir and Kh. Sihan, to Sheikh Abbas. The 52nd Division will be disposed facing north-east and east with its left astride the northern portion of the Anzac Ridge. The 53rd Division will concentrate in the area Jebaliye-Sheikh Redwan-Meshahera—(the village of Jebaliye and the shrine of Sheikh Redwan are north of Gaza). G.O.C. 53rd Division will detail the necessary troops to take charge of and control Gaza unless parties of the enemy are still holding out in the town at nightfall, in which case this work will be taken on the following morning.

In any case, all commanders will take measures to keep their troops clear of the town until G.O.C. 53rd Division reports that the necessary measures for its control have been established.

12. In the event of the action not being brought to a conclusion within the day, the troops will hold the ground gained and will consolidate their positions during the

night, preparatory to continuing the action on the following morning. In this event, divisions will be watered in accordance with the instructions contained in O.Z. 2/21 of the 10th April. The water dump (filled *fanatis*[71]), established in the neighbourhood of Tell el Ahmar-Mansura will, however, be available for troops of the 52nd and 54th Divisions if necessary; also for any troops of the 74th Division who may have been called on by the G.O.C. 52nd Division in accordance with the conditional authority given above in para. 8. The use of the water dump for this purpose will be at the discretion of G.O.C. 52nd Division. Every endeavour is, however, to be made to ensure that this water dump is not drawn upon unnecessarily and that in all cases in which it is possible animals are sent back to water at the divisional water areas referred to in the instruction above quoted, and that water is brought up from those areas is for the troops.

13. Instructions are being issued separately with regard to supply arrangements after divisions reach positions referred to in para. 11 above.

14. The Casualty Clearing Stations will remain at Deir el Balah Station and the main dressing stations as stated in amendment to Eastern Force Order No. 40, dated April 15th 1917. Any change in the above locations will be notified to all concerned. The positions of divisional advanced dressing stations, as altered from time to time in accordance with the requirements of the situation, will be notified to D.D.M.S. Eastern Force without delay.

15. The date left blank in the above orders will be notified in due course.

16. Eastern Force Headquarters will remain in its present position.

17. Acknowledge.

G. P. Dawnay
Brigadier-General, General Staff, Eastern Force.

Issued at 11.35 p.m.[72]

On April 16, the Essex Field Artillery Brigade was ordered to march at midnight and support the attack of the 163rd Infantry Brigade (1/4 & 1/5 Norfolks; 1/5 Suffolks; and 1/8 Hampshires) on the Sheikh Abbas Ridge, which was to commence at dawn.[73] Up to April 16 the two Norfolk battalions were at In Seirat, taking their turn in the trenches of the defensive position, in support or in reserve. During the night of the 16th-17th the 163rd brigade moved to the assembly position at Sharta, with orders to again carry the Sheikh Abbas ridge at dawn. The general line of attack was now to face north-eastwards, with its left on the sea and its right on the Wadi running from Khirbet Sihan to El Azaferieh.[74]

The assault commenced according to schedule and the capture of the Sheikh Abbas ridge on the 17th was effected without much difficulty by the brigade assigned the task. The Turks had only a few outposts there and the 8th Hampshire and 5th Suffolk battalions, preceded by the two tanks, and supported by the two Norfolk battalions, established themselves on the ridge and consolidated the position. The Turkish main line was along the Gaza-Beersheba road. During the consolidation there was a good deal of shell fire, and "A" Company of the 1/5th Norfolk under Captain Birkbeck received a good deal of the enemy's attentions, though fortunately casualties were few.

Two. The Sinai Peninsula and the Failures at Gaza   83

Sheikh Abbas Ridge, a key feature in all three battles of Gaza (Fair and Wolton, *The History of the 1/5th Battalion: "The Suffolk Regiment"*).

The night of the 17th–18th and the whole of the 18th were spent in this position. The rest of the line had also attained its first objectives without serious difficulties.[75] Orders for the general attack on the 19th were issued so late on the 18th that they did not reach the men till nearly midnight, with the result that most of the night had to be spent in preparations for attack and distributing rations and water, all of which might well have been done during the day, had orders been issued earlier. The orders contemplated the attack and capture of Gaza and the formation of a new line beyond it. There was to be a heavy bombardment from 5:30 A.M. for two hours before the infantry assault commenced.[76]

"The Battery [(Essex) 'B,' 271st Brigade, Royal Field Artillery] marched out with the infantry column at midnight, travelling in an easterly direction, and accompanied by tanks."[77] After something like a five mile march the guns were brought into action, ready to commence a bombardment as soon as the light became strong enough to observe the fall of shot. During this march to the position, silence was, of course, strictly enjoined on the troops, in order that the Turks should not discover the movement; this precaution was, however, negated by the spluttering roar emitted by the tanks, which, in all probability, was heard in Gaza itself, as they floundered over the ground, leaving in their wake a trail of sparks.[78]

At dawn the 163rd Brigade (54th Division — 1/4 &1/5 Norfolks, 1/5 Suffolk, and 1/8 Hampshire) occupied the Sheikh Abbas Ridge without requiring the support of the batteries on the right flank, and consolidated their position by digging in on the edge of the cliff. One of the tanks, which had done valuable work in clearing the enemy off the ridge, was struck by a shell and burnt out. Prior to the attack, the

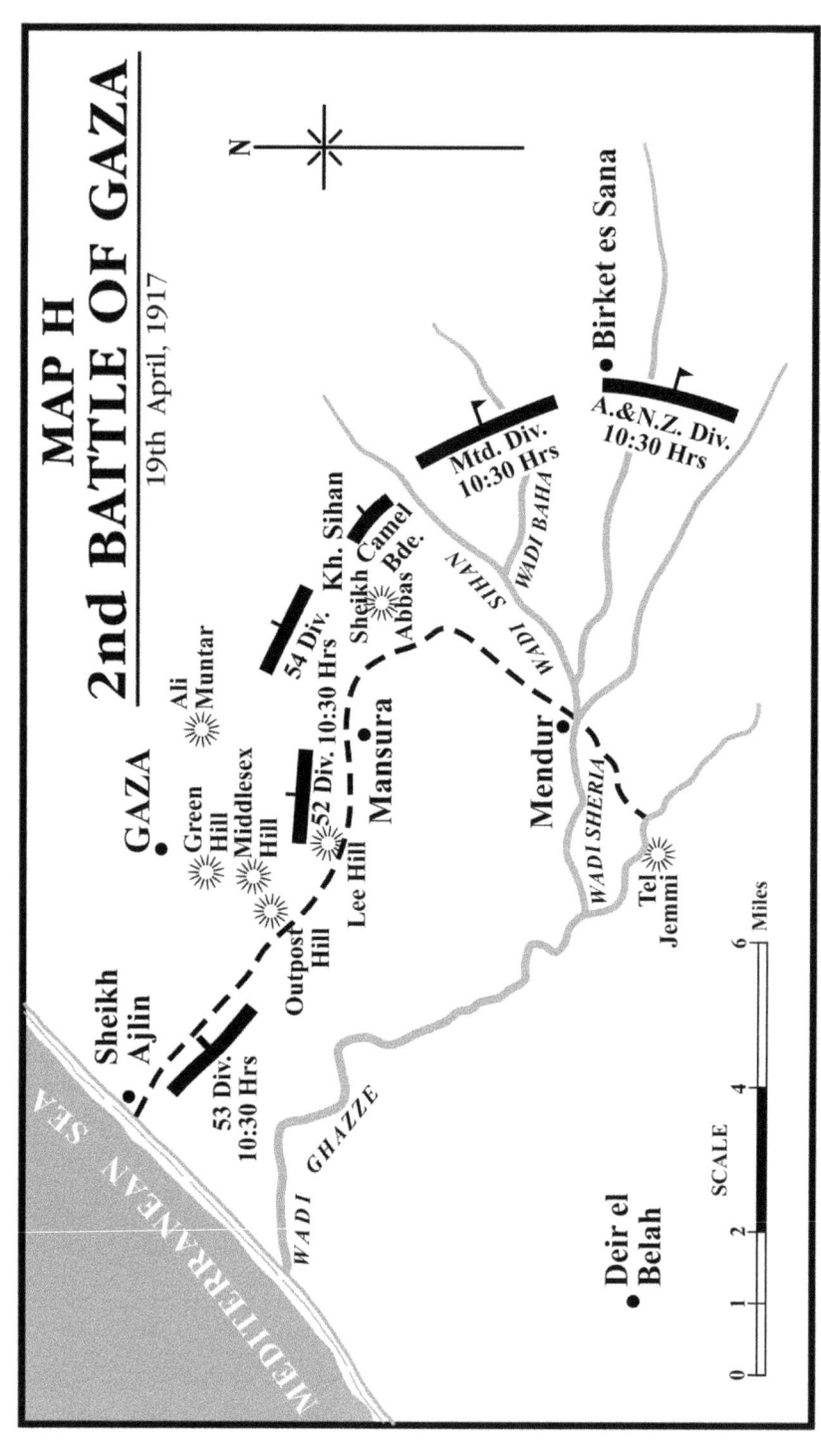

infantry had secured to their packs pieces of bright tin, cut from biscuit boxes and so forth, which glinted in the sun, so that their progress could be followed accurately by battery commanders.[79]

Petrie describes the attack:

> The 163rd brigade was to attack about Khirbet-el-Bir with the 52nd division on its left. In the front line were the 1/5th Norfolk on the right, the 1/4th Norfolk on the left, and the 8th Hants in support, with the 5th Suffolk in reserve. The four battalions were ready at 5 A.M. for the advance, which was to commence at 7.30 after a heavy bombardment for two hours. To the bombardment the Turks had made little or no reply, but when the infantry moved forward it soon became apparent that the British artillery had done very little harm, and the attack was met by what Captain Buxton describes as "a perfect hell of artillery and machine-gun fire." The British artillery could not give them adequate support, as they had already fired away a great part of their ammunition, and, moreover, the range of 6,000 yards was excessive. Thus, with little support, the infantry had to cross some 1,700 yards of undulating country in full view of the Turks awaiting them in trenches and well-wired redoubts beyond the Gaza-Beersheba road. At 7.30 the two Norfolk battalions advanced. Watching the first stages from brigade head-quarters, Captain Buxton writes that "it was a magnificent sight to see them going over in extended order as if on a field day."[80] Each battalion covered a front of about 900 yards. The right of the 1/5th Norfolk was directed on a Turkish redoubt which soon began to give trouble. The first low ridge was crossed by 8.30 and the second, about 500 yards further on, was reached. The 8th Hampshire now moved with one tank against the redoubt on the right of the 1/5th Norfolk. On the opposite flank, the left of the 1/4th Norfolk, the other tank advanced on another redoubt, but unfortunately was hit by a shell and put out of action. The 1/5th Norfolk disappeared over the second ridge and communication between the battalions became very difficult. The tank with the 1/5th and the 8th Hants was presently set on fire, but not before it had inflicted heavy damage on the enemy and sent back twenty prisoners taken in the capture of the redoubt, which was held by a party of the 1/5th Norfolk men and some of the Camel Corps. All this time the British had been suffering very heavy loss from the Turkish artillery, machine-gun, and rifle fire which the British artillery, at a range of 6,000 yards, was unable to keep down. At about 10 A.M. Lieutenant Buxton, who had gone out to get information for brigade head-quarters, telephoned what he had seen from a shell hole in which he had ensconced himself. In his own words:

> "It was quite obvious what had happened. The advance had been held up just below the Turkish line, and one could see our men lying out in lines, killed or wounded. The 1/5th Norfolk 'B' company, under Captain Blyth, had captured Tank Redoubt and had held it for some time, till all ammunition was spent. No support came up, and so those who did not get away, sixty in all, were captured in the Turkish counter-attack. My second tank, under Captain Carr (that with the 1/5th Norfolk on the right), had done very well in getting into the redoubt. The first tank had had a direct hit and was burning. It was obvious that our attack here had failed, and that most of our men had been killed. So I waited a bit longer, and when things were a shade quieter, got out of my shell-hole and ran back over the rise. There I came on about forty men of our brigade of all regiments. Major Marsh, who was O.C. 8th Hampshire, was there too, and Lieutenant Wharton of the 1/4th Norfolk. These men were just stragglers and all collected there. We decided it was no good going on then, so we started to dig ourselves in. This was all early in the morning — about 9. Marsh had a telephone line so I phoned back to Brigade H.Q. and gave them all the news. There were a lot of dead men and wounded all round us. Some of the latter we got

behind our lines, in case the Turks tried a counter-attack. We were about forty men and one Lewis gun, and no one on our left or right for several hundred yards. The place we were holding was the top of a rounded hillock. The Turks kept us under pretty good machine-gun fire all day. Marsh and I lay in a rifle pit and ate dates and biscuits for a bit. We allowed no firing, as we wished to keep all our ammunition in case of a counter-attack. About 4 in the afternoon the 5th Suffolk were sent up to support us and to consolidate the position we had held. This was really a great relief. About 7 P.M. the brigadier came out after dusk and saw the place. He ordered us to retire during the night right back to our starting point, for it would not have been possible to hold this advanced position as long as there was no one on our flanks at all.

"During the day a few stragglers joined us, among them Corporal Burtenshaw and a private. He told me that Captain Birkbeck had been very badly wounded. I told the O.C. Suffolks whereabouts he was said to be. They promised to send out patrols to try and find him, but these did no good at all, as I afterwards heard."[81]

"A heavy fire [artillery] was kept up all day in support of this attack, the Brigade expending some three thousand rounds of ammunition."[82]

The Attack of Eastern Force

At 5.30 A.M. the bombardment began, the warships shelling the rear of the enemy defences and the heavy artillery concentrating on the most important points. At 7.30 A.M. both switched their fire respectively to north and north-west of Gaza, and north and north-east of Ali Muntar, to avoid endangering the infantry, which began its advance at this hour. At 7.20 the 18-pdr. Batteries established a barrage on certain points to be attacked. There were not enough guns to cover the whole front, and even as it was the barrage was thin.

The advance of the 54th and 52nd Divisions began punctually at 7.30 A.M. The 163rd Brigade on the right of the 54th Division was directed north-east, its right on a Turkish redoubt one mile north-west of Kh. Sihan, its frontage 1,500 yards. On its left was the 162nd Brigade, with its left on the point where the Wadi Mukaddeme crossed the Gaza-Beersheba road. The 161st Brigade was in divisional reserve. The Camel Brigade moved simultaneously on the right of the 54th Division against Kh. Sihan. On the left the 52nd Division advanced, its leading brigade, the 155th, moving along Es Sire Ridge, while the 156th followed, echeloned to the right rear and prepared to swing up to attack Green Hill and Ali Muntar. The 157th Brigade was in reserve to the eastern attack.

It was speedily evident that the fire of the warships, the heavy artillery, and the field howitzers firing gas—mainly directed during the preliminary bombardment, as it had been, against the trenches—had in no way silenced the enemy's artillery. From Mansura and the Sheikh Abbas Ridge the ground to the north-east drops very slightly, then rises again equally slightly as the Gaza-Beersheba road is approached. In sharp contrast to the country between the Mansura bluff and the wadi, this is remarkably open and devoid of cover. As the brigades of the 54th Division advanced they came under well-directed artillery fire and, on approaching the Turkish trenches, under intense machine-gun fire also. The attack was carried out with admirable steadiness, the leading battalions moving straight on their objectives, despite heavy casualties.

On the right the 163rd Brigade (Brig. General T. Ward), led by a tank directed on the Turkish redoubt one mile north-west of Kh. Sihan, gained a ridge 500 yards from the enemy's trenches at 8.30 A.M. Half an hour later the tank, followed by part of the right battalion, the 5/Norfolk, entered the redoubt, killing or driving out the garrison and taking 20 prisoners. The Turks immediately concentrated the fire of several batteries on the redoubt, destroyed the tank, and caused casualties so heavy in the ranks of the 5/Norfolk that the party was unable to withstand the counter-attack which followed. The remnants fell back to the ridge from which they had advanced. The 4/Norfolk on the left fared no better, and was pinned to the ground also about 500 yards from its objective, after losing two-thirds of its numbers. The 8/Hampshire had been thrown in and had also suffered very heavy losses without being able to carry the assault forward. These three battalions had lost 1,500 men, including two commanding officers and all twelve company commanders.

On the left the 162nd Brigade (Brig. General A. Mudge), attacked with the 4/Northampton on the right, the 10/London on the left, and the 11/London in support behind the centre. Heavy casualties occurred from the first from artillery fire from behind Ali Muntar, from machine-gun fire, and also from that of mountain guns which must have been close up among the enemy's entrenchments. The 4/Northampton was held up 500 yards from the enemy's trenches. A handful of men, including Lewis gunners, worked their way forward almost to the Turkish parapet, and shot down a number of enemy at pointblank range, but this small party was eventually destroyed. The 10/London made the greatest advance of that black day. The right half battalion, endeavouring to keep in touch with the 4/Northampton, became separated from the left and was held up in front of the Turkish works, but the left, faced by no connected lines of trenches, fought its way across the Gaza-Beersheba road at 8.30 A.M. By rifle and Lewis-gun fire it drove out of action a Turkish infantry gun, which was hastily withdrawn to the ridge north of Ali Muntar. A deed of extraordinary gallantry was accomplished by Sapper Sore, of the brigade signal section, in cutting the telegraph line beside the road. He climbed a pole and cut one wire, but was then brought to the ground by fire from a range of under three hundred yards. Undaunted he climbed up the pole again, cut a second strand, and was in the act of cutting the third and last when he was blown to pieces by a shell fired from a mountain gun a few hundred yards away. The left of the 10th London was now completely isolated, there being a gap of 800 yards between it and the right half battalion, while it was far ahead of the 52nd Division on its left. Two machine-guns were pushed out to cover the left flank on the Wadi Mukaddeme, but the position remained hopelessly exposed. The situation was somewhat eased by the subsequent advance of the 52nd Division's right, but the party was eventually forced to fall back across the road. A counter-attack by two Turkish battalions compelled the whole battalion to fall back another 600 yards, but was then brought to a standstill, the machine-gun sections on the Wadi Mukaddeme swinging round to fire north-east and doing considerable execution.

At 1 P.M. General Hare ordered the 161st Brigade (Brig. General W. Marriott-Doddington) in reserve to reinforce the line held by the 163rd Brigade. The 5/Suffolk of the 163rd, supported by the 6/Essex of the 161st, was ordered to make a fresh attack on the redoubt from which the 5/Norfolk had been driven. At 2.20 P.M. these battalions began their advance, but had not become seriously engaged before General Hare ordered the whole line to stand fast.

On the right of the 54th Division the Camel Brigade, reinforced by one battalion of the 161st Brigade, was to attack Kh. Sihan up to but exclusive of the redoubt a mile north-west of it. It had not been employed during the first phase and had come up the previous night to Dumb-bell Hill, due south of Sheikh Abbas. It advanced in conjunction with the original attack of the 54th Division, and men of the 1st Battalion on the left entered the redoubt at the same time as the 5/Norfolk, the leading companies having lost half their effectives. Almost immediately the tank, repeatedly hit by shells, burst into flames. The enemy's artillery killed most of the men who entered the redoubt; the few who remained were captured by the Turkish counter-attack already described. On the right the 3rd Battalion crossed the Gaza-Beersheba road and temporarily established itself on two hummocks known as "Jack and Jill," east Kh. Sihan. When the 4th L.H. [Light Horse—Australian][83] on its right was forced to give ground before a Turkish counter-attack, the men of the 3rd Battalion were likewise compelled to withdraw across the road, then slightly refusing its right.

At 3 P.M. General Hare, as already stated, ordered his division and the Camel Brigade to stand fast. He was concerned lest the strong counter-attacks in progress against the Imperial Mounted Division should uncover his right, in which case he considered it might be necessary to swing it back towards Sheikh Abbas. Moreover it was becoming apparent that, however gallantly the infantry might struggle, there was not a sufficient volume of artillery fire to carry the assault through positions strong in themselves and most stubbornly defended. Whenever a small breach was made the troops which had made it were so thinned by the enemy's fire as to be unable to resist the furious counter-attacks repeatedly launched by the Turks.[84]

Historians Fair and Wolton add: "A tank, which had been christened 'Sir Archibald Murray,' was hit by a Turkish shell just in front of our line, and catching fire was put out of action at once.... A tank pushed on to Tank Redoubt, and held it until it was occupied by 1/8th Hants. It was, however, put out of action by enemy artillery fire, and could not move from there.... The tanks had not given as much assistance as was expected, but a very large amount of artillery fire had been concentrated on them, and in that way they saved us many casualties."[85]

Private Jake Mortlock of the 5th Suffolk vividly recalled this action in Gaza II: "The Norfolks were mown down in swathes—still there when third attack was launched." When I asked him whether he ever thought that he would be killed, his reply was: "Yes—all the time."[86]

The 54th had progressed considerably in their attack on the Tank Ridge position to the southeast of the town, enfiladed by very heavy fire from Kh. Sihan — where the Camel Corps were held up — and from Middlesex Hill, which had defied the efforts of the 52nd Division. "Five or six tanks, which had been brought up with the utmost secrecy, were deployed to break a way through the wire and the trenches but just could not get up the sandhills they were expected to scale. With the tanks bogged down, the unfortunate Infantry had an even harder job than in the first battle, and, after suffering appalling casualties, they had to withdraw."[87] Of the few tanks, one had been knocked out in the first advance, another on Outpost Hill, and another on the "Tank Redoubt" in which the 8th Hampshires (163rd Brigade) had actually gained a footing, suffering enormous casualties, as also did the 4th Northamptonshires (162nd Brigade) and the Norfolks (163rd Brigade).[88] "The 4th Battalion the Northamptonshire Regiment were heavily engaged at the second Battle of Gaza, with a loss of 386."[89]

The commander-in-chief, in his official dispatch, said "the 54th Division, on the right of the main attack, had progressed, in spite of determined opposition and heavy casualties, as far as was possible until a further advance of the 52nd Division should prevent the exposure of its left flank. Reports received from the 54th Division stated that the situation was satisfactory and that no help was required in order to enable the ground gained to be held until further progress by the 52nd Division should render practicable a renewal of the advance." He added, "I should like to state here my appreciation of the great skill with which General Hare handled his fine Division throughout the day."

In the evening the brigade on Outpost Hill was forced to evacuate the hill. Orders were received to consolidate the ground won during the day in a readiness for a resumption of the attack at dawn. Total casualties had amounted to some 7,000.[90]

Captains Fair and Wolton, in their *History of the 1/5th Suffolks*, state: "In the November battle the corpses of the 19th April were still lying around, or in front of it [Tank Redoubt].[91] The Turks had made no attempt to bury them. Most of them lay in long lines where the cross fire had mown them down, but some had reached the wire, and a few were near the parapet.... We felt that their lives had been sacrificed in a gallant attempt to capture a position that was impregnable by day."[92]

The Situation at Nightfall on the 19th April

As the evening approached it was painfully apparent that there was absolutely no prospect of success on any portion of the front. The troops of the Eastern Attack had striven most gallantly to attain their objectives, the 54th Division in particular having expended itself without stint. At a few points the enemy's front-line trenches had been taken, only to be promptly recaptured by determined counter-attacks. There had been neither gun-power nor ammunition sufficient to carry the attack further. The 52nd and 54th Divisions had both lost heavily. One brigade only of the former was intact, while one brigade of the 54th had had comparatively light casualties, and the 74th Division had not been engaged.

Sir A. Murray at Khan Yunis had been anxiously following the progress of the battle. "Since it was evident," he wrote in his dispatch, "that the action could not be brought to a conclusion within the day, at 4 P.M. I issued personally instructions to the general officer commanding Eastern Force that all ground gained must, without fail, must be held during the night with a view to resuming the attack on the Ali Muntar position, under cover of a concentrated artillery bombardment at dawn on the 20th."

> Despite the injunction to abandon no ground, it was necessary to adjust the line of the 54th Division, since its leading troops, lying out in the open in face of the Turkish

defences, were in an impossible position. Under cover of the Camel Brigade, which had its right close to Kh. Sihan, the right was withdrawn to the neighbourhood of Sheikh Abbas, where it was in touch with a brigade of the 74th Division. On the front of the 52nd Division the line passed close to the foot of Outpost Hill, but the construction of a new position through Heart and Blazed Hills was begun. The 53rd Division maintained its hold on Samson Ridge, which represented almost the only gain of the battle not already attained in the first phase of the 17th April.

General Dobell issued orders for the renewal of the attack next day. When, however, he had heard from his divisional commanders what was the state of their troops and their ammunition supply, had learned that the casualties were estimated to be 6,000, he decided that a fresh assault would only result in further heavy losses, without hope of success. He therefore postponed the attack for twenty-four hours and reported to Sir A. Murray that in his opinion no further advance was possible, adding that General Chetwode and the divisional commanders all held the same view. Sir A. Murray was reluctantly compelled to agree that the decision was just, and, though as late as the 22nd he informed the War Office that he still contemplated a renewed offensive, the reinforcement of the enemy's position finally obliged him to abandon the project.[93]

Private Jake Mortlock, writing to his cousin, Jack Parker, with typical British understatement, described the Second Battle of Gaza thus: "We have been having some rather lively times out here lately with old Johnny Turk, but at present things are a bit quieter."

Captain Oskar Teichman, in his diary entry for April 22nd, wrote:

> We heard for the first time of the very heavy losses sustained by the Fifty-fourth Division on April 19th, and how the Norfolks had suffered on rushing a redoubt which was supposed to have been successfully gas-shelled; we also heard how some of our tanks had been lost, and of the changes taken place in the Higher Command. These facts, coupled with the news that the Turks had received another 14,000 reinforcements and the total number of casualties which our whole force had sustained, had rather a depressing effect upon us. We had had practically a complete week's fighting and digging, with little sleep and scarcity of water, and had apparently little to show for it except a retirement as far as our brigade was concerned.[94]

The Higher Command, however, concluded during the night that the projected attack did not offer sufficient chances of success to warrant the very heavy casualties which were bound to occur, and the only course open was to dig in on the line now held to await a more favorable opportunity. This could hardly arise until the army received substantial reinforcements.[95]

This, almost flippant, evaluation does not even begin to consider the profligate loss of life and limb occasioned by pressing ahead with an ill-conceived, foolhardy assault so soon after the troops had been so fully extended. Private Jake Mortlock, in his letter to his cousin, Jack Parker, writes of "chaps falling down asleep" from utter exhaustion after Gaza I.

As to the human cost, *The History of the Norfolk Regiment* gives the following harrowing tabulation: "The casualties in this disastrous attack of the 19th were extremely heavy in the Norfolk battalions, as shown below":

Two. The Sinai Peninsula and the Failures at Gaza

	Killed		Wounded		Missing		Total	
	Officers	Other Ranks	Officers	Other Ranks	Officers	Other Ranks	Officers	Other Ranks
1/4th Bn.	6[96]	49	11	312	1	99	18	460
1/5th Bn.	6[97]	13	9	401	4	229	19	643

"First Gaza" had been a disappointment; "Second Gaza" was a disastrous reverse. It finished all prospects of any further advance by the E.E.F. until much more artillery and substantial reinforcements could arrive. For the 8th Hampshire it meant settling down to a tedious period of trench warfare opposite Gaza, waiting for drafts. Still, this long wait was far from a time of inactivity, and the battalion carried out a most successful minor operation and became most proficient in patrolling and harassing the enemy.[98]

The British newspapers continued to call the catastrophe of Gaza II a triumph:

GAZA BATTLE
*****
British On the Road to Beersheba.
*****

The Secretary of the War Office made the following announcement last night:—
In continuation of the *communiqué* issued on April 20, reports received form the general officer commanding-in-chief in Egypt indicate that his troops have consolidated the ground gained and are now in touch with the enemy main position covering Gaza....
About 200 Turkish prisoners were captured on the 19th inst.[99]

The 5th Norfolk assaults from Sheikh Abbas, during the Second Battle of Gaza, April 19, 1917. Both Norfolk battalions were decimated —"cut down in swathes," to quote an eye witness. Private Jake Mortlock and his comrades-in-arms also took part in this battle (courtesy Joan Jarold).

After the Second Battle of Gaza

On 21 April, by order of Sir A. Murray, Lt. General Sir Philip Chetwode assumed command of the Eastern Force and Lt. General Sir Charles Dobell returned to England. Major General Sir H. G. Chauvel succeeded General Chetwode in command of the Desert Column, and Brig. General E.W.C. Chaytor replaced him in command of the Australian and New Zealand Mounted Division.

General Chetwode, like his predecessor, was of the opinion that, owing to the strength of the enemy's position, the renewal of a direct attack with the forces at the disposal of Eastern Force was not justified. In this view his subordinate commanders concurred. Sir A. Murray decided, however, to maintain, subject to minor tactical readjustment, the position gained on the northern and eastern side of the Wadi Ghazze — a totally illogical and mindless decision and reminiscent of the Western Front generals' mindset. The first problem was, then, to make this position secure; the second to reorganize the force, and particularly the infantry divisions, after its severe trials and frightful losses. The prospect ahead was not a pleasant one. The really hot weather was at hand and another summer was to be endured, if not in the heat of the desert, on its verge, where desert heat and winds were prevalent; while to the strain induced by these conditions that of the tedium of trench warfare was to be added.

There was, however, to be one important difference between the deadlock which had resulted here and that on the Western Front. In Palestine, as in France, each adversary had one flank upon the sea, but in this case, unlike that of the main theater, each had the other flank open. On the British right the power to maneuver was limited only by the difficulties of water supply; the Turks, with Beersheba in their possession, were even less constrained in this respect on their left.[100]

The Times of London reported:

TURKS REINFORCED IN PALESTINE
*****
BRITISH GAINS CONSOLIDATED

The War Office makes the following announcement about the operations in Palestine: —

The Turkish forces in Southern Palestine, who have been reinforced, hold a strongly entrenched position extending from Gaza in the direction of Beersheba (twenty-five miles south-east of Gaza on the Turkish strategic railway).

Reports from the commander-in-chief in Egypt state that the organization of the positions gained in front of the Turkish main line is proceeding satisfactorily.

Our artillery, assisted by aircraft cooperation, have blown up an ammunition dump in Gaza.

The Turkish advanced positions on the Gaza front were captured eight days ago.

The other side's version is carried below: —

TURKISH STORY OF BRITISH WITHDRAWAL.

Turkish report, April 22:—
The enemy defeated near Gaza withdrew his right wing. He is constructing new positions with the view to protecting that flank. The small number of prisoners taken in this fight proves that the struggle was of a desperate character. We captured a large number of rifles and some automatic guns.
Three of the armoured motor-cars which the enemy sent into the fight were destroyed.—*Reuters.*[101]

Naturally enough the reaction in London to the appalling results of the second attempt to take Gaza did not bode well for the commanding general responsible. It was therefore merely a matter of time before at least one more head would roll. General Sir Archibald Murray's second attempt on Gaza "found the Turks well prepared and was repulsed. His force was in any case inadequate for a full-blooded campaign in Palestine, as he tried to explain. Despite his earlier achievements the set backs at Gaza unfairly tarnished his record. He was now associated with failure and had to go."[102]

Murray himself obliquely blamed Lt. General Sir Charles Dobell, commander-in-chief of the Eastern Force, E.E.F., for the catastrophe, and on 21 April, "I interviewed General Dobell and informed him of my decision [to relieve him of his command], in which he concurred."[103] But Murray was no longer in a secure position himself, having led the War Cabinet to expect a stirring victory all he had delivered was a costly reversal and a humiliating defeat.

The Palestine campaign now settled into a stalemate along a line of entrenchments from Gaza on the Mediterranean to the water wells of Beersheba at the foot of the mountains thirty air miles to the southeast.[104] There was considerable bitterness among the frontline soldiers over what had transpired. The troops were bitterly disillusioned and very angry because General Murray had no idea how to break the deadlock and kept his headquarters in the comfort of the Savoy Hotel in Cairo, giving awards for gallant services to members of his large headquarters staff, many of whom had never even seen the front line.[105] Actually Murray did temporarily move to a train carriage at El Arish so as to be closer to Generals Dobell and Chetwode quartered at In Seirat.

It was during this period that Private W. Vincent Rumbelow, "D" Company, 1/5th Suffolks, was mortally wounded by a 5.9 shell burst (May 1, 1917) while "on light duties" as his comrades were detailed for a wiring party. Murray reported, "They directed artillery fire on the rear of our positions on the Mansura ridge, doing a certain amount of damage among the transport animals, and making any movement of camel transport during the day impossible."[106]

Although urged by his pal, Private Jake Mortlock, to come with their wiring party, "as the Turks will send over a few shells and we shall be lying about most of the day" he would not heed the argument and a 5.9 ("Jack Johnson or coal box") shell mortally wounded him. His sister, Marjorie, remembered the fateful day the postman delivered the tragic news, and said that their parents' nightly

Mansura Ridge, Gaza I. This is the general location of Private Rumbelow's mortal wounding by a "Jack Johnson"—5.9-inch artillery shell, May 1, 1917 (Fair and Wolton, *The History of the 1/5th Battalion: "The Suffolk Regiment"*).

prayers to the Almighty to bring "Vin" safely home ended with the terrible telegram, and never again did she see them kneeling by their bed.[107]

Private Mortlock's grief is not readily detected in the letter he penned in the rear of the Sheikh Abbas Ridge relating the tragedy, but the loss of his best pal was a terrible blow to him — not to mention his sister, Gwen, who was engaged to be married to Vin. "One of the Best" was Jake's tribute written on the back of the photograph. W. Vincent Rumbelow's premature death also had unforeseen repercussions with regard to the family ownership of the ancient Freckenham Manor, as his surviving brother was a cripple and not able to manage such an onerous task.

After the Disaster of Gaza II

Kearsey writes, "There was position warfare now in front of Gaza from the Wadi Ghazze at Tel Jemmi on our right through Sharta and Dumb Bell Hill to Sheikh Abbas, then in a north-westerly direction by Mansura, Blazed Hill, Heart Hill, Samson Ridge, to the sea to Sheikh Ajlin."[108]

Sometime during this period of the campaign, Reg Lane — now a subaltern in the Egyptian Labour Corps—experienced some lighter moments, as he recounted to the author some forty-odd years afterwards. One involved finding and returning stolen horses to a Bedouin sheikh, who expressed his gratitude by inviting him to accompany him and his party hawking. The second related to a Royal Flying Corps' pilot-officer who landed where Lane was supervising a detail. Mutual introductions followed and Lane apologized for not being able to entertain the airman, but told him to repair to the Officers' Mess and partake of some liquid refreshment on Lane's mess account. Some little while later the fellow rejoined his aircraft, bid his farewells, donned his pilot's helmet and goggles to fly off into the far blue yonder. When Lane eventually went to the mess he discovered that the intrepid aviator had consumed six triple-brandies at his expense.

Captain Lane also said that when he and his unit were posted to, and arrived in, France that the question of the Egyptians wearing boots arose. In their native land none wore footwear, but conditions in Europe were quite dif-

Left: Private W. Vincent Rumbelow, "One of the Best," as his close friend Jake Mortlock described him. Engaged to be married to Jake's sister, Gwen, Vin was mortally wounded on Mansura Ridge on May 1, 1917, died five days later and was buried at El Arish Military Cemetery. *Right:* Private Reg Lane gained weight after a promotion. He ended the War in France with the commissioned rank of captain (both images Mortlock family photographs).

Three general service officers, possibly friends of Reg Lane (Mortlock family photograph).

ferent. It was a knotty problem, as the men practically refused to be encumbered by army boots. However, some genius discovered that as long as the fellows were issued with them, that was sufficient. So they tied the laces together and marched along happily with the boots around their necks.[109]

Trench Warfare Stalemate

"Six months of trench warfare followed"[110] the Gaza II debacle during which the Turkish defenses did not become less formidable while the British spent a great deal of time and physical effort perfecting theirs.

During these "six months of trench warfare" Private Jake Mortlock had a well-nigh miraculous escape while manning a front line trench when a bomb — mortar or hand-thrown — hit the trench wall and fell between his feet. The explosion blew him down, but he suffered no wounds at all. Another intriguing anecdote he shared with me: such was the highly tempered steel of the bayonet's blade that if struck by a bullet it would bend at a right angle to itself, and could be straightened out by the soldier wedging a few inches' length from the tip into an immoveable object, then applying the right amount of leverage. He also said that the ambulances were unsprung iron-tired wagons which would jolt the wounded painfully.[111]

Lt. Colonel Thomas Gibbons, of the 1/5th Battalion of the Essex Regiment, in his admirable military history, details this interval of trench warfare and supplies valuable insights into the workings of the routine.

> On June 12th the 54th Division relieved the 52nd in the Coastal Sector, which stretched from the sea at Sheikh Ajlin, on the left to Lees Hill inclusive on the right, a frontage of about 7,000 yards. The 161st Brigade relieved the 157th of the 52nd Division in the right sub-sector, the 5th Essex taking over from the 5th Argyle and Sutherland Highlanders, who held the salient of Lees Hill and Blazed Hill and a considerable length of line across the Kurd Valley. The position was well organised in two lines of trenches connected by frequent communication trenches (which stood well in the hard ground) and there were some good dug-outs. There was also a most convenient dry wadi bed running laterally in rear of the whole Battalion Section, in which ration, water and R.E. dumps were established, easily accessible by pack transport. Observation and field of fire were alike excellent, but the trenches on the forward slope of Blazed Hill looked very conspicuous from the front and a really heavy bombardment could easily have demolished them. They were a little over 500 yards from the enemy's front line on Outpost Hill, which was part of the same ridge, but separated by a saddle, from which started two wadis, one running to the right round our flank and down the Happy Valley, and the other round the left of Blazed Hill, breaking through the line on our left and following the Kurd Valley. The Battalion moved in lines of platoons in fours straight up the broad Kurd Valley and was met by guides from the outgoing battalion, who led companies straight to their posts, making the relief an easy and pleasant one. Advance parties from companies and Battalion Headquarters had, of course, made themselves acquainted with the line. Brigade Headquarters were behind the crest of Queen's Hill, another feature of the same ridge, about a thousand yards to the rear. It had the rather rare advantage of a good view of a great part of the enemy's front line.[112]

A paraphrased account of Colonel Gibbons continues: A very deep gully led from Brigade Headquarters to the Battalion Section and this made excellent covered communication, while the lateral wadi-bed before-mentioned afforded excellent ground for inspections of reliefs, movement of ration and working parties, and so on, very different from the same thing carried out in cramped and narrow trenches. Battalion H.Q. were comfortably ensconced in the proverbial "deep dug-out" (where, according to popular song, the colonel could always be found) dug into the side of the gully, with orderly room and signal office close by. Sections of the Machine Gun Company and Trench Mortar Battery were attached. Considerable new drafts began to arrive and were a welcome addition to the working and fighting strength of the battalion, which was responsible for a line nearly a mile long — as the trenches ran.

The ground in front was regularly patrolled and listening posts were established at night outside the wire. There were excellent snipers' posts and the enemy were thus prevented from taking any liberties.

Captain Teichman's diary gives the following information regarding Sir Archibald Murray's replacement:

> *June 15th.* We heard to-day for the first time that General Allenby had taken over the E.E.F. More French troops arrived, and also the Sixtieth Infantry Division, which had come from Salonika.
>
> *June 16th.* It was said that the "man-power" General had arrived, and that after combing out the "indispensables" in Cairo and Alexandria, he was about to do the same at Kantara; it was considered by some that he should be able to collect at least a division from that place![113]

Col. Gibbons recounts a very unfortunate accident which occurred on June 20, when Sgt. Chapman, one of his best non-commissioned officers in the battalion, was shot dead by a friendly sentry while accompanying Capt. Carlyon Hughes on a tour of the posts. This was unfortunate, as a similar thing had happened two nights previously, when Pvt. Smith, of "C" Company, was the victim. In both cases the sentries were men of new drafts and were probably a bit "jumpy"; but it was really cruel luck that shots fired in the pitch dark should on each occasion have proved fatal.

The weather in July was intensely hot and the men suffered from it severely. Flies were, however, well kept down by the strict attention to sanitation and the use of sprayers in the trenches. The Turkish artillery was frequently active, Col. Gibbons relates, varying their targets in a rather perplexing way; one never knew where they were going to start next, and a few casualties ensued. Also, the enemy used some indirect machine gun fire at night — a more annoying thing than artillery fire, as it silently swept the slopes of the hill, searching, it would seem, principally for the ration convoys who had revealed themselves coming over a saddle in the rear by their dust, which showed up plainly in the extra-ordinarily bright moonlight. These parties' timetable had to be altered in consequence, much to the annoyance of the quartermaster's and transport departments. "The moon was so bright that the enemy working parties were more than once dispersed by well-aimed rifle fire at over 500 yards range."[114]

Lt. Colonel Gibbons goes on to mention the arrival of quite a few native Indian officers who were attached to British units to learn trench warfare and its routine:

> During our tour on Blazed Hill we had several parties of Indian native officers, each under a British Special Service Officer, attached to us for an insight into the methods of trench warfare and routine. Each party stayed for a week. They belonged to the Hyderabad and Mysore Lancers. They were very keen and always wanting to go on patrol, at which class of work they were very good....

Some Turkish deserters complained of brutal treatment by non-commissioned officers, particularly towards Christians and Armenians, of whom they appeared to have considerable numbers. Another complaint was that men were allowed to purchase their discharge and immediately afterwards pressed into service again.[115]

Lt. Col. Gibbons goes on to relate that two Bulgarians serving with the Turkish Army defected to the Allied lines and

> gave valuable information about the enemy, pointing out positions of "*mitrailleuses*," etc. They came in early one morning and were seen in the light of the dawn by the Turks, who opened a brisk fire at them. The enemy's army was a queer mixture of real stout fighters, "*pukkah*" Turks — soldiers by nature and by choice, as their fathers had been before them — and every type of scallywag under the sun who had been forced into their service.... "Whizz-bangs" were particularly trying, and *minenwerfer* were also used from Outpost Hill — huge canisters on the end of poles, which could be distinctly seen by daylight hurtling through the air. One man from Thaxted country remarked, "Dalled if they ain't hurling *trees* at us now!" The range was evidently a little too long for these weapons, for they seldom reached the front line — which was just as well.[116]

It was during this period that Lt. Colonel Anthony Rawlinson, making a train trip, related:

> The rail journey from Cairo to Suez via Ismailia is no joy ride in summer, even in peace-time, and rail travelling is certainly no *more* comfortable in war-time. However, on this occasion I was lucky in that I enjoyed a perfectly unique military show from the train between Ismailia and Suez. Somewhere in these parts the Australian

A *Minenwerfer* (mine-thrower), known to British soldiers as "Moaning Minnies" owing to their onomatopoeic flight path (Fair and Wolton, *The History of the 1/5th Battalion: "The Suffolk Regiment"*).

cavalry were training, and soon after leaving Ismailia I became aware that a cavalry advance in line, on a large scale, was in progress parallel to the railway and about level with the train. This was the Australians training for the advance which they eventually made against the Turks, with results that proved beyond dispute the value of cavalry in open country.... I would have liked — and, in fact, I longed — to see those concerned and to congratulate them on the show.[117]

British Prime Minister David Lloyd George gives a very concise account of the collective decision to replace Sir Archibald Murray:

> In reviewing the course of the campaign on April 23rd, the War Cabinet came to the conclusion that it was desirable to introduce more resolute leadership into the command of the Egyptian Expeditionary Force, and with the concurrence of the War Secretary and the C.I.G.S. [Chief of the Imperial General Staff] decided to make a change in the chief command of this army. In regard to the choice of a successor to Sir Archibald Murray, it was pointed out that General [Jan Christiaan] Smuts had expressed very decided views as to the strategical importance of Palestine to the future of the British Empire. He would therefore be likely to prosecute a campaign in that quarter with great determination, and there was strong feeling that he would be one of the most suitable selections for the chief command of the Egyptian Expeditionary Force. On the other hand, the War Cabinet were aware that there was a growing opinion in favour of the retention of General Smuts in a central position in this country, with a view to the utilisation of his great qualities in the higher conduct of the war.
>   General Smuts was a standing disproof of the theory tenaciously held by the British War Office (despite the classic example of Oliver Cromwell) that no one was competent to hold high military command without long training in the regular army....[118] I however came to the conclusion that with Murray in command no results could be expected and I pressed Robertson to find a more enterprising commander. He recommended General Allenby. I heartily concurred in his recommendation. I felt that his [Allenby's] experience and qualities as a cavalry leader specially fitted him for the Palestinian campaign. On June 5th, 1917, the War Cabinet decided ... that General Allenby should be appointed as commander-in-chief of the British Forces in Egypt, and that arrangements should be made for him to take over the command as soon as possible. The policy to be adopted in that theatre of war would not be settled until General Allenby had assumed control. Before Allenby left for Egypt, I had an interview with him and impressed on him that we wanted a determined attack to be pushed against the Turks, with the object of driving them out of Palestine. They were known to be getting war-weary, and a succession of defeats might well drive them out of the war altogether. I told him in the presence of Sir William Robertson that he was to ask us for such reinforcements and supplies as he found necessary, and we would do our best to provide them. "If you do not ask it will be your fault. If you do ask and do not get what you need, it will be ours." I said the Cabinet expected "Jerusalem before Christmas."[119]

General Sir Edmund Allenby

The entry for Field Marshal Edmund Henry Hynman Allenby, First Viscount Allenby of Megiddo (1861–1936), was compiled by the eminent military historian, Cyril Falls.

Two. The Sinai Peninsula and the Failures at Gaza

Postcard photograph of Field Marshal Lord Allenby of Megiddo (Mortlock family photograph).

He assumed command of the Egyptian Expeditionary Force at the end of June 1917, and, as soon as the move could be carried out, transferred general headquarters to the Palestine border, close behind the front. He came like a fresh breeze to the somewhat dispirited troops. As he drove from camp to camp for brief visits of inspection he contrived to impress his personality upon them. The independently minded Australians took to him at once and gave him their full confidence. It was a promising beginning to his command. He received most of the reinforcements he demanded, bringing his army to a strength of seven infantry and three mounted divisions."[120]

CHAPTER THREE

A Change at the Top, Then Success at Beersheba and Gaza

During May 1917 the two Norfolk battalions received reinforcements totaling two officers and 382 other ranks. Their historian goes on to record that casualties were small — two killed and four wounded between the two battalions. June and July were uneventful from the point of view of fighting, such few casualties as occurred being the result of shelling by the Turks. Further reinforcements of 175 men for 1/4th and 245 for the 1/5th came out in July. Up till the 26th August there was the usual routine of trench warfare. Even then nothing noticeable occurred till the 163rd Brigade was sent from the resting area into the front line, with 5th Suffolk, 1/4th, and 1/5th Norfolk in that order from right to left.[1]

Allenby and his party travelled *via* Paris and Rome to Brindisi, where they embarked on a Royal Navy cruiser, HMS *Bristol*, on June 25, arriving at Alexandria two days later. A biographer wrote:

> His predecessor, Sir Archibald Murray, was still in Cairo, and remained for a few days after Allenby's arrival. Murray had broken up the commander-in-chief's mess, and had got rid of house and servants shortly before Allenby's arrival. After about a week at an hotel Allenby took over a house, the Villa Heller, at Gezira, and engaged Murray's chef, a Frenchman, proprietor of a cafe at Alexandria, who had been called up for service in the French Army. He was discovered occupying one of the most expensive suites at Shepheard's Hotel. Within less than two months he was cooking excellent meals in a hut on the Sinai Desert.
>
> Allenby's arrival undoubtedly caused some "alarm and despondency" at headquarters in Cairo. His reputation was not a comfortable one for a staff which had become accustomed to the fleshpots of Egypt.[2]

Lt. Colonel Badcock was in Cairo when Sir Edmund Allenby arrived, and he recorded his impressions in the "Personal Reminiscences" section of his book:

> On June 13, 1917, news reached G.H.Q. that General Murray was being succeeded by General Allenby (as our chief-to-be then was). He arrived at Cairo on Wednesday,

Three. A Change at the Top, Then Success at Beersheba and Gaza

Apsley House. The 5th Suffolks were here in August 1917 (Fair and Wolton, *The History of the 1/5th Battalion: "The Suffolk Regiment"*).

June 27, and within less than forty-eight hours he had made the acquaintance of every officer in every branch at G.H.Q. He came round our Directorate, for instance, accompanied by General Campbell [the deputy quartermaster general], he went to each person's office, shook hands with you, and had a few minutes' chat about your work and so on. I cannot adequately describe the far-reaching effect this simple act had on all such small fry like myself; you felt instinctively that there was nothing you would not try your best to do, and from the date of his arrival as our commander-in-chief a totally different atmosphere permeated our whole existence.

He went everywhere, saw everything, and possessed moreover that faculty—as wonderful as it is rare—of always remembering everyone he had ever met. His first great act was to make the acquaintance of all his officers at G.H.Q.; his next was to transfer G.H.Q. from Cairo to the desert.[3]

Allenby, by moving his headquarters from the luxury hotel room in Cairo that Murray had used to the front lines, had become as visible as any British commander during the entire war.

When Sir Edmund Allenby took over the Army on the Palestine Front, known at this time as "Eastern Force," it comprised three mounted divisions (Anzac, Australian, and Yeomanry) and four infantry divisions (52nd, 53rd, 54th, 74th). The Anzac Mounted Division consisted of two Australian Light Horse brigades and the New Zealand Mounted Rifle Brigade, the Australian Mounted Division of two Australian Light Horse brigades and a yeomanry brigade, and the Yeomanry Mounted Division of three yeomanry brigades. There was also a brigade mounted on camels (the Imperial Camel Corps Brigade) and an independent yeomanry brigade (7th Mounted Brigade). The 52nd (Lowland), 53rd (Welsh), and 54th (East Anglian) were first-line Territorial divisions which had fought at Gallipoli and in the campaign across the Sinai Desert; the 74th was formed of dismounted yeomanry units, and had taken as its divisional badge a broken spur.

A fifth division the 60th (London) was in process of arrival from Salonika; it was composed of second-line territorial battalions, and had fought in France before transfer to the Salonika front. A sixth division, the 75th, was being formed in Egypt from Territorial and Indian battalions from India and elsewhere. The material of the force was magnificent. The men, for the most part, were seasoned troops, who had not suffered the crippling casualties of the Western Front, and who still retained a good proportion of the personnel with whom they had begun the war. Such men were veterans, with nearly three years of experience. At present they were discouraged and cynical: they had lost faith in the Higher Command and in themselves, and were, like the Israelites of old, weary of the hardships of the desert. Moreover, they were weak in numbers, having received few reinforcements from home. "The force was in the doldrums, becalmed and dispirited, held between failure and success. It needed the wind of Allenby's tremendous personality to fill the sails and give it steerage-way."[4]

Another historian observed, "Allenby took over and devoted the first three months to intensive preparations for an autumn offensive, when the season would be suitable. The command was reorganized, the communications developed, and his own headquarters moved forward from Cairo to the front."[5] Some radical changes also took place on the opposing side.

> The volatile situation in Russia exercised a detrimental influence on the Caucasian Front. Revolution was coming, and its insidious backdrag was destroying the Russian armies. Their discipline slackened, and they began to break up with defeatism, and desertion. The Grand Duke Nicholas was recalled to Moscow and the spring offensive postponed. All through the spring and summer of 1917 the Russian armies gradually disintegrated. They crumbled to pieces, and, like dust before a wind, they were gone. The danger was over in that area. The enemy were gone, but away in the south a new danger reared its head. The British were preparing a big offensive — which if successful would threaten Syria with invasion. Urgent orders came from Constantinople to send every gun and man available, and posting General Mustafa Kemal to the Syrian front.
>
> The German High Command, at Enver Pasha's urgent request, had sent General von Falkenhayn to organize a new force, the *Yildirim*, "the Thunderbolt," as it was to be called. Its headquarters would be Aleppo; it would be stiffened by a large number of German officers and men. Mustafa Kemal was posted to command the 7th Army.[6]

When the 60th (London) Division arrived in Palestine from Salonika they found the Turkish Army holding very strong defensive line stretching from the Mediterranean Sea at Gaza to just beyond Beersheba — a distance of roughly thirty miles, roughly along the main Gaza-Beersheba road to Beersheba. Gaza had been transformed into a formidable modern fortress, heavily entrenched and wired, offering every facility for repulsing an attack. The remainder of the enemy's line consisted of a series of strong localities, *viz.*: the *Sihan* group of works, the *Atawinek* group, the *Baha* group, the *Abu Hareira-Arab el Teeaha* trench system, and, finally the works covering Beersheba. These groups of works were generally 1,500 to 2,000 yards apart, except that the distance from *Abu Hareira-Arab el Teeaha* group to Beersheba was about four and one-half miles. The whole defensive line was a now strong modern fortress, heavily entrenched, garrisoned by seasoned troops, and protected with barbed wire, "and offering every facility for protracted defence."[7]

Fair and Wolton wrote, "On the 14th June an artillery bombardment of Umbrella Hill gave us a great sight. The 8-inch shells falling on the parapet sent the many-coloured sandbags high in the air on a column of white sand, and the air soon became white with dust. The whole hill seemed to be shaken, but when the bombardment ceases there it remained very much the same...."[8]

"On the 26th of June the 1/5th Suffolks relieved the 1/4th Norfolks on Samson's Ridge — the most prominent feature on that particular sector, which gave an extensive view of the country behind Gaza. Every afternoon the white houses of Gaza caught the sun, and looked like a fairy town to our sand-weary eyes. The ridge naturally came in for a commensurate amount of attention from the Turkish artillery. It particularly concentrated on the reverse slope immediately below the crest-line, apparently convinced that some one *must* be there. Fortunately there were no bivouacs, stores, or men there, and the chief result of this firing was an interesting collection of shrapnel shell-cases and splinters of shells littering the sand, and giving it the name, 'Samson's Necklace.'"[9]

After carefully sizing up the situation, Sir Edmund Allenby arrived at the conclusion that before any decisive advance could be made it would be necessary to double the railway line, and the water pipe-line east of the Suez Canal. So he asked the British government for a considerable quantity of railway making material,

Lt. General Erich von Falkenhayn was the architect of the blood bath of Verdun and commander of the German Asia Corps in the Middle East ("Yilderim" [Thunderbolt]).

water-pipes, etc. In addition he requested the maintenance of his present divisions fully equipped and at full strength; for two additional fully trained divisions; and for a large addition to his aircraft and artillery.[10] The British military authorities actually commandeered a sizeable stock of steel pipes from the American Oil Company for use in piping water to the front line. The company concerned, however, received a complete reimbursement for the wartime emergency seizure of their property.

Royal Engineer Corporal Frederick Mills wrote in his diary: "Friday, July 5th, 1918. Kantara. Met Jack Isaacs of Ramsgate, who expects to go back to the front with the Northamptons.

"On July 6 the Commander-in-Chief, General Sir Edmund Allenby, visited the Brigade observation post on Kurd Hill. The following day one section of our battery went forward in order to cut wire on Outpost Hill, two lanes being cut. At night harassing fire was carried out by bursts of fire on selected parts of the enemy's line, all field batteries and 4.5 howitzers in the coastal sector being engaged.... Registration of targets was completed very carefully on July 19 and 20, by all batteries, with and without aeroplane co-operation. This drew heavy retaliatory fire from the Turks, which developed into mutual bombardment."[11]

On 12 August three corps were formed: the XX Corps, commanded by Lt. General Sir P. W. Chetwode, hitherto in command of Eastern Force; the XXI Corps, commanded by Lt.-General E. S. Bulfin, who had come from Salonika in command of the 60th Division; and the Desert Mounted Corps, commanded by Lt.-General Sir H. G. Chauvel, previously in command of the Desert Column. The distribution of the troops between the three corps was as follows. Desert Mounted Corps: Australian and New Zealand Mounted Division, Australian Mounted Division and Yeomanry Mounted Division. XX Corps: 10th Division (nominally G.H.Q. troops), 53rd Division, 60th Division, 74th Division and four brigades heavy artillery. XXI Corps: 52nd Division, 54th Division and three brigades heavy artillery.

The 7th Mounted Brigade, of two regiments only, was retained as Army troops. In the first week of September was formed the "Composite Force" from the Imperial Service Indian troops; the 1st Battalion, British West Indies Regiment; and detachments from the French and Italian contingents. It had about 3,000 rifles and six squadrons, but was without artillery or second-line transport.[12]

Trench warfare almost always entailed the soldiers being confined in narrow, cramped and unhygienic quarters, which tended to spawn problems. One of the afflictions most of the troops suffered was infestation with lice — an aspect rarely mentioned by most military historians or commentators. Private Jake Mortlock related that at one deinfestation center, shirts cast on the ground actually moved due to the vast numbers of these parasites within the fabric.[13]

The troops underwent extensive training throughout the summer. As Rifleman May of the London Irish Rifles recorded:

> We were engaged on a programme of training to desert conditions, including what was known as "water discipline"—gradually reducing our intake each week. Everything was done to bring us to peak condition for the autumn operations which all knew were ahead of us.
>
> The final exercise included advancing close up to a live barrage — our first introduction to this somewhat over-rated form of amusement. The theory was that if one could arrive on the enemy post a split second after the last shell from our own barrage, then one could clobber the Turk before he had time to pick up his battle-axe. Word from Olympus was: "One casualty from your own guns will save you twenty from the enemy." As the Australian remarked—"Too true, cobber, but who wants to be 'the one' at the dress rehearsal?"[14]

The Royal Norfolk's historian records the following incident: On September 3 a raid by the Turks on the new trenches near the sea was stopped by artillery fire before it got within 300 yards of the trenches. There was a certain amount of bombardment by both sides, but the only other excitement was the capture of two Turks by the 1/4th Norfolks in a fig grove and the surrender to them of a Turkish deserter.[15]

The extensive training introduced by Allenby progressed throughout the summer and early autumn — in particular it concentrated on the raw Indian drafts brought in to fill the places of the battalions hastened to France. But, as Lieutenant Robert Wilson, of "D" Squadron, the Royal Gloucester Hussars, recorded, there were some lighter moments:

> El Arish [Sinai] 23 September, 1917
>
> I have just returned from Alexandria after 7 days leave which I enjoyed very much and did me a lot of good.... I found the regiment had moved back nearly forty miles from the line, where peace reigns supreme; we can't even hear a cannon and very rarely see an aeroplane. We are living in a date and fig orchard; the former are not quite ready but the latter are just right. They make a welcome addition to our already excellent rations....
>
> On 1st September 1917, I was naturally thinking about the opening of the partridge season at home. We were resting by the sea at El Arish, and had rolled the beach to make a cricket pitch that we surrounded by one strand of barbed wire. I was the first to go down to the sea for a bathe the next morning and I noticed something hanging on the barbed wire. To my surprise I found it was a quail and on looking around, I found another one. I took them up to the cook-house and asked the cook to serve them up on a piece of toast but not to bring them up until the Colonel, who I would arrange to be sitting next to, came in for breakfast. After the cook had pushed a dish of sticky porridge in front of the Colonel, he came to me and said, "And what can I get you, sir?" "I think I should like a couple of quail on toast." He accepted my order and soon, produced them. The Colonel was very puzzled but I was not giving the game away. I was earlier still the next morning and, to my joy, I found four quail. So up to the cook-house again, and this time I told the cook he could ask the Colonel what he would like for breakfast. He came to me first and I repeated my order of the day before. Then he asked the Colonel who said, "Are there any more of those damned quail about?" The secret could be kept no longer. After breakfast hordes of Arabs

arrived over the desert and proceeded to erect miles and miles of nets and the following morning there were literally thousands of quail being collected. This was their migration and it lasted about a fortnight. One squadron had two quail per man for tea every day and the sergeants' and officers' messes had them all day long. The only problem was getting them plucked and ready for cooking.[16]

Also during this month, the 1/5th Suffolk historians stated, their battalion was relieved by the 10th Battalion the London Regiment on 29 of September 1917. The regiment,

a day or two before, had received warning of the impending operations. The battalion then moved to its previous camp by the sea at North Belah, and commenced collecting the equipment and doing the training for the assault. A model of our objective — the El Arish Redoubt — copied from the very excellent aeroplane photographs, was made exactly to scale, and every man to take part in the assault was given his place, his equipment, and practiced his job. Officers made frequent visits to Samson's Ridge for reconnaissance, and that spot, already highly unpopular with its garrison, became even more so as the Turk increased his fire on it. There was a continuous procession, and traffic had to be regulated into "up" and "down" trenches. Fortunately the Turk did not see very much — apparently just enough to make him believe that a relief was pending — so in compliment to his observers he increased his fire slightly, but not seriously.

While at this camp the battalion had an opportunity of seeing "The Rose of Gaza" by the Divisional Concert Party at Sheikh Shabasi, and every one enjoyed it immensely. The battalion marched to the performance, arrived early, and secured front seats.[17]

Compulsory attendance for this show was initially highly unpopular, according to Private Jake Mortlock, but afterwards all were glad to have been present.[18]

The coming of October coincided with a regimen of more elaborate training in preparation for General Allenby's planned offensive, now that he had in hand the promised additional forces with which to prosecute it. Model trenches and practice attacks on them, with reorganization of companies on a platoon basis, i.e., riflemen section, Lewis gun section [Jake's], etc., were the order of the day up till the 14th, when the 163rd Brigade moved up to first line, where it had much difficult patrolling work to do. It relieved the 156th Brigade in the left sub-sector, the 8th Hampshire being on the extreme left touching the sea, the 1/4th Norfolk in the center from Hereford Ridge to Cairo Ridge, and the 1/5th Norfolk on the right on Samson's Ridge. During the last ten days of October working parties were supplied from the left and right battalions, but the 1/4th Norfolk was kept intact, ready to counter-attack in case of emergency.[19]

The most effective way to achieve surprise is to plant false information in advance. Allenby was determined to deceive the enemy over the nature and timing of the initial assault. Here he was unexpectedly helped by the Turks' newly arrived German advisers. "I had myself fought against Allenby's divisions at Vimy Ridge [sic] and had little doubt that he would employ the methods used in France of preceding his attack by an overwhelming artillery barrage," Major Franz von Papen said in his memoirs a third of a century later. The Turks

Aerial photograph of the El Arish Redoubt (Fair and Wolton, *The History of the 1/5th Battalion: "The Suffolk Regiment"*).

made this useful item of information widely known, as the British discovered by an intercepted signal. British Intelligence took a famous initiative on October 10 when Lt. Colonel Richard Meinertzhagen, reconnoitering No Man's Land, deliberately attracted fire from a Turkish patrol; he feigned injury and in making his escape seemed accidentally to drop field glasses and a haversack, which the

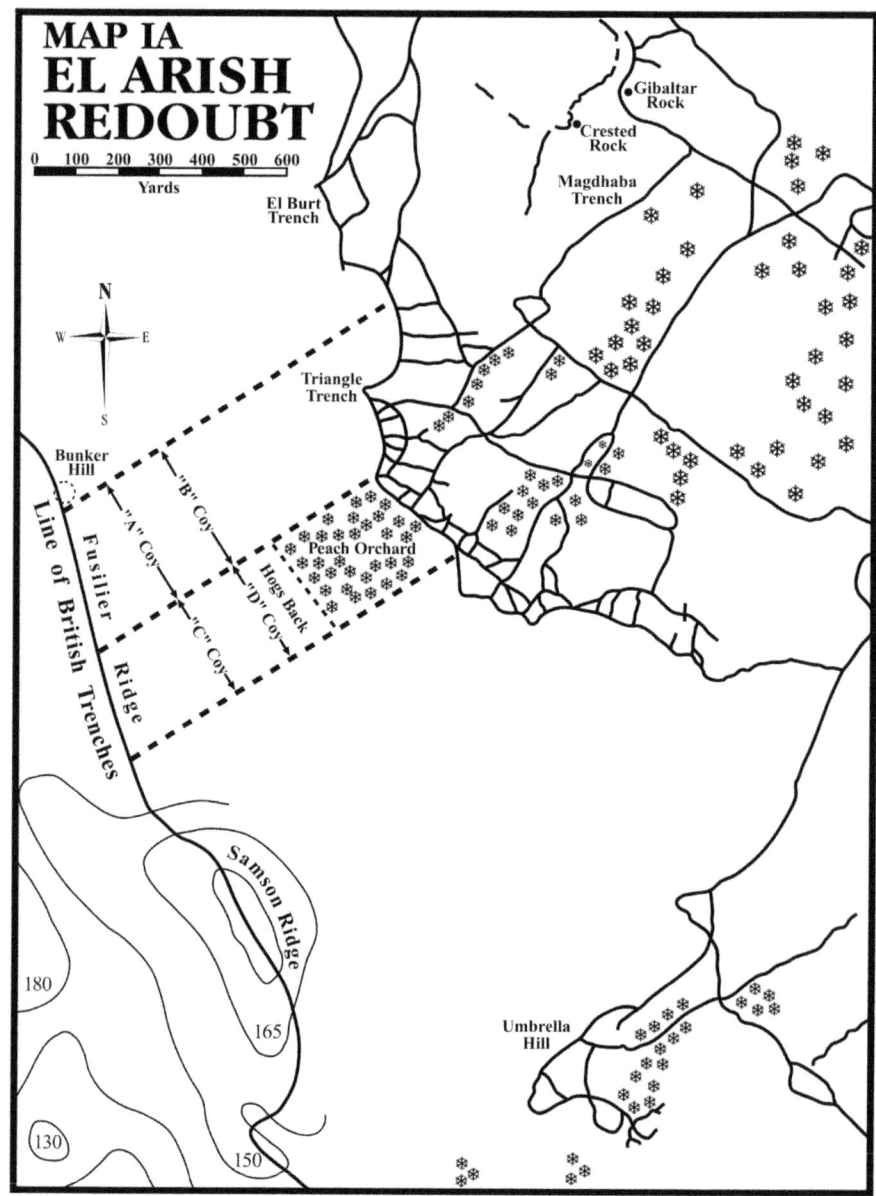

Turks duly seized. British Prime Minister David Lloyd George lavished high praise on Meinertzhagen:

> There is the famous ruse by which he [Allenby] deceived the enemy into the belief that his first assault would be on Gaza with a feint attack on Beersheba. This was suggested to him by a brilliant young officer called Meinertzhagen who subsequently,

Three. A Change at the Top, Then Success at Beersheba and Gaza 111

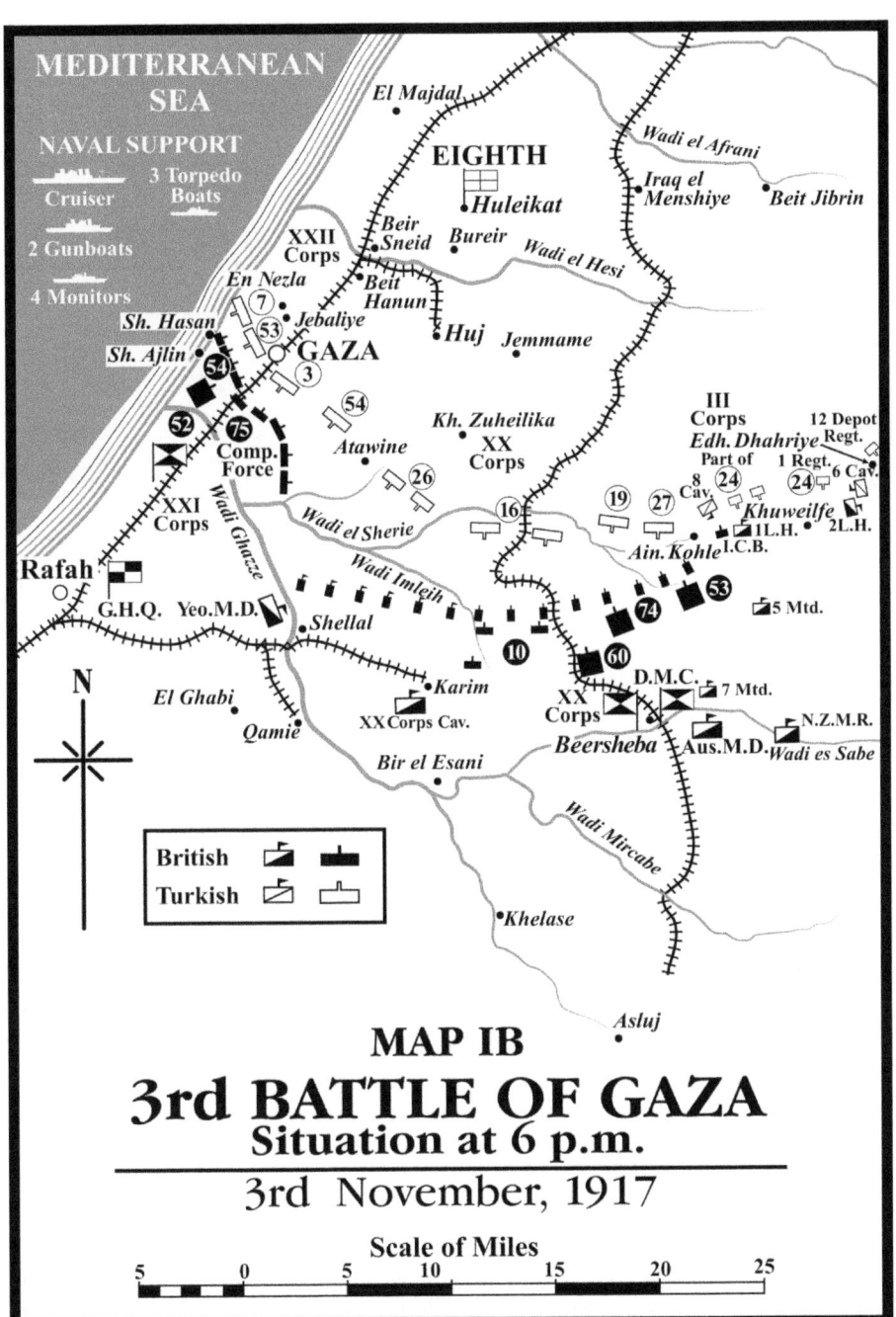

MAP IB
3rd BATTLE OF GAZA
Situation at 6 p.m.
3rd November, 1917

Model of the El Arish Redoubt (Fair and Wolton, *The History of the 1/5th Battalion: "The Suffolk Regiment"*).

at the risk of his life, successfully carried it out. But Allenby had the intelligence to perceive the value of the plan. Great leadership does not consist merely in the invention of schemes but in the selection and execution of the best. Meinertzhagen's device won the battle. Needless to say he never rose in the war above the rank of colonel. I met him during the Peace Conference and he struck me as being one of the ablest and most successful brains I had met in any army. That was quite sufficient to make him suspect and to hinder his promotion to the higher ranks of his profession.[20]

Major Vivian Gilbert, of the 2/20th Battalion, the London Regiment, summed his commander-in-chief up thus:

A commander-in-chief's work takes place *before* the attack; he makes his plans which are carried out by corps and divisional commanders, and he really has very little to do during the actual fighting — providing, of course, that everything goes well. Allenby's plans were usually entirely successful, so that he was free to be up in the firing line to encourage us during any particularly trying operation. His nickname in the army is "the bull." He is a tremendous fellow, over six feet tall, with a voice that corresponds. When he shakes hands his grip causes you to stretch your fingers for some little time afterwards. When he smiles his approval it makes you feel rather proud. I do not imagine people often attempt to deceive him. He has a combination of those qualities men admire most in a leader: personal bravery, knowledge of his job and a consideration for the man in the ranks.[21]

In Bruce Feiler's recently-published work, *Walking the Bible: A Journey by Land through the Five Books of Moses*, one of the ancient natives the author chanced upon in Gaza gave the following account of the first two attempts to take Gaza and the successful third battle for the city, and related key people and important events connected to these.

Three. A Change at the Top, Then Success at Beersheba and Gaza 113

Dunes south-west of GAZA from Samson Ridge.

A panoramic view of Gaza Battlefield I.

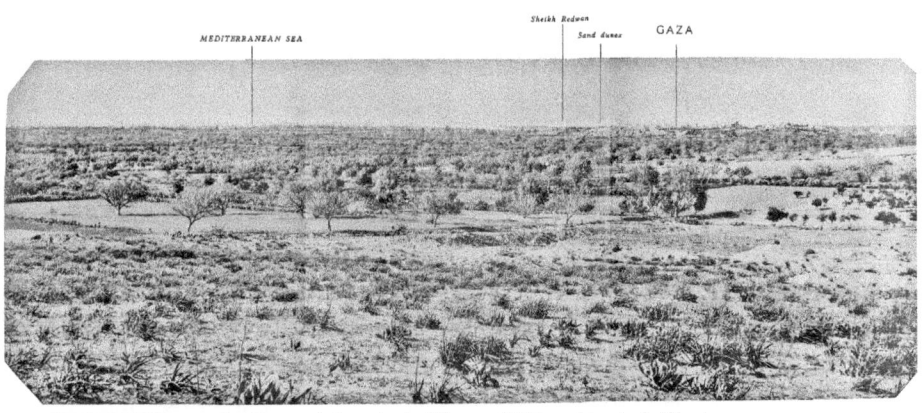

Looking north from Lee's Hill over GAZA and Lambeth Wood.

Gaza Battlefield II (both images from MacMunn and Falls, *Official History of the War: Military Operations: Egypt and Palestine. 2 Vol., Vol. II [Part1]*).

Archibald Murray was here in 1917, during the First World War. The British were trying to take Palestine from the Turks. They came from the south, from Egypt, and wanted to go to Jerusalem. To do so, they had to cross this area. It took them three months to come all the way from the Suez Canal to here. They built a train [railway]. They built a road. They built a pipe [laid a pipeline]. They brought water all the way from the Nile, because they needed steam for the train and water for thousands of horses. *In three months!* But they had to get through Gaza, which was controlled by the Turks. And one famous general helped them do that. Do you know which one?"

"Allenby?"

"Ah you make a mistake."

"Archibald Murray!" He grinned.

"But I've never heard of him," I pleaded.

"That's the point," Rami said. "One of them is famous, one of them is not. General

Murray got the British Army here in three months from Egypt, but then they bogged down for *eight months*. Twice they attacked Gaza, and twice they were defeated, despite using tanks and gas shells. Over eleven thousand British soldiers died. Finally, General Allenby arrived and hatched a plan.... And as always, Gaza was the key," Rami said. "Take it and you take the land. Six weeks later he took Jerusalem."

We drove a few miles to a large concrete memorial in the shape of a giant *A*, built to commemorate the ten thousand soldiers of Anzac, the Australian–New Zealand Army Corps, who died in the 1917 attacks on Gaza. From the overlook we had a clear view of the surrounding area; Gaza, the Mediterranean, the Sinai, the Negev, the mountains around Hebron. The afternoon light was changing to dusk, and the colors—pale yellow, powder blue, egg-plant purple reminded me of the Nile.[22]

Royal Engineer Corporal Fred Mills wrote in his diary on Tuesday, October 23, 1917, on the banks of Suez Canal: "Had a good supper tonight, eggs with bread and butter. It was a bit like home but the eggs were cheaper, four for 5d [five pence]."

Allenby and his staff finalized their plans and at 9 P.M. on October 24 the following order was issued from Corps H.Q.:

XXI CORPS ORDER No. 11

24th October 1917.

Ref. Maps: Palestine 1/63,360; Gaza 1/20,000; Trench Map 1/10,000.
1. The disposition of the enemy is given in the attached sketch.
2. The Corps Commander intends to attack the enemy's right flank from Umbrella Hill (inclusive) to the Sea, on a night (X—1X) and at an hour (Z) to be named later. The furthest objectives to be seized and consolidated will include Umbrella Hill, El Arish Redoubt, Magdhaba Trench, Gibraltar, Island Wood, Rafah, Yunis, and Balah Trenches and Sheikh Hasan. Advanced posts are to be sent to occupy trenches in G. 21, 22, and 28. Every endeavour is to be made to push beyond the limits of these objectives provided the tactical situation is thereby improved.
3. The attack will be carried out under the orders of Major-General Hare, commanding the 54th Division. The following troops will be placed at his disposal for this purpose:—
54th Division
52nd Divisional Artillery
156th Infantry Brigade 52nd Division
412th Field Company R.E. 52nd Division
1st Lowland Field Ambulance
211th Machine-Gun Company
1 Battery 9th B.M. Artillery Brigade.
After the capture of Sheikh Hasan, 1 mobile section of 9th B.M. Artillery may be withdrawn under Corps instructions.
4. The attack on Umbrella Hill is to be carried out as a distinct operation and some hours in advance of the main attack.
5. A bombardment of the enemy's defences from Fryer Hill via Outpost Hill to the Sea will be carried out from X-6 day onwards. His wire will be cut during this bombardment from Middlesex Hill to the Sea.
6. The attack will be supported by the Royal Navy, the Corps Heavy Artillery, Tank

Three. A Change at the Top, Then Success at Beersheba and Gaza 115

Detachment, and such guns of the Machine-Gun Companies in the Edinburgh and Carnarvon Sectors as can be spared from defensive purposes. From X-3 day (inclusive) all demands for naval co-operation will be made through the Senior Naval Officer, Marine View.

7. The routes and objectives of the tanks will be:—

(*a*) 1 tank Philistine Hill–Magdhaba–Crested Rock–Island Wood.

(*b*) 1 tank El Arish Redoubt–Magdhaba, then as in *(a)*.

(*c*) 1 tank Rafah Redoubt; Rafah, Yunis, Balah Trenches–Sheikh Hasan. Not to move north of Rafah Redoubt before Z+55, nor of John Trench before Z+110, nor of Balah Trench before Z+125.

(*d*) 1 tank Rafah Junior–Rafah Redoubt–Rafah, Yunis, Balah Trenches–Sheikh Hasan. Times as for *(c)*.

(*e*) 1 tank Beach Post–Cricket Redoubt–Gun Hill–Sheikh Hasan–Trenches in G. 21, 22, and 28. Not to move north of Beach Post before Z+55, nor of Cricket Redoubt before Z+110, not to reach Gun Hill before Z+120.

(*f*) 1 tank Sea Post–Beach Post–Cricket Redoubt–Gun Hill–Sheikh Hasan–Trenches in G. 21, 22, and 28. Times as for

(*e*) All tanks will return to Sheikh Ajlin on completion of duty. The H.Q. Tank Detachment will be at Marine View. Two tanks will be in reserve at Sheikh Ajlin.

8. A contact aeroplane will pass over the line as follows:—
5.45 A.M. Umbrella Hill to Rafah Trench (both inclusive),
6.45 A.M. Rafah Trench to Sheikh Hasan (both inclusive).
Flares are to be lit by troops in the furthest objectives of the lines named, when called upon by Klaxon horn.

9. The following troops will be in Corps reserve:—

(Q.10) Regent's Park	"	Cdr. Brig.-Gen. C. R. Harbord.
"	"	I.S.C. Bde. (less 2 squadrons).
"	"	Corps Cavalry Regiment.
Regent's Park	"	Cdr. Brig.-Gen. Hamilton Moore.
"		157th Infantry Bde.
"		413th Field Coy., R.E.
"		2nd Lowland Field Ambulance.
(T.5) Wadi Simeon		Cdr. Brig.-Gen. H. J. Huddleston.
"	"	232nd Infantry Bde.
"	"	Sections 495th Field Coy., R.E.
"	"	1 Section 123rd Field Ambulance.

The G.O.C. Sheikh Abbas Sector may call upon 2 battalions of the Corps Reserve troops at the Wadi Simeon for the defence of his line, notifying Corps H.Q. of his action.

10. The following subsidiary operations will be carried out on the dates and by the formations stated:—

Night	Formation	Operation
X-8/X-7	75th Division	Advance our line from direction Mansura to the Donga
X-2/X-1	75th Division	Raid on Outpost Hill
X-1/X	Composite Force	Advance our line towards Atawine Redoubt.
X/X+1.	75th Division	Raid on Outpost Hill.

11. From X-6 to X-2 day (both inclusive) the official time will be sent out daily at 2 P.M. on the telephone by the General Staff to all concerned. From X-1 day (inclusive) watches will be synchronized at 2 P.M. at Advanced Corps H.Q. Representatives will attend from all Divisions, O.C. Heavy Artillery, and the I.S.C. Bde. The G.O.C. 54th Division will arrange for synchronization with O.C. Tank Detachment.

12. Advanced Corps H.Q. will be established on Raspberry Hill at 4 P.M. on X-1 day.

E. T. HUMPREYS
Brigadier-General, General Staff, XXI Corps.

Issued at 9 P.M.[23]

General Allenby could call upon considerable naval firepower to prepare and support his planned assault. "The naval assistance provided by Rear-Admiral T. Jackson, was given by the cruiser *Grafton*, the French coast-guard ship, *Requin*, the monitors *Raglan* (14-inch), *M.15* (9.2-inch), *M.29, M.31,* and *M.32*." Also in attendance were "the British destroyers *Staunch, Comet,* and the French *Arbalete, Voltigeur, Coutelas, Fauconneau,* and *Hache*; the river gun-boats *Ladybird* and *Aphis*; three seaplane carriers, and a number of auxiliary craft."[24]

On this day R.E. Corporal Fred Mills, on the banks of the Suez Canal, wrote: "Thursday, October 25th, 1917. Changed a £1 note for Egyptian money. Its value was $97^{1}/_{2}$ Piastres."

Artillery at Gaza III

Regarding the artillery deployed at Gaza Three — thanks to the bullying of "The Bull," as General Sir Edmund Allenby was then known — the concentration of this type of ordnance was the greatest of any "sideshow" and on the scale of frontage equal to the Western Front. As Brigadier General Sir Hugh Simpson Baikie, Royal Artillery, stated:

> After commanding the starved artillery at Helles [Gallipoli] it was my good fortune to command the artillery of the 21st Army Corps [54th (East Anglian) Division belonged to this Army Corps] at the third Battle of Gaza, in November, 1917,[25] and also at the great Battle of the 19th September, 1918, in which the Turks in Palestine were finally crushed, and I think it may add emphasis to what I have said if I contrast the artillery support of the two campaigns and show the results which ensued.[26]

> The Royal Norfolks' historian relates, "On November 1st General Allenby was ready to renew the attack on the Gaza position, which had failed so disastrously in April. On that day the 163rd Brigade began moving up from Marine View to the assembly positions, which were reached by all units by 2.30 P.M. The brigade took no part in the first phase of the operations, which consisted in a turning movement by Beersheba on the Turkish left."[27]

Now the hour rapidly approached for General Sir Edmund Allenby to attempt a masterstroke, and in some way to redeem the two previous disasters. His basic strategy differed little from that of his predecessor — but his personal dynamism, man-on-the-spot direction, and easy accessibility stood to contribute enormous influence on the outcome.

Three. A Change at the Top, Then Success at Beersheba and Gaza

Major Gilbert skillfully put into words the eager anticipation of a momentous event:

> Is there any time so exciting and stimulating as those last few days before zero? Only the commander-in-chief knew which day the attack was to be launched, but we felt it must be imminent. The great army machine was working at such feverish pressure that something must happen soon. We had all received our orders; each branch of the service knew what was required of it. All we were waiting to know was, "the day."[28]

Sir Edmund Allenby's army would be enjoying the largest concentration of firepower away from the European theaters—both army field and howitzer batteries, plus the naval guns of the fleet, which, due to their great mobility, were able to enfilade many enemy positions.

While the bombardment itself was from Outpost Hill to the sea, a distance of 6,000 yards, the frontage of the attack was little over 4,000 yards. Sixty-eight heavy guns to 4,000 yards, or one to every 60 yards, is exactly the proportion employed on the first day of the Battle of the Somme (1 July 1916). The weight of artillery, it need hardly be said, increased greatly in subsequent operations on the Western Front—e.g., one heavy gun to 28 yards in the Battle of Arras, one to 27 yards on 8 August 1918. But when we take into account the naval artillery and the enormous weight of its projectiles—one monitor had a 14-inch gun, *Requin* two 27.4-cm. (10.8-inch), *Grafton* and another monitor each two 9.2-inch, without counting the secondary armaments of the big ships or the large number of guns of 4-inch and over carried by the small—this bombardment must be reckoned a very heavy one by any standard. Figures as to naval ammunition expended are not available, save that two 6-inch monitors fired 192 rounds on 30 October alone, and that the *Requin* sailed for Port Said on 2 November, having used all her supply.[29]

"The defences of Gaza were bombarded from October 20 onwards, and Allenby launched the attacks which opened the Third Battle of Gaza on October 30,"[30] Hart writes. Winston Churchill's historical account states, "Feinting at Gaza in the last week of October, he stormed Beersheba by a surprise attack by two infantry divisions and a wide turning movement of cavalry and camelry."[31]

Allenby boldly attacked Beersheba on the night of October 31, with a full moon illuminating the way. A daring cavalry charge by the Australian Light Horse allowed the British to capture the city and its critical water wells intact. The next day, British artillery prepared an attack on Gaza with 15,000 shells. Falkenhayn had little choice but to stage a fighting withdrawal, allowing British forces to enter Palestine and capture Jaffa, Jerusalem's chief port, on November 16.[32]

Tanks and the second use of gas-shells by the Egyptian Expeditionary Force added an edge, and a considerable amount of aircraft were at the general's disposal. German and Turkish accounts are unanimous in entirely discounting the beneficial strategic contribution the gas-shells lent to the occasion.[33]

Beersheba had to be captured before nightfall, or both men and horses would be without water. Chauvel[34] was ordered to mount a light horse attack from the south. It was their first cavalry charge.[35] The light horsemen galloped for Beersheba, through artillery, and then machine-gun, and finally rifle fire. They swept over the Turkish trenches and stormed them from the rear with rifle and bayonet. Beersheba was taken, and at minute cost, either in men or in the horses they loved.[36]

On this day Royal Engineer Corporal Fred Mills' wrote in his diary: "Monday, October 28th, 1917. Kantara. Lots of wounded came down today. The band of the Rifle Brigade came and gave a concert at the canteen at 3 P.M. Started with 'Land of Hope and Glory' then all popular songs; it quite livened things up. I thought of Wellington Gardens [Ramsgate], a hammock chair and a cigar."

The capture of Beersheba, though a necessary preliminary to the attack on the left of the main Turkish line, was in itself a complete operation. The fighting in the hills which followed it may be considered as part and parcel of the attack on the Sheria position by the XX Corps, and will be described with it in the next chapter. We turn now to the operations of the XXI Corps on the other flank at Gaza, which were to follow the Beersheba attack and precede that of Sheria. The date of the assault on the Gaza defenses was not fixed until the results of the fighting at Beersheba were known. Sir Edmund Allenby hoped that the Gaza operation would attract the Turkish reserves, thus easing the task of XX Corps; he therefore intended to begin it from twenty-four to forty-eight hours before the Sheria attack was launched. If the Turks did reinforce their right at the expense of their left, the capture of the Sheria position would be so much the easier, and the mass of the British mounted troops, passing behind the enemy's flank, would have the opportunity of making a vast haul of prisoners and guns, perhaps of virtually destroying the opposing force.

But the commander-in-chief was not in the grip of any fixed idea such as that which the Turks reproach his opponent, Kress von Kressenstein. He waited on events to exploit them. Though his original attack at Gaza was primarily a feint, he was prepared, if his cavalry failed to envelop the enemy's left completely, to transfer his weight to the coast, where advancing troops could be supplied more easily. What actually happened was rather outside his calculations, but he was quick to profit by it. The Turks, who had been so much concerned for the safety of Gaza and had massed their greatest strength on that flank, now, after the capture of Beersheba, became anxious regarding the Hebron road. Their anxiety was increased by the bold conduct of Lt. Colonel Newcombe's little detachment, which seemed to presage an advance up the road. They did not, indeed, weaken the Gaza front — where their reserve division was at once drawn into the battle — to secure the road, but they moved considerable forces eastward from Sheria. Thus they depleted quite as much as if they had reinforced Gaza, and locked up nearly half their force in the Judean Hills, where it took no part in the fighting for a week after the capture of Sheria.

Three. A Change at the Top, Then Success at Beersheba and Gaza   119

"D" Company (Suffolk) Lewis gun crew and crowd; Private Jake Mortlock is standing third from left. Private Freddie Turner is seated immediately in front of him (Mortlock family photograph).

Then Sir Edmund Allenby transferred his attention to that portion of the enemy's force remaining in the coast plain, which was so weakened that two infantry divisions and the mounted troops—all that could be fed—sufficed to defeat and pursue it, and hustled it northward to Jaffa.[37]

The attack of XXI Corps was to be against the enemy's works from El Arish Redoubt, half a mile west of the Rafah-Gaza road, to Sheikh Hasan on the shore. Owing to the distance between the British and Turkish trenches, General Bulfin had suggested to Sir Edmund Allenby that the attack should be made at night. It appeared that the risk of loss of direction and disorganization in the darkness was less serious than that of exposing the troops to machine-gun fire in daylight during their crossing of the heavy sand of No Man's Land. On the right flank the final objective was only 500 yards behind the Turkish front line, but on the left it was 2,500. The whole attack was to be carried out under the orders of Major General S. W. Hare, commanding the 54th Division, at whose disposal were put, in addition to his own division, the artillery, the 412th Field Company R.E., and the 156th Brigade (Brig. General A. H. Leggett) of the 52nd Division. The capture of "Umbrella Hill," a dune just west of the Rafah-Gaza road which overlooked the main objective, was to be a distinct operation, carried out some hours before the main attack. Certain earlier subsidiary operations were to be carried out on the right of the 54th Division by the 75th, which was to advance its line in the Happy Valley between the Es Sire and Burjabye ridges and was to raid Outpost Hill. On the right of the main operation the Composite Force, which had taken over the front on the right of the 75th Division, was to advance the line in the direction of Atawine Redoubt on the Gaza-Beersheba road. On the following night the 75th Division was again to raid Outpost Hill.

The advance of the line in the Happy Valley from the track known as "Watling Street" to Lee's Hill was successfully accomplished by the 75th Division during the night of the 26th, before the general bombardment began. The raid on Outpost Hill was made by the 3/3rd Gurkhas of the 233rd Brigade, 75th Division, at 3 A.M. on 1 November. It was large enough to induce the Turks to believe, when the attack on Umbrella Hill was launched the following night, that this was but another raid of the same nature. After a short but intense bombardment, a party consisting of two British and three Gurkha officers and 220 riflemen, under the command of Captain W. G. Bagot-Chester, entered the enemy's defenses on the hill. The garrison was overwhelmed, a number refusing to quit their dug-outs, in which they were bombed. Twenty-six were killed with bayonet or *kukri* and 16 prisoners brought in. The losses of the Gurkhas were 2 killed and 23 wounded.

Private Mortlock had an intense admiration for these warriors. Among his anecdotes were that "they were the only ones who were cheerful on Gallipoli." That "they would only draw their kukris in order to shed blood"—so when he asked to see one the Gurkha made a droplet of blood show on a finger. He told of them going off into the night, returning with grisly specimens of their nocturnal activities—slain enemies' ears kept in their haversacks.[38] Traveling to Malta he shared a hospital-ship ward with several Gurkhas suffering with frostbitten toes occasioned by the frigid weather on the Gallipoli peninsula.[39]

The attack on the Gaza defenses by the troops under the command of Major General Hare was divided into four phases, the first or preliminary, against Umbrella Hill, having its own "Zero" hour, at which an intense bombardment was to open. Ten minutes later the artillery was to lift, maintaining fire at reduced rate on the approaches to Umbrella Hill, and units of the 7 and 8/Scottish Rifles, 156th Brigade, were to assault the position. The second phase was the capture of the enemy's front line from El Arish Redoubt to Sea Post on the shore. This attack was to be carried out by the left of the 156th Brigade, the 163rd Brigade (Brig. General T. Ward) and the 161st Brigade (Brig. General W. Marriott-Doddington) less one battalion in divisional reserve. In the third phase of the attack, the 163rd and 161st Brigades were to force their way deeply into the southwest defenses of Gaza. The fourth and final phase, beginning 90 minutes after Zero, was to be made along the shore and carried out by 162nd Brigade (Brig. General A. Mudge). Its objectives were "Gun Hill" and Sheikh Hasan, the latter over 3,500 yards from the British front line at Sheikh Ajlin.

The Palestine Tank Detachment had at this date eight tanks, of which two were to be held in reserve during the operations. None were to be employed in

Three. A Change at the Top, Then Success at Beersheba and Gaza 121

the first phase against Umbrella Hill. In the second, two tanks were to support the infantry against El Arish Redoubt, with further objectives north of it. The other four were to attack with the 163rd and 161st Brigades, and after assisting in the capture of the trenches on their front, and in some cases flattening out wire, were to advance to Sheikh Hasan carrying Royal Engineers stores.

The greater part of the ground over which the attack was to be made consisted of seashore sand that extended a considerable distance inland. This differs from the desert sand of Northern Sinai, which also appears in places south of Gaza, in that it supports no vegetation except an occasional tuft of grass. It was extremely tiring on the feet, which sank at each step to the ankles, but it was, on the other hand, of little value from the point of view of cover, as no revetment would hold up under bombardment. The enemy's trenches, even where built up by sandbags, which was generally the case only in redoubts, were blown in by the British artillery, and in many cases almost disappeared. The Royal Engineers of the 52nd and 54th Divisions laid a number of wire tracks across the sand prior to the attack, in addition to working for several weeks on a water supply to the front line. The wire tracks were required chiefly for the evacuation of the wounded, supplies being brought up by camels and by a tramway which ran through the dunes.

The wire covering the Turkish front was fairly strong, but there was comparatively little farther back, though some of the switch lines were wired. The defenses of Gaza were held by two divisions, the 53rd from the shore to the eastern face of the town, then the 3rd. The 7th Division, Eighth Army reserve, was close at hand and might be expected to reinforce the front promptly. The artillery of the XXII Corps consisted of 116 guns, including the divisional artillery of the 7th Division. Six large naval guns had been located by British artillery observers, as well as several batteries of 150-mm. howitzers. Though the activity of the Turkish batteries was apparently diminished by 1 November as a result of the British neutralizing fire, the frontal attack to which Major General Hare's force was committed was a formidable undertaking if the defenders were sufficiently resolute.[40]

A signaler with a Royal Engineers' unit vividly described a sandstorm during the lead-up to Gaza III:

> Our final preparations for the advance took place in a sandstorm. For three days we were working with goggles over our eyes and handkerchiefs round mouth and nostrils. The job was recovering and loading cable ready for the dash up. It was impossible to see a man 20 yards away; there was sand all over our perspiring bodies, sand on every mouthful of food we ate, and a sip of tepid water left sand on our lips. Half the fellows were suffering from dysentery pains and passing blood. The storm passed, and we had a clear and beautiful night. We washed, and we stretched ourselves under the stars utterly content with just the absence of physical discomfort. I have had the same feeling in miniature when a tooth has stopped aching. The noise of the bombardment added a pleasurable touch of excitement. We felt things were afoot.[41]

The Attack

Historians MacMunn and Falls describe one scene of the attack: "Umbrella Hill, just west of the Rafah-Gaza road and on the fringe of the sand-dunes, was defended by a network of trenches, and was an advanced work in the enemy's system, connected by three long communication trenches with the main line in rear. It was known to be held by a battalion of the 138th Regiment, about 350 strong. The wire round it had been thoroughly cut by the British artillery during the preceding days."[42]

The 7/Scottish Rifles (Lt. Colonel J.G.P. Romanes), with a company of the 8th Battalion of that regiment attached and a second acting as carriers, assembled before 10 P.M. on 1 November in rear of the British front line. At 10:50 a covering patrol advanced into No Man's Land, but unfortunately was observed by a Turkish outpost which, despite the fire of Stokes mortars, had remained in Fisher's Orchard south of the work. The alarm was given and brisk machine-gun and musketry fire opened from the trenches on Umbrella Hill. The intense British bombardment began at 11, causing the Turkish fire to slacken and enabling a tape to be laid whereon the troops formed up. Rocket signals by the enemy brought down a Turkish barrage, which did not, however, cause serious loss.

The assault took place at night preceded by an intense artillery bombardment and accompanied by a creeping barrage. The infantry advanced with great dash and quickly seized their objective, sustaining only light casualties. However, the Turks shelled their lost position heavily, inflicting 103 casualties by the time twenty-four hours elapsed.

An inside-out umbrella was chosen as the first Divisional Sign for the 54th (East Anglian) Division. According to Private Jake Mortlock it was selected because units of the Division "turned Umbrella Hill inside out."[43] At night on the 20th, a strong raid on the enemy's position at Umbrella Hill was made by the 5th Bedfords (162nd Brig., 54th Div.) with the assistance of an intense artillery bombardment, in which all the batteries in the sector took part; an immense amount of ammunition was fired. Over a

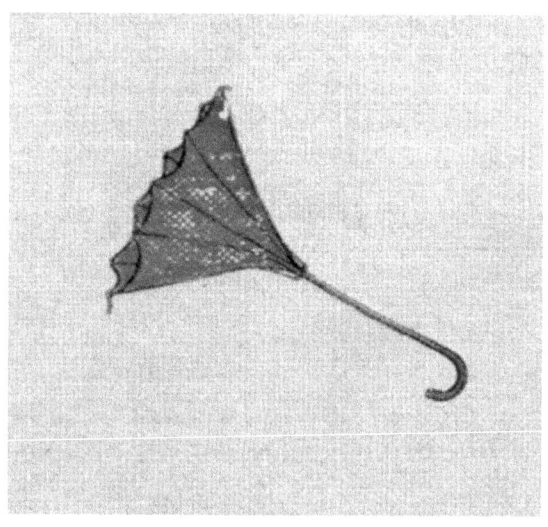

The 54th Divisional sign, an inside-out umbrella, makes reference to Umbrella Hill (Fair and Wolton, *The History of the 1/5th Battalion: "The Suffolk Regiment"*).

Three. A Change at the Top, Then Success at Beersheba and Gaza   123

hundred Turks were bayoneted, some prisoners taken, and several machine guns destroyed or captured. The Turks replied with a very heavy fire all along the line, and particularly concentrated for over three hours a terrific shelling by 5.9 howitzers upon Battalion Headquarters at Hereford Ridge, close to the "jumping off" place of the infantry attack. This part of the line ran through sand dunes, and the heavy bombardment simply obliterated that portion of the trench system, causing severe casualties in the battalion holding the line, and among the returning raiding party.

Gunner R. V. Stone, one of the telephonists, distinguished himself in this action by conspicuous gallantry and devotion to duty, while engaged as telephonist to Lieut. F. L. Tibbs, artillery liaison officer, to whom he was of great service. He was later awarded the Military Medal.[44]

"Zero for the second series of operations was 3 A.M. on the 2nd November, by which time the Turkish artillery activity that had followed the capture of Umbrella Hill had, as anticipated, died down. On the right, at El Arish Redoubt, the 156th Brigade's section of attack carried out by the 4/Royal Scots was completely successful."[45]

Lt. Colonel Thomas Gibbons, who faithfully recorded the part his battalion played in these operations, wrote:

> On the morning of November 1st we were informed that it was "Zero—1 day." In other words the attack was to take place in the small hours of the following morning. At 3 P.M. General Hare saw all officers and spoke a few final words of advice and encouragement. At 4 P.M. I saw each company on parade. They were ready "to the last button" and full of confidence. They knew well that they had a tough proposition in front of them but I could see from their faces they were quietly determined to carry it through.
>
> "A" and "D" Companies (Franklin and Deakin) were to attack the Rafah Redoubt, Deakin being in command. B Company and two platoons of "C" were to take the Zowaid trench, led by Frank Bacon. "C" Company, less two platoons, were in battalion reserve under Colvin and were given a point of assembly behind a slight rise about two-thirds of the way across and almost equi-distant from the two works to be assaulted. The 1/6th Essex were to attack Beach Post and Sea Post. The 1/7th Essex were then to carry the operations a stage further by attacking Cricket redoubt and the Rafah-Belah trench. The tanks were to support the 1/5th in the attacks on both their objectives, afterwards concentrating to the north of Rafah redoubt ready to take part in the second stage in support of the 1/7th. They carried a good load of material for consolidation. The 1/4th Essex were in divisional reserve. The third stage was to be an attack on Sheikh Hasan and Tortoise Hill by the 162nd Brigade, moving by the sea coast.[46]

Col. Gibbons goes on to relate that a well-attended short religious service was held at 4:30 P.M., following which, at 5 P.M., "the battalion went to sleep. Rest was essential, as we knew we had some disturbed nights in front of us."[47] At 11 P.M. the troops ate a good hot square meal accompanied by a pint of beer. At the same time Umbrella Hill was stormed and held by a brigade of the 52nd Division.[48]

Mr. E. W. Masterman, secretary of the British Palestine Society, gives his account of some part of the action: "At the western end on the morning of November 2nd, British infantry advanced and captured a hill nicknamed 'Umbrella Hill,' some 500 yards west of the Dir el-Belah-Gaza road and proceeded to take the whole of the Gaza first line defences between there and the sea. In this attack they were assisted by the 'Tanks.'"[49]

Lt. Colonel Gibbons continues his account: "Thirty minutes after midnight the soldiers of the 1/5th Essex left their bivouac to take up their position of assembly just to the rear of the front line. Careful selection of the latter sought to avoid confusion which often occurs in night operations of this nature. The heavy enemy bombardment of the recently captured Umbrella Hill continued until after midnight but by 1 A.M. eased up markedly. The Turks apparently were undecided as to what to do next, so decided to take a pause, and let the adversary decide for them — which they did."[50]

Now we come to, possibly the most detailed account of an infantry assault in the annals of war, as Colonel Gibbons resumes his commentary:

> At 2.20 we reported all ready at the position of deployment in front of the wire and it seemed a long wait until 2.55, when we were timed to start. Silence reigned supreme and we stood unscathed on ground, which an hour before had been a veritable inferno. It was a good start. The tanks had been got over safely and at 2.55 the companies moved off. At three precisely, the artillery commenced. The moon had just disappeared and the light got very bad. The smoke and dust of the fire made a thick fog and the compass had to be relied upon for direction. Battalion Headquarters was in the front line trench, an advanced headquarters under Evans, followed "A" and "D" Companies to establish as soon as possible the new headquarters in "Rafa Junior," an off-shoot of the redoubt. They laid a wire forward as they went. This was soon cut, and for some time I was without any information. Worse still, the carefully buried line to Brigade Headquarters also refused to work and remained on strike to the end of the proceedings. After about half-an-hour a runner got back to say that the enemy's front line was in our hands. Lancaster, who had been told off to check the direction, had been killed, also Evans our invaluable scout officer, who was shot dead just outside the enemy's parapet. The Turks had put up a wonderful fight, many of them lying in forward positions in the open to avoid the bombardment, and meeting our men with the bayonet. Still the reports were very confusing, as both attacking parties claimed to be in the Rafa redoubt. No word was received as to the Zowaid trench. Runners lost their way in the thick haze and it was impossible to tell exactly what the situation was.
>
> The air seemed filled with fine sand and smoke, which hung about like a thick ground fog and made it very difficult. Reports came in from the right that the attacks on El Arish Redoubt and the El Burj trench had been repulsed. I was very anxious about Zowaid, which joined El Burj. The reports, however, proved incorrect. It was now broad daylight and the enemy was firing furiously from his second line. The 6th had taken Beach and Sea Posts with little trouble. The 7th had taken Cricket redoubt, but had not succeeded in their attack on that very important trench the Rafa-Belah. The tanks had broken down and neither had reached even its first objective. The loss of their support was a serious blow to the 7th.
>
> The morning wore on and still no definite news of Zowaid. But a wounded man said he saw some of advanced headquarters personnel in Rafa Junior and it was

decided to move Battalion Headquarters to its new position. The enemy kept up a brisk fire from his second line (which it will be remembered commanded the first and was in full view) and we were held up half-way across by a very persistent machine gun, which afforded a convincing argument, to my discreet mind, for altering our course by way of Beach Post, to which there was a more covered approach. This route also took us away from the direction of Zowaid trench, of which I was still doubtful as to the occupiers, as a good deal of fire came from that direction.

I am afraid these peregrinations of our little band of headquarters may appear to the reader as rather affected by undue caution; but I confess I had no mind to walk across the front of a possible enemy trench at a distance of 300 yards. Zowaid trench was occasionally visible through the haze, but shewed no sign of life, and was not at that time being shelled, though it got a terrible dusting later. To cut a long story short we eventually reached our new position via Beach Post, and made our home in a shell hole. I had found poor Lancaster about half-way across, quite dead, with a smile on his handsome face. I took off his signet ring and sent it afterwards to his wife.

As I entered Rafa redoubt I was surprised to meet Frank Bacon being carried out, his foot badly shattered by a bomb. He was too much knocked about to stop and question as to how he got there, but the situation was gradually cleared up by further enquiry. An extraordinary thing had happened. The two attacking parties, going to divergent points, necessarily moved independently. Deakin, making straight for his objective — Rafa Redoubt — suddenly saw a swarm of men clambering up the steep sandy slope which led up to the work. It was "B" Company, whose objective was the Zowaid trench, and who had lost direction in the darkness and struck Rafa instead. How it happened will probably never be known; Lancaster alone could, perhaps, have told. But it can be safely conjectured that compasses proved unreliable with so many steel rifle barrels and steel helmets in the vicinity.

Deakin did not take long to make up his mind. He quickly realized that whoever the attacking party were and whichever position it was he was needed elsewhere. He told me afterwards that he thought he himself might have lost his direction and it was the 6th Essex storming Beach Post in front of him. Acting on this supposition he changed direction and felt for the next work on his right, which proved to be Zowaid trench. All the works were very much alike in that light; all were sited high, and had low ground behind them. Once you are in trenches it is very difficult to tell the plan of the position you are in. Hence it is not so surprising that I received, from Zowaid, a sketch of Rafa, shewing the parts of that trench which had been taken. It should be explained that officers of each party had been supplied with sketches of their objectives on which to make their reports.

Deakin's presence of mind saved the situation, but the change of direction had taken time, and the barrage had lifted some minutes before he arrived. The Turk was manning his parapets and it was only really good leadership and resolution that enabled the assaulting column to fight their way in. The casualties were heavy. Deakin's leg was broken by a bullet and he dropped outside the work. But Franklin carried on, and Wray, who was also wounded, and other officers and non-commissioned officers. Sergt. Watsham, Corpl. Jarrold and Pte. Long greatly distinguished themselves. Sergt. Cooper, D.C.M., fell gallantly leading his platoon after they had swept over the front line.

The second line lay on the low ground and those detailed for its capture — what was left of them — gallantly carried on and occupied it; but none of them ever got back. Support was not forthcoming from the right as expected and the position was untenable. However, the main trench on the high ground was won and held; though subjected to a murderous [assault] from howitzers and *minenwerfer*. The Turks had held on to it with the utmost tenacity and had to be bombed out by working along the trench. It was splendid work, and the way successive difficulties were overcome reflected the greatest credit on "A" and "D" Companies and their leaders.

Meanwhile, Bacon had made good the redoubt with his company and a half, although it was considered a big enough job for two companies. They got in close up to the barrage, but the Turks stuck to their machine guns, two of which were captured, as well as a British Lewis gun, taken in one of the first two battles. At the bottom of the rear slope two *minenwerfer* were silenced and deserted, but here again the low ground was untenable, without support which was expected from the left. It is to be feared that the unfortunate mistake above referred to was partly responsible for this. Part of the 7th Essex were to pass by the right of Rafa redoubt and attack the Rafah-Belah trench in flank whilst another part attacked it from the direction of Cricket redoubt. When the right half of the 7th arrived they shouted — to make sure — "Is this Rafa?" The answer, in all good faith was, "No, Zowaid!" The result was that the Rafa-Belah trench was not attacked in the way intended by the brigade scheme. The enemy held it, and from it played havoc in the ranks of the 7th [Essex] and the 10th Londons, who were making for a further objective in conformity with the rest of their brigade, who were moving by the seashore.

The result was that although the front line works were captured and held and the 162nd Brigade had also captured the Sheikh Hassan position far to the north, the Rafa-Belah trench still held out. It was effectually blocked from the Rafah redoubt end, where Archer did great work with his Lewis gun, fighting it himself almost single-handed after Sergt. Alloway, his most efficient gun non-commissioned officer, had been killed and most of his team knocked out. C.-S.-M. Wilson did splendid work in helping to organize and consolidate the position. Richmond and Lockwood, I remember, were conspicuous too, in Rafa redoubt; but it is hardly fair to mention names, there were so many others.

The Turks still shelled us very heavily, especially with *minenwerfer*, from the direction of "Island Wood," behind Zowaid, but our guns could not locate them. I had repeated messages from Franklin in the latter place and they were evidently suffering severely. It seemed likely that the enemy might counter-attack Zowaid, which proved, perhaps, a more difficult place than Rafa to hold. Its capture would have made Rafa more or less of a trap, particularly as the enemy held the Rafa-Belah trench. I therefore reinforced Zowaid with Colvin and the remainder of his company. I had little fear for Rafa as it had a good field of fire to the north, which could be improved by digging another trench during the night. The enemy contented himself with bombarding it, and occasionally opening heavy rifle and machine gun fire upon it, without following it up, and it appeared to be more "wind" than anything else.

The pioneers connected up two or three holes and made Battalion Headquarters a little more commodious. The entrenchment H.Q. became rather crowded with men from other units who had apparently lost their way. They were organized into working parties as there was plenty of work for everybody. During the night a complete new trench on the northern slope, the dead were buried, and the trenches cleared of debris and strengthened with materials brought up by carrying parties from Brigade Headquarters. The enemy made one counter-attack during the night, but only a few determined men reached the work and these were disposed of.

Soon after dawn both works were subjected to a furious bombardment, but if the enemy thought we were to be shelled out after a night's consolidation he reckoned without his host. Zowaid got it perhaps worse than we did, and our gunners were still unable to silence those elusive *minenwerfer*. During the day I was obliged to leave owing to wounds in the hands which I had received the previous morning.

Avery, my M.O. (who had been doing splendid work under heavy fire) insisted on my having further treatment and a tetanus injection, and I very reluctantly handed over the command to Franklin, who was fetched from Zowaid, Colvin taking over that place. I had every confidence in my successor, but it was galling to have to leave the battalion once more when they were "going through it." However, it was the fortune of war. The Brigadier subsequently sent for Wilson, who was waiting, and he took over the Battalion at midnight.

My sad trudge back to the Field Ambulance was relieved by one amusing remark which I heard from a carrying party going up to the line. I was dressed in a "Tommy's" uniform with no prominent badges of rank, and, I fear, did not look my best. "Poor old — —," one of them remarked to the other. "I call it a shame to send old blokes like him up there."

The capture of Rafa redoubt and Zowaid trench was a feat of which the battalion may well be proud. That the enemy offered a determined resistance was shewn by the fact that our casualties in the action were two officers and 73 other ranks killed, seven officers and 172 other ranks wounded and nine other ranks missing. The killed included, besides those already mentioned, such good non-commissioned officers as Sergts. H. Byles, N. Bruce and D. Ambrose, Corpl. P. Anderson, and L./Corpls. H. Quilter and Tasker.

It afterwards transpired that the enemy had drawn a whole division into Gaza to reinforce the defence. Thus, the attack not only succeeded in capturing its objectives but also achieved completely its primary objective, which was to keep the enemy's forces tied to Gaza, and to draw his reserves into that place.

The main attack on the enemy's left at Sheria took place at dawn on November 6th and was completely successful.

"The account of the capture of the town of Gaza on November 7th and the subsequent advance through Philistia, I must leave Wilson to tell, as I was *hors de combat* until December 22nd."[51]

Here the account is taken up by Major W. E. Wilson.

During the afternoon of November 3rd, I received a wire from 54th Division, ordering me to take command of the battalion, Colonel Gibbons having been wounded. I left the nucleus camp at Belah a little later, being ordered to report at Divisional Headquarters on my way. I saw the G.S.O. (1), Colonel Garsia, who informed me of the situation and impressed upon me the importance of the battalion holding on to their positions, particularly Rafah redoubt, which he explained was practically the key position of the whole line. He added that counter-attacks and heavy bombardment must be expected. On arrival at Ajlin Mosque I reported myself at Brigade Headquarters and proceeded to Rafa redoubt where I arrived at midnight.

The night was still, not a sound to be heard; the moon almost at the full, lighting up the sand like day. I found that both Rafa and Zowaid had suffered severely from our previous bombardment. Rafa especially looked like an old clothes shop, the burst Turkish sandbags, many of them made with shirts and other clothing being strewn everywhere. In both works the men were busy with the consolidation of the position. Nothing of interest occurred during the night, in fact the stillness of the whole front was uncanny. This peaceful state of affairs continued, as far as we were concerned, until about 10 o'clock on November 4th, when, without warning, the Turks opened up a heavy fire with 5.9 H.E. ["Jack Johnsons"] on Rafa redoubt. As hour after hour went by no cessation of the hostile fire took place, in fact it rather increased in intensity during the afternoon. Considering the great amount of shell fired at us it was extraordinary that the casualties were so light; this may probably be accounted for by the fact that a great percentage of the shells buried themselves in the sand before exploding.

The men worked with a will on the work of consolidation during the day, but the new work was quickly spotted by the Turkish observers, and more often than not demolished.

As darkness came on the Turkish fire changed to 77mm and 4.2 shrapnel. This was aimed principally at the rear of both Rafa and Zowaid to hinder movement. In this it was effective, and some difficulty was experienced in bringing up water and supplies. The Camel Transport not being able to reach the post it became necessary to detail fatigue parties for this work. The Turkish fire continued with varying intensity all through the night, changing to 5.9 H.E. as morning broke. On the following day, November 5th, the bombardment was heavier than ever, and I felt that if something were not done to check the Turkish gunners we stood the chance of serious casualties. About 10 o'clock I spoke to the brigadier and explained the position to him, and he promised to do his best to arrange for artillery support.[52]

Our Suffolk historians continue the story: "The 5th Battalion of the Suffolk Regiment [163rd Brigade, 54th Division] charged the trenches at El Arish, sweeping into the third line. A singular testimonial to the Battalion was found in the Turkish positions at El Arish in the shape of an order from General Friedrich Kress von Kressenstein. 'I have inspected your trenches,' the order ran, 'and am well satisfied with them. They are excellent, and if these trenches cannot be held, then it is no use digging any trenches.'"[53]

On the right of the 163rd Brigade the 5th Suffolk entered the western half of El Arish Redoubt at the same moment as the Royal Scots entered the eastern. Keeping close to an accurate barrage, it over-ran the whole objective with little loss, but was withdrawn from the third line owing to its exposed position, and proceeded to consolidate the second. The 8th Hampshire split into two bodies, one of which swung right-handed into Triangle Trench, outside its objective. The other captured Burj Trench. The 4th and 5th Norfolk in the second line lost direction also, in part owing to their companies being misled by the mistake of the Hampshire in front. On a ground spouting dust and smoke and covered by a maze of shallow trenches, some confusion followed, and only small bodies reached Gibraltar and Crested Rock, to fall back when they found themselves isolated.... The other companies, seeing troops in front assaulting what should have been their objective, thought these must be the 6th Essex at Beach Post and that they themselves were too far to the left. They therefore wheeled right-handed and entered Zowaid Trench,[54] apparently supposing it to be the front line of Rafah Redoubt. On the left the 6th Essex, which made no mistake, captured Beach and Sea Posts with slight casualties. The battalions passing through to the objectives of the third phase suffered from these mishaps, and became involved in heavy and confused fighting in Rafah Redoubt and Rafah Trench. Eventually Cricket Redoubt was captured with the aid of the tank from Beach Post.

Cricket Redoubt having been taken, the other misadventures had fortunately no serious effect upon the progress of the fourth phase, the attack by the

Three. A Change at the Top, Then Success at Beersheba and Gaza

162nd Brigade, except on the extreme right, where the 10th London had to turn the enemy out of Rafah Redoubt, which had only been partially penetrated. This battalion lost touch with the barrage and suffered heavy loss. The brigade was also deprived of the assistance of the few tanks allotted to its support, which had been put out of action in the previous phases. The attack was, however, completely successful. There was a sharp struggle for Gun Hill, which was taken with the bayonet.

By 6 A.M. the brigade was ready to assault Sheikh Hasan, and went forward after a quarter of an hour's bombardment, capturing this place without much difficulty and taking 182 prisoners. The tank at Cricket Redoubt, which had been disabled, was now repaired sufficiently to bring up a load of engineers' stores to Sheikh Hasan, but was again put out of action soon afterwards. The tanks had contributed to the success of the attack, but their casualty list was high, and in the opinion of some observers they prematurely alarmed the Turks at the beginning of the second phase, which might otherwise have taken them completely by surprise.

Lt. General Friedrich Kress von Kressenstein. Gaza III was a case of "third time unlucky" for this most capable commander.

The two reserve tanks which were ordered forward at 4 A.M. to support the infantry north of Rafah Redoubt were unfortunately loaded on top with sandbags as well as other R.E. material. In both cases the sandbags were set afire and the tanks temporarily put out of action. It had nevertheless been, generally speaking, a notable achievement on the part of the tanks, which were, with three exceptions, worn and obsolete Mark I machines, survivors of the Second Battle of Gaza. This was the detachment's last employment.

It had been intended that if possible the Imperial Service Cavalry Brigade should exploit the success. To clear a way for the cavalry a company of the 4th Northamptonshire was ordered to capture Lion Trench, three-quarters of a mile northeast of the shrine at Sheikh Hasan. The task was carried out by 7:30 A.M. and the wire cleared from the beach. Twenty minutes later, however, the enemy in considerable numbers attempted to surround Lion Trench, and the company, which was so far forward that little artillery support could be given to it, was forced to withdraw.[55]

Large bodies of the enemy were now seen advancing in open order on Sheikh Hasan from the north and northeast, and at 8:57 A.M. a barrage was put down by the whole of the Corps Heavy Artillery on a line 3,000 yards long, running north and south, about two miles east of that point. This barrage, which had been prepared and registered with aerial observation by Brig. General H.A.D. Bailkie in case the enemy's reserve division about Deir Sneid advanced to counter-attack, scattered the Turks in all directions and caused heavy casualties. After the counter-attack had broken down, a new attack on Lion Trench was ordered, but later cancelled by Major General Hare, and the 4th Northamptonshire, which had been assembled to make it, was employed instead in the afternoon in an attack on Yunis Trench. The battalion reached its objective, but was driven back by another Turkish counter-attack. Turkish troops in large numbers moving across the ridge in the direction of Sheikh Hasan were apparently screened from the British ground artillery observers by the smoke, but were caught by the fire of the monitors and destroyers and suffered terrible loss.

The enemy's heavy batteries shelled Sheikh Hasan throughout the day, but as a result of the British fire and the infantry advance, all his artillery, with the exception of a few mobile guns, was withdrawn by night to northeast of Gaza. The British consolidated their position during the night, and the Turks were heard working hard to strengthen Turtle Hill. The weather, as the result of a *khamsin*, became extremely hot and dusty on the 3rd, and the troops suffered severely. A new attack on Yunis Trench at 4:30 A.M. by the 4th Essex was momentarily successful, but the battalion, which was not disposed in sufficient depth, was ejected by a counter-attack and lost heavily during its withdrawal.[56]

At 2:30 A.M. on November 2nd, the 5th Suffolk, with "D" company of the 1/4th Norfolk attached for carrying purposes, formed up on the right outside the British wire, with the 8th Hants on their left. Between 2:30 and 3 A.M., both these assaulting battalions were advancing on Half-way House unmolested by a barrage, for the Turks believed them to be nothing more than a strong patrol. At 3 A.M., having passed Half-way House, the 5th Suffolk got into hand-to-hand fighting without much loss on the way. The 8th Hants were not so fortunate. In the mist and the smoke of exploding shells their leading wave got split, part going to towards El Arish, and part towards the Susan trench at El Burj. However, both battalions reached and occupied the objective trenches.

Meanwhile, the 1/4th Norfolk had formed in support at 2:15 A.M. on the rear of the 8th Hants, slightly to the right, with "B" Company on the right, "C" on the left, and "A" in the rear of "C," all in lines of sections in file. The machine-guns and light trench mortar were in the rear of "C" under 2nd Lieutenant C. M. Collier, who was killed shortly after the advance began. As the battalion advanced at 3 A.M. it ran into the enemy's barrage, which had gone over the 8th Hants. They had heavy casualties from this, and, owing to the split in the 8th Hants, two companies ("B" and "C") of the 1/4th Norfolk, followed the right of the 8th Hants towards Triangle trench, which was to the right of their proper direction. The orders were to follow the 8th Hants in touch with 1/5th Norfolk, which they were unable to find, though they were in touch with the 5th Suffolk on the right. At 3:55 A.M., when they should have passed through the 8th Hants to attack their proper objective, the Crested Rock, they found themselves involved in hand-to-had fighting in El Arish, and eventually occupied trenches there. "A" Company ("D" company was carrying for the 5th Suffolk) got into a trench still farther to the right.

The duration of the fighting at El Arish upset all calculations and rendered impossible the intended attack on Crested Rock. The 1/4th Norfolk appears to have gotten right into the area of the 5th Suffolk on the right and found it impossible to locate themselves. The 1/5th Norfolk had formed up at 2:50 A.M. on the left rear of the 8th Hants, who had already reached Half-way House. They too lost direction as they advanced at 3 A.M., lost touch with the 1/4th on their right, and arrived opposite the line Zowaid–El Burj instead of Zowaid–Rafa. Here their right flank was in the air, as was the left of the 1/4th. They were caught in the barrage at 3:30 A.M. when waiting to pass through, and it was too late to correct the direction. Some confusion resulted, but Captain Gardner and Lieutenants Cumberland, Catherell, and Pallett (all of whom became casualties) penetrated with small bodies of men to Island Wood, Gibraltar, and even to Crested Rock. Captain Gardner, at Island Wood with a small party, was forced by want of support to retire. Two officers with him did not return and were missing. The battalion took up the line Susan Trench–Zowaid. The situation was obscure throughout, and the units were much mixed up. Eventually a line was consolidated as follows, counting from right to left:

> 1/5th Suffolk–Grace trench, Gertrude trench, Craig post, Rook trench.
> 1/8th Hants, from El Burj towards Violet trench.
> 1/4th Norfolk, from Bertha trench to the junction of Grace and Violet trenches.
> 1/5th Norfolk, from El Burj to Zowaid.

The brigade had fallen considerably short of attaining its objective, a result due to darkness and confusion. The casualties of the Norfolk battalions were: 1/4th. Killed, 2nd Lieutenants C. M. Collier and W. S. Giles (both Royal Warwick attached to 1/4th Norfolk; Wounded, 2nd Lieutenants Geldart, Lucas, and Jewell, and 102 other ranks; and Missing, four other ranks. Unfortunately the casualties for the 1/5th were not entered in the diary.[57]

During the morning of 5 November, Major Wilson, C.O. *pro tempore* of the 1/5th Essex, reported that "a message was received to the effect that the 8th Hants would relieve us at Rafa and Zowaid. About 4 o'clock, as the Turkish fire again increased in intensity, I again spoke to the brigadier, and asked for artillery support, and some half-hour or so later we heard our heavies strafing the batteries which had paid us so much attention, and after that, except for the 77 shrapnel, the Turkish fire diminished appreciably."[58]

Mr. E. W. Masterman, secretary of the British Palestine Society, gives his account of some part of the actions: "The eastern line having now completely given way, the attack on Gaza was renewed at midnight on the 6th, and the city was captured without much opposition; the British left wing—Scottish infantry—pushing forward through the heavy sand dunes with great energy the same night towards the mouth of the Wady Hesy."[59]

Royal Engineer Corporal Frederick Mills' diary entry reads: "Wednesday, November 7th, 1917. Kantara. Gaza taken but oh! The wounded. Its awful. A lot of English nurses have arrived today, the first white women I have seen for sometime. We are in the desert.[60]

A headline in *The Times* (London) of Monday, November 5, 1917 read:

TURK DEFEAT AT GAZA.
******
ADVANCE ON FRONT OF THREE MILES.
*****
444 PRISONERS TAKEN.
*****

The War Office has issued the following communiqués
Regarding operations in Palestine:—

November 3.—On the night of November 1–2, after heavy bombardment, our troops attacked the western and south-western defences of Gaza and captured the Turkish first-line defences on a front of 5,000 yards. We took 296 prisoners and five machine-guns. Three counter-attacks have been driven off and heavy losses inflicted on the enemy.[61]

An article in *The Times* (London) on November 5, 1917 read:

THE BRITISH SUCCESS NEAR GAZA.
FOUR COUNTER-ATTACKS REPULSED.
(From W. T. Massey.)
BEFORE GAZA, Nov. 3.

Yesterday's strong attack on the system of trenches west and south-west of Gaza aimed at improving our position before the town, and its full success was made apparent by the desperate attempts by the enemy to regain the lost ground. Last night and this morning the Turks four times counter-attacked to recover their positions, throwing large numbers of men against our new line, which has eaten into an extremely important part of the defensive chain round the town. Each counter-attack was strongly delivered, but Scottish and East Anglian troops, who took and held the trenches, with the aid of well-sustained fire of our batteries, broke up every advancing line with rifle and machine-gun fire. The enemy fell back, leaving large numbers of dead and wounded in front of our new works.[62]

The Times (London) of Tuesday, November 6, 1917 reported:

GEN. ALLENBY'S SUCCESS.

TANKS IN GAZA ACTION.

TOTAL OF PRISONERS
NOW 2,636.

Three. A Change at the Top, Then Success at Beersheba and Gaza   133

The Secretary of the War Office makes the following announcement:—
The operations against Gaza are continuing, and we are in contact with the enemy north of Beersheba. The total number of prisoners captured by us from the commencement of these operations is now 207 officers and 2,129 other ranks.[63]

THE TURKISH ACCOUNT.

Turkish report, Nov. 4: — In Syria two out of five enemy aeroplanes, which unsuccessfully bombed Haifa, fell into the sea, as a result of damage. The wrecked machines sank after the occupants had been rescued by an enemy monitor.

Sinai Front: — On October 30 strong hostile attacks were delivered in which the enemy made lavish use of poison gas. With the exception of one small sector, which the enemy captured, all our positions were maintained, and great losses inflicted on the enemy. The battles are continuing.

A British captive balloon, which had broken loose, was shot down over Askalon.

One enemy infantry division which attacked our main positions on the left wing was repulsed.—*Reuters.*

ALL OBJECTIVES GAINED.

Valuable Help from the Navy.
British Headquarters, Nov. 2.

Following up the success against the extreme Turkish right, we engaged his opposite flank last night, capturing all our objectives, including strong trench systems and redoubts.

This part of the Turkish line had been subjected to somewhat rough treatment by artillery during the past six days, but what preceded must have seemed child's play compared with the regular drum fire which burst forth at 11 at night. These bombardments of extreme intensity may be regarded as normal happenings on the Western Front, but here they are quite without precedent. Even at the Dardanelles the Turk never experienced such a deluge of fire as was concentrated for a few minutes upon Umbrella Hill, a strongly organized position 500 yards from our lines on Samson's Ridge, south-west of Gaza.

There was, however, little left of organization when our men swept upon it, and they met with little opposition, the few casualties that occurred being in the main the result of shell fire when the Turkish batteries learnt that the position was lost. Although the rest of the enemy position between Umbrella Hill and the sea had not been treated so severely by our fire the assaulting troops attained all their objectives.

They were assisted in their task by several tanks. These Leviathans were not entirely at home amid the shifty sand dunes, but nevertheless nosed their way into the enemy lines, making themselves as obnoxious as they best know how. With supreme indifference to machine-gun and rifle fire, they lumbered over the entanglements, parapets, and trenches, contributing greatly to the capture of El Arish Redoubt and Beach Post, which latter is stated to be heaped with corpses. The moonlight exaggerating their huge and seemingly unwieldy bulk, the Turks must have regarded them as veritable sons of Eblis. Our bag included one mortar, many machine-guns, and over 300 prisoners, including nearly 30 officers. The unusually high percentage of officers captured in recent operations suggest that the Turks have found it necessary to stiffen the ranks with additional officers.

Still there is no denying that the enemy has so far shown a very stubborn spirit. He hangs on to his positions to the very last. For instance, a case is reported of a single machine-gunner, although completely surrounded, refusing to yield, and it had been impossible to knock him out when he was last heard of.

Captured Turkish trenches El Arish Redoubt, the scene of bitter fighting during the Third Battle of Gaza, November 1917, and where Private Jake Mortlock mortally wounded a Turkish sniper (Fair and Wolton, *The History of the 1/5th Battalion: "The Suffolk Regiment"*).

Our Flying Corps collaborated with the infantry with conspicuous success and helped to silence many of the enemy guns by bombing. Of course, they were unceasing in their efforts in conjunction with the artillery throughout the preliminary bombardment, yesterday they were the means of bringing Turks massing on a certain sector under heavy and destructive shelling. Two enemy guns were caught in the open yesterday by our heavies, which demolished both guns and crews.

Nor must the work of the Navy, cooperating in the present offensive, be overlooked. We have several monitors and destroyers in position before Gaza, and their fire played a valuable part in the preparatory bombardment, as their position enables them to enfilade a good part of the Turkish lines, and the accuracy of their fire is appreciatively recognized. They are also doing valuable work in shelling the Turkish communications in the rear, and are known to have severely damaged a bridge over the Wadi Hesi (north of Gaza).

One interesting detail of yesterday's fighting deserves mention — namely, the participation of the Italians attached to one of our brigades, which fought with great gallantry.

Meanwhile, on our right we have secured the hills to the north of Beersheba, where we are consolidating our new positions. — *Reuters.*

Probably the most difficult strongpoint to take, and the one gauged by many to be the key to Gaza was the "Hill of Ali Muntar, where Samson is said to have carried the gates of Gaza on one occasion."[64]

More captured Turkish trenches El Arish Redoubt (Fair and Wolton, *The History of the 1/5th Battalion: "The Suffolk Regiment"*).

Trench Fighting in the El Arish Redoubt

Private Jake Mortlock, of "D" Company, 1/5th Suffolks, recounted at some length his own experiences in the fighting for the El Arish Redoubt.

> We had captured part of a Turkish communication trench and had sandbagged it off. [Private] Freddie Turner was hit and dropped down — I thought he was dead at that moment, but he was only concussed by the impact on [the] helmet which deflected the bullet, causing it to exit without touching a hair on his head; he fell as if dead. I knew the shot came from close by. I took a quick peek over the top ... hedge of prickly pear ... "twigged" sniper,[65] rifle trained on me! I swung my rifle up and fired a snap shot." The bullet hit the man in upper chest and came out of his back — he rolled down and fell into the trench. A Turkish Sergeant-major. He was in a pretty bad way.... A Turk with a bullet-smashed knee was also in trench with them. It [the wound] had been dressed, but the dressing needed changing. The soldier became in so much pain that he began crying out: "Docktor Allemagne!" "Docktor Allemagne!" [Or, possibly "Docteur Allemand!" "Docteur Allemand!" Pierre van Paasen renders the Arabic "Allaman."[66]] presumably imploring his German M.O. [medical officer] to come and relieve his suffering. However, this constant calling out got on our nerves and we had to threaten to knock him out.[67]

In a letter penned in Alexandria several weeks, later Private Mortlock informed his cousin, Jack Parker: "I had a fortnight in the worst part of it, and then I had a dose of Sand fly fever[68] which put me in the dock for three weeks."

The Times reported on progress from Beersheba:

> November 3. — Our advance yesterday covered a depth of 800 yards at Umbrella Hill on the right of our attack, and amounted to 2,000 yards at Sheikh Hassan, on the sea shore west of Gaza. Scottish and East Anglian troops shared the honours of the fighting. In the course of yesterday the enemy made four counter-attacks, which were all repulsed with heavy loss. All our gains were maintained, and the new positions have now been consolidated.
>
> On our right flank infantry dislodged the enemy from Abu Irgeig station, eight miles north-west of Beersheba, and the enemy had to beat a precipitate retreat. Also on our right flank Yeomanry, supported by the Light Horse, had a brush with the enemy cavalry in the hilly region some miles north of Beersheba, the Turks being driven in the direction of Dhahe Riveh, losing a few prisoners and two guns.
>
> The Turkish communications in the rear of their right flank appear to have suffered heavily from the fire of our heavies and naval guns.
>
> We blew up ammunition dumps at Beit Hanun, Sheikh Hassan, and Deir-Sineid (north of Gaza), and the railway was so damaged near the Wadi Hosi that several trucks were derailed.—*Reuters.*[69]

> ENEMY REPORT ON THE LOSS OF BEERSHEBA.
>
> Turkish report, Nov. 3: — A British attack was launched on October 31. Our troops, which had advanced as far as Beersheba, retired before greatly superior enemy forces to their principal positions after repulsing all the enemy attacks. Seven officers, including a lieutenant-colonel, and a 100 men were captured.
>
> A battle took place on November 2 in front of Gaza in which two armoured motor-cars were destroyed by our artillery.—*Reuters.*

There is no confirmation of the statement concerning the capture of prisoners at Beersheba referred to in the Turkish communique.

Three. A Change at the Top, Then Success at Beersheba and Gaza

The Times (London) reported on Thursday, November 8, 1917.

GAZA TAKEN.
RAPID ADVANCE FROM
BEERSHEBA

The Secretary of the War Office made the following announcement last night concerning the operations in Palestine:—

General Allenby reports that our troops captured Khuweilteh (11 miles north of Beersheba) soon after midnight on November 5/6, and that repeated counter-attacks throughout the whole of yesterday were repulsed.

Further to the south our troops advancing in a north-westerly direction from the neighbourhood of Beersheba carried the whole of the Turkish defences south of the line Tell-el-Sheria-Abu Hareira, capturing both these last-named places. This is an advance of nine miles from the position of departure [the line Tell-el-Sheria-Abu Hareira is about eight miles in length, Abu Hareira being 12 miles south-east of Gaza].

"Uncle" Jack Parker corresponded throughout the war with two soldier cousins, Bob Jaggard and Jake Mortlock and, kept all their letters throughout his life (Mortlock family photograph).

General Allenby states that throughout the operations the troops displayed magnificent dash and endurance. Estimates of captures are not yet available, but on one portion of the front of operations six guns have been taken.

Turkish Report

Nov. 6:—

SINAI FRONT.—There was violent artillery fire on the Gaza sector, and weak artillery fire on the sectors of the Western (Beersheba) front.

PREPARING THE VICTORY
THE INDOMITABLE SPIRIT OF THE MEN
(From W. T. Massey.)
BEFORE GAZA, NOV. 5.

The Turks attempted to attack our position near Gaza last night and put up strong artillery fire, but our reply was overwhelming, and the enemy infantry dispersed with heavy loss.

The bombardment of the defences of Gaza continues from sea and land, the trenches being torn and crushed.

Many landmarks familiar to our troops for months, such as Ali el Muntar, the hill up which Samson carried the gates of Gaza, is now changed beyond all recognition.[70]

CAPTURE OF GAZA
******

A SWIFT ADVANCE IN
PALESTINE
******

Gaza has been taken by the British forces in Palestine under General Allenby. His troops after the capture of Beersheba, to the south-east of Gaza, on October 31, advanced rapidly north and north-west across the valleys through the Judean hills. On Monday night [sic] they carried the Turkish line of defences half way between the two towns.

The outer line of defences of Gaza on the west and south-west were taken on the night of November 1-2, with the aid of tanks and enfilade fire from warships. Gaza was captured yesterday morning, but no particulars have yet been received.

GENERAL ALLENBY'S ADVANCE
20 MILES NORTH OF GAZA
ENEMY CASUALTIES 15,000

The Secretary of the War Office makes the following announcements concerning the operations in Palestine:—
November 10 — General Allenby reports that on the 9th instant mounted troops moved forward rapidly and have captured another 400 prisoners and 10 guns.

Our line now runs in a south-easterly direction from two miles north of Hamameh (two miles from the coast and four north-east of Ascalon) to two miles north of Arak-el-Menshia, on the central railway — generally 10 to six miles north of the Wadi Hesi. Ascalon has been occupied by infantry and artillery.[71]

Two artillery observation balloons were available, of which one was shot down by Turkish shrapnel.[72]

"B" Battery, 271st (Essex) Brigade, 54th (East Anglian) Divisional Artillery, claimed the distinction of being the first battery past Gaza in pursuit of the retreating enemy. Although they fired on the Turco–German forces, their retirement was rapid, and the last stragglers were soon beyond the range of the guns.

To maintain the momentum of the advance necessary to prevent the enemy from organizing his scattered forces, transport for munitions and supplies became of the utmost importance. "The 54th Division remained at Gaza, and gave up all its transport to assist in the forward move, and was able to maintain itself without transport on a supply of five days' rations in depots close at hand."[73]

R. E. Corporal Fred Mills' diary entry reads: "Saturday, December 7th, 1918. Kantara. Jack Isaacs came down. His regiment [Northamptons] is going close to Cairo tomorrow.[74]

The Wells of Sheria

Light Horse Trooper Davison wrote: "On the morning of November 6th, with no news of our missing camel convoy, the attack on Sheria was launched. We all knew of the wells Sheria contained, and that, unless we captured the place before nightfall, many of us would die of thirst." The Turkish forces were "holding on to Sheria like grim death, because they realised that if they gave it up they would have to retreat over many miles of waterless desert with a depleted transport." Likewise, the Australians needed the precious element so badly that they "fought that day as men fight for their lives.... The smell of water, cold and sweet, was released on the dusty air. Standing weary and patient, out among the ridges, the horses smelled it, and a whinny ran from line to line."[75]

Private William Johnson, of the 2nd Battalion, 22nd London Regiment, 60th (London) Division, relates what happened to him and his unit:

It happened in Palestine on November 7th, 1917. The day is Wednesday. We are hard on the heels of the Turk. Gaza has fallen, we have taken Beersheba, and are now on the way to Sheria. There are wells at Sheria, and we are very thirsty!

From dawn all Tuesday we have ploughed through sand and sun, no food to speak of — a nibble of bully and biscuit; and, though warned at the start to hang on to our water, there isn't a man with a fly's bath in his bottle when we come to a halt in the evening. The grit on my teeth! The mud on my tongue! Lord! I can taste it now! Trekking the best part of a month, we are tired, ragged, verminous, and itchy with septic sores. Now we have halted and we know we are close to the Turk. Petulantly through the twilight half-spent bullets whine out their last breath overhead. Nobody cares; we are too fagged out to heed them. Dropping our packs, we unload the mules and feed the poor brutes a mouthful of corn.

We stretch our backs on the warm sand. Our aching backs! Oh, for a little green apple to quench this blistering thirst! Our spirits are low with fatigue and thirst and dirt. This hopeless, unending misery, this ultimate futility! Would I could sleep for ever. Would I could wake up in the morning and know all this for a nightmare. Ah me, have we not dreamed thus a thousand times through twenty unthinkable months! I sleep. Four hours seem but a minute before I am awakened with the toe of a corporal's boot.

"Get dressed!"

I rise and shiver, hating that corporal. I dress as a dog might shake himself. It is dark, but away to the left the sky glows red. I hear crackling sounds. The air is full of whistling lead.

"What's up?"

"Moving off."

I groan and drag my stiff legs over to my mule and tug and punch him into his harness. Taking his cue from me, he shows his teeth in a succession of mighty yawns.

Shadowy forms are everywhere moving to and fro in the darkness; tired, expressionless faces show palely out of the gloom and pass.

"Stack packs!"

Ah, we're in for it now. Grimly I smile as I hump my clobber in a pile and pitch it in with the rest. I meet Silburn on the way.

"Another stunt, Sunbeam?"

"Dunno, Gunga. Looks like it."

"What's that light over there?"

"Johnny's getting breezy. Blowing up his ammunition dumps."

"Best thing he can do with 'em," I grumble. "Why not let him get on with it!"

"Fall in for rum!"

"That's about corpsed it!" mutters Tich Webster, divining that not for nothing is he to get a noggin of rum in the Plain of Sharon. But the rum is good — dashed good it is! It stings our leathery tongues and stops our shivering. It calms my damnable nerves. I join a little group; Baker is there, the Welsh miner, our last remaining tenor, the red-headed, unquenchable "Scrounger."

"What's doing, Scrounger?"

"Oh, nothing much. Clearing snipers. Colonel can't sleep."

I smile skeptically. "Who told you that?"

"Harold," says Baker.

"A knowing bird, that mule of yours, Scrounger?" sneers Holland.

"He is," replies Baker. "Fed on bully and four-by-two, is Harold. In return for which he tells me things."

"He's a b-blatant liar," growls Durant. "That's w-what he is. It's b-bullets 'e wants, not b-bully!"

Then Durant is ashamed of himself. "Sorry, Baker. M-my n-nerves," he says, and turns away.

"I suppose you didn't ask him if we're getting any water tonight?" enquires Evans.

"I did," answers Scrounger. "And he kicked me in the — —!"

I go. Yes, as always, the officers will know all there is to be known when we start. We shall know nothing. We batten on rumours. Rumours! And are led like lambs to the slaughter. My blood boils. Are we such cowards we may not be told?

"Fall in! No noise! No talking!"

We line up. Bombs and additional bandoliers of ammunition are doled out. Ten rounds are loaded into the rifle magazines. Things look bad. Contrary to orders, I slip a cartridge "up the spout," adjusting the safety-catch.

Now we are shuffling out over the plain. Someone coughs; entrenching tools, haversacks, empty water-bottles clatter and rattle; here and there an iron-shod heel strikes a flint, igniting a shower of sparks; a man stumbles — and that man surely curses. Rob and I march side by side. We talk little. A Yorkshireman is Rob. His calmness reassures me. His sturdy bulk is a tower of strength to me. *Vive le rum!*

We trudge on in silence. I think of those at home — all warm and clean in bed. Perhaps they turn restlessly now and then and think of me. May they sleep deep and long to-night. *We* have work to do. Keep your eyes skinned, lad. Steady and cool! Don't fumble. Strike — swift as the lightning! I feel braced up and fit. God bless the distillers of rum!

I glance at Rob. His face in the dark is bloodless and dirty; there are streaks of grime on the cheeks where sweat has dried in the night; and a four-day growth of beard gives him a strangely spiritual expression. I think: This might be the face of Christ! A distant look in his eyes has Rob. *I know.* He's away and playing on his old violin.

"How feeling, Rob?" But Rob makes no reply.

Then the silvery voice of Baker, just behind me, breaks the silence, singing:

"How lovely are the Messengers
That preach us the gospel of peace! ..."

"Put a sock in it, Baker!" says a sergeant, irritably.

The roar of the burning dumps grows louder; and flames, leaping into view, send out cascades of sparks; we hear the crack of rifles; bullets whistle shriller, filling the night with little spiteful devils. We stop to unload the mules. I strap on my chest and back two wallets of spare Lewis gun magazines. The weight of them! We are leaving the mules behind. *I* am the mule — a proper soldier now!

And now, suddenly, we enter a world writhing in its last agony.... Deafening crashes, flames and smoke, unearthly boomings and rumblings! Above this din comes the splutter of machine guns; and, from a towering structure to the left, massive fragments of masonry are being pitch-forked into the night! It is grand! The Turk is blowing up the world!

"Shiverin' saints!" comes a voice.

"Strike me pink!" says another; and I catch a glimpse of an illuminated face uplifted for a moment in the glare..

Now we are off at the double. We zig-zag about; then, swinging to the right, plunge over the edge of a deep but narrow *wady*, and fall into dust and darkness. We regain our feet, bewildered, shaken. Officers dart hither and thither, shouting orders. "Steady now, boys! Steady! Lock-up, lock-up! Keep together! ... For God's sake, don't bunch up!"

Then out of the gloom and the confused medley of men emerges the colonel. I see him in the light of the conflagration. Like the rest, he has a steel helmet on his head; but he wears no tunic, his shirt-sleeves are rolled up past his elbows. How clean and neat and fresh he looks! His hair, sleek and parted, shines in the glare. He is lean and tall; his face is red. He carries his head as though his neck was stiff. His gait seems a shade unsteady. He waves a cane in his hand, and, in the crook of his other arm, he hugs a football! Borton is laughing!

"Twenty-second Queen's!" he bellows. "It's your turn now to cover yourselves with glory! Follow me!"

"Stone me paralytic!" gasps Tich.

He leads us along the *wady,* every gun in creation going mad at us. In that dusty inferno we are merely shadows. We come to an opening in the *wady*. Borton gets across, but not so others following; they seem to stagger and wilt and crumple up and fade away into the gloom. A murderous fire from concealed machine guns sprays death along that alley....

"Stand fast!" cries the colonel. "Now quickly in twos and threes!"

Rob and I plunge into the abyss. I hear a cry and Rob sinks into the dust. A momentary halt. I see heaving breasts all around me, and drawn, white faces. I hear curses unmentionable. I curse unmentionably too. But there's one man as cool as a water-melon—a man with a stiff neck, and a football under his arm!

"Fix bayonets!" yells the colonel. And the shining things leap from the scabbards and flash in the light as they click on the standards. They seem alive and joyous; they turn us into fiends, thirsty for slaughter. We scramble out of the *wady*.

"Charge!" And away goes the colonel, flourishing his ludicrous cane!

The hail of lead! We greet it with a blood-curdling shout, ripping our throats; and, surely as I have eyes, there's Borton driving ahead, taking the hill at a bound, and kicking the football!

Breathless we gain the top. The Turks have bolted. Torn tents flap in the wind; pots and pans are about our feet. Away now from the flaming dumps we pick our way at a walk, peering into the dark, bayonets ready to stab. Then I go sprawling over a vessel of porridge standing among the remains of a weed fire. I rip out an oath as an ember burns me. Scrambling up, a sticky mess, I flounder over something that is warm and groans as I clutch it. Again I stagger forward, and a strand of barbed wire catches me in the leg. I tear myself out of its grip. Near me, Scrounger Baker trips over a tent rope, and attempting to rise, is shot. A raking fire sweeps the darkness, but still we advance. The ground is rough and treacherous. Men are falling. Where's the colonel? Has he also stopped one? I hear his voice! God save Borton! *We* know him. The mad major of Gallipoli! He'll fetch us through, this man with a broken neck!

Suddenly the darkness lifts, paling to grey, and a ridge looms out ahead.

"Down! Down! Down!" and flat as a sack I go. Men are moving on the skyline. What use to take aim! I blaze away madly, striving to silence those swine on the ridge. I sweat. I gibber with glee when a form flings up its arms, dances a second between earth and sky, and vanishes. A little ahead of me, on rising ground, lie two pals working a Lewis gun; its bark, its spiteful rat-tat-tat, is music to me.

Spells of the tensest concentration are followed by moments of terrible fatigue. My strength ebbs away; I feel unutterably weak; I could sleep. There succeed intervals when my senses seem to stalk abroad, icily alert and alive; periods when my mind is a whirling wheel, my brain a furnace white-hot, my pulse a sledge-hammer. When my nerves seem about to snap there come instants of exquisite calm. Death! What does it matter? I am alone. Surrounded by friend and foe, I am alone in the world! But the will to live wells up — the desire to live is a torment, a torture, a devilish, damnable agony!

A man nearby groans and rolls over. A yard or so away an officer lies quiet as though sleeping. I see a friend writhe and twist. A sergeant, rising from the ground, staggers forward, shot in the back! I hear sobbing. No stretcher bearers here. Vaguely, as in a dream, I am conscious of flashes and rumblings overhead and regular crashes and slams to our rear. Where's *our* artillery? Where are the guns? Bring up the guns, O God!

The barrel of my rifle blisters my fingers; then the bolt sticks fast, fouled by grit. I tear and swear at it, and my hand goes stiff with cramp. The reeking breech sickens me. Now I become aware that the gun ahead is silent, and motionless the men beside it; one on his back with his eyes open, his hand outstretched as though beckoning; the other, his head on his arm. I look at the thing in a daze. It is getting lighter. A clammy sweat breaks out on me. *I* am a Lewis gunner! Turning my head, I gaze at the ridge. My hand shakes as I grip my rifle and take aim; but the bolt is jammed, the trigger limp. I lie there panting....

"You're a coward — a dirty, crawling coward! That one gun ... that one gun might stop those ... curs!"

A stone, struck by a bullet, jumps from the ground and hits me on the knuckle. It stings me to terrible anger. Next to me, Tom Rolls gives a yell as blood spurts from his wrist and splashes me in the face. I spring to my feet and race to the gun, heaving aside a corpse to get to it. I lie down to the gun between the two dead men, and ... I feel fine! But the magazine will not rotate. I strain and strain at it. The cocking-handle is stuck fast. I squeeze the trigger. I change the magazine. I talk to it, swear at it, do impossible things to it. Then, glancing down the barrel casing to the sights, I see that the muzzle is frayed and torn and broken, and the gas-regulator blown clean away. The gun is as dead as the men beside it.

At this moment the colonel appears. His face is black and sweaty; his shirt is torn to ribbons.

"Don't just lie here!" he roars. "Come on! ... With me!" We scramble to our feet and follow him down a long, rocky slope in the half-light, but heavy fire breaks out anew. We cannot stand it, and are forced into the dust again. Ripping out the bolt of my rifle, I lick it clean, spitting out the grit. It is hot and scorches my tongue.

Now a worse enemy attacks. Shells scream about us, exploding overhead, on the ground, everywhere; they tear up the dust; they cover us with stones; the air is a hell of whizzing shrapnel. I see Harman with his back ripped open. We bite into the earth. Our mouths are full of muck. Not so Borton. He's on his feet (has he yet been off his feet?); he crouches, his neck thrust outwards. His grey-blue eyes are searching, searching....

"Ah, good!" he cries, and tossing away his cane, pulls out his revolver. "Now I have them! Follow me!" I go staggering after him down the slope. Had every man been shot he would have gone alone. Dimly ahead I see a hedge of stunted cactus swathed in smoke from which come flashes — white knife-like flashes. Then I see figures moving, and pausing, fire from my hip.

"Don't stand there like a palsied idiot!" shouts the colonel. "Come on!"

I go on. Something warm is coursing down my face and trickles into my eyes, half-blinding me. I stumble on — my head is bursting....

"*Camarade! Camarade!*" Men in grey-coloured uniforms and "pork-pie" caps are coming forward, their arms above their heads.

"Austrians!" the colonel's voice is hoarse and husky. He rams his revolver into a man's ear. Beyond — across the open — men run for their lives; and I, breathless, land up against the smoking nozzle of an artillery field gun, the point of my bayonet stuck into the tunic button of a burly Austrian bombardier; while the colonel, with a man or two, strives desperately — but without success — to get another gunner to turn his gun and fire on his fleeing comrades!

Daybreak! I stand panting before my prisoner, a breath from whose smoke-blackened mouth could bowl me over. He towers above me, smiling. I am trembling.

"Mercy, Johnny," says he quietly, dropping a sooty hand and holding it out to me. "You brave feller. You haf face all bloody! Have mercy!"

He smiles. He looks a decent sort. His glasses and ginger hair remind me of Baker. Scrounger Baker! Rob! It is touch and go with the Austrian. Blood for blood! He smiles. *Camarade!* I cannot kill him.... Next to me on my right, little Sid Avery has a similar problem confronting him, and quickly he solves it, as well as mine:

"Cigarettes ... or yer life!" puffs Sid.

When the 321 V.C.'s sat down to dine with the Prince of Wales on November 9th, 1929, one man present, Lieut.-Colonel Arthur Drummond Borton, V.C., D.S.O., might possibly have experienced just one tinge of regret. For had the great function taken place two days earlier it would have coincided with the twelfth anniversary of his winning the coveted honor.

I know just a little about the winning of that V.C., and the man who won it, but I doubt whether the colonel would recall the fellow he swore at during that most critical moment of his career.[76]

The 5th Suffolks' historians, Captains Fair and Wolton, in their work supply a vivid picture of the after-the-battle scenes:

On the 8th [November 1917] we moved by night to Sheikh Hassan and were joined by Capt. Althaus, Lieut. Ryley, and 40 men. The following days were spent in salvaging. Every one then had a chance to examine the Turkish trenches, get some souvenirs, and visit Gaza. The town which looked so beautiful from a distance, was composed solely of skeletons of houses, and every few feet were shell holes. The Grand Mosque had been battered by our artillery, and the S.A.A. [small arms ammunition] dump, which we knew to be there, had blown up. Enemy gun positions were well concealed — always in deep pits, and sometimes behind cactus hedges nearly twenty yards thick. Ali El Muntar, the highest point around Gaza, which dominated the landscape, was a mass of shell holes, and apparently there was not even an observation post there. The shelling must have prevented nearly all direct observation of our movements. The next crest was, however, a strongpoint, and well fortified and wired in. Tank Redoubt, opposite Sheikh Abbas, was an exceptionally strong place, with well-designed trenches, deep dug-outs, and three rows of barbed wire, but apparently it was flooded during the October rains. It must have been very uncomfortable then, as there appeared to be no drainage system out of the redoubt, although there was a good slope into it. The remains of hundreds killed on the 19th of April were lying round or in front of it. The Turks had made no attempt to bury them. Most of them lay in long lines where the cross fire had mown them down,[77] but some had reached the wire, and a few near the parapet. A burial party was busy in this

The Great Mosque, Gaza, November 1917. It was used as an ammunition dump by the Turks (Fair and Wolton, *The History of the 1/5th Battalion: "The Suffolk Regiment"*).

area for some time after, and many officers from the brigade spent the next few days helping to identify in any way possible those friends and comrades who had made the supreme sacrifice on 19th April. Identity discs in many cases were gone, but articles of clothing and oddments in pockets helped in many a case to establish identification. All were laid to rest in a common grave after an impressive service. We felt then that their lives had been sacrificed in a gallant attempt to capture a position that was impregnable by day. Truly it was said: "The best of our grand old Territorial Brigade lie here."[78]

Blackwell and Axe, the Essex gunners' historians, give a very similar account:

Large infantry burial parties were hard at work during the next few days, burying the dead and generally cleaning up the battlefield. The town, from which all the civilian population had been evacuated long since, was found to be in a deplorable condition. The greater part of the woodwork of the houses had been removed for use in the trenches or for firewood. Immense damage was effected by explosions of Turkish ammunition dumps collected in the mosques and public buildings, and detonated by British gunfire.[79]

A Royal Army Medical Corps officer attached to the Worcestershire Yeomanry, Captain Oskar Teichman, wrote in his diary of his visit to the battlefield, probably late January 1918:

On one occasion some of us made an expedition to Gaza with the C.O., riding out to the British trenches, where we were met by a gunner officer who had been in charge of a heavy battery during the siege, and who was to show us round the various positions. As our role during the first and second Battles of Gaza had been on the right flank, and as we had been engaged at Huj when the third Battle of Gaza was being fought, we had never seen the town at close quarters, and were curious to see the various positions, about which we had heard so much. First we visited one of the tanks which the Turks had captured during the second battle and the various hills where the Fifty-third and Fifty-fourth Divisions had fought so gallantly. Then we rode on to Ali Muntar, the most commanding of the enemy's positions, the top of which had been literally removed by our gun fire. On this hill we noticed that several of the ancient tombs had been partly opened by the explosions of our shells, and one was very tempted to get to work with a pickaxe and make some wonderful discoveries; however, the presence of certain unexploded shells, some partly and some completely buried in the ground, finally altered our intentions. We lunched under the hill amongst masses of spring flowers, while our horses grazed on the rich grass, thinking over the many battles which had taken place over these positions during the last three thousand years. The town of Gaza was next visited, which a year ago had been the second largest city in Palestine and was now deserted and mostly in ruins. In the upper town, however, the remains of some very fine buildings were still to be seen. We noticed that where houses still remained not a single door existed, as the timber from the latter had been utilized by the Turks in order to revet their trenches. The large mosque was found in ruins, and still showed signs of the enormous ammunition dump which it had contained.

During this period of rest at Belah, leave was freely given to Cairo, and was much enjoyed.[80]

A Turkish lady, school administrator Madame Halidé Edib, stated:

> By November the reverses at the front had begun. I was so absorbed with my work that I hardly realized that Syria could be taken at any moment by the enemy and that the whole place could be turned into a battlefield. I had an anxious letter from Saime Hanum, the head of the Damascus school, asking me to come and make a decision, as there was considerable fear among the people of Damascus.
>
> I started as soon as I could, and it was only in Reyak that I heard very serious news. Djemal Pasha's family had left the day before, and he himself was leaving quite soon; a German commander, Falkenheim [sic], was coming. The military activity on the line had stopped ordinary transport, but I travelled in a carriage full of cartridge-boxes.
>
> After a serious talk with the teachers that evening, I went to see Djemel Pasha at his headquarters. He was extremely sad, and not in the best of humour with his colleagues in Constantinople. He thought that his removal would upset the entire organization and order, in which he was not mistaken.[81]

Despite the arrival of General von Falkenhayn to revitalize the Turkish command, Allenby drove the Turks back upon Jerusalem, winning a significant victory at Junction Station on the 13th and 14th of November. He moved on Jerusalem on 8 December; the Turks withdrew the following day, and the city capitulated on the 9th; this was shortly followed by the triumphal entry of General Allenby. After a Turkish counter-attack was beaten off on 26 December, the victorious Allied forces were assured possession of the city, and Sir Edmund's successful strategy had laid the foundation for total victory in the succeeding year.

> *Secret*
>
> XXI CORPS ORDER NO. 14
>
> *18th November 1917*
> *Reference Map: 1 in. to 1 mile*
>
> 4. The 54th Division will act as a pivot to the operations of the rest of the XXI Corps and will hold and consolidate the places named below.
>
> It will move as follows: — Headquarters and two Brigade Groups, also Heavy Battery, area Ramle-Lydda; Headquarters at Lydda. A garrison of not less than one battalion is to be detached to Beit Dejan (L.24). One Brigade Group to Abu Shushe (D.27) sending one company to Junction Station as escort to prisoners.

Captain Teichman wrote:

> November 19th. We were now under Twenty-first Corps orders, and were told that during the coming operations no unit was to go within 5 miles of Jerusalem. Close to our bivouac was the Patriarch of Jerusalem's summer residence, which included a large orange garden, which was much appreciated. In the evening we left this pleasant spot in inky darkness and torrential rain, and proceeded by a goat-track to the village of Kezaze. A little further on we stumbled in the dark into Junction Station, which had recently been captured, and seemed to consist, in the dark, mainly of shell-holes and destroyed railway lines. The rain came down in torrents, and we spent a very wet night sleeping in the mud.[82]

Royal Engineer Corporal Fred Mills' diary reads: "Friday, November 29th, 1918. Kantara. I met Will Long of the 10th Middlesex (Lily Ryan's husband) in the Y.M.C.A. He is now in the Essex Regiment and has just come out of hospital.

Three. A Change at the Top, Then Success at Beersheba and Gaza 147

MAP J
Turkish Attack on
4/Northamptonshire Regiment
27th November, 1917

The following day. Our own concert party gave a turn in the R.E. theatre. The first in public, they were very good. General Lloyd [commander Canal Zone, Palestine Lines of Communication] was present with staff. Will Long came with me. They are called the 'The Decauvilles' after the light railway used by the R.E.s."

CHAPTER FOUR

Lloyd George's Christmas Present

While disasters were sustained by the Allies upon the Russian, French, and the Italian fronts, a wide-sweeping movement against the Turks in the East brought the famous cities of Baghdad and Jerusalem under British control. By these military exploits the Arab world was loosened from its Turkish moorings and the prestige of Great Britain in the East was restored.[1]

"The British army which had previously advanced from Egypt and defeated the Turks in the Sinai peninsula, penetrated victoriously into Palestine under the command of General Edmund Allenby and in cooperation with the Arab forces of Feisal and Captain Lawrence. Turkish resistance, organized and conducted by the German General von Falkenhayn, was stubborn but ineffectual. Jaffa fell to the British in November, and Jerusalem in December."[2]

Winston S. Churchill wrote: "A vigorous pursuit opened the port of Jaffa to the further supply of the British forces. Thus possessed of the coastal region, a new base, and an alternative short line of communication, Allenby advanced north-westward upon Jerusalem, continuing to drive the Seventh and Eighth Turkish Armies before him and compromising the eventual retreat of the Fourth. On December 8, 1917, the Turks abandoned Jerusalem after 400 years of blighting occupation, and the British commander-in-chief entered the city amid the acclamations of the inhabitants."[3]

However, something of the extreme bizarre transpired before this official entry by Allenby and his entourage. Two British Army sergeants, Hurcomb and Sedgewick, belonging to the 2/19th Battalion, the London Regiment, did not feel up to accepting the initial capitulation of the Holy City on December 9. Prior to this the same group of dignitaries had offered this to two army cooks of another battalion (2/20th) of the London Regiment looking for water.

Major Gilbert, of the 2/20th Battalion, the London Regiment, 180th Brigade, 60th (London) Division, however, recounted a much different version—claiming unique firsthand knowledge of that event. In this particular rendering a certain officers' cook, one Private Murch, very early on the morning of December 9, was detailed by the second-in-command to go in search of eggs and pur-

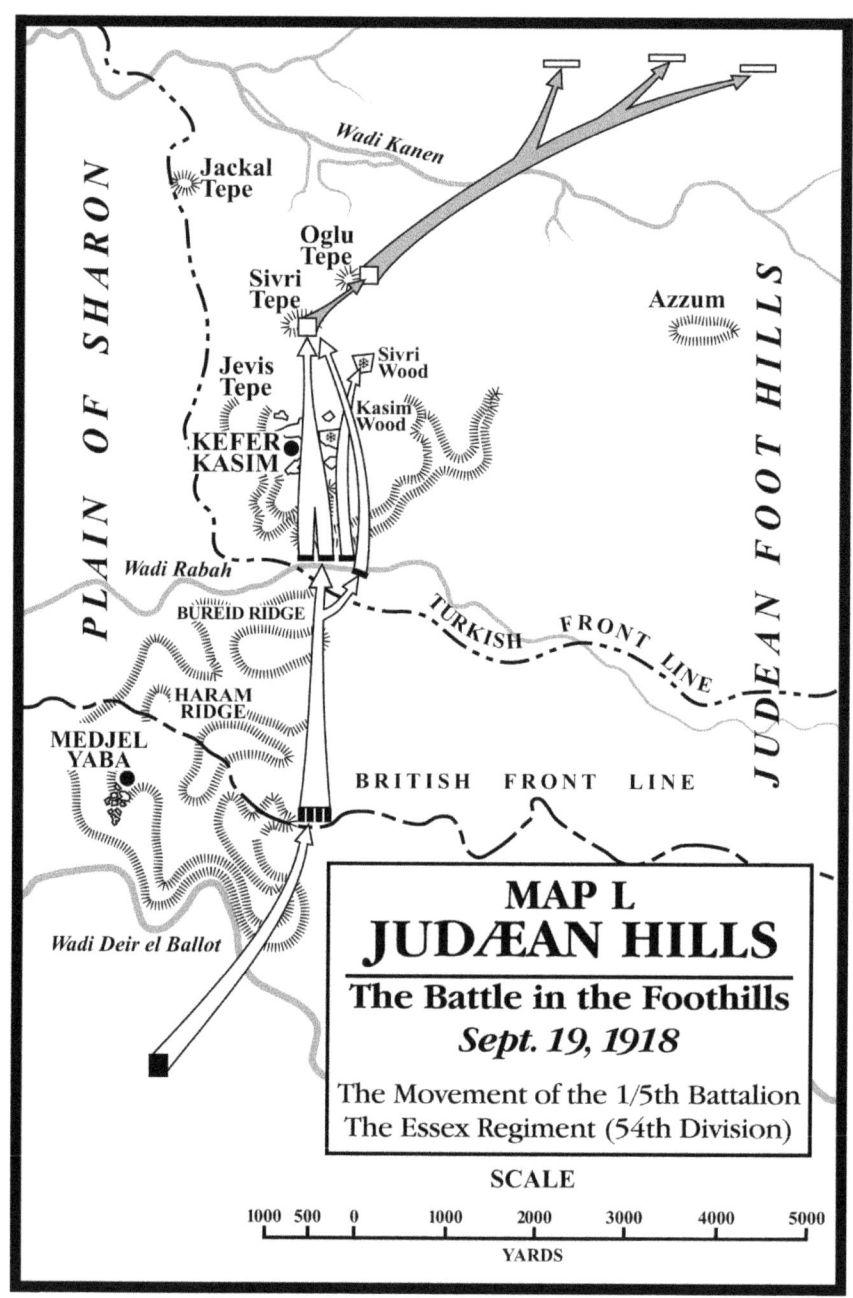

MAP L
JUDÆAN HILLS
The Battle in the Foothills
Sept. 19, 1918

The Movement of the 1/5th Battalion
The Essex Regiment (54th Division)

chase a quantity for breakfast. While on this errand he inadvertently stumbled into the party of dignitaries bent on handing over the city to "General Allah Nebi." Major Gilbert reported that he was at battalion HQ. when Private Murch, the egg-errand boy arrived, hot and out of breath, to be severely berated by the colonel.

> The perspiring private proceeded to relate his amazing adventures. Though he rambled a bit and was at times incoherent, the listeners finally determined "that one of the greatest events in the history of the world, for which thousands had given their lives and for which millions of pounds of English money had been poured out, had just taken place.

Sergeants Hurcomb and Sedgwick are offered Jerusalem (Massey, *Allenby's Final Triumph*).

When the man came to the end of his story, the colonel turned to us and said quietly, "Gentlemen, Jerusalem has fallen!"[4]

The colonel called Brigadier General Watson, who was the nearest general to Jerusalem, to relate the startling news. General Watson thus had the honor of accepting the surrender on the steps at the base of the Tower of David. However, Major General Shea, commander of the 60th Division, decided the honor rightfully should have been his. The keys to the Holy City, which had been given to General Watson by the mayor, were returned so that the whole ceremony could be repeated, Gilbert reported gleefully.

Rifleman Ernest May, of the London Irish Rifles—2/18th Battalion, the London Regiment—appears cynical about the story of the cook(s) and the sergeants.[5] The photographs of Sergeants Hurcomb and Sedgwick, together with a large group of dignitaries and a large white flag, would seem to offer incontrovertible evidence that the event really took place.

A 5th Suffolk soldier (Mortlock family photograph).

Colonel Badcock, in his "Personal Reminiscences," nicely summarizes this aspect: "And whilst on the question of water it may not be out of place to record another [the laying of the railway was one of many] great achievement by the Royal Engineers," the piping of water from Egypt to supply the foremost echelons of the E.E.F., and thus to eventually connect this vital supply with the Holy City herself.

Col. Badcock now addresses the more local aspect of the Royal Engineers' accomplishment: "I refer to the water supply of Jerusalem. It was primarily based on the system that history records had been initiated by Pontius Pilate! Between April and June 1918 some twelve miles of pipes were laid from south of Jerusalem, starting from the neighbourhood of Solomon's Pools between Bethlehem and Hebron, and the Holy City received a daily supply of nearly 300,000 gallons—a piece of work as great as it is romantic."[6]

Four. Lloyd George's Christmas Present

There is a very interesting prophecy with regard to the capture of Jerusalem. It is an old Arab saying and is over two hundred years old: "When the Nile flows into Palestine, then shall the prophet from the west drive the Turk from Jerusalem." When this prophecy was made it must have seemed an utter impossibility that the waters of the River Nile should ever flow over two hundred miles of arid desert into Palestine. But the pipe line across the peninsula of Sinai brought the Nile water from Kantara; and just before the capture of Jerusalem, this water from Egypt was being pumped into Palestine, north of Gaza, at the rate of thousands of gallons a day. *Fanatis* were filled with it, placed on the backs of camels and taken up to the troops in the line fighting for Jerusalem. Then again, "the prophet" in Arabic is *Al Nebi*, and General Allenby was known as *Al Nebi* by practically the entire native population. So this ancient prophecy was fulfilled to the letter; the waters of the Nile flowed into Palestine, and the prophet, *Al Nebi*, came from the west and drove the Turk from Jerusalem.

Chapter 12 of the Book of Daniel says: "Blessed is he that waiteth, and cometh to the thousand three hundred and five and thirty days."[7] The year 1335 of the Hegira is the year 1917 of the Christian era, the year in which Jerusalem was freed.

Major Gilbert succinctly summed up one aspect: "Nothing I think gave a clearer indication of England's intentions in Palestine than the order of the commander-in-chief that no British flag should fly over the conquered city, and no flag was flown save the Red Cross flag, emblem of succour to the distressed, and this proud pennant flew from the American Hospital in Jerusalem."[8]

Major Vivian Gilbert goes on to relate, rather amusingly, that the first things soldiers bought after the fall of Jerusalem were Bibles and matches. Cigarettes had been issued from the base but matches were not included. The Bibles were used as guidebooks to Palestine, which the soldiers were interested in learning more about. Many soldiers, in fact, were reported to be arguing about Biblical incidents when they were supposed to be sleeping.[9]

By December 10, Jerusalem was in the hands of the British. It capitulated to Allenby's force of British, French and Italian troops, after it had been entirely surrounded.[10] It was to the glory of British arms that the most venerated place of the Christian world came unharmed through the ordeal of battle.[11]

But it almost didn't.

Captain Marek Schwarz, an Austrian artillery officer, related that preparations had been made for a destructive policy towards Jerusalem. Orders were given to "blow Jerusalem to hell" in the event of the British entering the city. Schwarz' own battery was ranged on the Sheikh Omar mosque, but after the Turkish general fled, Schwarz spiked his guns and walked over to the enemy.[12]

An itinerant American missionary, Virginian Dr. W.H.T. Squires, who visited Jerusalem in 1921, recorded the account given him by Mrs. Fred Vester of life in that city prior to and at the time of its liberation. She worked as a Red Cross nurse; her narrative is vivid in its descriptive reality:

> As the war in this theater narrowed the suffering of all Europeans became more intense, until the climax came like a bolt. All European men were to be deported on a certain December day. The usual week's notice was given for preparation. As with the maids in Cana it was a week of desperation, agony, suspense and unspeakable anxiety and suffering. Deportation was usually merely a euphemism for assassination. The colony took itself to earnest and insistent prayer. The men prepared to depart, but they importuned the Throne of Grace as they had never prayed before. The European women had spent the war as Red Cross nurses, and the very hotel in which our party was quartered, just opposite the Jaffa Gate, was a hospital. The fateful morning came. The roar of the British guns to the west lulled somewhat. At any moment the men might be ordered to report for deportation. Mrs. Vester labored that eventful morning in the hospital, praying, hoping, weeping, despairing by turns. Let any wife and mother measure the bitterness of her grief. It was just by the stroke of ten by the Kaiser's clock over the way. She was binding the broken leg of a young Turk, when another nurse came quietly to the door and whispered in English:
> "The British are at the Jaffa Gate."
> She dropped the wounded soldier's leg and rushed into the street. There in the Kaiser's gap, astride a magnificent Arabian steed, like a statue a bronzed officer wearing the stripes of a colonel gazed down upon the motley crowd who curiously gazed up at him. In the hysteria of joy Mrs. Vester rushed to the officer's side, grasped his stirrup in her arms and kissed the soiled straps of harness weeping the while as if her heart would break.
> "What did he do?" I asked.
> "He did not move a muscle, but his expression seemed to say, 'Woman, are you demented?'"
> "Was it not silly of me," she added, but the tears stood in her eyes, and I confess that I felt a tightness in my throat.[13]

Sapper Bonser recalled of this time: "Three telegrams I handled stick in my memory. One from General Allenby to the 60th Divisional General [Shea] when Jerusalem was taken. It read: 'Congratulations. Psalm 122, v. 2.' I looked it up. 'Our feet shall stand within thy gates, O Jerusalem.' I thought it very decent of Allenby."[14]

General Sir Edmund Allenby made a triumphal entry into the Holy City on December 11. "Close by the Jaffa Gate, the iron doors of which were rarely opened, was seen the wide breach made in the walls in 1898 for the Kaiser's entry when he visited Jerusalem. Allenby passed that breach by and entered by the ancient gate."[15]

Preceded by aides-de-camp, Allenby had on his right the commander of the French, on his left the commander of the Italian detachment. At the base of the Tower of David, which was standing when Christ entered the city, the proclamation of military law was read. Every person was declared free to pursue his lawful business without interruption, and every sacred building, pious foundation, or customary place of prayer, whether Christian, Hebrew, or Moslem, was assured protection.

Another eyewitness of the memorable event, the special correspondent of the London *Times* with the British forces, described as follows:

> It was a picturesque throng. From the outskirts of Jerusalem the Jaffa road was crowded with people who flocked westward to greet the conquering general. Sombre-clad youths of all nationalities, including Armenians and Greeks, stood side by side with Moslems dressed in the brighter raiment of the East. The predominance of the tarboosh in the streets added to the brightness of the scene. Many of the Moslems joined aloud in the expression of welcome, their faces lighted up with pleasure at the general's approach. Flat-topped roofs and balconies held many, crying out a genuine welcome; but it was in the streets, where the cosmopolitan crowd assembled, that one looked for and obtained the real feeling of all the peoples. What astonished me were the cries of "Bravo" and "Hurrah" uttered by men who could have hardly spoken the words before....
>
> General Allenby entered the city on foot. Outside the Jaffa Gate he was received by the military governor and a guard of honour formed by men who have done their full share in the campaign. On the right of the gate were men from English, Scottish, Irish, and Welsh counties. Opposite them were fifty men afoot, representing the Australian and New Zealand horsemen who have been engaged in the Empire's work in the Sinai Desert and Palestine almost since the war broke out. Inside the walls were twenty French and twenty Italian troops from the detachments sent by their countries to take part in the Palestine operations.
>
> General Allenby entered by the ancient gate which is known to the Arabs as "The Friend." Inside the wall was a crowd more densely packed than was the crowd outside.
>
> The commander in chief, preceded by his aides-de-camp, had on his right the commander of the French detachment, and on his left the commander of the Italian detachment. The Italian, French, and American military attachés followed, together with a few members of the general staff. The guards of honour marched in the rear. The procession turned to the right into Mount Zion and halted at Al Kala (the Citadel). On the steps, at the base of the Tower of David, which was standing when Christ was in Jerusalem, the Proclamation of Military Law was read, in the presence of the commander in chief and of many notables of the city.
>
> Reforming, the procession moved up Zion Street to the barrack square, where General Allenby received the notables and the heads of the religious communities. The mayor and the mufti — the latter also a member of the Husseiny family — were presented, likewise the sheikhs in charge of the mosques of Omar and Aksa, and Moslems belonging to the Khaldieh and Alemieh families, which trace their descents through many centuries. The patriarchs of the Latin, Greek Orthodox, and Armenian churches, and the Coptic bishop, had been directed by the Turks to leave Jerusalem, but their representatives were introduced to General Allenby, as were also the heads of the Jewish committees, the Syrian Church, the Greek Catholic Church, the Abyssinian bishop, and a representative of the Anglican Church. The last presentation was that of the Spanish consul, who is in charge of the interests of almost all the countries at war, and is a very busy man.[16]

The ceremony over, the procession returned to the Jaffa Gate, and Allenby left Jerusalem.[17]

Major Gilbert, who rode in advance of his company, related: "Soon we reached the outskirts of the city and began passing the more modern Jewish buildings that lie outside the Jaffa Gate, and then at last we found ourselves inside the walls themselves—the first British troops to march through the Holy City! ... I looked back along the line of my company, and now every man's head was *up*, their eyes were shining, their arms swung by their sides. They were marching as men march on parade for an inspection by the king!"[18]

Lawrence of Arabia recalled that Sir Edmund Allenby "was good enough, although I had done nothing for the success, to let [Brigadier-General Gilbert] Clayton take me along as his staff officer for the day. The personal staff tricked me out in their spare clothes till I looked like a major in the British Army. Dalmeny lent me red tabs, Evans his brass hat; so that I had the gauds of my appointment in the ceremony of the Jaffa Gate, which for me was the supreme moment of the war."[19]

Murphy wrote in his history of the Suffolk regiment:

> While the elaborate parades, processions, speeches and celebrations marking the capture of Jerusalem took place the 54th (East Anglian) Division—less one brigade—was in the neighbourhood of Ludd, holding a portion of the line covering Jaffa. The 5th Battalion of the Suffolk Regiment, under Lt. Colonel Wollaston, D.S.O., was in reserve to the 163rd Brigade (Brig. General T. Ward), with two companies in the trenches at Yehudieh and the remainder, under Major Copinger-Hill, two miles away in the direction of Beit Nebala.
>
> On the 11th the Turks attacked Zeifizfiyeh Hill and Norfolk Post. The two companies under Major Copinger-Hill, moved up as local reserve, but the attack being easily repulsed were not called upon to act. That night the battalion, less these two companies, marched across to an olive grove behind Beit Nabala. On the following day six shells from a mountain gun fell right into the middle of the bivouac area, slightly wounding one man. On December 15th the whole line advanced, the battalion, under Major Copinger-Hill, participating with the 163rd Brigade in the capture of Bornat Hill, the highest point in the neighbourhood, and about 3,000 yards distant. "A" and "C" Companies, under Captains G. G. Warnes and A. A. Maris, were in the assaulting line, with "B" Company (Captain F. R. Althaus) in support, and "D" Company (Captain H. C. Wolton) in reserve. The battalion, emerging from the wood, soon came under machine-gun fire, but managed to reach the dead ground at the foot of the slope without much difficulty or loss. The assaulting companies, making use of the cover afforded by the rocks, quickly climbed the steep slopes of the hill, but in the meantime the Turks fled, the only prisoner taken being found fast asleep in a cave.[20]

The Battle of Jaffa and the Defense of Jerusalem; The Passage of the Nahr El Auja

Allenby's Army of British, Dominion, Imperial, and allied composition had now won both Palestine's capital and its second town. But Jerusalem and Jaffa were still within easy range of Turkish artillery, and the proximity of the enemy's forces exposed them to some slight risk of recapture by surprise attacks. It was therefore imperative to push back the enemy forces on either flank of the Allies' frontage as soon as possible. Formal orders to this effect were issued by

Four. Lloyd George's Christmas Present

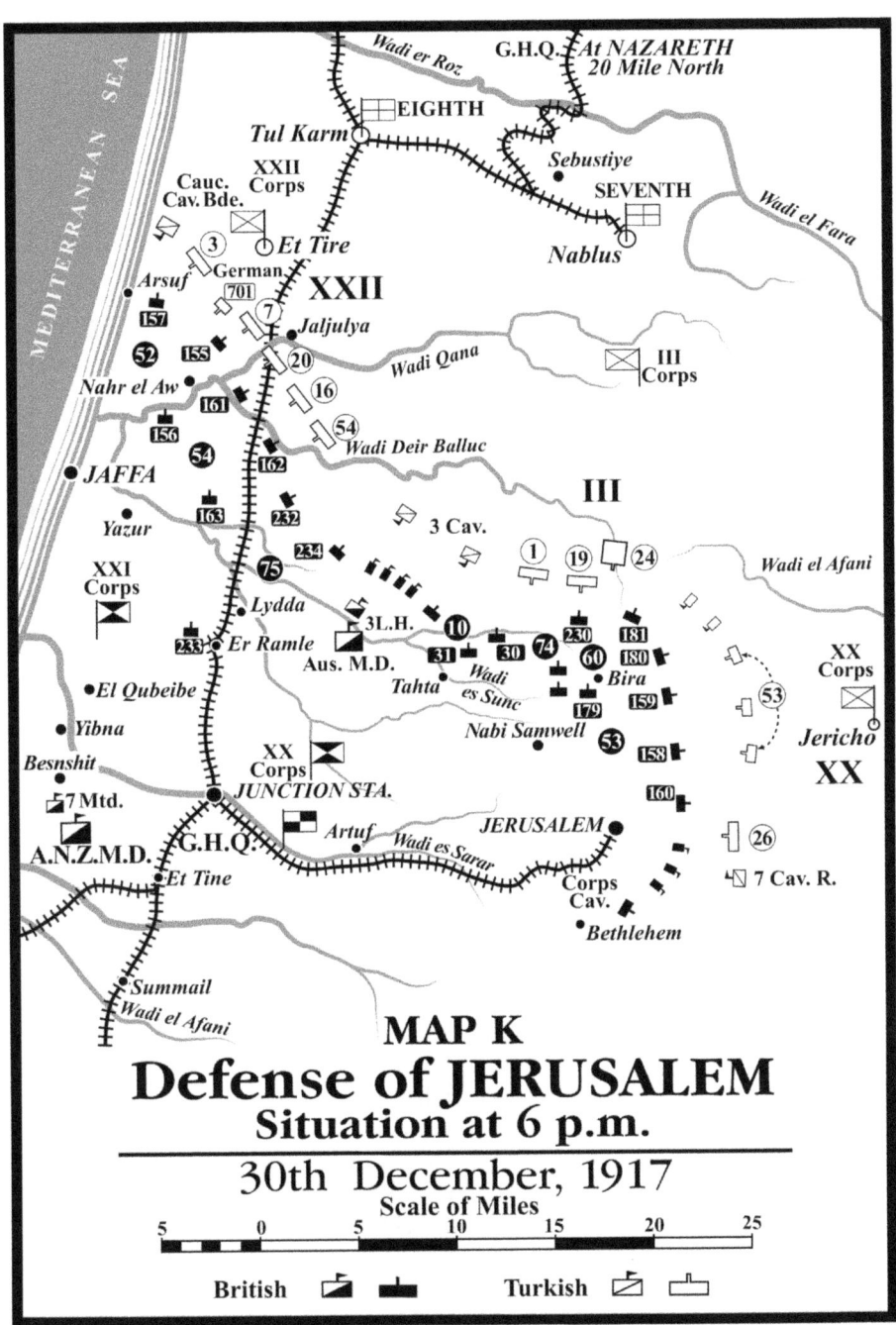

MAP K
Defense of JERUSALEM
Situation at 6 p.m.
30th December, 1917

MAP M
THE BATTLE OF JAFFA

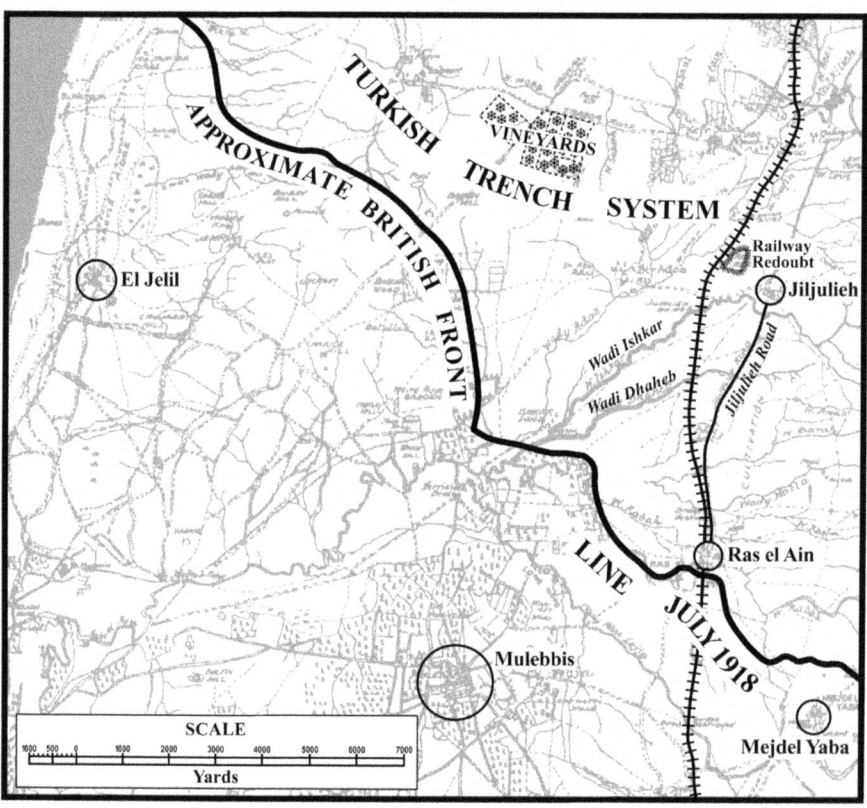

General Headquarters on 18 December, but plans for the two operations had already been drawn up and accepted by Sir Edmund Allenby; the XXI Corps had actually begun a minor preliminary operation a week earlier.

There had been no action of importance in the plain and foothills since the events described earlier but for a determined attack on the morning of 1 December upon the 2/4th Hampshire of the 233rd Brigade, which had then just entered the line east of Lydda under the orders of the 54th Division. A strong party of Turks crawled up the slope at Sheikh Gharbawi, west of the village of Midie, and under cover of overhead machine-gun fire assaulted the two companies holding this position. The post was reinforced by a company of the 3/3rd Gurkhas, and after heavy fighting the Turks were driven back.

On 7 December General Bulfin took over command from General Chauvel, the Australian and New Zealand Mounted Division remaining in the forward area until the 52nd and 75th Divisions were established in the line. By the 11th the front of the XXI Corps was held by the 75th Division on the right, east of the railway; the 54th Division was in the center, astride it, and the 52nd Division was on the coast. The 75th Division's line, from south of Midie to southeast of Beit Nebala, was held by the 232nd Brigade, with the 58th Rifles attached, covered by the South African Field Artillery Brigade and one battery of the 37th Brigade. Soon after dawn, as the first step in the preliminary operation, the 2/5th Hampshire occupied Midie, encountering no opposition. The 2/3rd Gurkhas then pushed forward patrols towards Budrus, two miles north-northwest of Midie, and after a Turkish counter-attack had been beaten off by artillery fire, captured the village about noon.

While the attack of the 232nd Brigade was in progress, the enemy bombarded Kh. Zeifizfiyye, a few hundred yards northwest of Beit Nebala, on the right flank of the 54th Division, with four batteries. This hill was held by a company of the 4/Norfolk. At 9 A.M. an attack at least a battalion strong was launched against it, and about thirty of the enemy succeeded in entering the trench on the summit. An immediate counter-attack by the 4/Norfolk restored the position, and the enemy was caught in flank during his withdrawal by machine guns at Nebala and Deir Tureif. Over fifty Turkish dead were afterwards found on the field, while casualties of the 163rd Brigade were 55.

The object of the 232nd Brigade's advance had been to secure gun positions within effective range of Kh. Ibanne, northeast of Beit Nebala, a ridge which dominated all the plain about Lydda, and to enable the 75th Division to cooperate with the 54th in an operation to capture the line Kh. Ibanne–Et Tire. The XXI Corps was now well provided with heavy artillery, two heavy artillery groups with 22 more heavy guns and howitzers and a sound-ranging section having arrived from Gaza by 13 December.

The advance was carried out on the 15th, when the 75th Division attacked the Turkish positions from the village of Qibye[21] (also rendered "Kibbia") a mile northeast of Budrus, to Kh. Ibanne, and the 54th from thence to Et Tire. The C Heavy Artillery Group of two 60-pounder and one 6-inch howitzer batteries cooperated, first by counter-battery work, and then by the bombardment of any positions with which it was called on by the infantry to deal. As a preliminary the 2/3rd Gurkhas of the 232nd Brigade, supported by the South African Field Artillery Brigade, attacked the Qibye ridge, south of the village, at 6 A.M., and took it without great difficulty, afterwards capturing the village itself.

The main attack on Kh. Ibanne, launched at 8 A.M., was carried out by the 2/5th Hampshire on the right and the 58th Rifles on the left. So swiftly did these battalions advance over the broken ground and up the steep hillside that the Turks withdrew their machine guns early to avoid losing them, and the casualties only amounted to 18. Fifteen prisoners and a machine gun were captured.

The 163rd Brigade of the 54th Division likewise reached its objective, but suffered much more severely. The Turks kept up heavy machine-gun fire, and mainly from this cause over one hundred and fifty casualties were suffered by the brigade. Now the way was cleared for an attempt to advance the line nearer the shore by crossing the Nahr el Auja.

The river Auja was a formidable obstacle, forty to fifty feet in width [at this point] and ten feet deep, with banks generally soft and muddy in this wet season. The northern bank commanded the lower and much flatter ground to the south. The village of Sheikh Muwannis, which had been occupied by the British in November and lost to a counter-attack on the 25th, was in a particularly dominating position, with a view all the way to Jaffa; while Kh. Hadra looked down on to the river almost to the sea. Since the November fighting the enemy had entrenched the high ground on the right bank, and also established works on the left covering the villages of Fajja and Mulebbis, at Hadra Bridge, and at Jerishe. The bar at the mouth was now the only place where the river could be crossed without military bridges or boats, as the bridge at Hadra and the mill dam at Jerishe, which had played a part in the November operations, had been destroyed.

General Bulfin's plan entailed carrying out a twenty-four hours' bombardment of the Turkish trenches and batteries and then attempt the crossing of the 'Auja by night. Time was of the essence, as the river was daily swelling with the rains and the south bank becoming more and more marshy. Twelve pontoons, with twelve Weldon trestles, were demanded by General Bulfin to achieve the planned strategy.[22]

A few days before General Bulfin launched his assault, Corporal Fred Mills wrote in his diary:

> Sunday, November 25th [1917]: Got a day pass for Ismailia. Started from camp 9 A.M. and caught the 9.20 train from Kantara. Return fare 6 Pt. [piastres]. Arrived at Ismailia after a fifty-minute journey across the sand. By the Suez Canal there is a fine station and a road runs directly in front of it for a long way with tall palm trees on each side. At the end is the Salt Water Lake with a small jetty going out into it. Motor boats and yachts and quite a little harbour. Along the bank of the lake is a lovely park called the Wilderness. Trees, cactus, flowers of all sorts and *grass!* The first grass I have seen here. The flowers were lovely, funny to see them in November. A lot of people in the park, mostly European and Jews, some playing tennis. There is quite a nice quarter for them with fine roads and houses. The shops were open and nearly all understood English. Bought Christmas presents at an Indian shop. The native quarter was a collection of mud huts in a filthy condition. Fowls, ducks, turkeys, pigs all in the hut with the people. Tons of sugar canes about, sold in the street from barrows. They break them across their knees and chew them from the middle. The shops were awfully dirty. We had our food at an Australian canteen, a lovely place out in the open under the palms. The cakes were just like Benoits [a Belgian cake shop in Mills' hometown] in peacetime. Cream cakes and fancy cakes with icing all over. I thought how different it was at home, plenty of sugar here. Caught the 9.25 P.M. for Kantara arriving in camp 10.20 P.M. after a most enjoyable day.[23]

CHAPTER FIVE

Advance, Delay, Advance: The Judean Hills and the Jordan

According to Blackwell and Axe, "On December 14 orders were received at our Brigade Headquarters from the 54th Divisional Artillery to make a reconnaissance for artillery support of the 161st Infantry Brigade [exclusively battalions of the Essex Regiment—1/4th, 1/5th, 1/6th, and 1/7th] in a contemplated attack on Mulebbis (Petah Tikwah). This clean and well-ordered little Jewish village was four miles directly north of our present position, and, as it turned out, was to provide our quarters for the greater part of the period prior to the final push from the Jaffa-Jerusalem line."[1]

Gurney adds, "At about this time our companion battery (A/271) was heavily engaged in operations undertaken jointly by the 75th and 54th Divisions for the capture of Klibannfa Kh. Bornat and 'A' Battery was in action all day, firing some 1500 rounds." At the commencement of the fight, Major H. R. Wilson was with the battalion commander, observing from Tureif, Lieut. V. S. Laurie observing from the forward observation post under a railway culvert near Wilhelma[2] Station and providing flank observation of much value. "Pursuing the Turks northwards up the coastal plain, the 4th [Northamptonshire Regiment] reached the outskirts of Jaffa. Here the 54th Division took post to cover the left flank of the force advancing on Jerusalem, and, while doing this, the 4th Battalion distinguished itself greatly at Wilhelma, where, on 27th November, though only four hundred strong, it decisively repulsed an attack by three thousand Turks. A few days later saw the fall of Jerusalem."[3] Captain Teichman recorded:

> December 2nd. Soon after dawn we were on the move, and descended the road to Ramleh; the latter appeared to have some fine buildings, particularly the well-known clock-tower, and was known in Biblical times as Arimathea. Leaving this town on our left, we marched across country, through cultivated fields, to the neighbourhood of Ludd, and bivouacked in the adjoining village of Surafend; however, on account of watering difficulties, as the horses of three brigades had been congregated at the latter spot, we moved at dusk into the olive grove just outside Ludd itself. Here also there were certain difficulties in connection with the water supply, and being the only M.O. with the brigade, it fell to me to make arrangements about drinking water,

Judean Hills. No. 15 Platoon Lewis gun section crew, spring 1918. Standing, left to right, are Sgt. George How, Pvt. A. Cobbold, and two unknown men. In front are Pvt. Jake Mortlock, L/Cpl. Charlie Bolton and Pvt. Bob Jaggard (Mortlock family photograph).

and also to procure water for the horses and camels in the unit, of which I was now in charge. It was always necessary on these occasions to have a totally different watering place for the camels, as horses would never drink from the same source; the camels, however, were obliging in that they only required a drink once every three days.

During the next two weeks we remained camped in the olive grove outside Ludd with all the horses belonging to our brigade, while the latter was fighting in the hills. It was hard work for our men in the plain, as each had six horses to groom, water, feed and exercise, and, as usual, the old septic-sore trouble made its appearance again. We sent up supplies daily to our field ambulance, and for the time being lived in comparative comfort in the olive grove.... Owing to the large number of dead horses and camels in the vicinity of Ludd, the jackals, as usual, made the night hideous with their shrieks and laughter. The old town of Ludd was of considerable interest, especially the early Christian church of St. George. On December 10th we heard that Jerusalem had surrendered, and the Jews and Greeks living in Ludd were hilarious in their rejoicings. On the following day the Fifty-fourth Division, who were fighting in the north, to the west of our line, were attacked, but drove the enemy back; this was followed by heavy artillery fire on both sides.

During our stay in the olive grove Fritz visited the neighbourhood of Ludd daily, and we witnessed some good air fights. On one occasion a motor-lorry was entering Ludd from Ramleh; the two drivers were buying oranges at a neighbouring stall, and while so doing some natives commenced to loot the contents of the lorry. Fritz came over, dropped his bomb, and killed the natives, obviously a just punishment for the latter. One morning the Third Australian Light Horse Brigade in their camp at Surafend suffered considerably, having eighty horses killed while at water.... On December 15th the whole of the brigade led horses and transport, together with a comparatively small number of officers and O.R.'s, left Ludd for Deiran; as we rode out we could see the Fifty-fourth Division heavily engaged a few miles to the north.

We took the road through Ramleh, crossing the Jaffa-Jerusalem road, and for the first mile or so our route lay amongst wheat and olive groves; a little later we found ourselves riding through miles and miles of orange groves heavily laden with fruit. These were the famous Jaffa oranges, and appeared to be cultivated most carefully.... It seemed to us indeed a land of peace and plenty. Homely looking white farmhouses, with red-tiled roofs, peeped through the foliage, and cleanly dressed, fair-skinned European Jews came out of their houses as we passed. The largest oranges, of superb quality, were being sold at forty for a shilling, but there appeared at that time no objection to our men picking as many as they liked without payment. When one looked at these large orange farms and the cheerful well-fed European inhabitants, one could not help thinking with some amazement of the stories which had been circulated in the East, describing how the Turk had maltreated all but the Mohammedan population in Palestine.

That night several of us walked into Deiran, where we repaired to the "hotel" Kliwitsky, an excellent restaurant, kept by a Russian Jew. We had not sat down to a meal at a table with a tablecloth for many months, and here we enjoyed a most excellent five-course dinner, served up in a spotlessly clean way. Dinner was followed by two sorts of port wine, made by the Jews, which was very much appreciated. The village of Deiran appeared to be populated by Jews from nearly every European country, who controlled the extensive orange, wine and almond trade in this fertile district. The houses were well built and the inhabitants seemed prosperous. There was an excellent water supply and pumping station, the water being laid on to every house, a thing which seemed to us hardly conceivable in Palestine. While at dinner, many Jews came in anxiously to inquire from us how things were going, especially those whose vineyards and orange groves were north of Jaffa and still in the hands of the Turks. On the following day we visited the village again, and were very struck, in the daylight, with its picturesque aspect. With its large number of cypress-trees and white houses it reminded one of an Italian scene. We were delighted to find the field cashier, generally a very elusive person, whom we had not seen for months, installed in the town hall.[4]

It was around this time that the 1/5th Suffolks' historians reported their battalion's transfer from the pleasant almond grove–sited camp at One Tree Hill to posts along the River Auja at "Northampton Castle" and West Mirr:

On February the 16th the battalion moved to the River Auja, relieving the Northants. The front was an ideal one. The swiftly flowing Auja springs in full maturity from a small depression in the plain near Ras-el-Ain and runs between banks of waving green reeds, noble trees, and orange groves until it reaches the sea. One of our posts was a pumping station with wooden palisades and castellated roof, rejoicing in the name of "Northampton Castle." This gave a wonderful view for miles over the Plain of Sharon to the north, to the sand-hills on the west, and to the Judean foothills on the east. The other [post] was at West Mirr, near the site of an old mill and bridge.

The names of the various camps and posts indicated their difference from the lines previously held by us. The reserve company and headquarters occupied Langdon Wood and Warley Wood. The outpost line ran from Lemon Wood, through Long Wood and White Gates, to Northampton Castle. The fields were bright green, the orange groves studded with gold, and the Turk invisible. Every one rejoiced at these pleasant places and life went by like a song.[5]

An American traveler, John Stoddard, visited this area at the turn of the century and recorded his impressions:

The River Auja, a tranquil scene (Fair and Wolton, *The History of the 1/5th Battalion: "The Suffolk Regiment"*).

Five. Advance, Delay, Advance

The usual approach to Palestine, it must be said, is not romantic. It was early in the morning when the steamer which had brought us from Port Saïd, in Egypt, halted before that celebrated seaport of the Holy Land, — now called Jaffa, but known in ancient times as Joppa. The city rises almost perpendicularly from the sea, and if that sea be rough, no traveler will forget his landing there; for, although one of the oldest cities of the world, Jaffa has as yet no harbour, and half a mile from shore, passengers are lowered from the steamer into little boats, manned by gesticulating, howling natives. These boats are then with difficulty guided through a semi-circular belt of rocks, some of which lift their savage tusks above the waves, while others lurk below the surface, ready to tear the keel from any vessel that encounters them. To one of these rocks, according to mythology, Andromeda was chained, until released by her deliverer, Perseus.

We found the surf which beats upon these reefs even more violent than our boatmen. There was a continual danger of capsizing, — a fate which, just at this particular place, appeared especially uninviting, since here it was that Jonah, when ejected from the ship, is said to have been swallowed by the whale.[6]

Blackwell and Axe add their account:

Jericho had been captured on February 21 by the 1st Australian Light Horse Brigade, following the fighting by the 53rd and 60th Divisions astride the road we had just left from Jerusalem. During this fighting progress was only possible, in places, in single file along tracks which were under accurate artillery and machine-gun fire. The 180th Brigade had successfully stormed Talaat ed Dumm, above the Good Samaritan's Inn, on February 20, although support from the 179th had been seriously delayed on account of the surpassing malignity of the terrain.

In taking Jericho, the Australian Brigade passed through the gorge of the Wadi Kumran, about 8 miles south of Jericho, and reached the Valley on the north-western shores of the Dead Sea. It took up a position along the Wadi Jofet Zeben nearby, and on the morning of the 21st started north across the slimy marl plain, and reached Jericho at half-past eight.[7]

Signals' sapper Harry Bonser recalled the one occasion he came face to face with the commander-in-chief, Lieutenant General Sir Edmund Allenby, somewhere in the vicinity of Haifa.

One hot morning, with a bandolier slipped over my shirt, and a coil of wire hung round the handle of my wire cutters, so that any enquiring red-tab might assume I was out mending a line, I set off on a fruit scrounge. A coil of wire and a blue armband were very useful passports in those days.

Plodding homeward with the spoil, I became aware of a mounted party approaching, and quickly detected the particular polish and aura of staff officers. There was nowhere to dodge, so I squared my shoulders and tried to forget the pomegranates bulging my shirt. Suddenly I realized that the leading horseman was the G.O.C. himself. He was spruce and polished; his equipment glittered, and his buttons shone.

I was tunic-less, covered with dust, and couldn't even have pretended to a lance-corporal that I'd seen any polish that morning, but I gave the regulation salute. The staff eyed me a trifle disdainfully, I thought, but General Allenby returned my salute with the precision of a full parade. There was no perfunctory lifting of the forefinger. The gesture was full and complete. It could not have been more so had he been taking the salute at the march past of a whole army. I thought that, too, rather decent of Allenby.

With spring we moved on to Birsalem.... G.H.Q. came to Birsalem, and we shifted

Aerial view of Haifa, an ancient port city, August 1918 (Mortlock family photograph).

onward, setting up a signal office by the side of the Turkish Railway near Wilhelma. It was fairly quiet but a Turkish battery at Kalkilieh used to shell fairly frequently. I remember being in the signal office one day when they kept our range for exactly an hour. They carried away every telegraph line we had, and as there was no proper dug-out the continuous whine and shatter were disconcerting. An Edinburgh fellow suddenly burst out: "Oh Christ! When the hell will they hit us?" I felt like that too.[8]

When granted leave from the front line, officers, and men found the Jewish and German colonists friendly, by and large, and ready and willing to meet the inner needs of the soldiers for a price.[9] "In fact, the rich red Palestine wine was a genuine bargain at a shilling for a pint mug-full; it is wonderful how our systems became gradually accustomed to this wine, to such an extent that mugs-full were in later days drunk as freely as beer in France."[10]

With regards to the German colony[11] of Wilhelma, Colonel Murphy stated that following a most cheerless Christmas Day: "The battalion [1/5th Suffolk], having gazed longingly awhile at the attractive village of Wilhelma,[12] welcomed the move thither on December 28. In this model German settlement, with its nicely furnished houses, well-stocked farms, and an abundance of firewood, a very pleasant month was spent. This was the only occasion on which the battalion occupied houses during its stay overseas."[13]

The 1/5th Suffolks' officer-historians, Captains Fair and Wolton, treat the reader to a much fuller account of this well-nigh idyllic interlude from the drudgery and danger of war:

> We looked longingly at the attractive village of Wilhelma, and welcomed the move to it on the 28th [December 1917]. This was a German colony founded by a religious sect, the Templars [sic], and was a model settlement. The houses were bright, well-furnished and airy, farms well stocked, and fire-wood plentiful. In fact it was quite like a corner of England. A farming company was at once formed that milked the cows and ran the dairy. Surplus stock was slaughtered, and altogether New Year's Day was a real holiday, with everyone in comfortable billets and enjoying a good rest after the trying times on the foothills.
>
> This was the first and last time since leaving England that the battalion had occupied houses. Furniture, including a bed and mattress, and protection against the weather were delightful novelties. As companies were detailed for outpost duty only once in four nights these blessings could be appreciated. The weather, which about New Year was very wet, increased our appreciation of our good luck. The pigs, fowls, and calves that the owners (who had been evacuated to Jaffa) were willing to sell, were quickly disposed of. Wheat was ground in hand mills, and home-made bread baked. With these luxuries we defied the weather and prayed for a long stay. Our genial padré [the Rev. E. D. Rennison], who was capable of appreciating these good things, was sent to hospital at Jaffa by a hard-hearted M.O., where he found a diet of bully beef and biscuits a poor substitute.
>
> The days were spent in digging trenches and drains, and making roads, and an

Wilhelma from the northeast. The arrow indicates the building where Jake Mortlock and his comrades-in-arms were billeted — a short-lived, but most welcome period of comparative paradise (Mortlock family photograph).

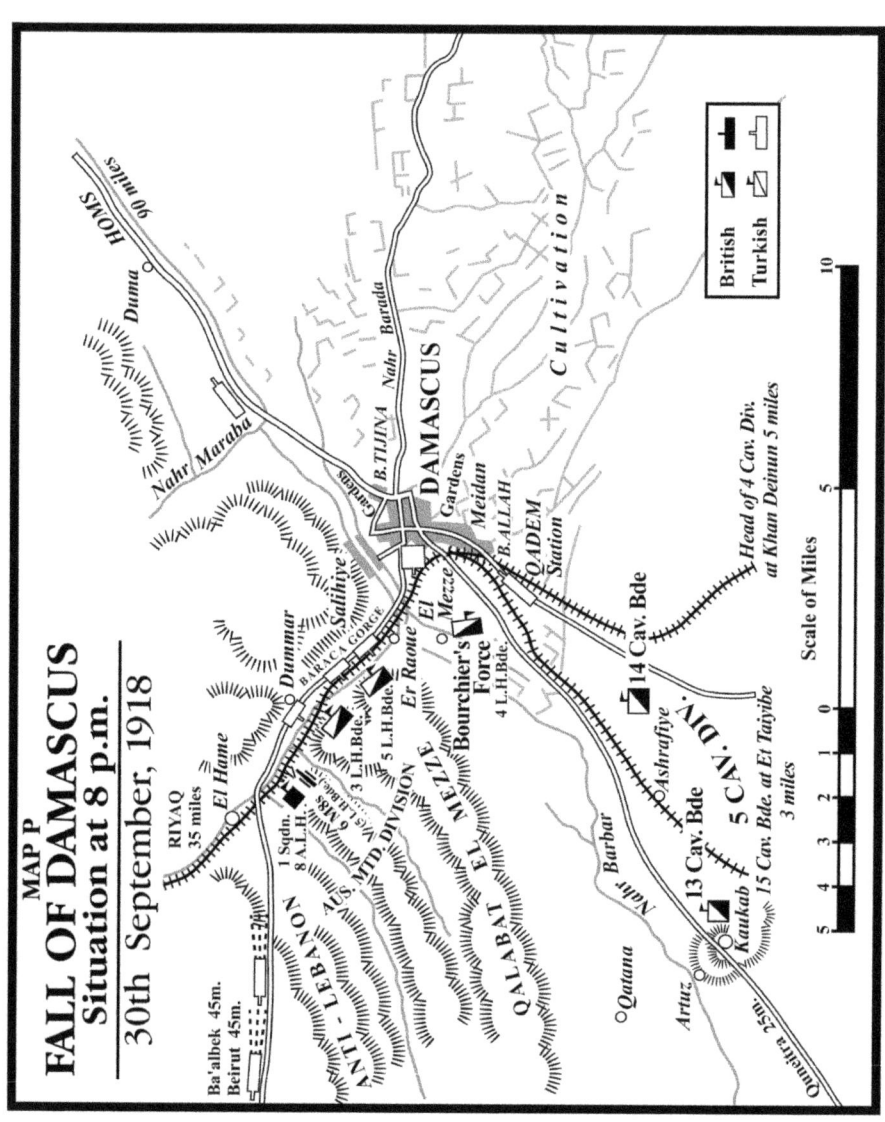

embankment for a light railway. The roads were excellent in fine weather, but after rain they were turned into quagmires, and dry creek beds became raging torrents. We kept a four days' emergency supply of rations in case the roads should be impassable. The transport, however, "delivered the goods" with unfailing regularity. A wonderful lot they were, with never a complaint or mishap, always cheery and always getting there. It was strange to see the sad-looking camels coming down the main street dragging their huge feet from the mud, into which they sank at every step, and which one felt sure they loathed with a deep and bitter hate.

On the 8th of January the Brig.-Gen. [A. McNeil] presented ribbons to those men who had been awarded decorations for gallantry in the third battle of Gaza. On the 14th we took over Station Post and Rantieh from the 1/4th Norfolks. Fortunately the weather, which had been very bad — heavy rain falling continuously — improved, and there was little trouble about the relief. About this time [late January, 1918] short leave to Jerusalem started; about six men at a time being allowed to go.[14]

Blackwell and Axe, artillerymen and historians, in this paraphrased and condensed version of the same period, paint a sobering picture:

Since the seizure of Mulebbis the enemy had not reached our line with shell fire, when one of his retreating 77mm. Batteries fired on our advanced outpost line for some hours. This state of affairs remained unchanged for several days. On January 7th, however, our front line was shelled in the neighbourhood of Fejja (eastern fringe of the town), and just over a week later (the 15th) a 5.9-inch or 10-cm. battery shelled Mulebbis itself, causing a few casualties among the inhabitants, but fortunately our battery's personnel suffered not at all.

The weather continued to be bad on and off, but the incessant and atrocious rainfall of the last month or so had tapered off to a great extent, and, consequently, in the more frequent intervals of sunshine, surroundings became brighter and drier, and spirits rose as a result.[15]

Harry Bonser, a sapper for the Royal Engineers, sadly recalled: "We trekked northwards, rigging up signal offices wherever we stopped, until we settled down in the Wadi Surar as a transmitting office to the divisions.... The next telegram was from the 163rd Brigade [54th (East Anglian) Division] reporting on how many men had died of exposure during the last twenty-four hours."[16]

Edmund Candler, late official eyewitness with the Mesopotamian Expeditionary Force, observed: "Nevertheless, our eyes were often on the past. The arid tracts where our own troops and General Allenby's were fighting, and the desert between, spanned the whole land of Holy Writ, from Jerusalem to Babylon, and from Babylon to Shush, the ancient Susa or the Shushan of the Bible."[17]

Private Mortlock and his comrades were here at Mulebbis, or Petah Tikwah (the Gateway of Hope), according to the Hebrew name. "On March 8th our line was slightly advanced and battalion headquarters moved to Short Wood, ten minutes from the Auja, and in the outpost line. The whole battalion was in the thick of orange groves heavy with golden fruit, and Jaffa oranges will find eloquent advocates throughout the battalion."[18]

Blackwell and Axe describe more artillery activity in the Mulebbis area:

March 12, 1918: At six o'clock the next morning, the entire No. 2 R.A. Group, which included our battery, opened a surprise bombardment on Mejdel Yaba, the 195th

H.A.G. [Heavy Artillery Group] assisting. The bombardment lasted ten minutes, and was continued for periods of two minutes each at intervals until 9 o'clock. The 162nd Infantry Brigade had meanwhile captured Mezeirah and Kh. Dikerim, and the 75th Division on their right had captured Deir Ballut. At 12 o'clock another bombardment was carried out on Sh. Barz ed Din, the 1/10th Londons [162nd Brigade, 54th Division] following up and captured both places without much opposition.[19]

Siegfried Sassoon wrote of his journey to Jerusalem:

March 12. Ramallah. Started at 9.30 [for Jerusalem]. (Twelve officers and baggage in a lorry [truck].) Reached 74th Division H.Q. at 4.30. The road climbed and twisted in the hills, which are wild and desolate, strewn with rocks and stones like thousands of sheep. Tractors going up with six-inch howitzers. Ambulances coming down. Leaving Ludd we passed a long procession of grey donkeys with blankets for the troops. At the first halt (Latron, at the foot of the hills) I munched my food in a ruined garden by a stream; frogs croaking and strange notes of birds; wild flowers out.[20]

In spite of opposition from the Ottoman government and growing anxiety among part of the local Arab population, by 1914 the Jewish population of Palestine had increased to approximately 85,000, or 12 percent of the total. About a quarter of them were settled on the land, some of it bought by national fund and declared to be the inalienable property of the Jewish people, on which non–Jews could be employed. Some were living in agricultural settlements of a new kind (the *kibbutz*), with collective control of production and communal life.[21]

Private Jake Mortlock told his cousin, Jack Parker:

We have had plenty of rain out here and this is a devil of a country for mud when it rains, you put your foot down and pick half of Palestine on it — so you can gess [sic] what it's like. But glad to say the weather is all right again now. I don't expect we shall get any more rain now for about another nine months, so must not grumble about what we have had.

We are quite near a Big Jewish Colony at present — modern houses, shops, and all that, and a very pretty place. Also some very pretty girls there — just like English. We can get a pass down there from the front line when we are off for the afternoon about twice a week. Go down there and have a good tea — eggs, bread, butter, cakes, and tea about 3d ["thruppence," 3 pence, 3 pennies] each — not so bad is it? Can get plenty of wine too quite cheap but it does not take much of that to make you silly. But it is a change to see a few civilized looking people now and then.

A few days later, on 19 March 1918, he wrote:

Dear Jack,

Thanks very much for your letter dated 14 Feb., jolly pleased to hear from you I only wish I could run over and see the same as I used to do and have a walk around the land for a bit of sport [Have to make up for?] lost time when the war is over. I am getting fed up with trying to shoot men — rabbits are more in my line — not so much chance of getting hurt with them.

Glad to say I am keeping quite fit and not having such a bad time — a lot better than this day a year ago in the first attack on Gaza when we were nearly dead for a want of a drink and so knocked up with marching that whenever we stopped for a minute the chaps fell down like logs sound asleep. Yes we are having quite a decent time at present we are out of the line for a spell and today we are having Batt [Battalion] Sports and a concert[22] to night. Last night I went to a divisional concert[23] in the town hall. It was jolly good. I have seen plenty worse shows in England and have paid to see them at that. But I don't suppose this will last long I expect you will be reading in the near future of another push in Palestine. But it all helps to win the war.

We had a terrific thunderstorm last Sunday afternoon hail stones as big as a potato and it came down so hard yo [sic] could hardly see ten paces in front of you and then when they melted the water rushed down the gully in torrents we pretty nearly all got washed away.

Two days after the date of the above letter, Ludendorff launched a massive offensive on the Western Front. "The enemy's attacks, which began on March 21st, were delivered on the maximum scale. Our defences were less complete and our resistance less effective than I had anticipated, especially in the southern (Fifth Army) area,"[24] wrote Hankey.

MacMunn and Falls say in their historical account:

The War Office had decided, before the German offensive was launched in France on the 21st March, to despatch large numbers of Indian troops to Palestine. Its object at that time was, however, not the relief of British troops for transfer to the Western Front, but the reinforcement of Sir Edmund Allenby's Army in accordance with the proposition of General Smuts, which had generally been accepted by the government. The 7th Indian Division had arrived in Egypt by the beginning of January; and although the government had decided against the transfer from Mesopotamia of the 13th Division, which General Smuts had suggested, they still had the intention of strengthening the E.E.F. by a second Indian division from that theatre. They had also, even before General Smuts's mission, informed the commander-in-chief that they would despatch to Palestine one of the two Indian cavalry divisions (which contained British regiments) in France, and subsequently determined to send all the Indian regiments from both divisions."[25]

On the very same day that Private Mortlock penned the above letter, another event occurred that was noted by his battalion's historians: "We learned the sad news of Colonel Wollaston's death from shrapnel fired during an air raid on London. He had commanded the battalion since August 1916. While critical of its methods in some details, he always had a deep affection for it, and a high admiration for the spirit that animated it. Considerate, tactful, and a kind friend to all with whom he came in contact, he was regarded by the men he led as a comrade who had shared their disappointments and successes, and who, understanding their weaknesses and virtues, was deeply attached to them. [As he was] a brilliant soldier and a gallant gentleman, the whole battalion felt his loss keenly."[26]

Captains Fair and Wolton resume their history of their battalion of Suffolk infantrymen:

Battalion training was continued at Garnett's Wood, and record entries were received for sports. The mule-back wrestling and the blindfold donkey race were the most amusing and popular items. Later cross-country running became popular. During this month [March] 2nd Lieutenants W. Emerson, R. F. Currington, A. Balfour, and F. J. Cottam joined the battalion. At the beginning of April we again moved into the front line among the orange groves, where we found the 1/8th Ghurka Rifles on our left.

On the 5th Major W. M. Campbell, of the Suffolk Regiment, who had recently commanded the 1/5th Norfolks, and had been second in command of the 4th K.O.S.B. [King's Own Scottish Borderers], assumed command of the battalion. He had been captured at Le Cateau during the retreat from Mons, and after being a prisoner in Germany for three years had effected a bold escape.

The quiet along the whole front continued. On April 10th on relief by the 2nd Loyal North Lancashires, we moved into reserve at Garnett's Wood, where we received warning orders for an advance up the Plain of Sharon. Details of this were worked out, but later the whole scheme was cancelled.

As a result of the situation in France, and the likelihood of an attack from the Turk, we devoted ourselves to organizing the defences of our front line. They had not been taken very seriously, and some of us, in our heart of hearts, had hoped for an opportunity for open warfare on the plain. With the possibility of German reinforcements reaching the Turk, and a probable reduction in our strength, defensive positions became a matter of common sense and urgency. So we dug and built for some weeks.

On April 24th Brig. General T. Ward, C.M.G. [Companion of the Order of St. Michael and St. George; "Call Me God"], who had been with us since Gallipoli, relinquished his command, which was assumed by Brig. General A. McNeil, D.S.O. [Distinguished Service Order].[27]

The Fair and Wolton account specifically alludes to "D" Company, 1st/5th Battalion, the Suffolk Regiment—the unit to which Capt. H. C. Wolton, Sgt. How, L/Cpl. Bolton, and Pvts. Burlham, Jaggard, Mortlock, and Turner belonged.

Early in May we went to Dikerin, among the rocks of the foothills, to be attached to the 161st [Essex] Brigade. Here "B" and "C" Companies provided working parties by and night, and specialized in the art of building stone sangars. "A" Company acted as guard to the guns in the Wadi Ballut, and "D" Company to the guns at Mezeireh. Near the latter was a charming little Roman temple.

During this time enemy planes displayed a very marked objection to our observation balloons. Three of them came down in flames in the same number of days, but were promptly replaced.

On May 23rd we took over the right sector of the divisional front, relieving the 4th Essex Battalion. This front was quite a novelty to us, being a series of small posts, each holding a platoon, and composed of sangars. These were on the forward of rocky hills, with precipitous wadis running up towards them, and were under direct observation from enemy posts, consequently most of them were not held during the day. Castle Hill alone was garrisoned. Observation posts were established along the rest of the line. The sangars had made slow progress, but were reasonable good cover.

Green Hill, occupied by "D" Company, was well detached, and so exposed to enemy observation that the garrison could not move about even the reverse slope of the hills by day. They spent their days lying low, undisturbed by surprise visits from headquarters, and unable to do any physical work. "B" Company were on Lone Hill; "A" Company on Castle Hill; and "C" Company behind Double Hill, near Ruin Hill. Headquarters were on the steep slopes of Boundary Wadi. The names fairly indicate the nature of the country. The versatile camel again aroused our respect by negotiating paths with rocky steps that were more suited to goats than to our lofty friends.

The canteen stores here were very good, and the C.O., transport and canteen officers arranged for a supply of bottled beer twice a week.[28]

Of the same area, Captain Teichman wrote on April 8, 9 and 10, 1918:

Our bivouac was a pleasant one, the country being covered with grass, dust being almost completely absent. A Taube [German airplane] was shot down near our camp during the afternoon, and it was said that fifty-seven had been shot down in the last three months. At night the batteries of the Twenty-first Corps were kept busy. On the following morning some of us rode out to a slight eminence known as Bald Hill, which had been the scene of some heavy fighting, as shown by the graves on it, a few months ago, whence we had a fine view of part of the line held by the Twenty-first Corps. Bearings were taken on various points, and landmarks were identified; below us lay the village of Mulebbis, with its little red-roofed houses, set among the trees, and beyond it on the right we could see the old Crusader fort of Ras El Tin, which at this time constituted part of our front line.

The Turkish railway almost up to this point was in our hands. Our shells could be seen exploding in the Turkish lines, and we identified the villages of Jiljulieh and Kalkalieh, with Kefr Kasim and Mejdel Yaba on our right. During the night the right hand division of the corps made an advance in the hills after a preliminary bombardment. On the following day the enemy counter-attacked, but were driven back. In the morning two of us rode through miles of beautiful orange and lemon groves and through orchards bordered by eucalyptus and pepper trees into Jaffa. It was an interesting and picturesque town, which had benefited by most of the modern improvements. All the guards of the various public buildings were supplied by French and Egyptian regiments. Just outside the town, along the coast to the north, was the

Supply Company Headquarters, Boundary Wadi (Fair and Wolton, *The History of the 1/5th Battalion: "The Suffolk Regiment"*).

Crusader castle of Ras el Ain (Fair and Wolton, *The History of the 1/5th Battalion: "The Suffolk Regiment"*).

flourishing German colony of Sarona, containing many large houses amongst the orange groves.[29]

Colonel Badcock eulogized the fruit of the groves and vineyards: "And weren't those Jaffa oranges good! Two shillings a hundred was the current rate of exchange for them, and I don't think I missed eating at least one a day from November 1917 till mid–June 1918. And besides, there were apricots, mulberries, figs, to say nothing of the grapes in the Jordan Valley west of Jericho."[30]

Lt. Col Badcock in this same region enjoyed pleasures such as only non-combatants can — like riding to hounds, in pursuit of a jackal rather than the traditional fox, and cricket.

> We contrived to get an occasional cricket match, and I only wish I had the score of one particular cricket match we played at the Horse Transport Depot at Ludd. My friend, Major H. B. Viney, M.C., who commanded this depot, provided all the gear, including the matting; he had converted a rough bit of land into an admirable parade ground, and except for a slight slope it made a very good cricket ground. I think my side won the match, our chief performers being E. R. Wilson (who for the past twenty-five years must surely rank as one of the finest slow-bowlers in English cricket), W. J. Whitty (an Australian Test Match cricketer), and an old Cambridge contemporary of mine, Major A. F. Leach Lewis, who at this time was D.A.A.G. at G.H.Q. The last-named played a great innings.[31]

General Sir Edmund Allenby — now, understandably, the darling of the prime minister, the War Cabinet, and the British government — received virtually all he asked for in reinforcements, replacements, substitutions, ordnance, and *matériel*.

As a result of these reinforcements and substitutions plans were afoot for the creation of a Third Army Corps. "However, the great German offensive of the 21st March and the consequent calls for troops for France at once put an end to the need for a third corps, and on the 19th March [*sic*] the commander-in-chief telegraphed that he no longer needed it."³²

Gilbert wrote, "The War Cabinet met again during the afternoon of March 27, Milner, Curzon and Churchill pressed Lloyd George to extend conscription to Ireland. But opinion was divided, and no decision was reached. It was also decided to send a further Division to France, and to order General Allenby to adopt the offensive in Palestine, in the hope of creating a major, if distant diversion."³³

Colonel Gibbons, of the 1/5th Essex, declared:

> During the month of April the serious position on the Western Front had necessitated the transfer of large numbers of troops from Palestine to France. The 52nd and 74th Divisions had gone intact, while in addition nine yeomanry regiments, five and a half siege batteries, ten British battalions, and five machine gun companies had been withdrawn from the line, preparatory to embarkation. To some small extent the gaps had been filled by Indian troops, which, however, had not seen service in the present war. During May the depletion continued, a further fourteen British battalions being withdrawn.
>
> As a result of these changes the enemy became much more active both in artillery and patrol work, the latter no doubt having for its chief object the identification of the troops holding the line and the shaking of the morale of the new units. On the 23rd, having completed our three weeks in the line, we were relieved by the 1/5th Norfolk Regiment [163rd Brigade] and went into bivouac in the orange groves near Mulebbis. It was a pleasant enough spot and a shady one, but the insects which infested the trees were rather a nuisance. The battalion was now employed in the war against mosquitoes, the chief measures of which were clearing and "canalising" the Wadi Ishkar (Issachar?) which ran in front of the line. Reeds and other growths were cleared and the banks cut straight to allow a free flow of water and any stagnant pools were covered with oil to stop breeding. This procedure was carried out for nearly a thousand yards to the front of the line in the plain, and was done in daylight, the banks and long grass giving good cover from view.
>
> During our stay in the orange groves I occasionally visited Ras-el-Ain, now occupied by our troops. It provided a good view of the enemy's positions on the foothills in front of Mejdel Yaba. The River Auja which rises there in several very strong springs, becomes a considerable stream almost at once, and its course is fringed with the most luxuriant growth of small trees, shrubs, grasses and flowers. Ras-el-Ain, seen from a distance, looks merely the gaunt shell of a castle, set bare in the plain, but a close approach reveals many hidden beauties. It is a favourite resort of the Mulebbis people in the summer, and altogether a delightful spot after the burning rocks of the hills. Alexander Jannæus fortified the place against the Syrians under Antiochus (B.C. 105–78) and constructed lines, probably along the course of the Auja, consisting, according to Josephus, of a wall with wooden towers and intermediate redoubts, but no trace of these remains. Herod built a town here, calling it Antipatris, in honour of his father, Antipater, son of Antipas....
>
> On June 6th the Battalion relieved the 1/5th Bedfordshire Regiment [162nd Brigade] in the front line in front of the River Auja. It was a delightful place, the trenches for the most part being in orange groves laden with fruit, and there were

good bathing facilities. There were also good fish in the river. The most effective method of getting them was by firing at them with a rifle. The bullet seldom hit them but they were stunned by the impact for several seconds, during which time they turned on their sides and floated on the surface, to be taken by a sandbag on the end of a pole. All ranks slept at night under mosquito-net "bivvies" and sentries had their faces and hands and knees anointed with anti-mosquito grease. The result of these precautions, and of the cleanliness of body and clothing made possible by the abundance of fresh water, was a good record of health, in contrast to Mejdel Yaba where sand-fly fever and other complaints were rife and malaria fairly common. The whole district is of course very unhealthy in summer, a fact frequently noted in historical records, and it speaks well for the efforts of the medical services that the health of the army was maintained in the way it was.[34]

All the seven infantry divisions in the force, with the exception of the 54th, now consisted of three British and nine Indian battalions, the so-called "Indian" divisions (3rd and 7th) being exactly the same in this respect. The 54th was allowed to retain all its British battalions intact, perhaps so the War Office should have one more complete British division on which to lay its hand in case of dire emergency. In June, to Sir Edmund Allenby's alarm, the War Cabinet decided not only to withdraw this division to France, but to take one of the mounted Australian divisions to use as drafts for the Australian infantry. However, both projects were dropped, though certain units of the 54th Division actually reached Qantara (Kantara, Egypt) before the transfer of the division was cancelled.[35]

About this time the dispatch of troops to France and the reorganization of the force prevented further operations of any size anywhere in Palestine, and — according to official records — rendered the adoption of a policy of active defense necessary.[36]

Lt. Colonel Maurice Hankey, secretary of the Supreme War Council, gives very precise details of the way this matter was wrestled with:

> Towards the end of June the War Office desired as a matter of urgency to withdraw the 54th British Division and Australian troops equivalent to a mounted division from Palestine to France. The man-power situation in France was parlous; the great need was for organised reserves; it was touch-and-go whether we should not lose Amiens, Paris and the Channel ports; Foch was continually calling on us for more divisions; heavy casualties must be expected. Troops had already been drawn from Home Defence, Italy and the Balkans as well as from Palestine itself.[37]

Colonel Hankey continues his account of the deliberations of the Supreme War Council: "On June 21st the Prime Minister agreed, rather reluctantly, that the 54th Division should be brought to France, but that the Australian mounted troops, who were supplied mainly from Australia, should remain in Palestine. On June 26th, however, they reversed this decision.... In fact, however, the new decision stood and the 54th Division took part in the final defeat of the Turks."[38]

Private Jake Mortlock of the 1/5th Battalion of the Suffolk Regiment recounted how he and his comrades had actually entrained for France when the order rescinding the movement directive came through. Thereafter he said the division became known as "Allenby's pets," as it was the only white infantry division that remained in the Palestinian theater.[39] The 1/5th Battalion of the Norfolk Regiment also actually entrained on June 27 and had "proceeded some distance before their orders were cancelled."[40]

All of the above information makes it abundantly clear the perilous turn of events on the Western Front — largely occasioned by the collapse of Russia, which enabled the Central Powers to transfer vast numbers of veteran troops from the Eastern Front to the Western. By the early part of the spring of 1918 the situation in France and Flanders had reached an acute crisis point — not only that, it was deteriorating daily. Soon Haig's army literally had its back to the wall, and reinforcements from all other British fronts were urgently needed to stem the relentless German tide.

Some of the Allies' best divisions were hurriedly shipped to France. In place of these seasoned soldiers were substituted untrained Indian troops with little or no knowledge of modern fighting methods. The adoption of such a drastic policy meant practically the re-making of the army before it could it could take the field in Palestine with any hope of success. Fortunately sufficient well-trained personnel were left to leaven the whole, but it was grueling work carrying out intensive training all through the summer months of 1918. In the case of the 60th Division, it was reduced to one white battalion to a brigade; the remaining nine battalions consisted of young Indian sepoy recruits. Woodard recorded, "Two Indian divisions had been sent from Mesopotamia, and Indians filled up his other infantry divisions, save one, the 54th Division, which after much agonising, the War Cabinet had left in Allenby's command."[41]

Siegfried Sassoon, in his largely autobiographical *Sherston's Progress*, recounts:

> April 8 [1918]. 7 P.M. In my bivouac near Sufa, after two days' marching. (About ten miles each day.) This morning we started from a point near Ramallah, over 3000 feet up.... Up at 5.15 and away by 7.40. Reached here 1.30. Passed General Allenby on the way....[42]
>
> April 10 [1918]. Left; left; left-right, left. 110 paces to the minute. Monotonous rhythm of marching beats in his brain. The column moves heavily on; dust hangs over it; dust and the glaring discomfort of the sky. Going up a steep hill the round steel helmets sway from side to side with the lurch of the heavily-laden shoulders. Vans and lorries drone and grind and blunder along the road; cactus hedges are caked with dust. The column passes some Turkish prisoners in dingy dark uniform and red fez, guarded by Highlanders. "Make the — — s work, Jock!" someone shouts from the ranks.... Through the sweat-soaked exhaustion that weighs him down, he sees and hears these things; his shoulders are a dull ache; his feet burn hot and clumsy with fatigue; his eyes are tormented by the hot glare of the airless road. Men in front, men behind; no escape. "Fall out on the right of the road...." He collapses into a dry ditch until the whistle blows again.[43]

Lt. Colonel Gibbons tells:

> Our working parties went nightly to the front line, and their efforts were much appreciated by its occupants, who were loud in their praises of the good work done

by the 5th.... The 5th Essex were to reap the benefit of their own labors when they relieved those self-same occupants the line in front of Medjel Yaba on May 2nd. The defenses there consisted of small works giving mutual support, and were designed for a mobile defense — where two companies were held in reserve.... Our Battalion Headquarters was in a large disused lime kiln on the edge of the wadi just in rear of the village of Mejdel Yaba which stood on a high rocky hill. The village itself was not occupied, except by observation posts on the forward slopes of the hill.

The surrounding country was so rock-strewn and rugged that the siting of the defensive works was a matter of much difficulty. The enemy shelled Medjel Yaba pretty regularly and made much dust in that venerable stronghold, but the company areas were well camouflaged and the works very lightly held by day, so that casualties were small.

"The human inhabitants of Medjel Yaba had of course departed, but the fleas were multitudinous — and aggressive. They came out of the houses in thousands to meet you as you approached, hopping over the stones and wagging their tails (metaphorically speaking), in anticipation of the visitor's blood. Consequently I did not explore the place as thoroughly as I should have liked," Colonel Gibbons confessed. "The house of the Sheikh is built against the wall of an old church now used as a stable."[44]

Captain Teichman's diary recorded the concluding days of his service in this theater of war. He was to finish his war on the Italian front, earning prestigious decorations. He wrote:

> While on one of these visits to Jerusalem, two of us suddenly received news that we had been granted leave to the U.K., as home leave is called in the Army. Many of us had had no home leave since we had left England in April 1915, and were naturally very excited at the prospect. The question was how to get down to Alexandria in order to catch the boat to which we had been detailed. The following morning, early, a passing Ford car, which was traveling from the Dead Sea to Jaffa, was stopped and commandeered, as it only contained the driver. The latter apparently was in a hurry to complete his journey, and we experienced a most thrilling descent as we zigzagged down the pass, whirling around the hairpin corners, often with a drop of hundreds of feet to the right or left. Our driver cheered us up by telling us how a few weeks ago the steering gear of a Ford car had refused to act on a similar road, with disastrous results to the occupants of the car. However, Latron was eventually reached, and we started on our journey from the railhead at Ludd on the evening of June 21st.
>
> Three days later we embarked on the transport *Rose*, in Alexandria harbour, one of a convoy of three small boats which were taking an infantry battalion en route to France, and a few officers on leave to Taranto. The three boats left the harbour at dusk, accompanied by five destroyers. There had been a considerable number of transports sunk outside the harbour, and consequently we had to stand to our stations for some two hours lest a similar fate should befall us; at the same time the destroyers emitted an enormous amount of smoke, which we imagined was to act as a screen. On account of this submarine menace we were compelled to wear our life-belts all day.
>
> After passing through the Corinth Ship Canal, about four days later, we emerged into the Straits, and were met by some French destroyers, which escorted us to Taranto, the latter place being reached after an uneventful journey. Taranto had at this time become an enormous rest camp, as it was the port of embarkation for all

troops proceeding to Salonika, Palestine, Mesopotamia and India. After a few days' delay the leave train was made up, and we travelled the usual route, along the east coast of Italy, and thence through Bologna to Genoa. Le Havre being reached after about ten days' railway travelling, the latter being broken by a couple of days' rest at Faenza and St. Germain au Mont d'Or, near Lyons.[45]

R.E. Corporal Fred Mills wrote in his diary: "Friday, July 5th, 1918. Kantara. Met Jack Isaacs of Ramsgate who expects to go back to the front with the Northamptons [54th Division]."

Blackwell and Axe tell us that in July, "B" Battery, 271st Brigade, Royal Field Artillery (1/2nd Essex Battery, R.F.A.), was deployed in the Jordan Valley—far from its division, which remained on the west flank. "Scattered about were whitened skeletons of horse and camel and stinking carcasses. Alone in this expanse one chances upon a grave with the simple indication 'Killed in action.' On the banks of the Jordan there were compensations. For the greater part of its sinuous length it was belted with a profusion of vegetation."

There was a regular profusion of trees of all kinds of graceful shapes and most varied hues. Willows, acacias, tamarisks and poplars stretched themselves to wondrous heights, and at their roots abounded marsh and aquatic plants, among which was the reed of Jerusalem, a kind of blossom-bearing bamboo. In places this thinned off into thickets of shrubs, and soon vegetation was no longer represented except by thin tufts of heather.

The battery only stayed at Jericho during the remainder of July 27, and on the next day went into action on the banks of the Jordan at Ghoraniyeh. "Here was a bridgehead which we were covering, but our occupation of this position was only until August 2. It was most unhealthy in this green belt, especially during the dank, clammy evenings, which brought out swarms of mosquitoes, and sickness was rife"[46] wrote Blackwell and Axe.

Lieutenant Robert Wilson, serving with "D" Squadron, the Royal Gloucester Hussars, described the Jordan Valley as "the Valley of Death" with its heat, mosquitoes and malaria.[47]

The Jewish Legion had some 5,000 soldiers under arms in Palestine, who, because of the pressures exerted by the anti–Zionist Jewish establishment, were known as "Royal Fusiliers," the 38th, 39th, and 40th Battalions, the last named being composed exclusively of Palestinian Jews. In August the so-called Jewish Legion was relocated to a site in the Jordan Valley, and for over seven weeks they languished in the sweltering heat.[48]

On August 17 twenty-three-year-old Captain Robert Ernest Eversden, Royal Flying Corps/Royal Air Force, wrote his mother from "somewhere in Palestine."

My dear,
It's topping to see the war again. The star-shells are faintly visible at night and the guns are distinct. I have trodden the road over which Mary and Joseph fled into Egypt, and saw Jaffa from the train 3 days ago. From my tent as I write, I see the low

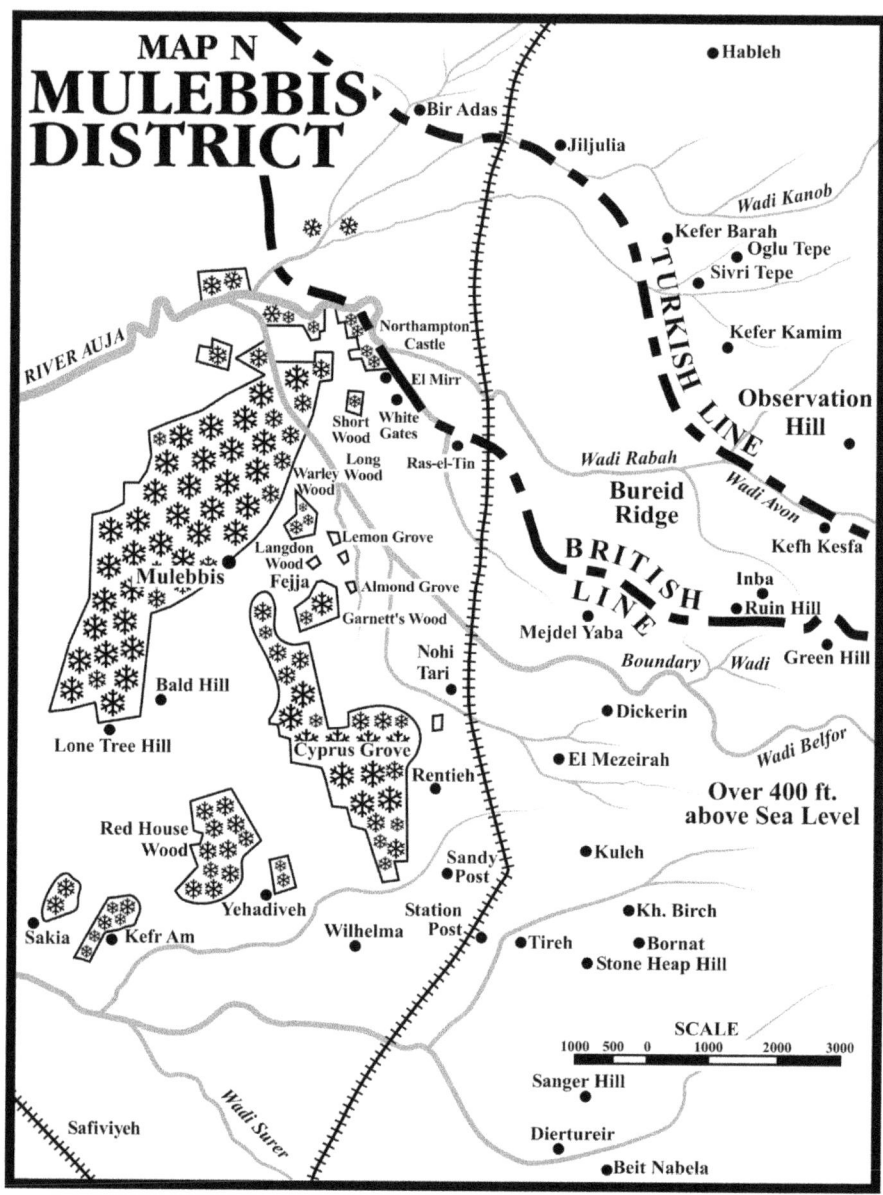

clouds hanging over the blue mountains which surround the Holy City, and from a height of 6,000 feet this morning saw the Dead Sea, and all the land of Palestine. A mile or so from the camp an ancient tower stretches leanly up from its surrounding bed of olive trees. It is a relic of the brave Crusader and bears upon its breast the effigy of St. George. How amazed the armoured saint must be to see, after all these centuries, British soldiers sweating past, marching on towards his Master's Tomb.

And across the fields there is an old Bedouin and his family, and on his land our fast scouts lie waiting for the call! He, with his dark skin, his hooked nose, his Koran and his knowledge of the Turkish Regime, sees the "infidels" making tennis courts and playing football between their bloody combats!

Heavens this is a fair country! Mother, after the sand and the flies, to see mountains, and fields, ploughs and corn, olive and orange groves, and to get your legs stung by thistles and nettles. Clouds and in the distance the blue sea....

Now, isn't this all ridiculous! I'm relapsing into my old sentimentality. Me! The cold-blooded me who races up after the poor unfortunate Hun! He (the Hun) is getting such a thick time here, dear. We shot one down yesterday. Shot his observer in cold blood and then shot off one of his planes, and then his fuselage — like a boy picking off flies' legs one by one!! All my love, dear.

Your affectionate son, Bob.[49]

In spite of all the poaching and rearranging his Army's contingents had been subjected to, Allenby made plans for an offensive. Originally he envisaged a limited campaign which would complete the conquest of northern Palestine while allowing most of the Turkish forces there to effect an escape. In August, however, he altered his plans. Sensing the inherent weakness of the enemy and confident of his own ability and that of the troops under his command, he planned a campaign of annihilation, which, if successful, would make the problem of occupying Syria a matter of supply alone.[50]

Colonel Gibbons, in his *With the 1/5th Essex in the East*, gives a detailed account both of daily life and of the training given the troops. It is almost incredible that this officer found the time to jot down the copious notes essential to compiling this work.

> We did a good deal of training on this historic ground, over which ebbed and flowed the struggles against the Syrians (B.C. 166) and the Romans (66 A.D.). Sometimes the tide flowed westward, as when Jonathan swept right down to Jaffa and took it; sometimes eastward, as when the Syrians rolled up to the walls of Jerusalem itself. The same thing repeated itself thirteen centuries later, with Saladin and Richard in the leading parts.
>
> We were able to form a battalion officers' mess at Beit Nebala, making a most comfortable mess room with spare bivouac sheets fastened together, with wagon poles for uprights and captured angle-iron pickets to hold up the sides, which were left open to let in the air. It is a good thing for all the officers of a battalion to get together, if only at feeding times. Companies and battalion headquarters are too much "on their own" when distributed in the line, and officers are apt to get "cliquey," a condition which is not conducive to the best battalion spirit.
>
> Particular attention was given to training the platoon as a fighting unit. On August 12th, Watts's platoon of "C" Company did a little scheme which was attended by the divisional commander and a large number of officers from other formations, and provided the occasion for a useful discussion on the platoon in the attack in hill country. The performers played their parts well. On the 18th a successful battalion sports meeting was held and on other days turn-out and driving competitions for the transport, cookhouse turn-out, etc.
>
> We left Beit Nebala on August 21st and relieved the 1/4th Northamptonshires in the left-central sub-section on a front of 1,500 yards. It joined our former Mejdel Yaba line, continuing it eastward. In front of us lay the Bureid Ridge, which was at

first occupied by our troops after the capture of Mejdel Yaba. The line was afterwards withdrawn to the one now held, as there were no covered communications with the ridge. The enemy had not occupied it, though he had a deep wadi — the Wadi Rabah — in rear of it and could have done so if he had chosen. It was patrolled by both sides at night. Enemy picquets were located in the hollows to the east of it, protected by barbed wire, also on the Umm el Bureid, a spur of it running north, which was held by day and night.

The latter had, as we discovered afterwards, an almost sheer face of rock just behind it, dropping to the Wadi Rabah, to which the picquet retired when the place was shelled, as it frequently was. The enemy appeared jumpy and often threw bombs a long distance from our patrols, also firing at the slightest sound and putting up Very lights. It was very difficult for patrols to avoid being heard, going over slippery rocks and treading in the rough dry grass. Propaganda leaflets were left in our old sangars on the ridge, and those were found, on subsequent nights, to have been duly collected. Small brushes with enemy patrols were frequent on the ridge, the latter generally retiring north into the Wadi Rabah. Some very good work was done by patrols led by Lucas, Lockwood, Foley-Whaling, Barnard, Archer, Wray, and Sergeants Rolph and French.

Two deserters came in on September 1st and two more on the 4th, including a warrant officer, who said that the enemy kept a reserve company north of the ridge, who had orders to occupy it in case of attack at night. The information gained by the patrols, added to reconnaissance by day with field glasses and telescopes, gave us a very good idea of the ground over which we were destined to attack, and proved of good value.

On the night of September 8th we were relieved by the 1/5th Bedfords and again recrossed the plain to Red House Wood, to rest and refit for the attack.

The commander-in-chief had decided to make his main attack, according to an official dispatch, "on the coastal plain, rather than through the hills, where the ground afforded the enemy positions of great natural strength and taxed the physical energy of the attackers to the utmost."

The hills around Kefr Kasim, in front of Mejdel Yaba, overlooked the plain and had to be included in the frontage of the main attack. The latter was entrusted to Lt. General Sir Edward Bulfin, K.C.B., who, we were proud to remember, had once commanded the Essex Territorial Infantry Brigade. The groves around us were teeming with troops. Every night the plain was alive with columns of every arm moving westward. There was little movement by day, and even if there had been the enemy had little chance of seeing it, for our ascendancy in the air was well nigh complete. During the last week in August the total number of enemy planes which crossed our lines was eighteen. During one week in June there had been over 100. I saw one brought down quite close to Divisional Headquarters with a bullet through its petrol tank. The pilot made good landing and was entertained at one of the divisional messes. I was told — I don't know how true it was — that the staff "did" him very well, in the hope of loosening his tongue, but that he turned out more than a match for them at the table. He talked freely about everything but the enemy, kept them up half the night, and got up in the morning with the only head of the party which didn't ache![51]

Lt. Col. Gibbons' account (paraphrased) continues:

A few nights after we left the line the 1/5th Bedfords had an officer shot dead on patrol on the Bureid Ridge. On the following night we saw and heard a regular battle going on the same ground. The report of this engagement was read at a brigade con-

Five. Advance, Delay, Advance

ference a day or two after. Our successors in the line stated that they were given to understand that they could walk about freely on the Bureid Ridge, but that when their patrol visited it they found it strongly held by the enemy. It is true that our patrols had walked about freely on the ridge, but, as the log book should have shown, they were frequently fired upon by enemy patrols, though it was never strongly held.

The next night the 1/5th Bedfords, after a short artillery bombardment, attacked the ridge in considerable force and met with strong resistance from enemy infantry. Presumably, on the strength of the report of this action, the Bureid Ridge was now stated to form part of the Turkish main system, wire was said to be known at one point and suspected at others, and a considerable length of enemy sangars appeared on the official maps. All this was contrary to the information supplied by our patrols, who regularly reported the ridge clear of any enemy works; it is only fair to these patrols to say that when the 1/4th Essex and ourselves advanced over the whole ridge in the attack which afterwards took place, there was no sign of wire, nor were there any prepared positions except our own old sangars on the northern slope.

What, I think, happened when the Bedfords attacked, was that the enemy, thinking their main positions were being attacked, sent out the reserve company of which the warrant officer had told us. However, it must be said that the action, in which the Bedfords took part with so much credit to themselves, had the important result of bringing down the enemy's barrage, the location of which led to certain alterations in the plan of attack which probably saved the Essex Brigade [161st] many casualties in the following battle. Another invaluable result was that the enemy's bombardment enabled our "sound rangers" to pinpoint the batteries themselves. Consequently, when the real attack came off every enemy battery had one of our "heavies" turned on to it, with excellent results, as we afterwards saw with our own eyes.[52]

CHAPTER SIX

The Final Stroke

Sir Edmund Allenby now had a massive force at his disposal, and one which required a colossal amount of supplying. Lt. General Sir Archibald Wavell, in his *The Campaigns in Palestine*, gives some idea of the extreme magnitude of this:

> The ration strength in the theatre, including all troops and over 80,000 Egyptians of the Camel Transport Corps and Labour Corps, was approximately 340,000. If, however, all labour working for and fed by the Army in the interior of Egypt, all followers, and all sick in hospital be included, a total of over 450,000 would be reached. The approximate number of animals was 62,000 horses, 44,000 mules, 36,000 camels, and 12,000 donkeys.[1]

On the opposite side, General Otto Liman von Sanders' account of political chicanery and lamentably poor military strategy pursued by Enver Pasha and the authorities at the Sublime Porte makes one fully sympathize with his situation. Because of the undue emphasis placed on operations in the East Caucuses, officers were even induced to volunteer for transfer to that theater by promises of "advantages of promotion and double pay." The departure of numerous such volunteers was natural, "because in the Army Group they received no pay and lived in anxiety about their families."[2]

He goes on to list a long catalog of grievances and his unheeded protests—his condemnation of the foolishness of opening another front, in Persia being but one. He cites his appeals to Berlin and correspondence with General Ludendorff—which included the prediction of an imminent "big attack in the coast sector."[3] In early August minor actions occurred, then a much bigger one astride the Jerusalem-Nablus road on the 12th-13th. "The fighting was severe and bloody and lasted until 4 A.M." The Turkish positions remained in their hands without loss of ground.[4]

General Liman von Sanders further elaborated that on August 19 a two-day enemy attack took place after extensive preparation by artillery, in the dune terrain of the coast, the left being directed against Birket Atife, and the 7th Division posted there under its brave commander, Nashui Bei, repulsed the assault after several bloody hand-to-hand actions. At the beginning of the war Nashui Bei became a Russian prisoner of war. After many adventures, he found his way back to Turkey via China. It appears that the British had learned of the exchange through their spies and wanted to test the efficiency of the new troops (Turkish 7th Division) in the open coast terrain.[5]

In the early days of September 1918 General Mustafa Kemal wrote to a doctor friend:

> Syria deserves pity. There is no governor, no commander. There is a lot of British propaganda. The British secret service is active everywhere. The population hates the government and looks forward to the arrival of the British. The enemy is strong in men and transport. We are like a thread of cotton before them. The British now think that they will defeat us by their propaganda, rather than by fighting. Every day from their aircraft they throw more leaflets than bombs, always referring to "Enver and his gang."[6]

Mustapha Kemal, statesman.

Egyptian Expeditionary Force Animal Numbers

An aspect seldom, if ever, stressed in military histories of the Middle Eastern theaters—Egypt, Palestine, and Syria, together with Mesopotamia—is the huge reliance upon beasts of burden. Brevet Colonel Badcock gives some interesting statistics—for instance, the 21st Corps had 13,206 camels, and 1,984 donkeys; the 54th (East Anglian) Division alone had 1,166 camels and an unspecified number of donkeys.[7]

Megiddo — The Annihilation of the Turkish Armies

"On September 19, 1918, began an operation which was both one of the speedily decisive campaigns and the most completely victorious battles in all history. Within a few days the Turkish armies in Palestine had practically ceased to exist,"[8] wrote Hart in *The Real War*.

Halsey's history states, "Armageddon overlooked the great plain of

Esdraelon, southwest of Nazareth. It was one of the most famous battlefields of the world. It was there that Barak defeated the Canaanites, and Gideon the Midianites; there Saul was slain by the Philistines, and there Napoleon, in 1799, defeated the Turks."[9] Over the centuries what Flanders had been to Prussians, French and British, Palestine was to the great kingdoms of the Nile, Euphrates, and Tigris. The paramount confrontation in battle usually occurred at Gaza when Egypt was threatened, or some one hundred miles to the north when the situation was reversed.

> Between the heights of Gilboa and Tabor, near the shores of Galilee and Mount Carmel, lies the Plain of Esdraelon (or Jezreel, or Armageddon), which is the Ramillies, the Fleurus, the Waterloo, the Po Quadrilateral, the Sedan, of the ancient world. Esdraelon had witnessed the victories of Thotmes over Hittites, of Gideon over Midianites, of Philistines over Saul and his sons, of a second Pharaoh over Josiah, King of Judah, and of Napoleon's Marshal Kléber, over the Turks.[10]

Blackwell and Axe help set the stage: "On September 18 the preliminary concentration was complete. The divisions detailed for the main attack, 60th, 7th, 75th, 54th and the French contingent, had actually taken up their positions, the troops previously holding the coastal sector having closed up on to their own fronts of attack to make room for them."[11]

Gilbert describes the beginning of the operation, which was an elaborate plan to camouflage actual troop movements with false information to deceive the Turkish forces. "We put up dummy tents, horse lines and ration dumps. We even made dummy horses from brown army blankets and bivouac poles.

The Valley of Jezreel has seen its share of conquerors down the ages (MacMunn and Falls, *Official History of the War: Military Operations: Egypt and Palestine. Vol. II [Part1]*).

We left behind convalescent soldiers and men unable to march, with orders to light camp fires and now and then fire off salvos from the Turkish guns we had captured in the earlier part of the campaign. For some days before the exodus we marched small bodies of men towards Jericho, trailing boughs of trees and thus raising clouds of dust. Empty lorries [trucks] constantly ran between Jerusalem and Jericho." The success of this deception was borne out by later captured documents that described concentrations of British troops in the Valley of the Jordan, along with reports of reinforcements. In reality, British troops were moving in the opposite direction.

By September 18 the troops were in position. The 60th Division's orders were to make a gap in the line for the cavalry. The 21st Corps was borrowed to aid this task. Gilbert reports that the newest models of airplanes had arrived from England and that road makers and railway workers were very busy preparing for the attack. "A constant stream of supply wagons and lorries ran all night piling up huge stores of shells and small arms ammunition behind the front. Special officers were stationed at all crossroads, and we worked strictly to time; the clock was our taskmaster. The traffic scheme was splendidly worked out and never a hitch occurred. During this time our water supply was developed to an almost unbelievable extent. Wells were dug wherever there was any sign of a yield; along the beach alone forty-five were sunk, each of them giving forth about three thousand gallons a day. We laid a pipe line near Jelil which supplied us with 20,000 gallons of water hourly. Certainly one of the richest legacies we left to Palestine was the improved water supply."[12]

The orders issued for the operation were clear and definite. The 21st Corps had to break through the enemy's defenses between the railway lines and the Mediterranean, to open a way through for the cavalry — simultaneously seizing the foothills southeast of Jiljulieh. The corps was then to pivot right, on the line Hableh-Tul Keram, then advance in a northeasterly direction through the hills, converging on Samaria and Attara, in order to drive the enemy up the Messudie-Jenin road into the arms of the cavalry at El Afule.

"At 4.30 A.M., September 19th, there began an intense bombardment of the Turkish positions by three hundred of our guns, and lasting fifteen minutes," Gilbert wrote. "The sound of the first gun was our signal to advance; and our men dashed forward at such a rate, that by 4.40 A.M. part of the enemy's line was already in our hands."[13]

Allenby's Plan of Attack

Before the operations began the XXth Corps was to take over the extreme right of the XXIst Corps' line from Berukin to Rafat, reducing the front of the XXIst Corps from 25 and a quarter miles to 21 and a quarter miles. The formations taking part in the attack and the frontages allotted to them were: French detachment (Colonel P. de Piépape), 5,900 yards; 54th Division (Maj. Gen. S. W. Hare), 9,500 yards; and 3rd (Lahore) Division (Maj. Gen. A. R. Hoskins), 11,300 yards.[14]

Massey further stated, "The big differences in the frontages allotted to the divisions were due to the fact that the fronts of the 54th and 3rd Divisions included the wide gap between Mejdel Yaba and Ferekiyeh which was only watched by the two divisions."[15]

The strategy never proposed assaulting along every yard of the Turkish line, but rather against various important tactical points of the enemy's defenses, and thus the plan enabled the attacking units to avoid an advance over bare, open ground which could be swept by artillery, machine-gun, and rifle fire by either flank.

The Battles of Megiddo/Armageddon, 19 September 1918

The Battle of Armageddon[16] actually took place — though not quite in the same way as the Biblical prophecy. Whatever one's theological feelings, the outcome of this event proved to be almost as profound.

Before going into detail regarding the defeat of the Canaanites, it is important to stress once more Canaanite supremacy in a regular set battle, because of their chariots and their regular infantry (chariots and multitude) [Judges, 4: 3], which consisted at least partly of heavily armed pikemen. The number of Sisera's chariots is given as 900. This number can be verified by comparing it with the number of Canaanite chariots quoted by Pharaoh Thutmose III as making up the armored forces of his northern Canaanite foes during the battle of Megiddo in 1468 B.C. Both numbers actually tally, since 924 chariots were the booty from the Megiddo battle, when the Canaanite coalition was somewhat larger and more prosperous.[17] What has been completely overlooked by historians and other commentators is that the 1918 Battle of Armageddon's composition faithfully followed the biblical prediction regarding its multi-national makeup.

"And when the thousand years are expired, Satan shall be loosed from his prison, And shall go out to deceive all nations which are in the four quarters of the earth, Gog and Magog, to gather them together to battle: the number of whom *is* as the sand of the sea" (*Revelation*, 20:8). Ezekiel the Prophet says: "And I will turn thee back, and put hooks into thy jaws, and I will bring thee forth, and all thine army, horses and horsemen, all of them clothed with all sorts of armour, even a great company with bucklers and shields, all of them handling swords" (Verse 4). "Persia, Ethiopia, and Libya with them; all of them with shield and helmet" (5). "Gomer, and all his bands; the house of Togarmah

Six. The Final Stroke

MAP O1
BATTLE OF ARMAGEDDON
Situation at 12 Midnight
19th-20th September, 1918

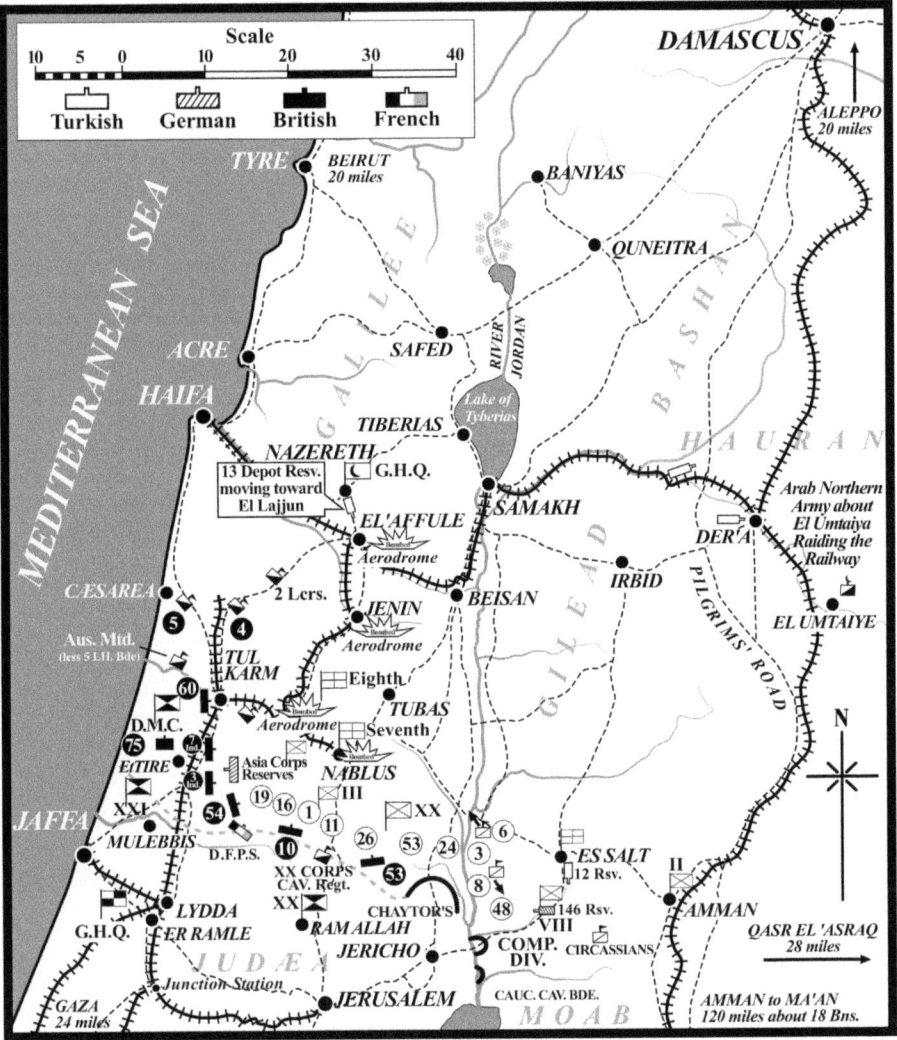

of the north quarters, and all his bands: and many people with thee" (6). "Thou shalt ascend and come like a storm, thou shalt be like a cloud to cover the land, thou, and all thy bands, and many people with thee" (Ezekiel, 4–6: 9).

Sir Edmund Allenby's strategy was to first break the enemy's trench system in the plain and then to move right and secure positions covering the Tul-

Karm-Nablus road from the north. This would open the way for the cavalry and screen the right flank during the first stage of its advance.

The Battle in the Foothills

Lt. Colonel Thomas Gibbons gives a very precise account of how he saw things (with some editing and paraphrasing):

> On September 14th the 1/5th Essex moved across to the hills again and bivouacked in a valley near Mezeireh, the next four days being occupied in studying the details of the attack, in bayonet fighting, and in practising the attack over rock country identical to the country on the front to be assaulted.
>
> I do not propose to go into details of the grand plan of operations. They are stated with wonderful clarity in the official despatch. But the root idea was as follows: — The enemy's line was to be attacked on a line running from the sea, along the whole width of the Plain of Sharon and for some distance into the foothills. The objective was to create a gap for the cavalry to break through on the plain and make straight for El Afule on the plain of Esdraelon, and Beisan — two important points on the enemy's lines of communication, forty-five and sixty miles distant, respectively, before the enemy could make his escape. Once the foothills north of Kefr Kasim were taken the XXI Corps was to swing to the right and advance in a north-easterly direction through the hills, so as to drive the enemy into the arms of the cavalry. At 4.30 A.M., September 19th, there began an intense bombardment of the Turkish positions by three hundred of our guns, and lasting fifteen minutes.
>
> The sound of the first gun was our signal to advance; and our men dashed forward at such a rate, that by 4.40 A.M. part of the enemy's line was already in our hands.[18]
>
> It will thus be seen that rapidity was the keynote of all the operations. Once the attack commenced the enemy [was] to be given no time to organize a retreat or to get away his guns. The frontage of the attack for the 161st Brigade was from the edge of the plain to Oglu Tepe. This line secured, the brigade was to advance to the hills to the north of the Wadi Kana, and another division was to carry on the pursuit. On our right was the 163rd Brigade and a detachment of French troops. On our left was the Lahore Division. The 162nd Brigade was in 54th Divisional reserve. It should be mentioned that owing to the great changes made in our order of battle by the despatch of British troops to France, the 54th Division was now the only complete white division on this front. All the others were Indian, with a sprinkling of British units forming part of their composition.
>
> The attack of the 161st Brigade was divided into six phases. The first was to take us over the Bureid Ridge to the line of the Wadi Rabah. The second to the crest of the hills to the north of it. The third to Jevis Tepe, to the west of Kefr Kasim, the village itself, and the cactus gardens to the east of it, called by us Kasim Wood. The fourth to Semer Tepe, north-west of Kefr Kasim, Sivri Tepe, a commanding position strongly fortified about a mile north of the village, and Sivri Wood, to the north-west of it on lower ground. The fifth to Jackal Tepe still further north, Kefr Barah, and Oglu Tepe. The sixth a further advance on the left, pivoted on the Oglu Tepe.
>
> The first three phases were entrusted to the 1/4th and 1/5th Essex, the last three to the 1/6th and 1/7th Essex. It was thus once more the good fortune of the 1/5th Essex to be in the leading line. In the advance over the plain at Suvla [Gallipoli] we were accompanied by the 1/7th. At the first battle of Gaza we were side by side with

the 1/4th. At the third battle of Gaza the 1/6th were up with us. And now the 1/4th and ourselves were once more to be shoulder to shoulder to kick off for the Essex Brigade.

On September 18th we were told the secret of "zero" day. It was to be on the morrow—the 19th. The divisional commander saw all officers in the afternoon. General Hare was not given to much talking. In a few words he impressed upon us the importance of our task, and the necessity of rapidity in the advance, in order that the high ground to the north of the Wadi Kanah might be captured as soon as possible to support the advance of the 3rd (Lahore) Division on our left, and to roll up the Turkish flank and secure the advance of the 10th Division through the difficult hill country on our right. We could all see that the general was quietly confident, and as he shook hands and wished us luck we felt his confidence was infectious.

All the details of the scheme — infantry, artillery, machine guns, trench mortars, communications, &c., were issued from Brigade Headquarters in a series of "Instructions" over the signature of Paris, the brigade major, and no instructions could have been clearer or more complete. Not only were they a model of lucidity and form, but the way they worked in practice showed a complete grasp of the needs of every possible situation. Although arranged in "phases" after the manner of trench warfare, the scheme was sufficiently elastic to allow of the best means being taken, by units already launched to the attack, to carry out the intentions of the commander, whatever emergencies should arise. In one important matter they differed from the ordinary trench to trench scheme of attack. After the initial phases the infantry were no longer tied to an artillery barrage, and the supporting artillery worked by the infantry and not vice versa.

The zero hour was fixed to coincide with the first peep of dawn. This made it possible after the first enemy resistance was broken to "see what he was up to" and act accordingly.[19]

The Battle of Sharon: First Phase

Disquieted by the advance of the 53rd Division east of the Damascus road, the enemy showed signs of rather more than his usual alertness that night. An increase in the number of rocket lights sent up all along his line bore witness to his nervousness. On the fronts of the 7th and 60th Divisions there were patrol encounters, which, however, caused no interference with the deployment; on that of the 75th Division there were long and heavy bursts of machine-gun fire. But only against the 54th Division was the Turkish artillery more than normally active. Here its scanty barrage was dropped on several occasions upon the British trenches and No Man's Land, the last being but a few minutes before Zero hour. At 4:30 A.M. there burst forth the terrific roar of the British bombardment, over a thousand shells a minute being thrown into the enemy's lines. The Turkish artillery replied promptly, but the intensity and accuracy of the British counter-battery fire caused its shelling to be ragged and intermittent. On the front of the 54th Division the enemy's barrage, which had already been put down and had hitherto been level, at once became wild. In many cases batteries soon ceased fire altogether, either because the guns had been destroyed or the detachments had been driven from them. The careful counter-battery study which had preceded the battle was now indeed repaid, and the British heavy artillery by its neutralizing fire gave full value for its superiority. Within a few minutes of the first discharge, while yet the earliest light of dawn had not pierced the pall of smoke and dust which overhung the lines, the assaulting infantry swarmed into the enemy's trenches.[20]

The Battle of Sharon: 19 September 1918

"The preliminary operation, carried out on the night of September 17-18, was designed [partly to] serve to distract the enemy's attention from the main attack in the plain. It was successful, after some hard fighting at some points,"[21] writes Wavell.

Not long after the noise of battle had died down in the hills the assault of the Twenty-first Corps opened with a great roar of artillery at 4.30 A.M. on the morning of September 19. The infantry began their advance at the same moment. Allenby did not believe in long preliminary bombardment — he put more trust in surprise; the Turkish wire, which was not strong, could be cut by hand, and it was important to give the enemy no time to think.

Simultaneously with the opening of the battle the Air Force set forth to bomb the principal Turkish headquarters. It was successful in completely interrupting all communications between the Eighth Army headquarters at Tulkeram and Liman von Sanders at Nazareth, besides greatly delaying communications with the Seventh Army. Fighting airplanes also patrolled over the principal enemy aerodromes and prevented their reconnaissance machines from leaving the ground. Thus the enemy commander-in-chief remained in almost complete ignorance of the grave events taking place on his front. The arrival next morning of a British cavalry brigade at his headquarters at Nazareth was his earliest intimation that something really serious must have happened to his army.[22]

The 54th Division had on its right the French battalions, which were now in the field on this front, in the centre the 163rd brigade, on the left the 162nd. The route of the 163rd was to be the Wadi Orwell and Ikba, so as to allow the French to use the Deben Wadi. On the left of 54th was the Lahore division. At 2 A.M. on the 19th the 1/5th Norfolk, who on this occasion were to head the attack (less "C" company) were ready, and the garrisons of the front trenches were withdrawn to allow the assaulting battalions to pass in front of the British wire, which they did in 3.45. The 163rd Brigade had two battalions (1/5th Norfolk and 8th Hants) in first line and the other two (1/4th Norfolk and 5th Suffolk) behind. At fifteen minutes after zero "C" company, which had been sent to support the 8th Hants, followed that battalion and received the benefit of the enemy barrage, which passed over it. It cost them a dozen casualties, of which half were due to a single shell. 2nd Lieutenant Wood received wounds from which he died the next day. Captain and Adjutant Walker was wounded as the battalion head-quarters moved to a better position. So far Turkish resistance, other than artillery fire, had not been strong. Presently a pause occurred, enabling the men to breakfast and the machine-gun detachment to come up.

The action of the Twenty-first Corps was exactly that of men pushing open a wide and heavy door of which the hinges were in the foothills and the handle by the coast.

Rightly, the greatest leverage was exerted at the handle end; here was the thickest concentration of troops and guns, and here were the leading cavalry divisions, ready to pass through the moment the door was even ajar.²³

The Main Operation Carried Out by the XXIst Corps

The intention of Major General S. W. Hare was to advance northward with the Détachement Français de Palestine et Syrie (D.F.P.S.) on the right, the 163rd Brigade (Norfolks, Suffolk, and Hants) in the center, and 161st Brigade (all Essex) on the left, pivoting on the Ra-fat salient, to a line from its apex through Crown Hill, northeast of Kufr Qasim. When this objective was reached (or sooner if the situation permitted) the 162nd Brigade (Bedford, Northants, two Londons) was to pass through the right of the 161st, move eastward on Bidya, and secure the crossings of the Wadi Qana south of Kh. Kefar Thilth. The D.F.P.S. (Colonel P. de Piépape) assaulted simultaneously the col west of Ra-fat from the southeast with one battalion of the Légion d'Orient, and Three Bushes and Scurry Hills with two battalions of the Régiment de Tirailleurs. The Légion d'Orient had taken its objective by 5 A.M.

The more difficult attack of the Tirailleurs was carried out with great dash and skill, Three Bushes Hill being stormed in face of considerable resistance by 5:10 and Scurry Hill by 5:45. Kh. Deir el Qassis, east of Scurry Hill, was soon afterwards occupied, but had to be abandoned owing to heavy shelling by guns beyond the reach of the French artillery. However, the detachment, having established itself on the western edge of the ridge, had accomplished virtually all that was required of it, and had captured 212 prisoners at light cost. During the night of the 19th it occupied Arara, northeast of Ra-fat.

The first phase of the attack of the 163rd Brigade (Brig. General A. J. M'Neill) was to be carried out by the 5/Suffolk on the right against a spur north of the Wadi el Ayun, which dominated the plain and was known to be used as an observation post for three batteries, and by the 8/Hampshire on the left against Kh. Ed Duweir and the high ground southeast of Kufr Qasim. The 5/Norfolk was subsequently to advance on the right of the 5/Suffolk and swing eastward against the village of Mesha, and the 4/Norfolk on the left was to be directed against the high ground west of Bidya.

The approach began at 4:20 A.M. So good was the timing that the British barrage began to move forward precisely as the infantry reached the Turkish trenches, but the first objectives were so speedily taken that companies had to pause to await the next lift. The whole of the first phase was carried through without difficulty, the only critical incident being the sudden counter-attack of a fresh Turkish company against the right flank of the 5/Suffolk north of the Wadi el Ayun. At this moment, however, a platoon of the 7th Tirailleurs appeared on Scurry Hill and opened up a devastating fire on the enemy, the survivors at once putting up their hands. A long delay now ensued owing to the 161st Brigade being checked in its advance upon the works north of Kufr Qasim, during which Brig. General M'Neill [163rd Brigade] was ordered by Major General Hare to assist an attack upon them from the southeast by clearing the enemy from the high ground at Kh. Sirisia.

A detachment of the 5/Norfolk was thus engaged when at 2 P.M. the brigadier learned that the whole works north of Kufr Qasim had fallen. He then ordered the 5/Norfolk to break off its engagement and move on Mesha, and the 4/Norfolk to advance on Bidya, driving the enemy off Kh. Sirisia on its way. Neither battalion met with any serious or prolonged resistance, but they were continually opposed by small parties and their progress after the fall of darkness was naturally very slow. By 3 A.M. on the following day the 5/Norfolk had occupied Mesha, while patrols of the 4/Norfolk, which was on high ground west of Bidya, had entered the village.

The 161st Brigade (Brig. General H.B.H. Orpen Palmer) was first to capture Kufr Qasim, the advance northward being carried out by the 5/Essex on the right. The killed numbered 14 only, but included two officers—Fenn, who had only recently joined, and who fell in the attack on the second objective, and Eames, who was killed by a shell in Kasim Wood. He had seen service in the ranks in France, and had a genuine taste for fighting. There were about 45 wounded. Portway, commanding "B" Company, was among the wounded, only stopping after being hit for the second time.

Lt. Colonel Gibbons and his men

> enjoyed our picnic meal on Sivri Tepe, tired but happy. We had a good view of the attack of the Lahore Division on Jijulia and Kalkilieh from the west. The frontal attack over the flat plain, so well known to our patrols, had been avoided, and they were taking most of the works in the flank, but the enemy put up a stubborn resistance. Everybody's knees were in a shocking state from the sharp rocks and prickly grasses, and I regret to say that many cardigans were minus their sleeves, which were used as knee protectors.[24]

For the advance northward the 4/Essex was on the left. The 7th and 6th Essex were then to move through against the works running south and west of Kefar Bara. The leading battalions quickly crossed the Bureid Ridge, taking 69 prisoners, reached the Wadi Raba, where there was a quarter of an hour's pause, and stormed the high ground south of Kufr Qasim, killing or capturing all the garrison. There was now another pause of fifteen minutes to allow battalions to reorganize and the 161st Machine Gun Company to take up positions from which it could cover the next advance by overhead fire.

By 7 A.M. Kufr Qasim and Jevis Tepe to the west of it were taken with little opposition. The 7th and 6th Essex then moved up to attack the next line of trenches, their right on Sivri Wood west of Crown Hill. Now for the first time there was obstinate resistance, especially on the left, but after re-bombardment by the divisional artillery the whole position was occupied. It could, indeed, have been taken earlier, but for an error committed by the headquarters of the 6/Essex, the commanding officer's messages asking for the artillery to lift not being sent off.

The 162nd Brigade (Brig. General A. Mudge), less the 11/London detailed as escort to the divisional artillery and to cover the gap between the division's left and the right of the 3rd at Ras el Ain, concentrated at 8 A.M. southwest of Kufr Qasim, suffering severely from long-range shelling. One battery of the IX Mountain Artillery Brigade had been pushed forward to the eastern end of Bureid Ridge to support its advance eastward. On hearing that Kufr Qasim was captured, Brig. General Mudge ordered the 4/Northampton and 10/London to move up north of it and face east, and at 9:30 directed them to begin their advance. A few minutes later he received a telephone message from divisional headquarters that the 161st Brigade was in difficulties at Sivri Wood and the works to the northwest. He had just ordered his leading battalions to advance between Sivri Wood and Crown Hill, clearing the wood en route, when he learned that the two Essex battalions had been ordered to renew their attack from the southwest, covered by a bombardment. It thus appeared that his own battalions and those of the 161st Brigade were about to assault the same objective by routes crossing at almost right angles and that the former would run into the latter's barrage. He therefore ordered the 4/Northampton and 10/London to stand fast, but his message was not received till after they had carried out the movement.

Fortunately their advance began before the 161st Brigade's attack was launched, and actually passed through its right. The 5/Bedford, having followed the 4/Northampton through Sivri Wood, came up on its left, and after a pause for reorganization the three battalions advanced steadily eastward. On reaching the south bank of the Wadi Qana, the troops of the 10/London saw below three howitzers of two different batteries, one team being already hooked in and having reached the road. Machine-gun fire killed several of the oxen and drove away the troops about the guns with considerable loss. In face of this fire one heroic man ran back to the battery position, stooped for a moment, and then dashed away. Soon afterwards there was a terrific explosion of the ammunition dump. The Northampton, after capturing Azzun Ibn Atme, reached Kh. Es Sumra during the small hours of the morning.

The 54th Division and the D.F.P.S. had thus successfully accomplished their task, having completely broken through the enemy's defenses on the right, and formed the pivot for the whole offensive movement on the left. About 700 prisoners, 9 guns, and 20 machine-guns had been captured at a cost of 535 casualties. Owing to the nature of the country, the troops under Major General Hare's command had had about the most difficult task of all in the early stages of the attack, but the resistance of the enemy had never been really stout.[25]

The same source records the exploits of the 93rd Battalion, the Burma Infantry — hitherto unmentioned: "The 93rd Burma Infantry reached the road two miles north-east of El Funduq at 3.10 P.M. and captured about 250 prisoners, a large proportion of them Germans."[26]

The training of men of the XXIst Corps during the summer consisted of instruction in the use of captured weapons. This proved very useful in the 54th Division when men of the 1/8th Hants (Hampshire), by skilful employment of captured machine-guns, so increased the volume of fire that they materially assisted in the advance of their battalion. Kefr Kassim's capture in the initial stages of the battle was effected at light cost by the bold handling of Lewis guns which were pushed forward to deal with enemy machine-guns. The 1/10th Londons of the 54th Division reached the high ground overlooking the Wadi Kanah as two 5.9 and one 4.2 howitzers were being limbered up. A section of the 162nd Machine Gun Company immediately came into action at 1500 yards and with their first burst shot down the gun teams. Under cover of this machine-gun fire and of Lewis-gun fire, the leading company of the battalion then charged and captured the three guns (howitzers) with their detachments.[27]

The 4th Cavalry Division was over the Iskanderunieh shortly after six and here they rested awhile. At 10 P.M. they were in the neighborhood of Hudeira, with patrols as far as the Musmus Pass, where the leading brigade had to beat down some opposition. The situation there was soon cleared up and a hundred prisoners were taken, and the whole division had moved up the defile by daybreak.

On descending the steep, narrow road from the hills on to the flat, an Indian cavalry regiment made a brilliant charge on the Plain of Armageddon.

The Musmus Pass has been a historic thoroughfare since Old Testament times (MacMunn and Falls, *Official History of the War: Military Operations: Egypt and Palestine. 2 Vol., Vol. II [Part1]*).

The 2nd Lancers, the leading regiment of the 10th Cavalry Brigade, came out of the pass at half-past five, just when it was sufficiently light to see across the patches of cultivation watered by a small stream. The advanced guard and the 11th Light Armoured Motor Battery reported that a battalion of infantry was in front of the road and appeared to be advancing to reach the slopes about Lejjun, apparently in ignorance that the cavalry was already in Nazareth, miles away to their rear.

As a matter of fact, the battalion had marched from Afuleh to hold the Musmus Pass. The infantry might have caused a good deal of trouble if they had got to the hills first, but they were too late. "Two squadrons of the 2nd Lancers immediately deployed, and with their shrill voices ringing over the plain they charged full weight into the infantry, killing forty-six with the lance, and accepting the surrender of the whole of the remainder, 470 in all, with their machine guns, automatic rifles, and rifles. Armageddon will take a proud place in the records of the regiment,"[28] Massey wrote.

Moir adds, "The 5th Battalion of the Suffolk Regiment moved into the attack at Megiddo on the 19th of September. The Battalion was on the extreme right."[29]

Capture of Observation Hill

The divisional commander, Major-General S. W. Hare, later commended the 1/5th Suffolk for storming Observation Hill.

Headquarters 54th Division.
My Dear Campbell,
    As your battalion has gone to the force in Egypt for good, I am writing to thank you and them for all they have done.
    I have known them now for three years, and they have always done well, and never better than last 19th September. The dash with which they took Observation Hill set the pace for the whole attack. I am very sorry to part with them, and wish them all the best of luck and safe home.
    Yours very sincerely,
    S. W. Hare, Major General. Commanding 54th Division.[30]

On the right of the attack — on which the movement was to pivot — was the 54th Division, with three or four battalions of Algerians and Armenians attached. The right of the divisional frontage was allotted to these battalions, the 163rd Brigade being on their left. The 5th Battalion (Suffolk Regiment) was on the right of the brigade attack, its objective — Observation Hill — being intended to form the pivot for the further movement eastward, which was to begin the same day.

At half-past four in the morning of the 19th, when objects could be distinguished about two hundred yards ahead, the bombardment opened. At the

Observation Hill, as its name suggests, is a commanding feature (Fair and Wolton, *The History of the 1/5th Battalion: "The Suffolk Regiment"*).

end of a quarter of an hour the attack was launched and broke through the Turkish defenses on the coast almost without a pause. As regards the 5th Battalion, the Suffolk Regiment, its line of advance lay across steep foothills, which rose three or four hundred feet above the dry ravines intersecting them. Barbed wire had been located in front of Khurbet Kesfa, and immediately when the barrage had lifted from the first objective, two platoons, under Lieuts. G. G. Oliver and D. Green, rushed these points. Having crossed the rock-strewn ridge, the two leading companies plunged into the Wadi-el-Ayun, and while they were clambering up the rocks on the further side an effective bombardment fell upon Observation Hill, which formed the second objective. Pausing under the crest-line until the barrage had lifted, they gained the summit exactly on schedule.

Numbers of the enemy were holding on to a knoll to the left which had not been attacked, whereupon Lieut. G. Hughes, gathering together a few men and directing them towards it, captured the post, with ten prisoners and a machine-gun. Once on the summit of Observation Hill, the men encountered stiff opposition, owing to the arrival of enemy reinforcements. While Captain Fox was engaging the enemy in front and on both flanks, a platoon of Tirailleurs, under Lieut. Morisson, came up on the right flank and cooperated with great effect, shooting the enemy down as they fled from the caves in the precipice on the northeast side of the hill.

Shortly after five o'clock Captain G. Kilner with his company moved across

Six. The Final Stroke

Turkish prisoners on Observation Hill (Fair and Wolton, *The History of the 1/5th Battalion: "The Suffolk Regiment"*).

the Wadi-el-Ayun to support the attack. The whole operation was an unqualified success. The 1/5th Suffolk alone captured over a hundred prisoners, including five officers, with three machine-guns and much war material, and buried a number of Turks and Germans. Killed were Lieut. N. A. Mackinnon; 2nd Lieut. P. T. Clarke, and five other ranks. Wounded included 2nd Lieut. W. Emerson and twenty-four other ranks. The following awards were made Major F. M. Campbell, Distinguished Service Order (DSO); Captain and Adjutant A. Fair, Military Cross (MC); and 2nd Lieut. G. Hughes, Distinguished Conduct Medal (DCM).

The 1/5th Suffolk remained in the positions it had captured until late in the afternoon, when it was withdrawn to the Wadi-el-Ayun. Here it anxiously awaited the arrival of much-needed water. The following day was spent on salvage work, and on the 22nd the battalion moved out onto the plain near Kefr Kasim, acting as reserve to the guard over the thousands of Turkish and German prisoners who had been collected in the ruins of the old Crusader fortress of Ras-el-Ain.

"The brigadier thanked the battalion for their work, and said that when he saw them running like hares for the top of Observation Hill he did not wait to see them arrive, but wired at once: 'Observation Hill taken.'"[31]

General Sir Edmund Allenby's own estimate of the comparative fighting strengths of the Allied and enemy forces when he launched his offensive was:

British — 12,000 sabres, 57,000 rifles and 540 guns; Turkish — 3,000 sabres, 26,000 rifles and 370 guns.

Other estimates give larger or smaller figures for the Turkish strength. In any case there was a clear preponderance on the British side, which Allenby skillfully increased still further on his actual front of attack by carefully camouflaged massing of his troops there, combined with a pretense of assembling troops for assault on another sector.

Allenby's Great Victory

British Prime Minister David Lloyd George admirably summed up Allenby's huge success:

> On September 19th, Allenby launched his great attack, planned with real military skill. His aim was not just to beat back, but to encircle and wipe out the Turkish forces in Palestine. The Battle of Megiddo was a brilliant operation, of a kind supremely satisfactory to a military commander. The available weight was so crushingly applied at successive key points, and the blows so swiftly and adroitly followed up, that with minimum losses on our side the whole of the Turkish forces opposed to us were killed, captured or dispersed.... Of all the Turkish forces in Palestine, with a ration strength of about 100,000, only a broken rabble of about 17,000 escaped [Allenby's] net and fled northwards. His tale of prisoners amounted to 75,000, while the total battle casualties of his forces were only 5,666.[32]

By the end of the summer, Arab and British forces were working in tandem, with the Arabs harassing Ottoman lines of communication and the British bringing air and artillery assets to bear. At the Battle of Megiddo in September, the British annihilated the Turkish Eighth Army, opening the roads to Nazareth, Haifa, Acre, and Damascus. In the war's final weeks, the Ottomans lost Beirut, Aleppo, and Mosul as well.[33]

Liman von Sanders' Critical Commentary

The German commander-in-chief of the Turco–German forces, Marshal Otto Liman von Sanders, wrote:

> The six German battalions with the Army Group, three of the Asia Corps and three of the 146th Infantry Regiment, had received no replacements since the spring of 1918, owing to the urgent need of men on the German west front. Battle losses and sickness had reduced their numbers considerably.
> The German aviators on the Palestine front had a very hard time against the British during the summer. The German machines were greatly inferior to the modern British types in speed and climbing ability. In two shipments of replacement machines almost all were found useless. Further replacements could not be furnished on account of their urgent need on the German west front. From spring to fall this

excellent body of fliers had lost fifty-nine pilots and observers. Air reconnaissance against the enemy ceased almost completely in September. As soon as a German machine appeared, it was attacked by such superior air forces that reconnaissance became impossible.

Colonel von Oppen, chief of the left group of the Eighth Army, asked me in Azzum on September 3rd to stop air reconnaissance on his front, as the sight of the now invariably luckless air fighting was calculated to further reduce the low morale of his troops. On September 19th the chief of the flying corps reported but five machines of the Army Group fit for use against the enemy.

At that time it was the intention of the headquarters of the Eighth Army, in case of attack in the coast sector, to send the 16th Division there which had but two infantry regiments. The division was holding a front of seven kilometers and was to be replaced by the Asia Corps. Colonel von Oppen declared it quite impossible to defend this part of the line with his small force and, moreover, it was to be expected that the division would arrive much too late. Even if placed in readiness at Serta before the beginning of the attack, the division had to make a march of sixteen kilometers to the edge of the coast sector at Kal Kilyas. Reserves from neighboring sectors, when called on for help, could be obtained only by still further weakening the overextended divisional fronts, and by leaving their defenses largely to machine guns. This method had heretofore been used with good results. It was the only method practicable for establishing supports.

At the beginning of September, I pondered the idea of a voluntary retirement to a position with the right abreast the Lake of Tiberias, center and left in the Yarmuk valley. Aside from Enver's instructions to hold Palestine, I gave up the idea, because we would have had to relinquish the Hedjas railroad and the East Jordan section, and because we no longer could have stopped the progress of the Arab insurrection in rear of our army. On account of the limited marching capacity of the Turkish soldiers and of the very low mobility of all draft animals, I considered that the holding of our positions to the last gave us more favorable prospects than a long retreat with Turkish troops with impaired morale. The lack of sufficient troops to establish rearward positions of support was fraught with danger for the retreat; it also was the cause of the collapse of the front. In my reckoning I made the mistake that while considering a possible step by step retreat of units, I had not calculated upon the collapse of whole divisions. During the entire campaign I had observed such failure of Turkish troops under my command but once, in the attack on July 14th, but never in defense.

On September 17th a deserter, a sergeant of an Indian company, came to the right group in the coast sector and stated that a heavy attack on that part was in contemplation for September 19th, which he wanted to escape. On the same day reports came that hostile Arabs were menacing the railroad north and south of Deraa, and that the line had been blown up in several places. I realized at once that these attacks on our only line of communications were the beginning of serious fighting.[34]

The British Attack on September 19

Liman continues his account:

On the night of September 18/19 the heavy battle opened on the front of the Seventh Army. At 3.30 in the morning of September 19th began a tremendous drum fire against the whole front of the right wing of the Eighth Army from the coast to the mountains. Shortly after daybreak squadrons of British fliers appeared over the houses of headquarters of the *Seventh* and Eighth Armies, over the tent camps of the various corps headquarters, and over the central telephone office of the Army Group in Affuleh; flying low they threw bombs on them and destroyed part of our wires. In the entire section between the coast and Jordan we had but the two anti-aircraft guns of the Eighth Army, so that the task of the enemy fliers was an easy one. Telephonic and telegraphic communication between Tul Keram and Nazareth ceased about 7 A.M. The wireless station of headquarters of the Eighth Army also ceased to respond when called. Between 9 and 10 A.M. headquarters of the Seventh Army wired from Nablus that Colonel von Oppen had reported that the front of the right flank group in the coast sector had been broken through, and that strong cavalry forces were advancing northward along the coast. I at once sent orders to Colonel von Oppen, through headquarters of the Seventh Army, to advance toward the railroad and road at Kal Kiliyas, toward the coast sector. Colonel von Oppen had anticipated the order and reported that he had put three battalions and two squadrons in a march toward Kal Kiliyas and Felamie.

We did not learn until later that the British had broken through in the western part of the coast sector before 7 A.M. without meeting with resistance. At that time they also occupied the height west of Et Tire and armed it with numerous machine guns. At Et Tire the weak 46th Division under Major Willmer [of Suvla fame] made an effective resistance and checked the hostile advance for a time. The greater part of the division was soon destroyed. Its only German regimental commander, Major Pfeiffer, here died a hero's death.

Up to this day [1927] no exhaustive account has appeared of the complete and sudden collapse of the 7th Division in the western part of the coast sector, and of the adjoining two regiments of the 20th Division. Though the force was very small for such a large sector, it had stood up well in prior battles. After two hours of drum fire they had completely disappeared on September 19th, before a hostile infantry attack had been launched. Nor did I ever during the retreat see officers or small parts of this division. After the transmission of the above orders to Colonel von Oppen the telegraph and telephone communications between Army Group headquarters and Nablus were interrupted for two hours, so that the scope of the above events could not be discerned there. It was assumed that the 7th, 20th and 46th Divisions were falling back to the prepared positions in rear.[35]

Allenby's Strategy

Planned with real military skill, Allenby's aim was not merely to beat backwards but to encircle and annihilate the enemy forces in Palestine. The Battle of Megiddo was a brilliant operation, of a kind supremely satisfactory to an army commander. It rated alongside the great military triumphs down through the ages: Agincourt, Arcola, Assaye, Austerlitz, Badajoz, Bannockburn, Blenheim, Bull Run, Cannae, Colenso, Crécy, Dettingen, Eylau, Fontenoy, Fredericksburg, Gettysburg, Friedland, Hastings, Heights of Abraham, Isandlwana, Jellalabad, Khartoum, Little Big Horn, Majuba Hill, Malplaqet, Manassas, Marathon, Minden, Naseby, Omdurman, Plassey, Poitiers, Poltava, Prestonpans, Quartre Bras, Rourke's Drift, Salamanca, Seringapatam, Stamford

Bridge, The Boyne, Talavera, Tours, Thermopylæ, Vimiero, Waterloo, and Yorktown.

The secretary of the War Council, Maurice Hankey, summed up the successful turn of events: "Allenby opened his attack in Palestine on September 19th, routed the Turks at Megiddo, and was in full pursuit with cavalry and aircraft, which, as in Macedonia, were wreaking frightful havoc. On the 23rd Haifa and Acre and Es Salt were occupied and on the 25th the Hejaz railway was cut by British cavalry at Amman. The plight of the Turkish Army was obviously desperate. Such was the position when I returned from leave on September 22nd."

On the same day he wrote in his diary, "September 23rd.... I think the Palestine victory is largely due to the action of the Committee of Prime Ministers last July in refusing to allow the transport of the 54th Division from Palestine to the Western Front. As [the chief of the Imperial General Staff, General Sir Henry Wilson] said to me this afternoon, the victories in Palestine and Salonika are most glaring examples of 'amateur strategy' — but he is very pleased all the same."[36]

General Allenby's Report

General Allenby gave the following official report on the fighting of 20 September at Armageddon:

Our left wing, having swung around to the east, had reached the line of Bidieh, Baka, and Messudiyeh Junction, and was astride the rail and roads converging at Nabulus.
Our right wing, advancing through difficult country against considerable resistance, had reached the line of Khan-Jibeit, one and one-fourth miles north-east of El-Mugheir and Es-Saweih, and was facing north astride the Jerusalem-Nabulus road.
On the north our cavalry, traversing the Field of Armageddon, had occupied Nazareth, Afule, and Beisan, and were collecting the disorganized masses of enemy troops and transport as they arrived from the south. All avenues of escape open to the enemy, except the fords across the Jordan between Beisan and Jisr-ed-Dameer were thus closed.
East of the Jordan Arab forces of the King of the Hedjaz had effected numerous demolitions on the railways radiating from Deraa, several important bridges, including one in the Yurmak Valley, having been destroyed. Very severe losses have been inflicted on the masses of Turkish troops retreating over the difficult roads by our air services.
A German airplane, later ascertained to have been carrying mail, landed in the midst of our troops in Afule. The pilot, who believed the place still to be in Turkish hands, destroyed the machine and its contents before he could be secured.[37]

A Virginian missionary, Dr. H. Squires, gave the following analysis:

It was up the Plain of Sharon, through the Pass of Megiddo and into the Plain of Esdraelon that the Philistines came and cut the kingdom of Saul in two. They defeated him on the rugged ridges of Mount Gilboa, where he and Prince Jonathan and his other sons made their last, brave fatal, but futile stand. This was the way Napoleon came and Allenby followed.

The Turks held the lofty hills from Hebron northward. Allenby slowly gathered the coastal plains under the British flag. The Turks supposed he would strike for Jerusalem. It would have been a long and bloody road, for a mountain country is always difficult to conquer and easy to defend. Allenby's strategy suggests to Americans the genius of Stonewall Jackson. While the Turks were consolidating their hold on the mountainous land Allenby pushed his cavalry through the Pass of Megiddo and poured his army upon the Plain of Esdraelon. It was a bold move, for had the Turks captured the pass of Megiddo, Allenby would have been isolated in a hostile land; but when the news came to Jerusalem that the English had fallen upon their flanks and threatened communications with Damascus and Constantinople, the Turks fled in dismay. An army half a million strong just melted away.[38]

Dr. Squires also heard the experiences of Moncera, the granddaughter of the first Evangelical Christian to live in Cana of Galilee. She told of the oppressive life experienced under Turkish rule after her father had been pressed into military service.

After their father's departure every squad that passed through Cana plundered the humble home of Moncera. Their neighbors escaped unwelcome visits by pointing the hungry soldiers to the home of the Protestant Christian. Time and again their little store of provision was swept bare. The cry of hunger from little lips that could not suffer in silence was forever in the toiling mother's ear and on her heart.

Through the dreadful year of 1917 the days grew ever darker. The pinch of poverty grew ever more acute, and starvation stalked boldly through all the war and famine-stricken countryside. The military authorities grew harsher and their exactions daily more burdensome. As the November days were drawing in the worst blow fell. A Turkish officer ordered the family to prepare for deportation. The girls would be taken to Constantinople, the mother and little boys would be sent to Syria. Finally came the announcement: "One week from today you depart."

Moncera told the story to her sympathetic guests in her little home. When she reached this episode her voice choked and tears streamed down her cheeks.

"It seemed as though our hearts would break. We cried by day, and prayed by night. I did not see how Jesus could forsake us! My grandfather trusted Him, and my father trusted Him, and now the burden was greater than we could bear. My sister and I asked God to deliver us from this shame and sorrow or else to strike us dead. How gladly would we have died!

"The week dragged its weary length of unutterable misery. It was, oh! So long in agony, and, oh! So short, when we thought of the dreadful deportation. The last night fell. Sister and I went to the housetop, for the days were still warm. We clasped our Testaments to our bosoms and we prayed as never before, and cried until we thought our hearts would break for very sorrow. We could not bear to think of tomorrow and the shame and agony to follow.

The night was clear and calm, not a cloud was in the sky, but we heard a peel of thunder that rolled ever so faintly over the hills toward Nazareth. And then another and another. We thought it must be a rising storm.

"As the weary hours passed the thunder grew ever louder and rolled longer. Sister cried: 'It's a battle in Esdraelon!' And she was right, for by midnight we could see the flash of fire reflected over the mountain summits. As the cannonade rolled nearer the flashes became continuous until the sky was aglow with frightful red like the world aflame. We did not, could not guess what it meant; but we watched, and hoped, wept and prayed.

"About 10 o'clock next morning the soldiers came to Cana as they had never come before. Some marched along the road from Nazareth, in perfect order; thousands upon thousands swarmed over the hills, every man running for his life. Some rode camels and asses and some drove dories and carts. No one noticed us now, though a few paused long enough to beg for food. And all that long day the roll of the guns came floating unceasingly over the hills. It was General Allenby! God heard our prayer; God saved us just in time! Again the tears rained down, tears of faith and gratitude that are precious in His sight."[39]

Megiddo (September–October 1918)

This was the engagement that ended Turkey's participation in the Great War. General Edmund Allenby's effective strategy in Palestine used battle-hardened soldiers, whose ranks included Armenians, Australians, Burmese, Egyptian, English, French, Indians, Irish, Nepalese, New Zealanders, Palestinians, Scottish, South Africans, Welsh, West Indians and Arab irregulars led by Lt. Colonel Thomas Edward Lawrence (Lawrence of Arabia).

Allenby deployed 57,000 infantry, 12,000 cavalry, and more than 500 guns against the Turks' 32,000 infantry, 200 cavalry, and 400 guns. With superiority in cavalry and mastery of the air, Allenby was well placed to overwhelm the numerically inferior and exhausted Turkish troops. His strategy, however, was based on mobility, surprise, and depriving the enemy of all communications by attacking the Turkish road and rail systems, particularly the Hedjaz Railway south of Damascus, the feeder line for supplies for the Turkish Fourth, Seventh and Eighth Armies.

There was, however, a critically dangerous moment when a deserting Indian soldier divulged Allenby's strategy of attack on the eve of its launching. Fortunately Liman thought the information was a plant, and his view seemed to be corroborated when flying columns of Arabs attacked Turkish communications east and west of the Jordan.[40] Liman would have had insufficient time to alter his overall deployments had he placed credence in the deserter's information (as Mustafa Kemal and others did), but he continued to anticipate Allenby's main thrust to be delivered in the Jordan River area. "When, therefore, the British attacked along the coastal plain at dawn on 18 September, after an artillery bombardment lasting only a quarter of an hour, surprise was achieved and the Turkish defences were swiftly overwhelmed."[41]

Royal Engineer Corporal Frederick Mills wrote: "Friday, September 20th, 1918. Kantara. A lot of wounded brought down from the line today, also Turkish prisoners. Heavy fighting."[42]

The retreating Turks were bombed repeatedly by Allenby's aircraft as they fell back from Nablus toward the River Jordan. The Turkish Fourth Army east

MAP O2
BATTLE OF ARMAGEDDON
Situation at 9 p.m.
24th September, 1918

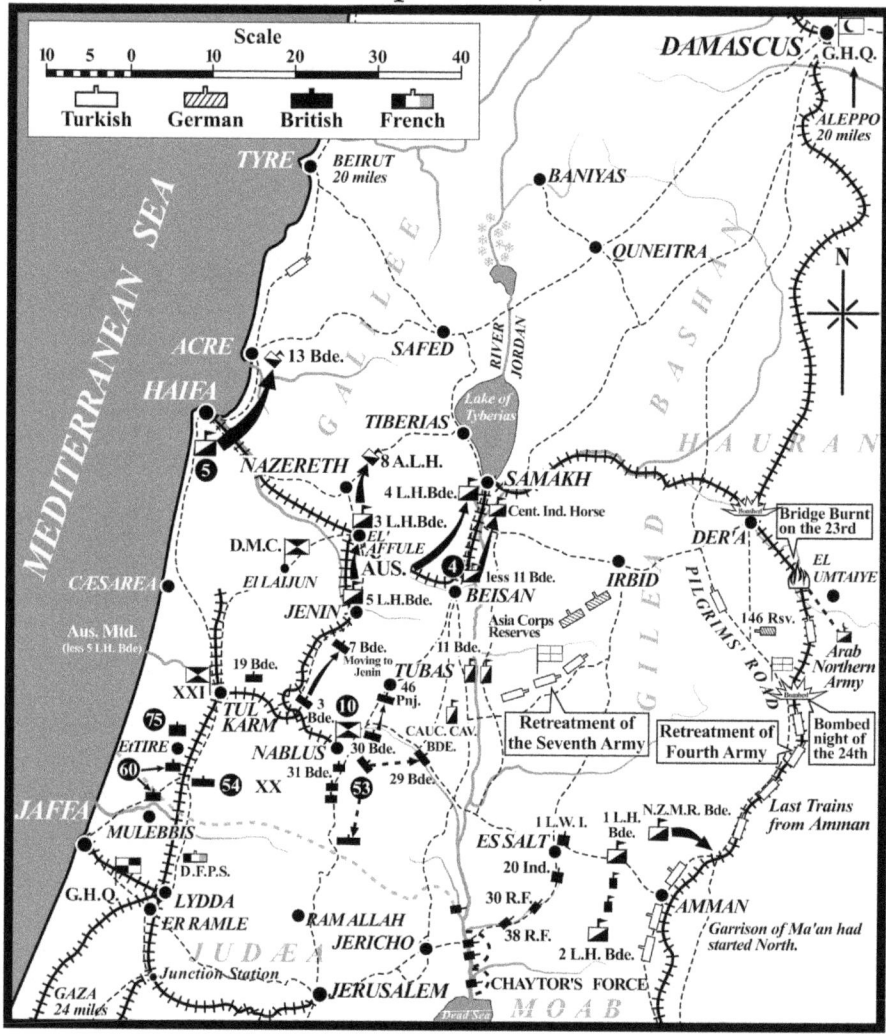

of the Jordan began retreating on 22 September, surrendering near Amman and at Damascus. By 1 October, the key cities of Beirut, Homs, Aleppo, and Damascus had fallen to Allenby's army, and for Turkey the war was over.[43]

On Sunday, 22 September, the British ambassador in Paris, the Earl of Derby, wrote in his diary:

Luncheon with Thornton and a large party at the Racing Club in the Bois de Boulogne. Not particularly amusing and a bad luncheon. It was held there because the Flying Corps Sports were on at the same place. Saw a lot of people I knew there including Jellicoe [of Jutland fame] who tells me his wife is very much better and will be quite all right in about a month's time. He tells me he heard from the Ministry of Marine that our successes in Palestine are simply gigantic and we have taken from 25,000 to 30,000 prisoners. I have not myself seen any confirmation of that. If it is confirmed I must say it gives a legitimate right to Lloyd George to crow as whenever Repington and Co. attack him in the press for these side shows something always comes off which shows we are hitting the Turk hard.

I do not quite like the Salonika news. I do not think it is a big enough success to really knock the Bulgar out but I really have seen nobody. I hope to see Clemenceau tomorrow morning."[44]

The Times of London reported on the successful attack:

GEN. ALLENBY'S
VICTORY
******

OUR CAVALRY IN
NAZARETH

Decisive success has crowned the brilliant offensive launched by General Allenby in Palestine last Thursday [19 September].

The Turkish main force west of the Jordan has been practically wiped out. East of the Jordan only small enemy detachments are holding out. No fewer than 18,000 prisoners have been taken, together with 120 guns, four aeroplanes, and large booty in material and rolling stock. For the escape of the remnants of the broken Turkish Army only the Jordan fords on a restricted sector remain, and these are for the most part impracticable for wheeled traffic.

By Friday night our cavalry had occupied Nazareth, Afuleh, and Beisan, at the Jordan bend of the Haifa-Damascus railway, where they proceeded to collect the disorganized masses of enemy troops and transport as they arrived from the south fleeing before the determined pressure of the Allied infantry.

On Saturday night our left infantry wing, with its center about Samaria, was shepherding the enemy on the west of the Jerusalem-Shechem road into the arms of the cavalry, who by this time were operating southwards from Jenin and Beisan.[45]

The Official History gives the following account:

21st September, 1918: The XXI Corps had thus completed one of the most successful operations of the war, at a cost which must, in the circumstances, be considered light. The total casualties were 3,378, of whom only 446 of all ranks were killed. The captures were about 12,000 prisoners, 149 guns, vast quantities of ammunition, countless transport wagons. The whole of the Turkish Eighth Army, with the exception of the German and a few Turkish battalions of the Asia Corps, had been destroyed.[46]

Lt. Colonel Thomas Gibbons, commanding officer of the 1/5th Essex, related:

A day or two after the battle I met the divisional commander [General Hare, 54th Division] at Brigade Headquarters, and he was good enough to say that he was thoroughly satisfied with the work of the battalion on the 19th. He fully appreciated the

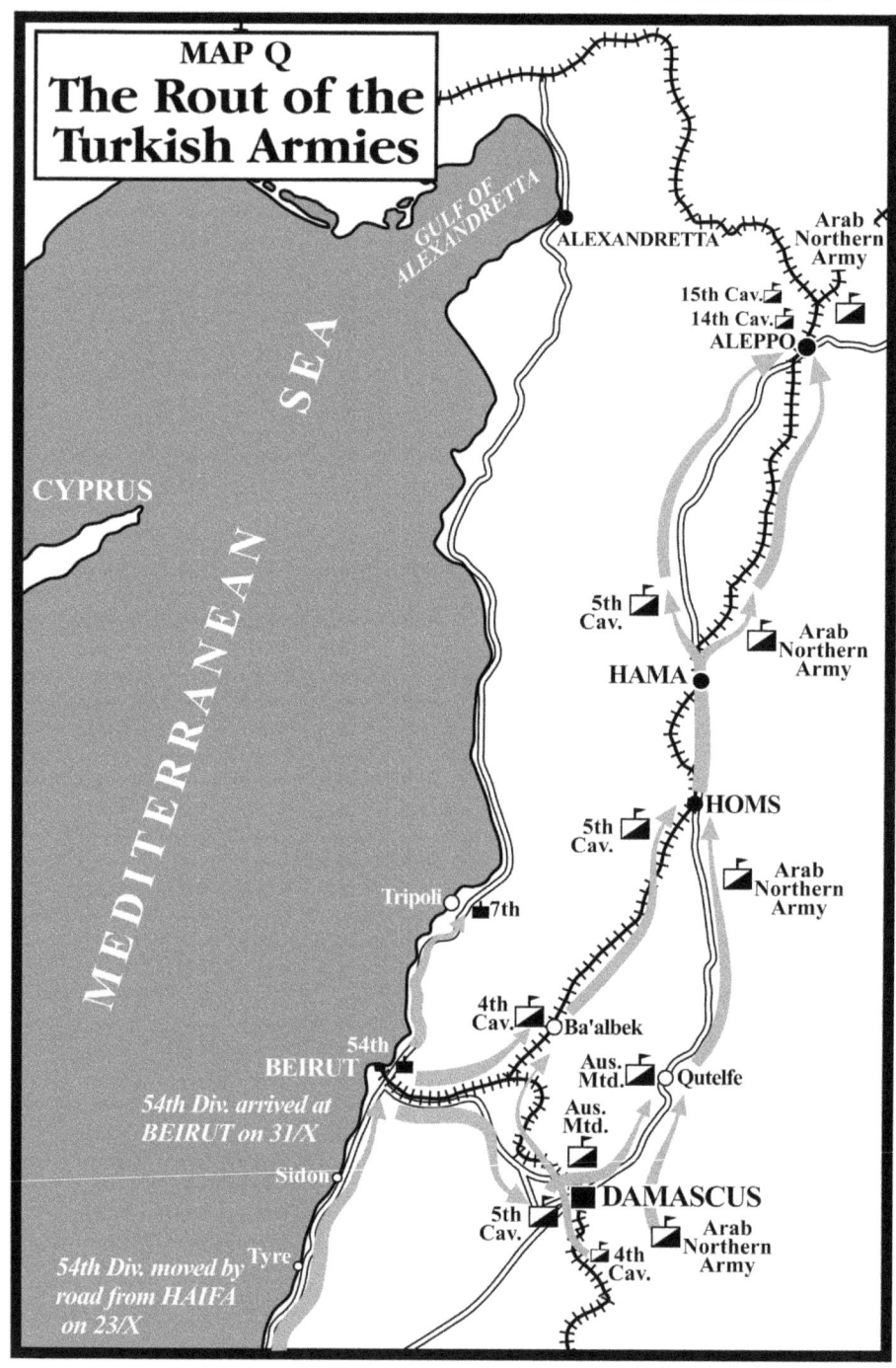

Six. The Final Stroke

Nazareth, where the Holy family dwelled (Stoddard, *John L. Stoddard's Lectures*).

strenuous nature of the operations and said the way they were carried out was "extraordinarily good." The brigadier [Orpen-Palmer, 161st Brigade] also spoke highly of the 1/5th. The operations had been essentially a section leaders' and soldiers' battle—a series of small actions—the broken ground calling for plenty of initiative and good fighting qualities on the part of the rank and file. Officers also had done very well, particularly in keeping their companies and platoons together on terrain which was conducive to disorganization and the breaking up of fighting units; and when asked to select an officer for an immediate award of the Military Cross I had some difficulty in making a nomination. I eventually recommended Lockwood, who had done consistently well on previous occasions, as well as the present one. Finn again proved himself an ideal battle adjutant. He never let me forget anything, and I have a shocking memory. It is a great asset for a battalion commander to be able to give his whole attention to the tactical situation without being distracted by the possibility of forgetting half-hourly situation reports, returns of captured weapons, estimated casualties, etc., etc.

Sergt. R. T. French led his platoon with much skill and pluck throughout the action. Sergt. Christopher Green displayed great dash, particularly in the capture of an enemy machine gun, which he rushed with the bayonet, and captured with a small party of men. L/Corpl. P. E. Byford had a similar feat to his credit. Under cover of Lewis gun fire he got in with his section and captured the gun with nine prisoners. Among the other section commanders, Sergt. Tyler, Corpl. L. W. Newman, and L/Corpls. John Gray, W. J. Ranson, and E. A. Lofts, with their Lewis gun sections[47] repeatedly broke up enemy parties opposing the advance, whilst among the "Nos. 1" of the guns the following were conspicuous for cool and skilful handling of their weapons: — Ptes. A. E. Cox, H. H. Smith, and A. Balaam. The latter was a holy terror to the Turkish machine gunners. The Lewis gunners can be fairly said to have deserved a very large share of the honours of the day. The ground suited them and they used it well. At the first Gaza battle on the level plain they never had a chance. They could only go on firing until they were knocked out by concealed machine guns, an ordeal they faced without flinching. At the last Gaza battle, the attack being in the dark, they were only used in defence against counter-attacks, a role in which they proved their value. It was not until the attack over the Judæan Hills that their efforts in the attack were rewarded with a full measure of success.

Other section leaders who were noted were L/Corpls. John Spaull, F. L. French, and K. T. Harrington. Pte. R. Lockwood, although twice wounded, continued to advance, and set a fine example of pluck and determination to his comrades. Pte. Daniel Hockley's work as a company runner was beyond praise. He repeatedly crossed fire-swept zones with messages and exhibited great pluck and endurance. Pte. A. J. Daveridge volunteered to carry a message to Battalion Headquarters through a heavy H.E. [High Explosive] barrage. He was knocked out for nearly half-an-hour by a shell, but succeeded in delivering his message.

Ptes. C. E. Hawkes and Frank Saville upheld the fine reputation of the stretcher bearers in going out and bringing in three wounded men under particularly heavy fire. The battalion, whilst in the Wadi Kanah, got some fresh clothes with which we were able to cover the nakedness of some of the worst cases. Hill fighting is very destructive to clothing.[48]

Capture of Damascus

Lawrence's unsigned letter in the *Palestine News* of October 10, 1918 claims that Feisal's Arab irregulars captured Damascus. The claim closely matches that in *The Times* of London on October 17, 1918. However, Lt. General Sir Henry Chauvel, commander-in-chief of the Desert Mounted Corps, and Brig. General Wilson, commanding officer the Third Australian Light Horse Brigade, both utterly refuted this claim.[49]

H. T. Massey, war correspondent of *The Times*, joins the chorus of voices weighing in on the subject:

There was some discussion as to who were the first troops to get into the city of Damascus. I have indicated that, if possible, British troops were not to go into the city, but if it was necessary that they should do so to make a complete capture of the Turks, and to settle the question whether Arabs or British took Damascus I give the report of Brigadier-General Wilson, of the 3rd Australian Light Horse Brigade, which is accepted as final. General Wilson says:

"Jemal Pasha, commander of the Turkish IVth Army, arranged to hold a meeting of the notables of Damascus at the Municipal Gardens at 4 P.M. on September 30, 1918, for the purpose of handing over the military governorship of the City to Shukri Pasha Ayoubi. The last-mentioned person was an Arab formerly in the Turkish Army and favourable to the Sherif of Mecca. There was in the City at this time a person of Algerian birth named Emir Said. This man for some time had been employed by the Turkish government in raising a volunteer force of Arabs to fight against the Sherif. Emir Said's sympathies were really in favour of the Sherif, but he disguised them and drew arms, ammunition, and money from the Turks.

"Some time prior to 2 P.M. on the 30th news was received in the city that the British cavalry were approaching. A report was also circulated that the Germans intended to burn the City before they left, and Shukri Pasha and Emir Said then went to Jemal Pasha and informed him that they would not allow the City to be burned. They advised Jemal Pasha to leave the City forthwith and said if he did not he would probably be attacked by the local Arabs. In Jemal Pasha's presence these people then produced a sherif's flag and displayed it at the Town Hall and declared for the sherif. Jemal Pasha left the City at 2 P.M. by the Beyrout road.

"On the night of Sept. 30–Oct. 1, this brigade bivouacked in the hills overlooking the village of Dumar about four miles north-west of Damascus on the Beyrout road. The road was during the night covered by six machine-guns, and heavy casualties were inflicted on the enemy trying to escape by this road, and the balance of them were turned back into the city. The Beyrout road was thus closed to the enemy from sunset on the 30th September. At 5 A.M. on October 1 the brigade descended to the main road at Dumar and marched along that road south-easterly into Damascus. The 10th Light Horse Regiment formed the advanced guard, Major Olden being in charge of the vanguard. On entering the north-western suburbs a good deal of rifle shooting was indulged in by the inhabitants, some shooting or sniping at the column. In a few cases the snipers were observed and their fire returned. To discourage the sniping Major Olden moved the vanguard at the gallop until he arrived at the Town Hall where he halted.

"The time was now between 6.30 and 7 o'clock. Major Olden then asked for the civil governor and was told he was upstairs. Major Olden dismounted and went into the Town Hall, where he found a large assembly of notables and people in uniforms as if arranged for some public function. Emir Said was sitting in the municipal chair, and when Major Olden asked for the civil governor, Emir Said rose and came forward as such and shook hands. Through an interpreter Emir Said said, 'In the name of the civil population of Damascus I welcome the British Army.' Major Olden said, 'What is all this rifle shooting going on?' and Said replied, 'That is the people welcoming you.' Major Olden then said, 'It must cease, as it may lead to misunderstanding.' Said answered, 'You may have no fear. I will answer in the name of the civil population that the City is quiet.' Major Olden then said, 'Who are all these armed men in uniform about the streets?' and Said replied, 'They are the police. What would you have them do?' Major Olden said, 'They can retain their arms for the present and assist in maintaining order and preventing looting. A large force of cavalry is following me up, and if my orders are not obeyed you will be held responsible.' Said replied, 'You need have no fear. We have been expecting the English for some days and have made preparations to receive them.'

"Emir Said then made a speech of welcome, and stated what they would be prepared to do to assist us. He then asked Major Olden to have refreshments. This Major Olden declined and asked for a guide to the north-east or Aleppo road. Emir Said detailed an officer called Saki Bey to act as such. This officer stopped with the brigade till the following morning. The advanced guard then moved on followed by the remainder of the brigade, passed through the City and moved to the north-east road, passing the English hospital en route. Touch was gained with the enemy rear-guard at the Wadi Maraba. Up to the time — about seven o'clock — that this brigade completed its passage through the City, thereby closing the only remaining available exit for the enemy, no member of the Sherif's Army was visible in any part of the City within the view of this brigade."[50]

This report would appear to settle the question as to whether Australian, British, or Imperial troops, or Arab irregulars were the first in Damascus. Solid evidence that the Australians were in the city some hours before the Arabs exists. So also was an Indian cavalry regiment, the advanced guard of the 14th Cavalry Brigade, which was well ahead of the leading Arab troops.[51]

However, Colonel Lawrence's account must be considered, and, in Appendix D of W. T. Massey's *Allenby's Final Triumph*, he speaks out.

The report of Colonel Lawrence written in Damascus for the General Staff is interesting. It is a very brief, modest document and is worthy of a man who during the long years of war remained in the desert to keep the Arabs true to our cause:

"The Arab force left Deraa on September 29 under Sherif Nasir and Nuri Bey Said, following up the 4th Cavalry Division on the right flank. We marched by the Hedjaz railway, and in the morning of September 30 came in contact with an enemy column of 2000 men and four guns retiring from Deraa. Our mounted men kept up a running fight with these till 4 P.M., when Sherif Nasir galloped ahead of them with thirty horses and threw himself into Khiara Chftlike, south of Kiswe, to delay the enemy, as General Gregory's brigade was just marching into Khan Denun. The Turks showed some fight, but were shelled effectively by the British while the Arabs hung on to their tail. The Arabs took about 600 prisoners, fourteen machine guns, and three guns.

"From Kiswe the Sherif sent a mounted force forward to get contact with his followers in the gardens east of Damascus, to find that his local committee had hoisted the Arab flag and proclaimed the Emirate of Hussein of Mecca at 2.30 P.M. Sherif Nasir with Major Stirling and myself moved into Damascus at 9 A.M. on October 1 amid scenes of extraordinary enthusiasm on the part of the local people. The streets were nearly impassable with the crowds, who yelled themselves hoarse and danced, cut themselves with swords and daggers, and fired volleys into the air. Nasir, Nuri Shaalan, Audi abu Tayi, and myself were cheered by name, covered with flowers, kissed indefinitely, and splashed with attar of roses from the housetops.

"On arrival at the Serai Shukri Pasha el Ayoubi was appointed Arab military governor, as all former civil employees had left with Jemal Pasha the previous day. Martial law was proclaimed, police organised, and the town picketed. The Rualla are behaving very well, but the Druses are troublesome. I have no orders as to what political arrangements should be made in Damascus, but will carry on as before till I hear further from you. If Arab military assistance is not required in further operations of Desert Mounted Corps I should like to return to Palestine, as I feel that if I remain here longer it will be very difficult for my successor.

T. E. Lawrence.

[P.S.] G.O.C. [general officer commanding] Desert Mounted Corps has seen above and agrees with my remaining with the town administration until further instructions.

T. E. L.

[P.P.S.] The Arab army since September 26 have taken 8000 prisoners and 120 machine guns.[52]

In London *The Times'* war correspondent, W. T. Massey, gives a contemporary account of events in that newspaper's issue of Monday, 7 October 1918:

Six. The Final Stroke 213

THE ENTRY INTO
DAMASCUS

JOY OF THE PEOPLE
UNRESTRAINED

HATRED OF THE GERMANS
(From W. T. Massey)

Damascus, October 1.—General Allenby's triumphant march northwards into Syria continues. Early this morning he drove the Turks completely out of Damascus, and now there is not one Turkish soldier in the city, nor a Turkish official doing duty.

Those British who entered this wonderful city today and whose emotions were not stirred by the enthusiastic greeting of the population must have been without a spark of national pride. I thought the people would receive us with their customary immobile features giving no outward visible sign of their inward feelings. I rode into the town with an armoured car officer at a time when the road was deemed unsafe, owing to snipers in the luscious gardens surrounding this fascinating and truly Oriental city. I was amazed at the heartiness of the welcome accorded to the British uniform. The city is far from taking out victory as an ordinary incident of life. The population threw off their stolid exterior, and received us with ecstatic joy. They closed the shops, put on festival dress, and acclaimed the day as the greatest in the 4,000 years' history of Damascus.

Only a few British officers have as yet entered the city, but each has been received with the same wholehearted fevour. [Lieutenant Robert Wilson, of the Royal Gloucester Hussars, spoke of particularly warm welcomes being offered by Damascene "young ladies in flimsy negligées jumping up to ride behind troopers on their horses, etc."][53] Here, at least, the people have seen what the British name stands for. They acclaimed the victors as their deliverers, and looked upon this Army as the saviours of down-trodden peoples in this part of the East.

This amazing tribute to Britain and British freedom lasted all day. At nightfall the population gave a firework exhibition with captured Very lights. Even the street of Saint Paul called Straight was illuminated from end to end. Opportunities for rejoicing were increased by the arrival of the Arab Army which operated on the right of our cavalry during the march from Deraa.

ARAB HORSEMEN'S DISPLAY

Soon after daybreak the Arab Army entered the city, and the streets became alive with picturesquely clothed figures mounted on light steeds almost overburdened with elaborately appointed saddlery. Arab horsemen and camelry dashed about the streets, proclaiming victory, making much noise, and continually firing their rifles. This lasted till midnight, and the inhabitants, tired out and happy, allowed the city to become normally calm.[54]

According to no lesser authority than the Australian War Memorial: "A patrol of the 4th Australian Light Horse, 4th Australian Light Horse Brigade, Australian Mounted Division, commanded by Sergeant Frank Organ, were the first Allied troops to enter Damascus." These were part of the units comprising "Bourchier's Force" operating directly west of the city under the command of Brig. General M.W.J. Bourchier.

Lt. General Sir Archibald Wavell adds his version to the train of events:

"At dawn next morning, October 1st, the 3rd A.L.H. [Australian Light Horse] Brigade, which had now received permission to enter the city, passed through on its way to the Homs road. These were the first of the British forces to enter Damascus. Soon afterwards Lawrence and his Arabs arrived, closely followed by the troops of the 5th Cavalry Division,"[55] Commanding, Major-General H.J.M. MacAndrew, 13th, 14th & 15th Cavalry Brigades; Essex Battery, Royal Horse Artillery; 11th Light Armoured Motor Battery; and No. 1 Light Car Patrol.

Thus by 26 September, when Allenby held a conference of corps commanders at Jenin, all Palestine was his. He had nearly 50,000 prisoners, the Turkish Seventh and Eighth Armies were reduced to a few small scattered columns, and the Fourth Army was in hasty retreat. There were estimated to be perhaps 40,000 Turks either between the British and Damascus or at Damascus itself. At his conference Allenby announced briefly that the Desert Mounted Corps would advance forthwith on Damascus, while the Twenty-first Corps would send a division (the 54th [East Anglian]) along the coast to Beirut, to be followed by another if necessary. Orders to this effect had already been issued.[56]

The Essex gunner-historians recorded:

> The capture of Damascus was the climax of the campaign. To us, who look back across the years upon the successive episodes of this great victory, what remains to be recorded must seem of minor interest and importance. The last heavy blow has been struck; the end of the drama is approaching. To commanders and troops, however, no such aspect of the operations can have appeared. They realized the fullness of their success, and perhaps guessed that no big battle remained to be fought in Syria; that, though progress might be slow, they could now go forward, based upon Syrian ports, and that until they reached the mountain masses of Taurus and Amanus no barrier could long check their march. Yet the very distances now stretching before them, so much greater than those traversed between Jaffa and Damascus, were impressive. The resources of Turkey were believed to be nearly exhausted, but the best information on this matter could only be vague. What effort the enemy would make to replace the armies which they had destroyed was uncertain. At the moment, therefore, the capture of Damascus brought no feeling that strenuous exertions were nearly at an end or that demands for sacrifice were soon to cease.
>
> Meanwhile ill-health was cause enough for anxiety, and the death in hospital of many officers and men who had passed unscathed through fight after fight was depressing to their comrades. Viewing the situation of his troops at the beginning of October, the commander-in-chief could congratulate himself upon the small number of battle casualties which his victory had entailed; yet the length of the daily lists showing the wastage from disease and the speed with which they mounted up made him realize that he had to bring his campaign to a close with a force crippled by sickness [initially a malignant strain of malaria was the chief cause of casualties]. About the 6th October came the wave of influenza which was experienced in every theatre and indeed all over the world. At once the hospitals and receiving stations established in Damascus were filled to overflowing with patients suffering from this scourge, which at first could not be differentiated from the malignant malaria. The Indian troops were only affected slightly less than those of European blood.[57]

General Allenby's triumphal entry into Jerusalem.

The Virginian missionary Dr. Squires paints a vivid picture of a most ancient metropolis:

> The white houses of Damascus are set in an oasis of living green, like a costly pearl in an emerald frame. The tawny desert stretches afar, filling the background of every landscape.... Damascus is one of the most attractive cities in the world. She boasts no history like Jerusalem, no art like Florence, no architecture like Athens. "What can be the attraction that draws one irresistibly?" I asked my ignorant self time and again. At last I grasped it. "It is human nature." In Damascus more than any place on earth man is frankly a human animal. Human nature stands forth naked, unabashed and unashamed. In the bazaars of Damascus everything is primitive, everyone is natural. One dresses, talks, bargains, buys or sells as he pleases. There are no traditions, no ethical standards, no public opinion. The bazaars present a scene unrivalled for variety and interest. The merchants of each guild gather into a quarter of their own. In the saddle market hundreds of men and boys work long hours on their leather, sitting cross-legged as they stitch, or selling straps to customers who seek their small booths. In the drapers' bazaar eager purchasers pass from tiny shop to tiny shop. The goldsmiths, joiners, sweets, silk, grocers, booksellers, spicers, turners, carpet, and many other stalls invite the visitor to linger. The traveler who enjoys the beautiful, who appreciates the antique, or who candidly seeks sensations will find here his desires.[58]

On Trek

"On Trek" is the apt title Lt. Colonel Thomas Gibbons gave to a concluding chapter of his admirable military history, and in it he describes the peregrinations of his battalion subsequent to the overwhelming defeat of the enemy.

> All details were arranged for the march northwards, wagon loads made up, etc. Camels were used for carrying the day's water and each Battalion had two G.S. [General Service] wagons on which it carried officers' kits (35lbs. each), orderly room boxes, mosquito bivouacs, two or three tents for orderly room, medical room, etc., some spare boots, and clothing and equipment, dubbin and oil, two large canvas water tanks, armourers', pioneers', and shoemakers' tools, and a few other indispensable things. The men were heavily loaded; full marching order and a bivouac in addition.
>
> On September 28th the brigade [161st] concentrated on the plain near Jijulia. An immense amount of digging had been done there by the Turks and it had evidently been designed as a strong point of resistance. It was inhabited, but the inhabitants looked in a wretched state. On the 29th the brigade marched to Kakon, headed by the brigade band (under Sergt. Ross, of the 1/5th [Essex]) and as we swung past the ancient Gilgal to its martial strains, through the long lines of wondering natives, one could not help feeling the elation of victory, tempered with sorrow for all those brave companions we had left behind, at Gaza, on the Auja, and in the hills, the fruits of whose sacrifice we were now reaping to the full. After a very hot and dusty march of 14 miles we reached Kakon. Kakon was an important military point from the earliest times. From it branches the most eastern of the three routes over Carmel to the plain of Esdraelon, *viz.* that by the plain of Dothan, the one more usually taken by invaders from the north and south. It was by this road that the company of Ishmaelites came from Gilead and bought Joseph from his brothers (Genesis, XXXVII.) The

route we were taking — round the promontory of Cape Carmel by the seashore, which the Crusaders called *Les Destroits*, was not so often used. As Napoleon said, it was a *"passage difficile à forcer s'il etait defendu."* But Carmel had already been cleared for us by the cavalry, and Haifa was in our hands, having been taken by the Mysore and Jodhpur Lancers on September 23rd....

On the following day [30th] we resumed our march due north, keeping to the plain. It was terribly hot and dusty but the men stuck it well with their heavy packs. The flies were innumerable, as they always were in the wake of the Turk. The country was strewn with dead animals and there were still a few Turks unburied, staring, black-faced and horrible into the sun.

Streams of prisoners were met coming in — all returning motor lorries were packed with them, but many had to march, and one pitied the long straggling columns of tired, thirsty, foot-sore men. The feeding and watering of the enormous number of prisoners was a big strain on the transport, and was in fact delaying the advance.

Soon after midday, after crossing the swampy bed of the Wadi el Khudeirah — the "Dead River" of the Crusaders — we reached our bivouac near Kurkur on a hill where were the remains of an extensive oak forest. This forest formerly spread over a great part of the plain of Sharon, at one time giving it the name of "Drumos" (Isaiah, XXVIII, XXXV, etc.) Strabo calls it "a great Forest," The Crusaders "the Forest of Assur," Tasso "The Enchanted Forest." ... Herod spent twelve years in building Cæsarea and making it a haven for his ships. The breakwater was 200 feet wide in twenty fathoms of water — no wonder half the rocky ridge seemed to have been taken away.... We now approached the "Crocodile River" of the Crusaders. Pliny speaks of the town and river of crocodiles at this; and a crocodile was killed here as late as 1902.

October 7th. Marching for a further four miles between the marshes and the ridge we came to the town and Jewish colony of Zimmarin. It was a stiff climb up to the town, the road enclosed by high hedges and several inches deep in white dust. Our bivouac was a very pleasant one, on the slope towards the sea. Provisions were obtained in the town and the more energetic set out for nearly three miles to the sea for a bathe.

The town seemed very full and was practically *en fête*. Most of the Jewish maidens had put on their best frocks and marched up and down the High Street giving the glad eye to the Essex boys, but the latter were not visibly impressed. There was evidently little fear of the "brutal and licentious soldiery" in these parts. The town boasted a hotel, which supplied very bad liquor, but little in the way of food, which had all been snapped up by the two other Brigades [162nd & 163rd] which had preceded us....

On October 7th the battalion marched through Haifa, and the whole brigade bivouacked on the plain to the east of the town, under the shadow of Carmel and between it and the Nakr el Mukuttah — the brook Kishon — which meandered through the level plain and emptied itself into the sea about two miles to the north. As we passed through Haifa we met many German and Turkish officer prisoners, very "beat," being helped along by their kindly Indian escorts.[59]

October 7, 1918, was also the date that advanced elements of General Sir Edmund Allenby's army entered the port city of Beirut. *The Times* of London in the issue of Friday, October 11, carried the following announcement:

The Entry Into Beirut

Town Held By British Infantry

The War Office made last evening the following announcement concerning the operations in Palestine and Syria:—

French and British warships entered the port of Beirut on October 6, finding the town evacuated by the enemy.

On October 7 British armoured cars, preceding our cavalry and infantry columns arrived, and on October 8 the advanced detachments of British and Indian infantry occupied the place, being received enthusiastically by the inhabitants.

The number of prisoners taken by the Egyptian Expeditionary Force (exclusive of those taken by the Arab Armies) has risen to over 75,000, and it is estimated that the entire strength of the Turkish 4th, 7th, and 8th Armies not more than 17,000 in all have escaped, this figure including about 4,000 effective rifles.

Many of the prisoners captured were in a lamentable state of exhaustion and are receiving such treatment and attention as is possible.

The prisoners taken by the Arab forces number about 9,000, so that the total captured by the Allies in Palestine and Syria since September 19 amount to over 85,000. Of these over 5,500 are Germans or Austrians.[60]

The paraphrased account of Colonel Gibbons resumes:

Everywhere abounded with signs of ancient habitation. The map was full of names of places most with the prefix "*Khirbet,*" or ruin. It was more a land of ruins even than Judæa. The whole country was studded with them; the remains of numerous small towns which formed, as Heeren says, "almost an unbroken city, extending along the whole line of coast," in the palmy days of Phœnician prosperity. After a very hard march we came to rest at Ras-el-Ain about five miles south of Tyre. Near the place were several immense reservoirs, which store the water of the springs which supplied the city of Tyre with water in the old days. According to Josephus, Salmazar IV had already destroyed the aqueducts in the year B.C. 726. In the middle ages Ras-el-Ain was called the Pools of Solomon.

Setting off next morning we left Tyre on our left. It was hard to believe that the small town on the small peninsula was really all that was left of the mighty city of King Hiram, the parent city of Carthage and Cadiz, the wonder of the East for luxury and magnificence, and the centre of commerce of the world. A narrow neck of sand connected the town with the mainland. At the time Alexander the Great besieged the city in B.C. 332 it was on an island. He filled up the straits and made the island into the peninsula it is now. But it was easy to realize why the prophet Ezekiel likened the city to a beautiful ship with her "masts of cedar, her sails of fine linen, blue and purple ... very glorious in the midst of the seas" (Ezekiel, XXVII; 3–26), and easy also to feel in imagination the force of the prophecy of the stern old seer: —"I will bring thee to ashes upon the earth in the sight of all them that behold thee" (XXVIII; 18).

Not that Tyre is at present a heap of ruins, though it has been that more than once. It is now a town of about 6,000 inhabitants (of whom nearly half are Christians), but its greatness is no more than a memory. Three hours' march brought us to the River Litani, the largest stream we had yet crossed — deep and placid, running between green banks, it might have been an English river. It was full of fish.... We pitched our bivouac a little to the north of the river to escape the mosquitoes, and resumed our march at 8 o'clock the next morning [October 29].... After crossing the

Wadi Khaiseran we passed the village of Surafend, the ancient Zarephath or Sarepta, where the prophet Elijah lodged with the widow whose "barrel of meal wasted not, neither did the cruse of oil fail," and whose son he raised [from the dead] (I Kings XVII; 16–22).[61]

[Thence to] Sidon, which is one of the oldest cities of the world and is mentioned in Genesis (X: 19) as the northern border of the Canaanites. Homer mentions its artisans as celebrated, especially in metallurgy. Its history is similar to that of many other towns we had come through. A fierce rivalry between it and Tyre prevailed for many ages, each in turn regaining its supremacy, generally by the complete destruction of its rival by a foreign conqueror.

It was a beautiful morning on October 31st when we marched out of Sidon with our bands playing.... For over two miles the road made a gradual ascent, passing through the delightful gardens which earned Sidon in olden days the title of the "Flower-crowned."

Another four miles took us round the promontory of Ras Jedra and two more to the village of El Jiyeh, where stood the ancient city of Porphyrion, so named from the fishing for the famous purple dye. Here Ptolemy was defeated by Antiochus the Great in B.C. 218. It is surrounded by beautiful gardens. The Khan on the outskirts of the village was called the Khan en Nebi Younes (the prophet Jonas). According to Musselman legend it was here that Jonah was thrown up by the whale.... Beyond is the Maronite village of Ed Damour, near which we pitched our bivouac for the night.

The Maronites are a sect of Eastern Christians who inhabit a great many villages in Lebanon. They are a sturdy lot, preserving a certain amount of independence, even now desisting the payment of tribute to the Turks. They acknowledge the Pope, but without giving up their own peculiarities. Among other things their priests insist on the right of marrying if they choose, and their laws allow revenge for murder.[62]

The 54th (East Anglian) Division on the coastal left wing reached Beirut, which Dr. Squires eulogized thus:

> Beyrout is a city of great and growing importance. Here the Orient meets the Occident, each with much benefit to the other. Crosses and minarets rise side by side. There are handsome boulevards with fine Parisian limousines upon them, and just around the corner caravans of camels are folding their long, ungainly legs after a sixty-day march from Baghdad or the fastnesses of Arabia.
>
> At the edge of town a fine Franco–Turkish military road begins at once its climb to the passes of Lebanon. Each turn lifts the traveler higher, and each pause discloses a view more extensive, comprehensive and interesting. Handsome country estates everywhere abound, elegant gardens, rich vineyards and numerous groves of mulberry trees closely pruned after the manner of the country.... Syria is more prosperous than she has been in centuries. There is surely poverty here, but at the elegant hotel as I watched the wealthy Syrians in full evening dress pouring their champagne and conversing with women who wore brilliant diamonds and ropes of pearls, I felt embarrassed at my dusty, rusty, travel-worn exterior. I thought of the heart rending pictures of starving Syrians that appeared in our papers last spring.[63]

The Advance to Aleppo and Conclusion of the Armistice

"Of the whole of the Turkish armies in Palestine and Syria, which had had a ration strength of over 100,000 on September 19th, only some 17,000 escaped north, and of these it was estimated that only 4,000 were effective rifles. The hostile forces in Northern Syria were in fact a mere rabble, without artillery, without transport and without organisation,"[64] wrote Wavell in *The Campaigns in Palestine*.

Damascus and Aleppo were captured, and the Turks surrendered on October 30. Within a few weeks the Turkish forces facing Allenby had been destroyed. British forces, suffering 5,666 casualties, had taken 75,000 prisoners.[65]

Banks gives this description: "In Palestine General Allenby, with elaborate deception and imaginative use of cavalry pushed the Turks (and the German 'Asia Corps') rapidly northwards into the Lebanon and Syria in the autumn of 1918. His advanced cavalry reached Aleppo before Turkish delegates concluded an armistice at Mudros [on the island of Lemnos] on 30 October, with the commander-in-chief of the British Mediterranean Fleet."[66]

Rudin adds in *Armistice 1918*: "The British Admiral, Sir Somerset Calthorpe, had been authorized by his government to discuss terms with accredited representatives of Turkey. The English had already arrived at an understanding with France and Italy with respect to their demands. On October 25 the British government instructed Admiral Calthorpe to conclude the armistice on the basis of the twenty-four clauses agreed to in Paris. The final terms were agreed to by Admiral Calthorpe and the Turkish delegates on a British warship at Mudros on October 30. Turkey was to end all hostilities Thursday noon, October 31."[67]

British Prime Minister David Lloyd George, in summing up, wrote:

> In reviewing this ultimate dramatic success of our arms against Turkey, it is very hard to escape the conclusion that, granted good generalship, we might have attained a similar victory years before. Granted that in 1918 the Turkish Army was becoming very inferior in quality; but our own force was a comparatively small one, of only seven infantry and four cavalry divisions, from which many of the finest units had been withdrawn to reinforce the Western Front and replaced by raw Indian levies that had seen no service. Twenty-two of the Indian battalions were in this condition, as were some of their commanding officers, and the *Official History* records that they were largely made up of recruits who had done no musketry. When they landed in Egypt they had hardly any signalers, few Lewis gunners, no bombers, and were deficient in a number of other respects, notably in officers who could speak Hindustani. Prior to the substitution of these for the experienced troops which Allenby sent to France in the spring of 1918 — upwards of 60,000 officers and men — our force in the Near East was far more potent than that which ultimately gained so striking and decisive a victory.
>
> Had we reinforced our Egyptian Army in 1916 with a few of the men we were wasting by the hundred thousand on the Somme, at a time when the Allies outnumbered the Germans on the Western Front by more than fifty per cent., we might have broken the Turkish power in time to save Rumania, equip Russia, and end the war two years before it finally dragged to its tragic close. In a Turkish campaign our sea communications gave us a definite advantage over the Central Powers. The railway accommodation was so limited and so broken that Germany could not have

reinforced the Turks, however desperate their plight might be. The military advisers who scorned the Palestine campaign as a futile and wasteful "sideshow" have a heavy reckoning to settle.[68]

On September 23rd, the secretary of the War Cabinet, Sir Maurice Hankey, wrote: "I think the Palestine victory is largely due to the action of the Committee of Prime Ministers last July in refusing to allow the transport of the 54th Division from Palestine to the Western Front. As the C.I.G.S. [Chief of the Imperial General Staff, Sir William Robertson] said to me in the afternoon, the victories in Palestine and Salonika are the most glaring examples of 'amateur strategy'— but he is very pleased all the same."[69]

The Essex gunners' war record a month later, on October 25 at Nebi Kasim, read:

> We arrived in a thunderstorm, and there stayed the night on the banks of the river. In crossing the Nahr el Kasimir we marched out of Palestine proper, some eighteen months after crossing the southern frontier at Rafa. It is believed that the 54th Division was the only division to do this without its order of battle being changed....[70]
> The 7th Division pushed on all night through very difficult country, following mountain tracks over which no wheels could move; their greatest hardship was shortage of water, many men having nothing but what they carried in their water-bottles for more than 24 hours.... Both these Indian Divisions 7th (Meerut) and 3rd (Lahore) had to rely for their water supply during this day's advance on the two specially organised Camel Transport Corps water convoys, each of 2,400 camels.[71]

MacMunn and Falls' *The Official History* goes into much greater detail:

> Once again the supply of water had been the hinge whereon all hung. In addition to the pipe-line to Jlil, constructed before the concentration took place, a pipe 7,000 yards in length was laid by the 14th Army Troops Company, R.E., working directly under the chief engineer of the corps, Brig. General R.P.T. Hawksley, from the mill-race near Ferrikhiye to Jaljulye, in eight and a half hours. This pipe had an output of 17,500 gallons per hour. Two water convoys, each consisting of 2,400 camels, were employed to carry water to the troops in the hills, and without them the 7th Division would not have been able to continue its advance on the 20th. Even with their aid, the leading brigade was, as we have seen, in difficulties for want of water, and Beit Lid would hardly have been taken that night had not the other brigades discovered local wells.[72]

Retrospective Analyses of Allenby's Triumph

The era's historians offer their commentary on the victory.

"The campaign in Palestine had been one of uninterrupted success since Allenby took over the British command. Australians, New Zealanders, Highlanders, Lowlanders, Indians, and, last but not least, British Territorials, or county regiments, had vied with one another in advancing the *Entente* power,"[73] said Halsey. Gilbert reported that on October 26, Aleppo was occupied. The combined troops had reached Homs and Tripoli, while the cavalry was advancing on Aleppo, thus capturing the city.[74]

Lt. Colonel Thomas Gibbons of the Essex Regiment wrote:

During the day's march on October 31st a message from Brigade Headquarters was passed back along the column. It read: "Hostilities with Turkey ceased at 12 noon today." It was not entirely unexpected, but it was welcome news for all that. The three Turkish armies opposed to us had been utterly destroyed.[75]

Between September 19th and October 26th 75,000 prisoners had been captured, including 200 officers and 3,500 other ranks German and Austrian, 360 guns had been taken, with the transport and equipment of the three armies. The captures also included over 800 machine guns, 210 motor lorries, 44 motor cars, 3,500 animals, 89 railway engines, and 468 carriages and trucks. The Turkish armies had been completely surrounded, and had in fact ceased to exist. "Such a complete victory," said Sir Edmund Allenby in his message to the troops, "has seldom been known in all the history of war."[76]

Megiddo: 19–21 September 1918

The culminating battle of the Palestine campaign brought British, Dominion,[77] and Imperial — along with largely token contingents of Armenians, Egyptian,[78] French, Italian, and Palestinian Jews — troops under Lt. General Sir Edmund Allenby, to bear against Turkish forces, stiffened by Austrian and German personnel, under the Prussian General Otto Liman von Sanders. A meticulously planned and faithfully executed offensive resulted in a stunning victory for Allies. The battle is also unique inasmuch as it marked the last use of massed cavalry in warfare.

Allenby's Palestine Campaign, and Megiddo in particular, won him his place as one of Britain's greatest generals. At the Battle of Megiddo he achieved surprise, shock, overwhelming victory, and relentless pursuit. In just under a month he advanced 360 miles, destroyed three Turkish armies, and took 76,000 prisoners and over 300 guns at a cost of 853 dead, 4,482 wounded, and 385 missing.[79] "The British had fought hard for every mile of their advance, for if the Turks were not always well equipped they were well led by their German generals."[80]

Winston Churchill wrote of Allenby: "With no more than 150,000 men he had expelled 170,000 German-led Turkish troops from fortified positions — Plevnas[81] — on which years of labour had been spent, and inflicted upon them most serious losses in men, guns and territory. No praise is too high for these brilliant and frugal operations, which will long serve as a model in theatres of war in which manoeuvre is possible."[82]

A portion of an entry in Frances Stevenson's *Lloyd George* mentions Allenby: "*March 19th 1919:* ... General Allenby came to lunch. He is a fine looking man, & one I imagine who would stand no nonsense. D. [David Lloyd George] was urging him to give the French the facts about Syria, that the French would not be tolerated there. I believe he did at a subsequent meeting between P.M., Clemenceau & Wilson.[83]

On Saturday, October 5, the British Ambassador in Paris, Lord Derby, wrote in his diary:

> It seems to me from what Lloyd George says that we are being rather petty complaining that the French do not give us enough credit for Palestine and for the part we have played in Salonika. I really do not see that that matters in the least. If they like to think France is doing everything let them do so. It cannot for one minute alter the fact that we have done all the fighting in Palestine; that the war with Turkey is ours and nobody else's. I asked him "suppose Turkey now asks for an armistice have you settled what the terms are to be?" His answer was that the soldiers knew what they wanted but as far as he knew the various foreign offices had never discussed the matter and he is determined to try and get it settled at the afternoon conference.[84]

Candler recalled, "The end was sudden and dramatic. Those of us who left Mesopotamia in the summer of 1918 only missed one week's fighting. It was Allenby who unlocked the door at Aleppo, but by this time the Turks were beaten to a standstill on both fields, in Palestine and Mesopotamia."[85]

The Armistice

Lt. Colonel Gibbons relates: "The men took the news of the armistice as they took everything else that came along, and allowed themselves to show no signs of excitement, whatever they felt. But after slipping off their heavy packs and taking a short rest they were soon busy with their writing pads, giving mail off until we got to Beyrout."[86]

The Essex gunners give this version of these momentous times (paraphrased):

> So that was the spirit of the Armistice. Visions of a care-free future conjured up. Sighs of relief. It was truly immense. A maze of different thoughts arose, the most prominent being the feeling of infinite relief at the finality of the whole business. In dim retrospect, the early days of Romford and France seemed associated with an era as far removed as the ancient history of Beirut. Happiness approached hysteria — the same emotions prompted the same actions as in the home towns on Armistice night. Bonfires on the slopes of Lebanon; music and merriment, cat-calls and cacophony; awed natives standing agape at the rapidly-disintegrated stolidity of the Britisher. The bottles of Greek-distilled "cognac" bought surreptitiously from dirty Arabs were unnecessary for intoxication. Laws and rules were blithely transgressed. All ranks were infected. Our colonel, hastily collecting a group of any soldiers from anywhere, led the singing of the national anthem, which tailed off hours later into detached crowds singing detached jingles. The horses wondered; the Arabs went *magnoon* (mad). With the Very lights and flares of infantry units were mingled the glare and dull thuds of our "C" Battery of howitzers firing sandbag wads with full charges in a royal salute. Ships' hooters sounding from the Bay of St. George, and the hazy peaks of Lebanon indulgently smiling down. Without a doubt this same Syrian scene was being enacted over half the globe. Pandemonium was allowed to reign. The boiler did not burst, but the safety-valve springs were severely over-worked![87]

The following day, November 2, was the anniversary of the last battle of Gaza, and was marked by the triumphal march of the brigade through Beyrout. The corps commander, Sir Edward Bulfin, took the salute in the main square at 11 o'clock, Gibbons recorded. "He said we were the best brigade on the march through, and it was a really good show. The 5th Essex was in front that day. We were in rather ragged condition but the men went with a fine swing, led by the battalion drums. Luckily the big drum took the strain. It was my chief anxiety. We only had three side drums left — and even if we had had more we lacked the drummers to play them. The inhabitants appeared delighted to see us; there was much cheering, applause, and throwing of flowers in the street. The 6th Essex stole a march on us by playing the *Marseillaise* past the French consulate, and got a tremendous reception from the balcony."[88]

Possibly this was the venue for Private Jake Mortlock's one and only bout of drunkenness, when "the ground kept coming up and hitting me in the face."[89]

Brevet Colonel Badcock wrote:

> *Beirut*.— Starvation was rampant amongst the poorer classes of Beirut when we occupied the town in early October. The XXIst Corps under General Bulfin did wonders to ameliorate conditions. The destitute poor used to make a regular practice of taking their poor starving little children and placing them on the doorsteps of rich people's houses in the hope that food might be forthcoming. It was pitiable to hear their cries. I'm afraid that more often than not these poor little souls never got many scraps of food that kind Samaritans may have handed out, for the parents generally lurked in the background and swooped like hungry vultures on any eatable that was given. In fact they used their children's dying cries as a decoy for themselves. Starvation is an appalling thing to see — it is only exceeded by thirst, so far as my limited experience goes.[90]

A Lebanese woman also witnessed the horrors of hunger in her midst:

> "The days of the war were prolonged, and so were the images of suffering. And the methods of violence and injustice were extended to all the Arab countries. It was enough to remember what my own eyes saw in Beirut of horrors, which people may not believe could ever happen to human beings. Poverty crept slowly over the land, a result of Ottoman policy to impoverish the Arab countries, particularly Lebanon. Death opened its jaws wide to devour the hungry. We used to rush to the windows and balconies to encourage those who were able to walk to pick up the food we threw to them, or else we would send to those who could not walk whatever pittance of food or drink was enough to sate their hunger.[91]

Lt. Colonel Gibbons also saw "little children walking the streets of Beyrout absolutely naked, like skeletons, thighs no bigger round than my wrists."[92]

Private Jake Mortlock wrote to his cousin, Jack Parker, on 4 November 1918 from somewhere in Syria:

Dear Jack

Thanks very much for your letter dated the 11th Sept which I received about a fortnight ago but have not had a chance to answer it before now as we have been on the trek all the time. Jee Old Boy we have had some stone-wall marches just lately — we have marched right out of Palestine and almost out of Syria. But its all for a good

Six. The Final Stroke

Junie Bay north of Beirut, the 5th Suffolks' last camp in Syria (Fair and Wolton, *The History of the 1/5th Battalion: "The Suffolk Regiment"*).

cause and the war looks a good bit nearer the end than it did when we started, Turkey and Austria throwing in.[93] I dont think Germany can hang out much longer on her own. Yes we have finished fight[ing] out here and we dont seem hardly able to realise it; get no more of Old Johnny's aeroplanes to worry us, and no more hiding in holes from shells or anything of that sort [and] can have a good night's rest now without having to stand-to in the middle of the night.

We are going to have a bit of a rest here I think anyhow I can do with one and then I should not be surprised if we found ourselves bit nearer home before long. We saw lots of interesting places on the way up [and] had a look round Beirut which is the biggest town in Syria over 200,000 population. electric trams and everything It is a rare place for wine too you can get all sorts of wine at practically every place you go in there.

Well Old Boy I was awfully sorry too [*sic*] hear about Poor Old Douglas and I know just how you feel about it for he was one of the most merry happy go lucky chaps I knew and you two had been the best of chums since you were nippers. Gee this war has something to answer for and I am like you I dont think things can ever be quite the same again But trust that we shall have some good times together when this is all over which I dont think will be long now.

The Day of Victory: Armistice Signed

In London both the monarch, King George the Fifth, and his prime minister, David Lloyd George, responded in the *Daily Telegraph* to the news that the war was over:

In response to the ovation by the enormous crowds which all day long gathered about Buckingham Palace, the King and Queen twice came out on the balcony. On the first occasion, obtaining a moment of comparative silence, His Majesty, addressing the people, said: "With you I rejoice and thank God for the victories which the Allied armies have won, and have brought hostilities to an end and peace within sight."

Mr. Lloyd George's important speech is reported on page three. Below are some of his principal points:

The issue is settled. It is the most miraculous change in history. The Turkish armies are annihilated, and the capital is now almost under our guns. Austria is shattered and broken. Germany has been hurled back, and the army which was once the most formidable in the world is now hardly an army at all. Its navy is certainly no longer a navy. The potent empire that threatened civilisation is headless and helpless. Its head, the Kaiser, and the Crown Prince, have abdicated. A successor has not yet been found. A regency has been proclaimed, but the regent has not yet been ascertained. A German National Assembly is to be summoned to determine the future government of Germany. Was there ever a more dramatic judgment in the history of the world? Whatever happens, we mean to have no Hundred Days after this peace.[94]

Chapter Seven

Backlash

Commenting on behalf of the Norfolk infantry battalions, their historian wrote: "The capture of Damascus was the climax of the campaign. To us, who look back across the years upon the successive episodes of this great victory, what remains to be recorded must seem of minor interest and importance. The last heavy blow has been struck; and the end of the drama is approaching."[1]

Royal Engineer Corporal Frederick Mills' diary entries read: "Friday, November 29th, 1918. Kantara. I met Will Long of the 10th Middlesex (Lily Ryan's husband) in the Y.M.C.A. He is now in the Essex Regiment and has just come out of hospital. *The following day* [30th]. Our own concert party gave a turn in the R.E. theatre. The first in public, they were very good. General Lloyd [commander Canal Zone, Palestine Lines of Communication] was present with staff. Will Long came with me. They are called the 'The Decauvilles' after the light railway used by the R.E.s."[2]

The officer commanding the 1st/5th Essex , Colonel Gibbons, chronicled the stay in Beirut and afterwards in this account:

> Beyrout was not an attractive place to spend winter, and the men found it slow. The ground which was cleared for football, & c., was nearly always unplayable owing to its wetness; no tents or huts were available for recreational purposes. So the news that the division was ordered back to Egypt was received with satisfaction. There was talk of us marching back as far as the railhead (some distance short of Haifa), but to the men's relief the idea was abandoned, and the sea route was decided upon. On December 2nd we embarked on HMS *Tagus*; the transport proceeding by another boat. The latter was named the *Ekaterinoslav*—and the transport personnel said it served her right too! She was not a floating palace. December 4th, disembarked at Kantara, housed at the Transit Camp on the west bank of the canal for the night. Next day proceeded by train to Helmieh, some nine miles from Cairo.[3]

Corporal Frederick Mills' diary entry reads: "Saturday, December 7th, 1918. Kantara. Jack Isaacs came down. His regiment [Northamptons] is going close to Cairo tomorrow."[4]

MacMunn and Falls said the 54th Division marched through Cairo on December 20, past the commander-in-chief.

In Palestine the infantry suffered heavy casualties[5] on certain occasions, the 54th Division being particularly unfortunate in this respect in the Second and Third Bat-

The 5th Suffolks march past Lord Allenby in Cairo (Fair and Wolton, *The History of the 1/5th Battalion: "The Suffolk Regiment"*).

tles of Gaza; but as a rule losses were not so great as to affect seriously the fighting quality of the unit. Good junior officers and non-commissioned officers nearly always remained, becoming craftier fighters and better leaders of men as they gained experience; and the spirit of the rank and file was not blunted by the prospect, on forming up for an attack, of one-third or two-thirds of their numbers being killed or wounded by nightfall.... Those who were serving on the Western Front in the summer of 1918 will recall the excellent impression made by the two divisions which arrived from Palestine, and also by the individual battalions which were distributed among a number of divisions and by the splendid battalions of the Machine-Gun Corps formed from Yeomanry regiments. The result of this training was a notable skill in the use of ground which reduced losses from the fire of machine-guns, the chief weapon which the troops of the E.E.F. had to face.[6]

The 54th (East Anglian) Division was but one of the contingents of Allenby's victorious army to return to Egypt following the Armistice of 11 November 1918. Captains Fair and Wolton chronicled the 1/5th Battalion of the Suffolk Regiment's experiences:

The battalion, quartered at Helmieh and having been detailed for duty on Christmas Day, celebrated that festival on the 24th, the 1/8th Hampshire Regiment lending a magnificent marquee for the occasion. On the 29th Captain A. Fair, M.C., relinquished the adjutancy which he had held for nearly twenty months, being succeeded by Captain C. M. Fyson. On January 5, 1919, the battalion sustained a great loss by the death of R.S.M. J. J. French, D.C.M., who had served with from before the war and had taken part in almost every one of its engagements.[7]

Now, of course, those lads who volunteered to fight in the war at its outbreak eagerly anticipated an early return to their native lands and happy reunions with their loved ones. However, as Colonel Gibbons and others related, this was to be a source of much frustration for some. "The scheme for demobilisation was a disappointment to many, who hoped that we might return to England as a unit, after our long sojourn in the East. It was evident that it was going to be a slow business, and during January [1919] only four officers and 88 other ranks were demobilised."[8]

Murphy wrote, "With the advent of the New Year demobilization, now in full swing, received a temporary check owing to an outbreak of rioting in Egypt. The troops were called out in aid of the civil power to protect persons and property, and to restore order in Cairo, Alexandria, and elsewhere."[9]

Sergeant George How of "D" Company, 1/5 Suffolk, was among many other 54th Division personnel had to stay behind on account of the student riots. Some Australian Light Horsemen also stayed behind — troopers of the 4th Australian Light Horse Regiment were among them.

Early in March 1919 the British arrested Egyptian nationalist Saad Zaghloul with two associates and banished all three to Malta. Demonstrations immediately took place up and down the country, followed by civil unrest and riots. The situation escalated to looting and random violence, which included the murder of British soldiers; mass action involved people of all walks of life, urban workers and *fallahin*, members of ethnic and religious minorities, and even women, something unprecedented in Egypt. Martial law was reinforced, and General Allenby sent from England to supersede Wingate as high commissioner. Allenby, without an Egyptian government, ruled by decree, and order was not restored until early April when the British, having concluded that the Allies in Paris would in any case recognize their protectorate in Egypt, announced Zaghloul's release and freedom to travel to Europe to make his case.[10]

Gibbons gives this explanation:

Corporal (later Sergeant) George How had to stay behind in Egypt to help control the deadly riots and looting which erupted in March and April of 1919 (Mortlock family photograph).

The anti–English, or Nationalist Party in Egypt, who had persistently believed in a German and Turkish victory, had been for a long time working quietly all over the country to bring about among the illiterate population a rising against the British occupation. All sorts of lies were spread about, and the industrious but ignorant *fellaheen* were made to believe that they would benefit by a declaration of Egyptian independence. The prime movers of this agitation were the extreme Moslem fanatics of the University of El Azhar, and the students. The former were opposed to the substitution of a Christian for a Moslem power as suzerains of Egypt, while the latter were out for official jobs. Neither had the slightest intention of doing anything for the *fellaheen*, for whom "independence" would only have meant a return of the tyranny of the Turco-Egyptian Pasha, from which they had been delivered by a benevolent British rule. But the agitation had been very cleverly worked, and for the first time the *fellaheen* had been induced to side with their former oppressors. Riots broke out in Cairo, and the worst elements of the populations took the opportunity of indulging in their favourite pastime of looting and outrage. The result was that the British soldier, who had always been most friendly and considerate to the "Gyppoes," had his demobilisation delayed, and was called upon to assist the civil power in the preservation of order — an unpleasant task to the soldier at any time, but doubly so when his one idea was to get back to England as soon as he could after nearly four years' exile from home. About March 12th the trouble broke out in the provinces, and Battalion Headquarters and 300 other ranks were ordered to Benha, an important junction on the railway, which crossed the Nile at this point, and the chief town of the Kalioubieh Province.[11]

Once the news of Saad Zaghloul's arrest and exile became public knowledge in Cairo, "university and secondary school students poured into the streets to demonstrate. They overturned trams, smashed windows and street lamps and paraded through Cairo chanting Zaghloul's name. The riots worsened as the students were joined by others more interested in looting than politics." On 11 March the student strikes spread to government offices, doctors and lawyers, causing business in the capital to come to a standstill in what amounted to a general strike. "Shops in central Cairo and the offices of Faris Nimr's Anglophile *al-Muqattam* newspaper were sacked. British troops were called out; several rioters were shot and many more arrested. To the astonishment of the vast majority of Anglo-Egyptians who had assumed that the *fellaheen* were impervious to student agitation, the trouble now spread to the countryside."

By far the most callous act happened in the Nile valley: "The worst incident for the British side was the murder of seven unarmed soldiers and one civilian returning by train from Luxor to Cairo. At each station that the train pulled into, carrying their mutilated bodies, a frenzied crowd shouted with joy when they heard the English had been killed until the bodies were taken off and buried at Minieh."

On 17 March, General Bulfin, who had taken over command of the Egyptian Expeditionary Force when Allenby left to go to Paris for the peace conference, arrived by car in Cairo to take charge of the situation. An energetic and powerful personality, he immediately issued the sternest of warnings to notables and civil servants, and, hastily collecting all the troops available — including an Australian division awaiting demobilization — dispatched mobile columns into every province where there was trouble. Aircraft bombed every suspicious gathering and armored cars and airplanes fired on any suspect groups near roads and railways. From then on the security situation improved and within two days trains were running again in the Delta. The pacification of Upper Egypt, where the trouble had been worse, took longer, and General Shea's punitive column did not reach Aswan until 18 April. But in most of Egypt the rebellion was over by the end of March, even if sporadic incidents continued.[12]

The Times (London) first reported the trouble in Egypt on Monday, 17 March 1919, as follows:

FATAL RIOTS AT CAIRO
******

GENERAL ALLENBY'S
******

WARNING.
******

(From Our Own Correspondent)
CAIRO, March 10.
The situation has developed since the announcement of the acceptance of Rushdi Pasha's resignation of the Premiership.
On learning of the arrest of Zaghloul and the three other Nationalist pashas associated with him — of whom Hamed Bassel Pasha is a Beduin notable in the Fayum — their adherents lost no time in stirring up trouble, and today the police and military were compelled to clear the streets by force, several members of the mob being killed or wounded.
The students of the higher schools, ever the ablest material in the hands of political agitators, as the history of Egypt during the past decade abundantly proves, went on strike yesterday. The movement began in the law schools and spread rapidly to the medical, engineering, and agricultural schools, and extended this morning to the secondary schools.
The students demonstrated yesterday at the railway station for an hour, believing that the four pashas would be leaving from it; the departure was carried out, however, quite quietly, without the knowledge of the public, and the pashas are now on their way to Malta. The students also demonstrated before the Governorate, where they were joined by the more adventurous element from El Azhar, who helped to smash tramway-cars, lamps, & c.
This morning the demonstrations continued before the chief government offices and in the main streets, where considerable damage was done to shops, trams, and street lamps. The newspaper offices received special attention, some being wrecked. At some points, for instance at the Governorate, the crowd was quite good humoured and listened amusedly to the futile efforts of some students to incite them to excesses. At other points, however, the demonstrators refused to move on or to desist from damaging public and private property.
The police, who meanwhile had been reinforced by British troops, had to charge and fire upon the mob, with the result that some of the demonstrators were killed and several wounded. Large numbers were arrested.
The Sultan's palace and his private residence are strongly picketed by British troops, who are also patrolling the streets, where at present things are somewhat quieter, though an undercurrent of excitement is evident everywhere.

March 11.
The demonstrations continued today, and it was again necessary to fire on the mob before it would disperse. The demonstrators so far are composed mainly of

government pupils, Azhar students, and the rabble which is always attracted on such occasions, the two last-named elements doing most damage.[13]

Egyptian Nationalism

Although Egypt was Arab in speech, its historical traditions as well as its geographical situation predisposed it less to any Pan-Arab nationalism than to a separate nationalism of its own. Though most Egyptians welcomed the final extinction of Ottoman suzerainty in 1914, and the accompanying change in the title of their immediate ruler from "khedive" to "sultan," many did not take kindly to the continuing and apparently strengthened British protectorate. Especially after the accession of the Sultan Fuad in 1917, the native Nationalist party increased its popular following and its demands for national independence. The leader of this party—the *Wafd*, Saad Zaghloul, a lawyer of peasant stock, insisted on Egypt's being represented at the Paris Peace Congress as a sovereign power; and his subsequent arrest and deportation to Malta by the British authorities precipitated an insurrection which was put down in 1919 only by the energetic campaigning of General Allenby at the head of a British army of 60,000 men.[14]

Colonel Murphy, in his *History of the Suffolk Regiment*, relates:

> On March 25 the 5th Battalion [Suffolks] was selected to furnish a guard of honour for General Allenby on his return from a flying visit to Paris, the guard being commanded by Captain H. C. Wolton, M.C. The following day the Rev. E. D. Rennison and Captain H. C. Wolton left to inspect the graves of those of the battalion who were buried in Palestine and Syria. By their good offices the greater number of these graves were located and visited, photographs being sent to the next of kin. On Sunday, April 13, the battalion marched to the Cairo garrison church, the first parade of the kind it had attended at a church since leaving Thetford. On May 5 the commander-in-chief inspected the battalion, sending it a message of appreciation, and on the 26th bestowed high praise on the guard of honour, under Captain E. D. Wolton and Lieut. E. E. Ladell, which had paraded at Zeitoun. During that month a draft of two hundred men arrived, an additional hundred being transferred from the 5th Bedfordshire Regiment [162nd Brigade, 54th Division].[15]

Lt. Colonel Gibbons tells us that:

> During May demobilisation was opened again, and by the end of the month we were back in Cairo, having been relieved in Benha by a battalion of the Kamoan Rifles. The officials expressed their regret at our departure, and their appreciation of the courtesy and good behaviour of the troops. The men were indeed to be congratulated on their conduct in very trying circumstances. Their imperturbable good humour and their admirable restraint were a great credit to the battalion—and to the British Army, if I may be allowed to say so.
>
> We [now] came under the command of Brig. General E. M. Morris, C.M.G. [Companion of the Order of St. Michael and St. George, "Call Me God"], commanding 31st Infantry Brigade in Cairo, and after one or two temporary billets were quartered

in the Nasrieh Schools, forming part of the Cairo garrison. The 4th [Essex] were at Kasr el Nil barracks.[16]

As for the Norfolk Regiment, "The two battalions of the Norfolk Regiment remained in Beirut most of November. On the 28th they embarked for Egypt, arriving at Kantara on the 30th.... From Kantara they entrained for Helmieh near Cairo, where we part from them on December 31, 1918."[17]

Major Vivian Gilbert, author of *The Romance of the Last Crusade: With Allenby to Jerusalem*, stayed on with the army of occupation for more than a year following the armistice. He wrote:

> I spent long, interesting days in Jerusalem steeping myself anew in all its wonderful history and romance. I bathed at Jaffa, visited the orange groves and cantered past the thriving Jewish colony at Richon which stands on the hills above Bir Salem, where Allenby's headquarters used to be.
>
> Sometimes I wandered through the twilight dimness of the bazaars in Damascus, full of the odours of spices, rich with gorgeous colours, and chequered with the bright pattern of brilliant sunlight that filtered through rents in the overhanging matting. I watched Bedoueen glide spectrally along with wild roving eyes like startled deer, and children, more beautiful than any in the East, play in the living mazes of the crowds. I sipped sherbet of roses cooled with snow from Lebanon, and drank Mocha coffee in quaint silver cups.
>
> One day I rode through the wheatfields by a bridle path, climbing from Esdraelon to the rocky foot-hills through thick brush and scrub with undergrowth of large purple thistles, mallows with blossoms like pelargoniums, stocks of hollyhocks, honeysuckle and convolvulus; then between the shoulders of the mountains into the cool of the dull green olive groves, with just a pause for a moment in which to gaze back over the moorland where a million flowers were scattered, poppies, pimpernels, anemones, the mallow, the narcissus and blue iris, "roses of Sharon and lilies of the valley." Strange to think that some of the fiercest battles of the world had taken place there; that Thotnes, Rameses, Sennacherib, Cambyses, Alexander, Pompey, Titus, Saladin, Napoleon and many another had led his armies where Allenby led us!
>
> It was harvest time when I received my orders for demolibilisation. The afternoon before I left Palestine for Egypt, en route to England, I climbed to the top of the Crusaders' tower near Ramleh. It is known as the Church of Forty Martyrs, and is all that now remains of the stately pile that Richard's warriors built to the glory of God so many centuries ago. Nearby is the burial place of England's patron saint, St. George, martyred in Ludd in the year 303.
>
> I wanted to be alone; I wanted to think for a time of all that had happened since the day when I first set foot in France. The war had called me and I had become a soldier. For over four years I had been constantly with men I had learnt to admire and trust. From second lieutenant I had become major; many of my friends had been killed or disabled for life; I had been through the horrors of a great war but had experienced much of its romance and adventure. I stood in the tower and turned my back on the Mediterranean Sea, looking towards where the Jaffa road, like a white ribbon, winds it way up into the hills of Jerusalem. We had fought over every mile of the way, but now the country was at peace and the people were free to return to their homes.
>
> In the fields below me they were gathering in the harvest, Christians, Jews, Moslems, Syrians, Bedoueen, Arabs—all gathering in the golden grain. The air was

filled with bees and butterflies, and small birds whose sweet song was periodically hushed as a great hawk hovered overhead.

In the distance I could hear a military band playing the latest popular dance tune; nearer an Arab boy was playing on his reed flute as he drove his goats to water. We had finished our crusade, peace and freedom were in the Holy Land for the first time for five hundred years—and it all seemed worth while.[18]

Major Gilbert lost three brothers in various theaters in the war, and a fourth was seriously wounded.

POSTSCRIPT

Back Home

Following his demobilization and return to farming the land at Manor Farm, Worlington, Suffolk, Private Jake Mortlock religiously attended the regimental reunions and subsequently the Old Comrades' Association annual dinners. Sometimes, when pressed, he even "went on parade." It was on one of the later ones—possibly late 1940s or early 1950s—the Suffolk Old Comrades and the Mildenhall British Legion paraded on Remembrance Day. As they marched through the town, Mortlock thought: "I was glad I survived when I saw all your smiling faces."[1]

Was his return to England all the way by boat, or to Taranto or Marseilles? Private Jake Mortlock never alluded to his demobilization, or how he was trans-

All Saints Church in Worlington, Suffolk contains a memorial to the twelve men killed in the Great War and another to the two who perished in the Second World War (Mortlock family photograph).

The Street in Worlington, Suffolk, the village Private Jake Mortlock left to go to war in August 1914 (Mortlock family photograph).

ported back home. However, unlike his great friend Sergeant George How, he was not detailed to stay behind to control the rioting Egyptian "students"—as he referred to them.[2] The mention of George How, demobilization, and the method of transportation home evokes the certain conclusion that How would not relish the prospect of a sea voyage.

The Great War stamped a heavy hand on the little parish of Worlington. Twelve of its men were buried "in some foreign field" (like the poet who penned those immortal lines) and their sad inscriptions grace a memorial in All Saints' Church to "Our Glorious Dead."

Referring specifically to the 5th Battalion, Lt. Colonel Murphy, in his *History of the Suffolk Regiment*, wrote:

> The beginning of July [1919] saw most of the original officers and practically all the men gone. Thus was broken up a battalion with a fine record, that had lived as one big family, with little crime and general good feeling; that had earned an individual message of congratulation from the commander-in-chief, and that carried as its motto the burning words, addressed to the 54th Division, which fittingly closed its history. In the peace procession held in London on July 20, 1919, the colours of the 5th Battalion were carried amongst the massed colours of the territorial units of the kingdom.
>
> In November, 1919, the cadre of the battalion arrived home from Egypt. At short notice a party of officers and men escorted the colours to the station, Bury St. Edmunds, and handed them over to the officer commanding the cadre as representative of the mobilized battalion. From the station the cadre proceeded to the Corn Hill, where it was officially welcomed home by the mayor on behalf of the borough. Thus ended more than five years of mobilized service, of which four years and five months had been spent overseas. On February 27, 1920, a reunion dinner was held at the Corn Exchange, Bury St. Edmunds. This proved to be the last representative gathering of the 5th Battalion, and was an overwhelming success, about eight hundred of all ranks attending. During 1921 the battalion, under the command of Major B. E. Oliver, had been open for recruiting, but the area allotted to it did not include Beccles and Bungay, as was the case before the war.
>
> At the end of the year the 5th Battalion was informed that, owing to the need for national economy, it was to be disbanded, a decision naturally received with great regret. Accordingly, the battalion plate and the balance of its funds were placed in the hands of trustees. The war trophies were handed over to the officer commanding the Stowmarket company, thenceforth to form part of the 4th Battalion, but with the proviso that they should be handed back to the 5th Battalion should it ever be resuscitated. On Sunday, December 4, 1921, the colours of the battalion were laid up in St. Mary's Church, Bury St. Edmunds, an impressive ceremony marking the conclusion of sixty-two years of service.[3]

Appendix A

Participants in the Palestine Campaign

Allenby, 1st Viscount of Megiddo and Felixstowe, Field-Marshal Sir Edmund (Henry Hynman). (1861–1936). High commissioner of Egypt from 1919 until 1925, Allenby was appointed special commissioner at the time of the 1919 Rebellion. He advocated Zaghloul's release from exile, realizing that this was the only way to ease the tense atmosphere in Egypt. Following this Allenby acted firmly to suppress a number of industrial strikes in April 1919 and to restore order to the cities.*

Bulfin, General Sir Edward Stanislaus. Commanded the 21st Corps at Gaza III and thereafter. Helped to put down dangerous riots in Egypt in March 1919.

Chauvel. Lt. General H. G. Commander of Desert Mounted Corps, Gaza Battles and Megiddo.

Chetwode, Lt. General Sir Phillip W. Took over from below after Gaza II.

Dobell, Lt. General Sir Charles. Commander at Gaza I and II. Relieved after II.

Falkenhayn, General Erich von. Commander of the German Asia Corps.

Hare, Major General Sir Steuart Welwood. Commanded the 54th (East Anglian) Division, Gaza and Megiddo.

Inglefield, Major-General Francis Seymour. Commanded the 54th (East Anglian) Division, and for a short period in Egypt.

Kemal, Major General Mustapha. Commanded Turkish Seventh Army in Palestine and Syria, later to become Ataturk, "Father of Modern Turkey."

Kress von Kressenstein, Major General Friedrich. Was in command of Turkish Armies at Gaza I and II. Replaced by Otto Liman von Sanders after Gaza III.

Lane, Reginald E.S. Corporal, D Company, 1/5th Battalion the Suffolk Regiment, and 2nd lieutenant, lieutenant, and captain, Egyptian Labour Corps, Egypt, Palestine and France.

Liman von Sanders, Otto. Astute German general chosen to replace Kress von Kressenstein after Gaza III; made the best use of what was basically inferior mate-

---

*Joan Wucher King, *Historical Dictionary of Egypt* (Metuchen, N.J.: Scarecrow Press, 1984), p. 130.

rial because of failure of Ottoman government to accede to his requests for reinforcements and replacements—unlike his opponent's treatment by his government.

Maxwell, General Sir John Grenfell (1859–1929). General and commanding officer of Egyptian troops in World War I, Maxwell brought to his post lengthy experience with Egypt and its administration. He was a sympathetic and effective commanding officer, and with Milne Cheetham, a strong opponent of British annexation of the country. Maxwell introduced martial law, while allowing certain civilian institutions to remain functioning, but this move was unpopular with the nationalists and with many ordinary Egyptians whose lives it affected. Despite Maxwell's assurances to the contrary, Egyptian soldiers were eventually drafted for the labor corps supporting the British war effort, which by 1916 had succeeded in repulsing two major Ottoman attacks on Egypt. Conscription and forcible seizure of draught animals caused great disruption in rural areas, as the men needed to farm and the animals needed to run agricultural machinery were taken. Sir Archibald Murray replaced him in 1916. He returned to Egypt in 1919 as a member of the Milner Mission.*

Mortlock, Private S. Jacob P., D Company, 1st /5th Battalion, Suffolk Regiment. Enlisted in March 1913; demobilized in 1919. Served at Suvla Bay and Anzac. Went "over the top" in all three Gaza battles, Sharon and Armageddon. Taken off the force as an invalid in Gallipoli in late October 1915, returning the next year.

Murray, Lt. General Sir Archibald. Sent out to command the Egyptian Expeditionary Force. Was responsible for advancing railway and water pipe lines in tandem with pressing on Gaza. Relieved of command following two failures to take Gaza.

Teichman, Oskar. Captain (later major), Royal Army Medical Corps attached 1st Worcestershire Yeomanry.

Wollaston, H.A. Lt. Colonel, Rifle Brigade. Commanding officer of the 1st/5th Battalion the Suffolk, in Palestine. Killed in an air raid, June 1917, while on leave in London.

---

*Joan Wucher King, *Historical Dictionary of Egypt (African Historical Dictionaries No. 26)* (Metuchen, N.J., and London: Scarecrow Press, 1984), p. 427.

Appendix B

Basic British Army Structure

The following model is based on an infantry arm; that of the cavalry differed considerably.

4 Sections = 1 Platoon; 4 Platoons = 1 Company

1 Section					
2 Section =	1 Platoon	2 Platoon	3 Platoon	4 Platoon	Company =
3 Section					260 Men
4 Section					

4 Companies = 1 Battalion; 4 Battalions = 1 Brigade

1 Company					
2 Company =	1 Battalion	2 Battalion	3 Battalion	4 Battalion	Brigade =
3 Company					4,960 Men
4 Company					

3 Brigades = 1 Division; 2 Or More Divisions = 1 Army Corps

1 Brigade =	1 Division	2 Divisions	Division	Army Corps =
2 Brigade	(A Division	Division (additional)	Division (additional)	(Minimum of
3 Brigade	Also Included Supporting & Ancillary Units, I.E.: Artillery, Engineers, Medical Corps, Etc., Making For A Total Of Around 20,000 Men.)			38,000 Men)

Adapted and expanded by the author from Wallace, *Kitchener's Army and the Territorial Forces*, 59.

APPENDIX C

Casualties

Unless otherwise defined, the numbers of killed and wounded include prisoners of war.

1917 Palestine Losses
BRITISH, DOMINION AND IMPERIAL TROOPS
killed and wounded   37,351
sick admissions   138,821
(of the sick admissions, 1,760 died)

In one battle alone — the 2nd Battle of Gaza in April 1917 — the Norfolk battalions suffered heavy losses, as reported in *The History of the Norfolk Regiment*. From the 1/4th Battalion, six officers* and 49 troops were killed; 11 officers and 312 troops were wounded; the missing included one officer and 99 others. Total casualties for the 1/4th were 18 officers and 460 troops. From the 1/5th Battalion, six officers† and 13 troops were killed; nine officers and 401 troops were wounded; and the missing included four officers and 229 troops. Total casualties for the 1/5th were 19 officers and 643 troops. In addition, it was noted that 3,330 camels and 245 donkeys were lost.

TURKISH AND GERMAN TROOPS
killed and wounded   35,118+
(plus multitudes sick, many of whom died, but no exact figures are available)

1918 Palestine Losses
BRITISH, DOMINION, IMPERIAL, AND ALLIED TROOPS
killed and wounded   25,705

---

*The six were Major W.H.T. Jewson; Captains W. V. Morgan, S. D. Page, and R. W. Thurgar; Lieutenant F. J. Cole; Second Lieutenant J. Levy. Petre, *The History of the Norfolk Regiment, 1685–1918: Vol. II; 4 August 1914 to 31 December 1918*, p. 147.

†Lt. Colonel Grissell; Captains A. E. Beck, G. W. Birkbeck, and E. H. Cubitt; Lieutenants E. J. Gardiner, and R. R. Plaistowe. Petre, *The History of the Norfolk Regiment, 1685–1918: Vol. II; 4 August 1914 to 31 December 1918*, p. 147.

Arab Irregulars
killed and wounded   432+

In addition, 247+ camels and 23 donkeys were lost.

Turkish and German Troops
killed and wounded   10,299+
prisoners of war   79,880

Megiddo/Armageddon Losses, 19 September–26 October, 1918

British, Dominion and Imperial Troops
killed and wounded   5,566

Arab Irregulars
killed and wounded   unknown

In addition, 82 camels were lost.

Turkish Troops
overall losses, including prisoners of war   75,000+*

Austrian and German (Asia Corps) Troops
killed and wounded   3,700

---

*Randall Gray, with Christopher Argyle, *Chronicle of the First World War, Vol. II: 1917–1921* (New York: Facts on File, 1990), pp. 282 and 286.

APPENDIX D

Order of Battle of the Egyptian Expeditionary Force, October 1917: Third Battle of Gaza

The following is based on MacMunn and Falls, *Official History of the War: Military Operations, Egypt and Palestine*, Vol. II, Appendix.

GENERAL HEADQUARTERS

Commander-in-chief: General Sir Edmund Allenby
Chief of the General Staff: Maj. Gen. L. T. Bols
Brig. Gen. General Staff: Brig. Gen. G. P. Dawnay
Deputy Adjutant General: Maj. Gen. J. Adye
Deputy Quartermaster General: Maj. Gen. Sir Walter Campbell

Attached:
Major General Royal Artillery: Maj. Gen. S.C.U. Smith
Engineer-in-chief: Maj. Gen. H.B.H. Wright

DESERT MOUNTED CORPS

General Officer Commanding: Lt. Gen. Sir H. G. Chauvel
Brig. Gen., General Staff: Brig. Gen. R.G.H. Howard-Vyse
Deputy Adjut. & Quartermaster Gen.: Brig. Gen. E. F. Trew
General Officer Commanding, Royal Artillery: Brig. Gen. A. D'A. King

Australian and New Zealand Mounted Division

General Officer Commanding: Maj. Gen. E.W.C. Chaytor, C.B., C.M.G.

1st Australian Light Horse Brigade: Brig. Gen. C. F. Cox, C.B.; 1st A.L.H. Regt.; 2nd A.L.H. Regt.; 3rd A.L.H. Regt.

2nd Australian Light Horse Brigade: Brig. Gen. G. de L. Ryrie; 5th A.L.H. Regt.; 6th A.L.H. Regt.; 7th A.L.H. Regt.

New Zealand Mounted Rifles Brigade: Brig. Gen. W. Meldrum; Aukland Mounted Rifles Regt.; Canterbury Mounted Rifles Regt.; Wellington Mounted Rifles Regt.

Artillery: 18th Brigade Royal Horse Artillery — Ayr, Inverness, & Somerset Batteries.
Engineers: Australian and New Zealand Field Squadron.

Australian Mounted Division

General Officer Commanding: Maj. Gen. H. W. Hodgson
3rd Australian Light Horse Brigade.: Brig. Gen. L. C. Wilson; 8th A.L.H. Regt.; 9th A.L.H. Regt.; 10th A.L.H. Regt.
4th Australian Light Horse Brigade: Brig.-Gen. W. Grant; 4th A.L.H. Regt.; 11th A.L.H. Regt.; 12th A.L.H. Regt.
4th Mounted Brigade: Brig. Gen. P. D. Fitzgerald; 1/1st Warwick Yeo.; 1/1st Gloucester Yeo.; 1/1st Worcester Yeo.

Yeomanry Division

General Officer Commanding: Maj. Gen. G. de S. Barrow
6th Mounted Brigade: Brig. Gen. C.A.C. Godwin; 1/1st Buckingham; 1/1st Berkshire; 1/1st Dorset
8th Mounted Brigade: Brig. Gen. C. S. Rome; 1/1st City of London Yeo.; 1/1st Middlesex Yeo.; 1/3rd Co. of London Yeo.
22nd Mounted Brigade: Brig. Gen. F.A.B. Fryer; 1/1st Lincs. Yeo.; 1/1st Stafford Yeo.; 1/1st East Riding Yeo.
Artillery: XX Brigade Royal Horse Artillery — Berks, Hants, & Leicester Batteries.
Corps Troops: Machine-Gun Corps— Nos. 2, 3, 11, & 12 Light Armoured Motor Batteries. Nos. 1 & 7 Light Car Patrols.

Attached to Yeomanry Division:

7th Mounted Brigade: Brig. Gen. J. T. Wigan; 1/1st Sherwood Rangers; 1/1 R. Glos. Hussars; 1/1st S. Notts. Hussars
Artillery: Essex Battery Royal Horse Artillery; Hong Kong & Singapore Mountain Battery
Imperial Camel Corps Brigade: Brig. Gen. C. L. Smith, V.C., M.C.; 2nd Imperial Battalion; 3rd (Australian and New Zealand) Battalion; 4th (Australian and New Zealand) Battalion

20TH CORPS

General Officer Commanding: Lt. Gen. Sir P. W. Chetwode
Brig. General Staff: Brig. Gen. W. H. Bartholomew
Dep. Adj. & Quartermaster Gen.: Brig. Gen. E. Evans, D.S.O.
General Officer Commanding Royal Artillery: Brig. Gen. A. H. Short, C.B.
Chief Engineer: Brig. Gen. R. L. Waller

53rd (Welsh) Division

General Officer Commanding: Maj. Gen. S. F. Mott
158th Brigade: Brig. Gen. H.A. Vernon; 1/5th Royal Welch Fusiliers; 1/6th Royal Welch Fusiliers; 1/7th Royal Welch Fusiliers; 1/1st Herefordshire Regiment

159th Brigade: Brig. Gen. E. S. Money; 1/4th Cheshire Regiment; 1/7th Cheshire Regiment; 1/4th Welch Regiment; 1/5th Welch Regiment

160th Brigade: Brig. Gen. V.I.N. Pearson; 1/4th Royal Sussex Regiment; 2/4th Royal West Surrey Regiment; 2/4th Royal West Kent Regiment; 2/10th Middlesex Regiment

Artillery: 265th Brigade, Royal Field Artillery ("A," "B," & "C" Batteries) 266th Brigade, Royal Field Artillery ('A,' 'B,' & "C" Batteries), 267th Brigade, Royal Field Artillery ("A" & "B" Batteries).

Engineers: 436th, 437th, and 439th Field Companies, Royal Engineers.

60th (London) Division

General Officer Commanding: Maj. Gen. J. S. M. Shea

179th Brigade: Brig. Gen. Fitz J. M. Edwards; 2/13th London Regiment; 2/14th London Regiment; 2/15th London Regiment; 2/16th London Regiment

180th Brigade: Brig. Gen. C. F. Watson; 2/17th London Regiment; 2/18th London Regiment; 2/19th London Regiment; 2/20th London Regiment

181st Brigade: Brig. Gen. E. C. Da Costa; 2/21st London Regiment; 2/22nd London Regiment; 2/23rd London Regiment; 2/24th London Regiment

Artillery: 301st Brigade, Royal Field Artillery ("A," "B," & "C" Batteries); 302nd Brigade, Royal Field Artillery ("A," 413th, & "C" Batteries); 303rd Brigade, Royal Field Artillery ("A," "B," & "C" Batteries)

Engineers: 519th, 521st, & 522nd Field Companies, Royal Engineers

Pioneers: 1/12th Loyal North Lancashire Regiment.

74th (Yeomanry) Division

General Officer Commanding: Maj. Gen. E. S. Girdwood

229th Brigade: Brig. Gen. R. Hoare; 16th Devonshire Regiment; 12th Somerset Light Infantry; 14th Royal Highlanders; 12th Royal Scots Fusiliers

230th Brigade: Brig. Gen. A. J. M'Neill; 10th East Kent Regiment; 16th Royal Sussex Regiment; 15th Suffolk (Yeomanry) Regiment; 12th Norfolk Regiment

231st Brigade: Brig. Gen. C. E. Heathcote; 10th Shropshire Light Infantry; 24th Royal Welch Fusiliers; 25th Royal Welch Fusiliers; 24th Welch Regiment

Artillery: 44th Brigade, Royal Field Artillery (340th & 382nd Batteries); 117th Brigade, Royal Field Artillery ("A," "B," & "C" Batteries); 268th Brigade, Royal Field Artillery ("A," 368th & "C" Batteries)

Engineers: 5th (Royal Monmouth) & 5th (Royal Anglesey) Field Cos.

Corps Troops

Mounted Troops: 1/2nd County of London Yeomanry

Artillery: 96th Heavy Artillery Group (15th, 91st, & 181st Heavy Batteries; 378th, 383rd, & 440th Siege Batteries)

10th (Irish) Division
(attached to 74th (Yeomanry) Division)

General Officer Commanding: Maj. Gen. J. R. Longley

29th Brigade: Brig. Gen. R. S. Vandeleur; 6th Royal Irish Rifles; 5th Connaught Rangers; 1st Leinster Regiment; 6th Leinster Regiment

30th Brigade: Brig. Gen. F. A. Greer; 1st Royal Irish Regiment; 6th Royal Munster Fusiliers; 6th Royal Dublin Fusiliers; 7th Royal Dublin Fusiliers
31st Brigade: Brig. Gen. E. M. Morris; 5th Royal Inniskilling Fusiliers; 6th R. Inniskilling Fusiliers; 2nd Royal Irish Fusiliers; 5th Royal Irish Fusiliers
Artillery: 47th Brigade, Royal Field Artillery ("A," "B," & "C" Batteries); 48th Brigade, Royal Field Artillery ("A," "B," & "C" Btys.); 263rd Brigade, Royal Field Artillery (75th & "C" Batteries)
Engineers: 65th, 66th, & 85th Field Cos., Royal Engineers
Pioneers: 5th Royal Irish Regiment.

21st Corps

General Officer Commanding: Lieut. Gen. E. S. Bulfin
Brig. Gen, General Staff: Brig. Gen. E. T. Humphreys
Dep. Adjutant & Quartermaster Gen.: Brig. Gen. St. G. B. Armstrong
General Officer Commanding Royal Artillery: Brig. Gen. H. A. D. Simpson Bailkie
Chief Engineer: Brig. Gen. R. P. T. Hawksley

52nd (Lowland) Division

General Officer Commanding: Maj. Gen. J. Hill
155th Brigade: Brig. Gen. J. B. Pollock-M'Call; 1/4th Royal Scots Fusiliers; 1/5th Royal Scots Fusiliers; 1/4th King's Own Scottish Borderers; 1/5th King's Own Scottish Borderers
156th Brigade: Brig. Gen. A. H. Leggett; 1/4th Royal Scots; 1/7th Royal Scots; 1/7th Scottish Rifles; 1/8th Scottish Rifles
157th Brigade: Brig. Gen. C.D.H. Moore; 1/5th Highland Light Infantry; 1/6th Highland Light Infantry; 1/7th Highland Light Infantry; 1/ 5th Argyle & S. Highlanders
Artillery: 261st Brigade, Royal Field Artillery ("A," "B," & "C" Batteries); 262nd Brigade, Royal Field Artillery ("A" & "B" Batteries); 264th Brigade, Royal Field Artillery ("A" & "C" Batteries)
Engineers: 410th, 412th, & 413th Field Cos., Royal Engineers

54th (East Anglian) Division

General Officer Commanding: Maj. Gen. S. W. Hare
161st Brigade: Brig. Gen. W. Marriott-Dodington; 1/4th Essex Regiment; 1/5th Essex Regiment; 1/6th Essex Regiment; 1/7th Essex Regiment
162nd Brigade: Brig. Gen. A. Mudge; 1/5th Bedfordshire Regiment; 1/4th Northamptonshire Regiment; 1/10th London Regiment; 1/11th London Regiment
163rd Brigade: Brig. Gen. T. Ward; 1/4th Norfolk Regiment; 1/5th Norfolk Regiment; 1/5th Suffolk Regiment; 1/8th Hampshire Regiment
Artillery: 270th Brigade, Royal Field Artillery ('A,' 'B,' & "C" Batteries); 271st Brigade, Royal Field Artillery ("A" & "B" Batteries). 272nd Brigade, Royal Field Artillery ("B" & "C" Batteries)
Engineers: 484th & 486th Field Companies, Royal Engineers.

75th Division

232nd Brigade: Brig. Gen. H. J. Huddleston; 1/5th Devonshire Regiment; 2/5th Hampshire Regiment; 2/4th Somerset Light Infantry; 2/3rd Gurkha Rifles

233rd Brigade: Brig. Gen. the Hon. E. M. Colston; 1/5th Somerset Light Infantry; 1/4th Wiltshire Regiment; 2/4th Hampshire Regiment; 3/3rd Gurkha Rifles

234th Brigade: Brig. Gen. F. G. Anley; 1/4th Duke of Cornwall's Light Infantry; 2/4th Dorset Regiment; 123rd Outram's Rifles; 58th Vaughan's Rifles

Artillery: 37th Brigade, Royal Field Artillery (389th, 390th & 405th Batteries). 172nd Brigade, Royal Field Artillery (391st, 392nd, & 406th Batteries); 1st South African Field Artillery Brigade ("A" & "B" Batteries).

Engineers: 495th & 496th Field Companies, Royal Engineers

Corps Troops

Mounted Troops: Composite Regiment (1 Squadron Royal Glasgow Yeomanry; 1 Squadron Duke of Lancaster's Yeomanry; 1 Squadron 1/1st Hertfordshire Yeomanry).

Artillery: 97th Heavy Artillery Group (189th & 195th Heavy Batteries: 201st, 205th, 300th, & 380th Siege Batteries); C Heavy Artillery Group (10th Heavy Batteries; 43rd 134th, 379th, 422nd, & 423rd Siege Batteries); 102nd Heavy Artillery Group (202nd Heavy Batteries; 209th, 292nd, 420th, 421st, & 424th Siege Batteries).

Machine-Gun Corps: "E" Company, Tank Corps; 211th Machine-Gun Company

GENERAL HEADQUARTERS TROOPS

Royal Flying Corps, Middle East
General Officer Commanding: Brig. Gen. W. G. H. Salmond

Palestine Brigade, Royal Flying Corps: Lt. Colonel A. E. Borton; 5th (Corps Artillery) Wing (Nos. 14 & 113 Squadrons, Royal Flying Corps); 40th (Army) Wing (No. 67 Australian Flying Corps; No. 11 Squadron, No. 21 Balloon Company).

Artillery: 8th Mountain Brigade, Royal Garrison Artillery (10th & 11th Batteries [3.7-inch howitzers]); 9th Mountain Brigade, Royal Garrison Artillery ("A" & "B" Batteries [2.75-inch] and 12th [3.75-inch howitzers] Battery.

Attached Desert Mounted Corps: 7th Mounted Brigade & Imperial Camel Corps Brigade

Attached XX Corps: 10th (Irish) Division.

Appendix E

General Allenby's Official Report

The following is General Allenby's official report of the fighting on the 20th of September at Armagedon:

Our left wing having swung around to the east, had reached the line of Bidieh, Baka, and Messudiyeh Junction, and was astride the rail and roads converging at Nabulus.

Our right wing, advancing through difficult country against considerable resistance, had reached the line of Khan-Jibeit, one and one-fourth miles north-east of El-Mugheir and Es-Saweih, and was facing north astride the Jerusalem-Nabulus road.

On the north our cavalry, traversing the Field of Armageddon, had occupied Nazareth, Afule, and Beisan, and were collecting the disorganized masses of enemy troops and transport as they arrived from the south. All avenues of escape open to the enemy, except the fords across the Jordan between Beisan and Jisr-ed-Dameer were thus closed.

East of the Jordan Arab forces of the King of the Hedjaz had effected numerous demolitions on the railways radiating from Deraa, several important bridges, including one in the Yurmak Valley, having been destroyed. Very severe losses have been inflicted on the masses of Turkish troops retreating over the difficult roads by our air services.

The entire fighting ability of the enemy had thus been completely destroyed — without the possibility of any recovery. A truly magnificent achievement, and a stirring victory to boot — one that will certainly hasten the end of the Central Powers, by ensuring an eventual Allied triumph.

APPENDIX F

The Egyptian Government

The following is from A.H. Hourani, *Minorities in the Arab World*:

In Egypt the line of political development was different [from other areas under Ottoman domination]. Under Muhammad Ali and his successors the country became even more free of control from Stamboul than it had been before. Their rule was comparatively favourable for the minorities. There was a gradual shift from the concept of theocracy to that of a nationalism which could include the Copts as well as Moslems; and the Copts continued, as before, to hold many positions in the government. The rulers welcomed foreigners who wished to live and work in the country; Armenians, Syrians and others found an official career open to their talents, and vast opportunities in the commercial and financial life of the country. The dynasty was receptive to Western culture, and under its aegis a veneer of Western ideas and refinement spread over the upper classes at least, but the enlightenment was much less profound than it seemed, and beneath the surface Islamic feeling and hatred of the Christian West continued to be strong.

When the British occupied Egypt, they carried further certain tendencies begun by the dynasty of Muhammad Ali. They ensured greater freedom of religious thought and expression, greater equality before the law (although far from complete equality). They opened the country still wider to foreigners, and made full use of Eastern Christians as government officials: for example Syrian Christians in both the Egyptian and Sudanese governments, and a small but important group of Armenians, of whom the most famous was Nubar Pasha. But contrary to what might have been expected, they neither attempted to use the Copts as instruments of government nor gave them in any way a privileged position. Individual Copts co-operated with the British, like Butrus Pasha Ghali, but in general there were fewer Coptic officials under the British than there had been in previous periods.

Just as the political development of Egypt differed from that of other Arab-speaking countries in the nineteenth century, so did its nationalist movement. Arab nationalism did not take deep root in Egypt; the popular movement was that for a separate Egyptian nation and state, which first became important under Arabi Pasha in the eighteen-eighties, appeared again at the beginning of the twentieth century under Mustafa Kamil Pasha, and finally expressed itself in the Wafdist movement of Zaghlul Pasha.

Like Arab nationalism, Egyptian nationalism had two faces. On the surface it was a lay movement which linked together Copts and Moslems, and it was much influenced by the ideas of French liberalism. This was much more than a catchword, it corresponded to the realities of the situation; no one can deny that the Copts, who pride themselves on being descendants of the ancient inhabitants of the Nile valley, are fully a part of the Egyptian community. Moreover, the refusal of the British to give them the place they thought themselves entitled to, drove them into opposition to Great Britain. There was, however, a difference between the articulate leadership and the inarticulate spirit of the movement; the latter was so much more Islamic than the former.*

---

*A. H. Hourani, *Minorities in the Arab World* (London: Oxford University Press, 1947), pp. 31–32.

Appendix G

Statement of Aims in Palestine Proclamation of December 11, 1917

Preceded by aides-de-camp, [General Edmund] Allenby had on his right the commander of the French detachment, on his left the commander of the Italian detachment. At the base of the Tower of David, which was standing when Christ entered the city, the proclamation of military law was read: "Every person was declared free to pursue his lawful business without interruption, and every sacred building, pious foundation, or customary place of prayer, whether Christian, Hebrew, or Moslem, was assured protection."

APPENDIX H

Norfolk Regiment Officers

The following is from Petrie, *History of the Norfolk Regiment, 1685–1918*, Volume II:

History of the Norfolk Regiment

... From May 21st 1915 both Norfolk battalions became part of the 54th Infantry Division, and with the 1/5th Suffolk and 1/8th Hampshire constituted the 163rd Infantry Brigade. On the previous day the 1/4th Battalion had been sent to Watford, which it left by special train on July 29th, 1915, for Liverpool, where it embarked on the S.S. *Aquitania* en route for the Dardanelles. It was commanded by the adjutant, Captain E. W. Montgomerie, owing to the illness of Colonel Harvey. On the same day the 1/5th Battalion embarked, also on the *Aquitania*. It had been doing further training at Watford since early May. Each battalion had 1,000 other ranks and the officers originally with them were the following:

4th Battalion	5th Battalion
Commanding Officer	*Commanding Officer*
Captain E. W. Montgomerie	Colonel Sir Horace G. P. Beauchamp
Majors	*Majors*
None	W.J. Barton
	T.W. Purdy
Captains	*Captains*
C.W.W. Burrell	A.E. Ward (Adjutant)
S.D. Page	F.R. Beck
B.M. Hughes	A.D. Pattrick
W.H. Jewson	A. Wright
J.F.K. Fisher	E.R. Cubitt
B. Boswell	A.G. Coxon
	A.H. Mason
	E.R. Woodward

4th Battalion	5th Battalion
Lieutenants	*Lieutenants*
T.W. Flatt	T. Oliphant
V.C.C. Corke	E.A. Beck
W.V. Morgan	G.W. Birkbeck
C.K. Bampton	E. Gay
	V.M. Cubitt
	E.H. Cubitt
	A.G. Culme-Seymour
2nd Lieutenants	*2nd Lieutenants*
R.P. Caton	R. Burroughes
C.H.B. Elliott	M.B.G. Beauchamp
H.J. Bradshaw	A. Beck
G.H.C. Culley	A. R. Pelly
S.G. Steel	M. F. Oliphant
R.E. Burrell	R. Adams
R.B.C.M.T. de Poix	W.G.S. Fawkes
S.J.M. White	W.C. James
R.W. Thurgar	M.B. Buxton
F.H. Collison	
C.A. Wood	
C.B.S. Spackman	
J.H. Jewson	
Quartermaster	*Quartermaster*
R.W. Moore	Hon. Lieutenant Parker
Medical Officer	*Medical Officer*
J.C.F. Hosken	Capt. R.G. Laden

The *Aquitania* reached Mudros without adventure on August 5, and the troops on board her were taken on smaller vessels, on the 9th, to Imbros, whence they proceeded, on the 10th, to the landing place of the 54th Division in Suvla Bay and bivouacked on the beach. Following the evacuation of the Suvla Bay/Anzac Cove enclave the two Norfolk battalions, with the 54th (East Anglian) Division, were redeployed to Egypt. Later, in Palestine, they were decimated at the Second Battle of Gaza, and the survivors and replacements made great contributions to the eventual triumphs of General Sir Edmund Allenby's campaign.

APPENDIX I

Royal Army Service Corps Officers, 54th (East Anglian) Division

54th Divisional Train: Cairo

Acronyms for Appendix I

A/Capt. = Acting Captain
D.S.O. = Distinguished Service Order
O.C. = Officer Commanding
R.O. = Research Officer
S.S.O. = Staff Supply Officer
Sub = Subaltern (Second Lieutenant)
(T.) = Temporary
T.F. = Territorial Force

Headquarters

Transport

O.C. Train	Lt. Colonel	Lt. Colonel H.D. Russell
Adjutant	Captain	A/Capt. A.C. Demetriadi
Interpreter		Temp. Lieut. C. Rofe

Supply

S.S.O.	Major	Major O.W.H. Briggs
R.O.	Captain	
R.O.	Sub.	Temp. 2nd Lieut E.H.N. Hyde

Headquarters Company (No. 921 Company)

Transport

O.C.	Major	Major (T.) H.P.C. Verschoyle
T.O.	Sub.	Temp. 2nd Lieut. L. A. Solomon
T.O.	Sub.	Temp. 2nd Lieut. E.D.J. Taunt

Supply

S.O.	Captain	A/Capt. J.S. Allen

No. 2 Company (922 Company)

Transport

O.C.	Captain	A/Capt. D. McFarlane
T.O.	Sub.	Lieut. G.D. Ross

Supply

S.O.	Captain	Capt. V. Deacon

No. 3 Company (923 Company)

Transport

O.C.	Captain	Capt. H. Hime
T.O.	Sub.	Temp. 2nd Lieut. T. Town

Supply

S.O.	Captain	Capt. R.C. Horton.

No. 4 Company (924 Company)

Transport

O.C.	Captain	A/Capt. A. Soutar
T.O.	Sub.	Temp. 2nd Lieut. R.J.A. Strudwick

Supply

S.O.	Captain	A/Capt. J.C. Kent.

Appendix J

Equipment on Company Establishment

Establishment of 1,200 Burden and 30 Riding Camels.

Articles	No.	Average Wastage Monthly	Remarks
Rugs, camel	2,400	—	perpetual repairs necessary in heavy-burden companies.
Hobbles, camel	1,230	200	If used
Cacolets, lying	3	—	{Includes six heavy-
Cacolets, sitting	3	—	{burden saddles adapted.
Saddles, pack complete with pads	1,194	100 sets	Depends on weather.
(Average life of pads on working camels, three months.)			
Straps, breast	1,244	100	Varies. Fifty will often go in day.
Collars, head	1,320	500	
Girths & ties	1,260	100/300	
Ropes, loading, pairs	1,200	600	If made of fibre.
"		10	If made of manila.
Muzzles	120	20	Establishment not enough
Nets, fibre, pairs	600	200	Rarely used.
Protectors, pad	120	20	Depends on nature of ground.
Shears, camel	18	—	
Saddles, camel	30	1	Apt to break at top of riding tree
Bags, sand	1,230	600	To carry two days reserve forage on a mobile scale
(Always in possession of a Camel Company.)			
Sacks, 5-bushel	1,350	200	Split and used in place of nose bags.
Cordage, hawser	1,320 fathoms	—	Establishment insufficient.

APPENDIX K

Field Marshal Lord Allenby's Letter

The following is a letter used as the foreword to The History of the 1/5th Battalion: "The Suffolk Regiment."

This history of the 1/5 Battalion, Suffolk Regiment, has been compiled by a committee of officers, most of whom — if not all — were in the battalion during the war. They are to be congratulated on their work.

The record deals lightly with dangers and hardships; but there runs through the book a deep note of unselfish patriotism, of devotion to duty, and of reverence for those who made the Great Sacrifice.

The book, though primarily written for members of the regiment, will be read eagerly by the general public. Gallipoli, Gaza, Jerusalem, are names that stir the blood; and the campaigns that centre on them have an interest that is magnetic.

Chapter I makes reference to the South African War. During the operations therein described I was often in close touch with the Suffolk Regiment, and I well remember many of the situations and incidents mentioned.

In the Great War, the 1/5 Suffolks came under my command in 1917 — as a unit in the 163rd Brigade of the 54th Division. They took a prominent part in the capture of Gaza, the pursuit to Jaffa, the fighting about Et Tireh, the break through in the Plain of Sharon, and the advance to Beyrout.

After the armistice the battalion returned to Egypt, and demobilisation began. Soon, however, the troubles of 1919 broke out; and demobilization was suspended. Then the war-worn troops were set the difficult and thankless task of restoring civil order. This work, calling for great tact and self-restraint, was carried out ably and effectively.

It speaks well of the high tone of the 1/5 Suffolks that, at the end, despite stress and toil of war, they had lost none of their smartness on parade. I remember the good impression made by the Guard of Honour which received me — on my return from a flying visit to Paris — in March 1919; and I recall the fine appearance of the battalion on the occasion of my last inspection in May of that year.

No finer body of men fought in the war; and these reliant sons of Suffolk have left a memory that all who knew them will cherish while life lasts.

Allenby, V. M. [Viscount Megiddo] • Cairo • 16th May/'23.

Chapter Notes

Introduction

1. Michael S. Neiberg, *Fighting the Great War: A Global History* (Cambridge, Mass.: Harvard University Press, 2005), p. 140.
2. Lt. General Sir George MacMunn and Captain Cyril Falls, *The Official History of the War: Military Operation; Egypt and Palestine*, 2 Vols. (London: H.M.S.O., 1928–1930), Vol. I, pp. 94–95.
3. The Atlantic liners *Britannia* and *Mauretania* were now running as hospital ships between England and The Levant. Their size prevented them from entering the Egyptian harbors, but they could go into Mudros on the Island of Lemnos. The sick and wounded from Egypt destined for England were therefore dispatched to Mudros in smaller ships and transferred to the great vessels. MacMunn and Falls, *The Official History of the War*, Vol. I., p. 74.
4. Ibid.
5. Ibid., p. 95.
6. Ibid., p. 88.
7. Ibid., p. 87.
8. Ibid.
9. C. T. Atkinson, *The Regimental History of the Royal Hampshire Regiment: Vol. II, 1914–1918* (Glasgow: Robert Maclehose, 1952), p. 114.
10. Lt. Colonel Thomas Gibbons, *With the 1/5th Essex in the East* (Colchester: Benham and Company, 1921), p. 30.
11. Ibid.
12. L/Corporal Thomas Part, *The Diary of Thomas Reginald Part: An Australian Soldier Who Fought in World War I* (Cumberland Park, South Australia: Jones-Carter Digital, 1997), p. 8.
13. Gibbons, *With the 1/5th Essex in the East*, p. 30.
14. Lt. Colonel Russell Gurney, *History of the Northamptonshire Regiment: Vol. I, 1742–1934* (Aldershot, U.K.: Gale and Polden, 1935), p. 327.
15. F. Loraine Petrie, *The History of the Norfolk Regiment, 1685–1918: Vol. II; 4 August 1914 to 31 December 1918* (Norwich: Jarrold and Sons, Empire Press, 1924), p. 138.
16. Capts. A. Fair and E. D. Wolton, *The History of the 1st/5th Battalion: "The Suffolk Regiment"* (London: Eyre and Spottiswoode, 1923), pp. 35–36.
17. Guthrie Moir, *The Suffolk Regiment*. Famous Regiments Series; ed. Lt. General Sir Brian Horrocks (London: Lee Cooper, 1969), p. 93.
18. Fair and Wolton, *The History of the 1/5th Battalion: "The Suffolk Regiment,"* p. 37.
19. Atkinson, *The Regimental History of the Royal Hampshire Regiment, Vol. II:1914–1918*, p. 263.
20. Edwin Blackwell and Edwin C. Axe, *Romford to Beirut, via France, Egypt and Jericho: An Outline of the War Record of "B" Battery, 271st Brigade, R.F.A. [Royal Field Artillery] (1/2nd Essex Battery, R.F.A.), With Many Digressions* (Clacton-on-Sea, Essex, England: R. W. Humphris, 1926), p. 7.
21. Housman, Laurence, ed. *War Letters of Fallen Englishmen* (Philadelphia: Pine Street Books, University of Pennsylvania Press, 2002), pp. 48–49.
22. John L. Stoddard, *John L. Stoddard's Lectures: Vol. II: Constantinople, Jerusalem, and Egypt.* 10 Vols. (Boston: Balch Brothers, 1905), p. 235.
23. Lawrence James, *The Golden Warrior: The Life and Legend of Lawrence of Arabia* (New York: Paragon House, 1993), p. 87.
24. General Sir Archibald Murray, *Sir Archibald Murray's Despatches (June 1916–June 1917)* (London: J. M. Dent and Sons, 1920), pp. 184–185.
25. Housman, ed. *War Letters of Fallen Englishmen*, p. 109. Lt. Fletcher was educated at Eton and Merton College, Oxford. He was a candidate for Holy Orders. He was killed in action during the first Battle of Gaza, March 26, 1917.
26. "Ismâîlîyeh (Ismailia), situated on the north bank of Lake Timsâh was the main centre of operations during the construction of the Suez Canal, but has to a large degree lost its importance. It has a governor of its own and con-

tains 10,373 inhabitants. The pretty gardens and plantations and the view of the blue lake lend the town an appearance of an oasis, with both European and Arab cultivation. Close by to this area is the site of the Biblical 'Land of Goshen.'" Karl Baedeker, *Egypt and the Sudan: Handbook for Travelers* (Leipzig: Karl Baedeker; London: T. Fisher Unwin; New York: Charles Scribner's Sons, 1914), pp. 179–180.

27. Lieutenant Siegfried Sassoon, *Sherston's Progress* (New York: Book League of America, 1936), pp. 132–133.

28. Jean Moorcroft Wilson, *Siegfried Sassoon: The Making of a War Poet; A Biography 1886–1918* (New York: Routledge, 1999), p. 448.

29. Francis Whiting Halsey, *The Literary Digest History of the World War, Compiled from Original and Contemporary Sources: American, British, French, German, and Other, Vol. 8; August 1914–October 1918* (New York and London: Funk and Wagnalls, 1920), p. 206.

30. Badcock, *History of the Transport Services of the Egyptian Expeditionary Force, 1916–1918* (London: Hugh Rees, 1925), p. 313.

31. Patrick J. Quinn, *The Great War and the Missing Muse: The Early Writings of Robert Graves and Siegfried Sassoon* (Selinsgrove: Susquehannah University Press. London and Toronto: Associated University Presses, 1994), p. 202.

32. Ibid., pp. 202–203.

33. Wilson, *Sassoon: The Making of a War Poet*, 457.

34. Sassoon, *Sherston's Progress*, 156–157.

35. Lena Ashwell, O.B.E. (Order of the British Empire) was the third daughter of Commander Pocock of the Royal Navy. Honorary organizer of Lena Ashwell Concerts at the front, 1914–1920; and chairman of the Lena Ashwell Players. Her principal parts included Mrs. Dane in *Mrs. Dane's Defence*, 1900; Ellen Farndon in *Chance the Idol*; 1902; Katusha in *Resurrection*; Pia and Gamma in *Dante*; Yo San, *Darling of the Gods*; Leah Kleschna, *Bond of Ninon*; Deborah in *The Shulamite*; and Iris in *Iris Intervenes*. She was manager of the Kingsway Theatre. Her publications include *Modern Troubadours*; *Reflections from Shakespeare*; and *The Stage, Myself a Player*, her autobiography published in 1936. (*Who's Who 1957: An Annual Biographical Dictionary With Which is Incorporated "Men And Women of the Time."* London: Adam and Charles Black; New York: Macmillan, 1958, p. 101.) The concert party was made up of soprano, contralto, instrumentalist, tenor, baritone or bass, entertainer and accompanist. All were professionals and some 600 artists were involved throughout the war period. Concerts were free in the camps. (Lena Ashwell, *Myself a Player*. London: Michael Joseph, Ltd., 1936, pp. 11–12.)

36. Wilson, *Siegfried Sassoon: The Making of a War Poet*, p. 456, and endnote 120 on p. 576. Plate 51, between pp. 280 and 281, which depicts them, names them as "Lena Ashwell Concert Party, Y.M.C.A., Egypt."

37. Blackwell and Axe, *Romford to Beirut, via France, Egypt and Jericho*, p. 53.

38. Gibbons, *With the 1/5th Essex in the East*, p. 30.

39. Sapper F. T. Mills, *Great Uncle Fred's War: An Illustrated Diary, 1917–1920*, researched and edited by Alan Pryor and Jenifer K. Woods (Whitstable, Kent: Pryor Publications, 1985), pp. 34 and 38.

40. Joyce Marlow, ed. *The Virago Book of Women and The Great War, 1914–1918* (London: Virago Press, 1998), p. 259.

41. Badcock, *A History of the Transport Services of the Egyptian Expeditionary Force*, p. 319.

Chapter One

1. Robert Henry Wilson, *Palestine 1917*, edited by Helen Millgate (Tunbridge Wells: Costello, 1987), pp. 40–41.

2. The equivalent of 2½pence; 26 centimes; or 5 cents. Karl Baedeker, *Egypt and The Sudan: Handbook for Travellers* (Leipsig: Karl Baedeker. London: T. Fisher Unwin. New York: Charles Scribner's Sons, 1914), p. 1.

3. Fair and Wolton, *The History of the 1/5th Battalion: "The Suffolk Regiment,"* pp. 38–9.

4. "Alexandria, called *Iskanderîeh* by the Arabs and Turks, the second town of Egypt and one of the most important commercial cities on the Mediterranean, is situated at the western extremity of the Nile delta, on the narrow sandy strip separating Lake Mareotis from the sea.... In 1907 the population amounted to 332,246 (now estimated at 400,000), of whom about 60,000 were Europeans (Franks), chiefly Greeks (24,600) and Italians (15,916), but including some Britons, French, and Austrians, and a few Russians, Germans, etc. The Mohammedans live chiefly in the northern and western quarters of the city, and the Europeans in the eastern quarter and at Ramleh. The town has a governor of its own." The city boasted many fine hotels, clubs, restaurants, cafés, and other facilities, calculated to make wealthy expatriate Europeans feel at home. The existence of a "British Club" is likely to have a similar effect on Britons. Arab coffee was served at various cafés at ⅟₁₀ 1 piastre per cup (2–5 cents). German beer was obtainable, and the city possessed several confectioners of some renown. A thriving seaport since time immemorial "is entered and cleared annually by upwards of 2,000 steamers, about half of which are under the British flag." Baedeker, *Egypt and The Sudan: Handbook for Travellers*, p. 11.

5. The author's uncle, Ord. Telegraphist Al-

bert Joseph Brown, Royal Navy, married a French woman in Cairo and settled there, and apparently that was the last any of the family ever heard of him.

6. Sassoon, *Sherston's Progress*, p. 133.
7. Blackwell and Axe, *Romford to Beirut, via France, Egypt and Jericho*, pp. 27, 28 and 32.
8. L/Corporal T. R. Part, *The Diary of Thomas Reginald Part: An Australian Soldier Who Fought in World War I*, p. 15.
9. Lt. Frank Apperly, "Medicine and War," *Journal of the American Medical Association* Vol. 119 (May 1942), pp. 349–351.
10. Gibbons, *With the 1/5th Essex in the East*, p. 31.
11. Ibid., pp. 31–32.
12. Ibid., pp. 32–33.
13. Ibid.
14. Ibid., pp. 36–37.
15. Ibid., p. 37.
16. Fair and Wolton, *The History of the 1/5th Battalion*, p. 40.
17. Victor Horsley was educated at Cranbrook and London University. He was a professor of pathology at University College Hospital, London, and fellow of the Royal Society. He died on active service in Mesopotamia, 16 July 1916, age 59.
18. Housman, ed., *War Letters of Fallen Englishmen*, pp. 139–140.
19. Ibid., pp. 138–139.
20. Blackwell and Axe, *Romford to Beirut, via France, Egypt and Jericho*, pp. 27–29.
21. Geoffrey Moorhouse, *Hell's Foundations: A Social History of the Town of Bury in the Aftermath of the Gallipoli Campaign*. (New York: Henry Holt, 1992), pp. 56–57.
22. Fair and Wolton, *The History of the 1/5th Battalion*, p. 40.
23. Gibbons, *With the 1st/5th Essex in the East*, 38.
24. Blackwell and Axe, *Romford to Beirut, via France, Egypt and Jericho*, p. 30.
25. Private Mortlock—with considerable hyperbole—claimed to have witnessed young, barefooted Egyptian boys raising sparks with the hard-skinned soles of their feet while riding on the back of trams. Interview, February 2, 1965.
26. Blackwell and Axe, *Romford to Beirut, via France, Egypt and Jericho*, pp. 40–1.
27. W.H.T. Squires, *Peregrine Papers: A Tale of Travel in the Orient* (Norfolk, Va.: W.H.T. Squires, 1923), pp. 188–189.
28. Badcock, *A History of the Transport Services of the Egyptian Expeditionary Force*, p. 298.
29. Ibid., 297–299.
30. Sir Llewellyn Woodward, *Great Britain and the War of 1914–1918* (London: Methuen and Co., 1967), pp. 116–117.
31. Flora Armitage, *The Desert and the Stars: A Portrait of T. E. Lawrence* (London: Faber and Faber, 1956), p. 97.

32. Robert Graves, *Lawrence and the Arabian Adventure* (Garden City, N.Y.: Doubleday, Doran and Co., 1928), pp. 65–66.
33. Jay Winter and Blaine Baggett, *The Great War and the Shaping of the 20th Century* (New York: Penguin Studio, 1996), p. 122.
34. Byron Farwell, *The Gurkhas* (New York: W.W. Norton, 1984), p. 107.
35. Lt. General Sir Archibald Wavell, *The Palestine Campaigns: Part of the Series Campaigns and Their Lessons*, edited by Major General Sir Charles Callwell (London: Constable, 1928), p. 41.
36. Shepheard's Hotel was owned by the Egyptian Hotels Company and had 400 rooms (180 with bathrooms), separate sites for families, a famous terrace with bands on Saturday, garden, restaurant, bar, post and telegraph office, and other amenities; it was open all year. (Baedeker, *Egypt and The Sudan: Handbook for Travellers*. Leipzig: Karl Baedeker, 1914, pp. i, 35.) "Shepheard's was out of bounds to all but officers and gentlemen, but there were plenty of other hotels where the Egyptians would give you a great spread." (Moorhouse, *Hell's Foundations: A Social History of the Town of Bury in the Aftermath of the Gallipoli Campaign*, p. 58.) Shepheard's Hotel functioned largely in the same fashion until 1952 when it was destroyed by fire. The present day Shepheard's is not even located on the same site and has little, other than the name, in common with the original.
"The old Shepheard's Hotel, where Englishmen at ease took their gin and tepid Scotch on the verandah, is gone." (Linda Steet, *Veils and Daggers: A Century of National Geographic's Representation of the Arab World*. Philadelphia: Temple University Press, 2000, p. 146.)
37. Situated in the city east of the Nile between the main Cairo Railway Station (Gare Centrale) and the Abdin Palace. To the immediate southwest were the Ezbekiah Gardens which Major Gilbert mentions. "Ezbekiyeh Garden, or simply Ezbekiyeh, on the site of the former Ezbekiyeh Lake and named after the heroic Ezbek, the general of Sultan Kâït Bey (1468–96) who brought the general and son-in-law of Bayazid I as a captive to Cairo. A mosque, now vanished, was erected in 1495 in honour of his victory. The fine gardens, which have several entrances (admission half a piastre), were laid out by M. Barillet, formerly chief gardener to the city of Paris. They cover an area of 20 and a half acres and contain a variety of rare and beautiful trees and shrubs. Crows and kites are here very numerous. In the centre of the garden is a roller skating rink. English military bands play on Tuesday and Friday evenings during the summer." (Baedeker, *Egypt and The Sudan: Handbook for Travellers*. Leipzig: Karl Baedeker, 1914), pp. 42 and 51.

38. Major Vivian Gilbert, *The Romance of the Last Crusade: With Allenby to Jerusalem* (New York: D. Appleton, 1923), pp. 69–70.

39. Alan Pryor and Jenifer K. Woods, eds. *Great Uncle Fred's War: An Illustrated Diary, 1917–1920* (Whitstable, Kent: Pryor Publications, 1985), p. 40.

40. André Raymond, *Cairo*, translated by Willard Wood (Cambridge, Mass.: Harvard University Press, 2000), pp. 323–324, and elsewhere.

41. Captain R. Hugh Knyvett, *"Over There" With the Australians* (New York: Charles Scribner's Sons, 1918), pp. 97–98.

42. "Egypt was the hub of a wheel whose spokes radiated into the western oases, where the Senussi were met and repulsed, into Gallipoli, across the Sinai Desert into Palestine and Syria, and south to Aden and the Sudan. It was the great rest and recreation center for troops of the Gallipoli and Palestine campaigns. The beginning of the war found William Jessop, British by nationality, but with American Association training, directing a small city Y.M.C.A. at Cairo under the auspices of the American International Committee. He became chief secretary for Egypt and promoted activities in every direction from that base." (*Service with the Fighting Men: An Account of the Work of the American Young Men's Christian Association in the World War*, Vol. II. Editorial board William H. Taft, et al. New York: Association Press, 1922, p. 397.)

43. Knyvett, *"Over There" With the Australians*, p. 84.

44. *Service with the Fighting Men: An Account of the Work of the American Young Men's Christian Associations in the World War*, edited by Taft, Harris, Kent and Newlin (New York: Association Press, 1922), pp. 411–412.

45. Ibid., Vol. I.

46. Alexander Aitken, *Gallipoli to the Somme: Recollections of a New Zealand Infantryman* (London: Oxford University Press, 1963), p. 2.

47. E. Gorman, *With the Twenty-second: A History of the Twenty-second Battalion, A.I.F.* (Melbourne: H.H. Champion), p. 15.

48. A. B. Facey, *A Fortunate Life* (Ringwood, Victoria: Penguin Books Australia, 1981), p. 248.

49. Peter Mansfield, *The British in Egypt* (Holt Rinehart and Winston, 1972), pp. 213–214.

50. F. K. Crowley, ed., *A New History of Australia* (Melbourne: William Heinemann Australia, Ltd., 1974), p. 320.

51. Part, *The Diary of Thomas Reginald Part*, pp. 8–9.

52. Sapper H. P. Bonser, "A Sapper in Palestine," in *Everyman at War: Sixty Personal Narratives of the War*, edited by Charles B. Purdom (London: J. M. Dent and Sons, 1930), pp. 312–313.

53. Blackwell and Axe, *Romford To Beirut, via France, Egypt and Jericho*, p. 32.

54. Captain C.E.W. Bean, *From Anzac to Amiens* (Canberra: Australian War Memorial, 1928) (*Argus*, 21 January 1915), p. 66. From John F. Williams, *Anzacs, The Media and The Great War* (Sydney: University of New South Wales Press, 1999), p. 59.

55. Correlli Barnett, *The Great War* (New York: G. P. Putnam's Sons, 1979), p. 166.

56. Knyvett, *"Over There" With The Australians*, p. 151.

57. Part, *The War Diary of Thomas Part*, p. 18.

58. It is the author's opinion that either the figure for divisions or the figure for total troops is an error—for, according to his calculations, as they stand they make for divisions of nearly 31,000 troops, half as much again as the normal absolute maximum.

59. Lt. Col. A. Kearsey, *The Operations in Egypt and Palestine, 1914 to June 1917: Illustrating the Field Service Regulations* (Aldershot: Gale and Polden, 1919), p. 12.

60. Murray, *Sir Archibald Murray's Despatches, June 1916–June 1917*, p. 190.

61. Kearsey, *The Operations in Egypt and Palestine*, p. 30.

62. John Grigg, *Lloyd George: War Leader 1916–1918* (London: Penguin Books, 2003), p. 149.

63. This soon acquired the nickname of "Bill Harris."

64. Colonel J. W. Wintringham, *With the Lincolnshire Yeomanry in Egypt and Palestine, 1914–1918* (Grimsby, Humberside: Lincolnshire Life, 1979), pp. 30–31.

65. Ibid.

66. The reader should refer to Map C to ascertain Suez Canal locations mentioned in the text.

67. Lt. Colonel Anthony Rawlinson, *Adventures in the Near East, 1918–1922* (New York: Dodd, Mead and Company, 1924), pp. 14–15.

68. Gurney, *History of the Northamptonshire Regiment, Vol. I, 1742–1934*, p. 327.

69. *Service With the Fighting Men: An Account of the Work of the American Young Men's Christian Association*, Vol. I. Eds., William Howard Taft, Frederick Harris, Frederic Houston Kent and William J. Newlin (New York: Association Press, 1922), p. 72.

70. Badcock, *A History of the Transport Services of the Egyptian Expeditionary Force*, p. 95, details the number of camels allocated to each division. "In first half of 1916 approx. 4,000. First half of 1918 approx. 1,200. The steady reduction was due to the improved possibilities of using wheeled transport, as the general advance went on and the forces moved from desert sand to the harder ground and roads." In his foreword, he

stated: "In the history of that ancient land [Egypt] it is probable that no greater demand was ever made on the 'ship of the desert' to carry freight across its native element, and the management of 40,000 burden camels alone was a gigantic undertaking."
71. Knyvett, *"Over There" with the Australians*, pp. 154–155.
72. Fair and Wolton, *The History of the 1/5th Battalion*, p. 42.
73. Ibid., p. 43. Also alluded to by Australian signaler, L/Cpl. Thomas Part, in his *The War Diary of Thomas Part.* Colonel Badcock, in the "Personal Reminiscences" section of his book *A History of the Transport Services of the Egyptian Expeditionary Force, 1916–1918*, pp. 302–303, states that H.R.H. "was at G.H.Q. for several weeks about this time (March 1916)."
74. Badcock, *A History of the Transport Services of the Egyptian Expeditionary Force*, pp. 302–303.
75. Part, *The Diary of Thomas Reginald Part*, p. 10.
76. Badcock, *A History of the Transport Services of the Egyptian Expeditionary Force*, p. 302.
77. Brig. General Vincent J. Esposito, *A Concise History of World War I* (New York: Frederick. A. Praeger, 1964), p. 200.
78. Siegfried Sassoon, *Sherston's Progress*, p. 153.
79. Knyvett, *"Over There" With the Australians*, p. 87.
80. Fair and Wolton, *The History of the 1/5th Battalion*, pp. 43–44.
81. Lord Maurice Hankey, *The Supreme Command, 1914–1918*, Vol. II (London: George Allen and Unwin, 1961), p. 531.
82. Blackwell and Axe, *Romford to Beirut, via France, Egypt and Jericho*, pp. 48–49.
83. Robert Henry Wilson, ed. Helen D. Millgate, *Palestine 1917* (Tunbridge Wells, Kent: Costello, 1987), p. 81.
84. Private Mortlock. Interview, 1 August 1966.
85. Fair and Wolton, *The History of the 1/5th Battalion*, pp. 44–45.
86. Gibbons, *With the 1st/5th Essex in the East*, 41.
87. Ibid., 40.
88. Fair and Wolton, *The History of 1/5th Battalion*, p. 46.
89. Ibid.
90. Gibbons, *With the 1/5th Essex in the East*, p. 46–47.
91. Kearsey, *The Operations in Egypt and Palestine, 1914–June 1917*, p. 32.
92. Wavell, *The Campaigns in Palestine*, p. 59.
93. Badcock, *A History of the Transport Services of the Egyptian Expeditionary Force*, p. 323.
94. Captain Oskar Teichman, *The Diary of a Yeomanry M.O: Egypt, Gallipoli, Palestine and Italy* (London: T. Fisher Unwin, 1921), p. 218.
95. Possibly 1914 might have rated higher for Private Jake Mortlock, who gobbled his army dinner and then bicycled home thirty-something miles to enjoy a second one in the evening.
96. Fair and Wolton, *The History of the 1/5th Battalion*, p. 48.
97. Private Mortlock. Interview, December 26, 1965.
98. Blackwell and Axe, *Romford to Beirut via France, Egypt and Jericho*, p. 52.
99. Ibid.
100. Ibid.

Chapter Two

1. Woodward, *Great Britain and the War of 1914–1918*, p. 116.
2. Kearsey, *The Operations in Egypt and Palestine*, pp. 18–19.
3. Private Jake Mortlock. Interview, Christmas 1966.
4. Blackwell and Axe, *Romford to Beirut, via France, Egypt and Jericho*, p. 54.
5. Badcock, *History of the Transport Services of the Egyptian Expeditionary Force*, p. 47.
6. Blackwell and Axe, *Romford to Beirut, via France, Egypt and Jericho*, pp. 54, 60.
7. Ibid., pp. 61, 62.
8. A single sheet of canvas that did little to shield people from the sun. Wintringham, *With the Lincolnshire Yeomanry in Egypt and Palestine, 1914–1918*, pp. 30–31.
9. Blackwell and Axe, *Romford to Beirut, via France, Egypt and Jericho*, pp. 63–64.
10. Fair and Wolton, *The History of the 1/5th Battalion: "The Suffolk Regiment,"* pp. 51–52.
11. Private Jake Mortlock. Interview, Christmas 1966.
12. Blackwell and Axe, *Romford to Beirut, via France, Egypt and Jericho*, p. 65.
13. Badcock, *History of the Transport Services of the Egyptian Expeditionary Force*, p. 314. "Deir el Belah was an attractive place too at first, with its orchards of apricot trees, pomegranates, etc."
14. MacMunn and Falls, *The Official History of the War: Military Operations; Egypt and Palestine*, Vol. II, Part 2, pp. 286–287.
15. Badcock, *A History of the Transport Services of the Egyptian Expeditionary Force*, Introduction, pp. 9–10.
16. Ibid., p. 158.
17. Kearsey, *The Operations in Egypt and Palestine, 1914–June 1917*, p. 35.
18. Ibid.
19. Ibid., pp. 35–37.
20. Ibid., pp. 70–71.
21. David Lloyd George, *War Memoirs of David Lloyd George: Vol. IV, 1917* (Boston: Little, Brown, and Company, 1934), pp. 88–89.

22. "And Samson lay till midnight, and arose at midnight, and took the doors of the gate of the city, and the two posts, and went away with them, bar and all, and put *them* upon his shoulders, and carried them up to the top of an hill that *is* before Hebron." *The Holy Bible* (King James Version), The Book of Judges, 16: 3.

23. *El Muntar* ("the watch tower") is thought to be the eminence to which the strong man of Israel (Samson) "took the doors of the gate of the city, and the two posts, and went away with them, bar and all." Halsey, *The Literary Digest History of the World War*, Vol. 8, p. 213.

24. Halsey, *The Literary Digest History of the World War*, Vol. 8, pp. 209–210.

25. MacMunn and Falls, *The Official History of the War: Military Operations; Egypt and Palestine*, Vol. I, pp. 283–284.

26. Ibid., p. 288.

27. Ibid., pp. 289–290.

28. Petrie, *The History of the Norfolk Regiment, 1685–1918: Vol. II*, pp. 141–142.

29. MacMunn and Falls, *The Official History of the War: Military Operations; Egypt and Palestine*, Vol. I, p. 293.

30. Teichman, *The Diary of a Yeommanry M.O.*, pp. 121–122.

31. MacMunn and Falls, *The Official History of the War: Military Operations; Egypt and Palestine*, Vol. I, pp. 301–302.

32. Halsey, *The Literary Digest History of the World War*, Vol. 8, p. 210.

33. Blackwell and Axe, *Romford to Beirut, via France, Egypt and Jericho*, p. 68.

34. Ibid.

35. Gibbons, *With the 1st/5th Essex in the East*, p.66.

36. MacMunn and Falls, *The Official History of the War: Military Operations; Egypt and Palestine*, Vol. II, Part 1, p. 303.

37. Wavell, *The Palestine Campaigns*, p. 82.

38. Grigg, *Lloyd George: War Leader 1916–1918*, p. 149.

39. Captain Reginald Lane recalled the incident almost fifty years later. Interview, 5 May 1966.

40. Captain Reginald E.S. Lane (corporal, D Company, 1/5th Battalion, the Suffolk Regiment, at the time), Egyptian Labour Corps, 1917–1919. Interview, November 5, 1965.

41. Private Jake Mortlock. Interview, 27 March 1967. Mortlock had a very low opinion of British generals for ordering frontal assaults "in broad daylight" and for being generally out of touch with the frontline troops. "All the generals ought to be shot" was his declared wartime panacea, although he did develop a great admiration for Sir Edmund Allenby.

42. Ibid. Interview, November 5, 1965.

43. "On the 25th March two brigades of the 54th (East Anglian) Division, 162nd and 163rd, occupied the Sheikh Abbas Ridge without opposition, but retired with the army after two days and one night sustained by a single issue of water." Moir, *The Suffolk Regiment*, p. 103.

44. Private Jake Mortlock. Extract from letter to his cousin, Jack Parker, of Beck House Farm, Beck Row, Mildenhall, Suffolk.

45. Blackwell and Axe, *Romford to Beirut, via France, Egypt and Jericho*, p. 84.

46. *The Times* (London), Saturday, April 7, 1917, p. 5a and b.

47. *The New York Times*, Tuesday, April 3, 1917, p. 5, c. 5.

48. Ibid., cc. 5 and 6.

49. Ibid.

50. Captain O. Teichman, *A Diary of a Yeomanry M.O.: Egypt, Gallipoli, Palestine, and Italy* (London: T. Fisher Unwin, 1921), pp. 124–125.

51. Ibid.

52. *The Times* (London), Monday, April 2, 1917, p. 8b.

53. Lloyd George, *War Memoirs of David Lloyd George: Vol. VI, 1918*, pp. 201–202.

54. Ibid., p. 202.

55. Lloyd George, *War Memoirs of David Lloyd George: Vol. IV, 1917*, p. 89.

56. Ibid.

57. Quoted in Lt. General Sir Archibald Wavell's *The Campaigns in Palestine*, p. 80.

58. *The Great Events of the Great War*, Vol. 5, eds. Charles F. Horne and Walter F. Austin (Washington, D.C.: National Alumni, 1923), p. 402.

59. Ibid., p. 81.

60. Teichman, *The Diary of a Yeomanry M.O.*, pp. 122–123.

61. Captain Basil H. Liddell Hart, *The Real War, 1914–1918* (Boston: Little, Brown, and Company, 1930), p. 208.

62. Atkinson, *The Regimental History of the Royal Hampshire Regiment: Vol. II, 1914–1918*, p. 266.

63. General Sir Archibald Wavell, *Allenby: A Study in Greatness* (New York: Oxford University Press, 1941), p. 188.

64. General Archibald Murray, *Sir Archibald Murray's Despatches (June 1916–June 1917): With Specially Prepared Maps, and Portraits* (London: J. M. Dent and Sons, 1920), p. 153.

65. *The New York Times*, Sunday, April 15, 1917, I, p. 14, cc. 1 and 2.

66. Wavell, *The Campaigns in Palestine*, p. 83.

67. Ibid., pp. 83–84.

68. Teichman, *The Diary of a Yeomanry M.O.*, pp. 127–128.

69. Other references to this vessel suggest that it was a French coast guard ship; all agree on the armament.

70. MacMunn and Falls, *The Official History of the War: Military Operations; Egypt and Palestine*, Vol. II, Part 1, p. 424.

71. "The reserve water for the army was carried in copper cisterns called 'fanatis,' each holding about fifteen gallons. These metal containers were suspended by rings from each side of the camel's pack saddle, 30,000 camels being employed for this purpose alone." Gilbert, *The Romance of the Last Crusade: With Allenby to Jerusalem*, p. 89.
72. MacMunn and Falls, *The Official History of the War: Military Operations; Egypt and Palestine*, Vol. II, Part II (Appendices), pp. 424–427.
73. Blackwell and Axe, *From Romford to Beirut, via France, Egypt and Jericho*, p. 84.
74. Petrie, *The History of the Norfolk Regiment, 1685–1918: Vol. II; 4 August 1914 to 31 December 1918*, pp. 143–144.
75. Ibid., 144.
76. Ibid.
77. Blackwell and Axe, *From Romford to Beirut via France, Egypt, and Jericho*, p. 84.
78. Ibid., p. 85.
79. Ibid.
80. Petrie, *The History of the Norfolk Regiment*, p. 145.
81. Ibid., pp. 144–146.
82. Blackwell and Axe, *From Romford to Beirut via France, Egypt, and Jericho*, pp. 84–85.
83. Possibly one of these dead troopers supplied Pvt. Jake Mortlock with the black leather belt with the large brass buckle, to which the author was to become painfully familiar!
84. MacMunn and Falls, *The Official History of the War: Military Operation; Egypt and Palestine*, Vol. I, pp. 337–340. *This redoubt, subsequently known as "Tank Redoubt," was, as has been stated, outside its objective, but the 163rd Brigade appears to have swung slightly to its left, though, as we have seen, men of the 5/Norfolk also entered the redoubt. P. 340.
85. Fair and Wolton, *The History of the 1/5th Battalion*, "The Suffolk Regiment," p. 62. This redoubt, subsequently known as "Tank Redoubt," was, as has been stated, outside its objective, but the 163rd Brigade appears to have swung slightly to its left, though men of the 5/Norfolk also entered the redoubt. MacMunn and Falls, *The Official History of the War*, Vol. I, p. 340.
86. Private Jake Mortlock. Interview, 19 April 1967.
87. Ibid., p. 59.
88. Fair and Walton, *The History of the 1/5th Battalion: "The Suffolk Regiment,"* p.59.
89. Gurney, *History of the Northamptonshire Regiment, Vol. I, 1742–1934*, p. 327.
90. Gibbons, *With the 1/5th Essex in the East*, pp. 81–2.
91. "The Norfolks lay there in swathes just as they'd been hit." Private Mortlock. Interview, 2 December 1967.

92. Fair and Wolton, *The History of the 1/5th Battalion*, p. 83.
93. MacMunn and Falls, *The Official History of the War*, Vol. I, pp. 346–348.
94. Teichman, *The Diary of a Yeomanry M.O*, pp. 140–141.
95. Ibid., p. 82. Also, Murray, *Sir Archibald Murray's Despatches*, pp. 163–164.
96. Major W.H.T. Jewson; Captains W. V. Morgan, S. D. Page, and R. W. Thurgar; Lieutenant F. J. Cole; Second-Lieutenant J. Levy. Petrie, *The History of the Norfolk Regiment, 1685–1918: Vol. II; 4 August 1914 to 31 December 1918*, p. 147.
97. Lt. Colonel Grissell; Captains A. E. Beck, G. W. Birkbeck, and E. H. Cubitt; Lieutenants E. J. Gardiner, and R. R. Plaistowe. Ibid.
98. Atkinson, *The Regimental History of the Royal Hampshire Regiment, Vol. II: 1914–1918*, pp. 268–269.
99. *The Times* (London), Monday, April 23, 1917, p. 8e.
100. MacMunn and Falls, *The Official History of the War*, Vol. I, p. 351.
101. *The Times* (London), Wednesday, April 25, 1917, p. 6b.
102. Grigg, *Lloyd George: War Leader 1916–1918*, p. 149.
103. Murray, *Sir Archibald Murray's Despatches (June 1916–June 1917)*, pp. 164–165.
104. Bevin Alexander, *How Great Generals Win* (New York: W. W. Norton, 1993), p. 174.
105. Ibid., footnote.
106. Murray, *Sir Archibald Murray's Despatches (June 1916–June 1917)* p. 151.
107. Marjorie Drackett-Case (*née* Rumbelow). Interview, May 1, 1968.
108. Kearsey, *The Operations in Egypt and Palestine, 1914–June 1917*, p. 39.
109. Captain Reginald E. S. Lane. Interview, 5 November 1959.
110. Gurney, *History of the Northamptonshire Regiment, Vol. I, 1742–1934*, p. 327.
111. Private Jake Mortlock. Interview, 20 August 1963.
112. Gibbons, *With the 1/5th Essex in the East*, p. 86.
113. Teichman, *The Diary of a Yeomanry M.O.*, pp. 154–155.
114. Gibbons, pp. 86–87.
115. Ibid., p. 88.
116. Ibid., pp. 88–89.
117. Lt. Colonel Anthony Rawlinson, *Adventures in the Near East, 1918–1922* (New York: Dodd, Mead and Company, 1924), pp. 14–15.
118. Lloyd George, *War Memoirs of David Lloyd George: Vol. IV, 1917*, p. 91.
119. Ibid., pp. 90–94.
120. *The Dictionary of National Biography, Vol. 26: 1931–1940*, edited by L. G. Wickham Legg (London: Oxford University Press/Geoffrey Cumberlege, 1949), pp. 9–11.

Chapter Three

1. Petrie, *The History of the Norfolk Regiment, 1685–1918: Vol. II; 4 August 1914 to 31 December 1918*, p. 149.
2. General Sir Archibald Wavell, *Allenby: A Study in Greatness* (New York: Oxford University Press, 1941), p. 187.
3. Badcock, *The History of the Transport Services of the Egyptian Expeditionary Force*, p. 316.
4. Ibid., p. 189.
5. Captain B. H. Liddell Hart, *The Real War, 1914–1918* (Boston: Little, Brown, and Company, 1930), p. 307.
6. H. C. Armstrong, *The Grey Wolf: The Life of Kemal Ataturk* (New York: Capricorn Books, 1961), pp. 67–69.
7. Gilbert, *The Romance of the Last Crusade: With Allenby to Jerusalem*, pp. 78–79.
8. Fair and Wolton, *The History of the 1/5th Battalion*, p. 68.
9. Ibid.
10. Hankey, *The Supreme Command, 1914–1918*, Vol. II, p. 685.
11. Blackwell and Axe, *Romford to Beirut, via France, Egypt and Jericho*, p. 91.
12. MacMunn and Falls, *The Official History of the War*, Vol. II, Part II, p. 16.
13. Private Mortlock. Interview, 6 July 1968.
14. Ernest May, *Signal Corporal: The Story of the 2nd London Irish Rifles (2/18th Battalion, the London Regiment) 1914–1918* (London: Johnson Publications, 1972), pp. 53–54.
15. Petrie, *The History of the Norfolk Regiment, 1685–1918: Vol. II*, p. 149.
16. Wilson, *Palestine 1917*, pp. 86–87. (Shades of *Exodus* 16: 13; *Numbers* 31–33; *Psalms* 78: 26–31, and 105: 40.)
17. Fair and Wolton, *The History of the 1/5th Battalion*, pp. 72–73.
18. Pvt. Jake Mortlock. Interview, 18 September 1967.
19. Petrie, *The History of the Norfolk Regiment, 1685–1918: Vol. II, 1918*, p. 149.
20. Lloyd George, *War Memoirs of David Lloyd George, Vol. VI, 1918*, pp. 202–203.
21. Gilbert, *The Romance of the Last Crusade*, pp. 195–196.
22. Bruce Feiler, *Walking the Bible: A Journey by Land through the Five Books of Moses* (New York: William Morrow, 2001), pp.343–345.
23. MacMunn and Falls, *The Official History of the War: Military Operations; Egypt and Palestine*, Vol. II, Part 1, pp. 76–77.
24. Ibid., pp. 65–66.
25. General Sir Ian Hamilton, *Gallipoli Diary*, Vol. II (New York: George H. Doran, 1920), pp. 287–288.
26. Ibid., p. 288.
27. Petrie, *The History of the Norfolk Regiment, 1685–1918: Vol. II, 1918*, pp. 149–50.
28. Gilbert, *The Romance of the Last Crusade: With Allenby to Jerusalem*, p. 83.
29. MacMunn and Falls, *The Official History of the War: Military Operations; Egypt and Palestine*, Vol. II, Part 1, p. 65.
30. Liddell Hart, *The Real War, 1914–1918*, p. 307.
31. The Rt. Hon. Winston S. Churchill, *The World Crisis, 1916–1918*, Vol. II (New York: Charles Scribner's Sons, 1927), p. 47.
32. Neiberg, *Fighting the Great War: A Global History*, p. 148.
33. MacMunn and Falls, *The Official History of the War: Military Operations; Egypt and Palestine*, Vol. II, Part 1, p. 77 fn.
34. Lieutenant-General Sir Harry "Chauvel was appointed to command the Desert Mounted Corps in June 1917, becoming the first Australian corps commander, although not of an Australian Corps since the Desert Mounted Corps contained New Zealand, Indian and British Yeomanry regiments as well as Australian light horse." Jeffrey Grey, *A Military History of Australia* (Cambridge: Cambridge University Press), pp. 113–114. Also in T. B. Millar's *Australia in Peace and War: External Relations 1788–1977* (New York: St. Martin's Press, 1978), p. 74.
35. Several sources cite Magdhala, in the Sinai, as being the first. Author.
36. F. K. Crowley, ed., *A New History of Australia*, p. 340.
37. MacMunn and Falls, *The Official History of the War: Military Operations; Egypt and Palestine*, Vol. II, Part 1, pp. 63–64.
38. Corporal Herman Walters, an American Army infantry veteran of the North African and Italian World War II campaigns, stated that the Gurkhas were paid a bounty per ear.
39. Pvt. Jake Mortlock. Interview, 19 April 1967.
40. Ibid., pp. 66–69.
41. Sapper Harry Bonser, *Everyman at War: Sixty Personal Narratives of the War*, pp. 313–314.
42. MacMunn and Falls, *The Official History of the War: Military Operations; Egypt and Palestine*, Vol. II, Part I, p. 69.
43. Private Jake Mortlock. Interview, November 3, 1968.
44. Blackwell and Axe, *Romford to Beirut, via France, Egypt and Jericho*, pp. 94–95.
45. Ibid., p. 70.
46. Gibbons, *With the 1/5th Essex in the East*, pp. 95–96.
47. Ibid., p. 96.
48. Ibid.
49. *Source Records of the Great War*, Vol. V, edited by Walter F. Austin and Charles F. Horne (Washington, D.C.: National Alumni, 1923), pp. 403–404.

50. Gibbons, *With the 1/5th Essex in the East*, p. 96.
51. Ibid., 96–101.
52. Ibid., pp. 103–104.
53. Fair and Wolton, *The History of the 1st/5th Battalion*, p. 85, and Moir, *The History of the Suffolk Regiment*, p. 104.
54. This is one version of the affair. The other is that the officers realized what had happened and that Zowaid Trench was not being attacked, and therefore decided to attack it themselves. Owing to the heavy casualties sustained by them it was not possible to clear up this point. In any case considerable delay was caused. MacMunn and Falls, *The Official History of the War: Military Operations; Egypt and Palestine*, Vol. I, Part 1, footnote p. 72.
55. "On 31 October the attack was resumed and the Turkish positions turned and taken in the third Battle of Gaza, in which the battalion had 215 casualties." Gurney, *History of the Northamptonshire Regiment, Vol. I, 1742–1934*, p. 327.
56. MacMunn and Falls, *The Official History of the War: Military Operations; Egypt and Palestine*, Vol. I, Part 1, pp. 71–74.
57. Petrie, *The History of the Norfolk Regiment, 1685–1918: Vol. II*, pp. 150–151.
58. Gibbons, *With the 1/5th Essex in the East*, p. 104.
59. *Source Records of the Great War*, Vol. V, edited by Walter F. Austin and Charles F. Horne (Washington, D.C.: National Alumni, 1923), pp. 403–404.
60. Mills, *Great Uncle Fred's War*, p. 42.
61. *The Times* (London) Monday, November 5, 1917, p. 2b.
62. *The Times* (London) Monday, November 5, 1917, p. 2b.
63. *The Times* (London) Tuesday, November 6, 1917, p. 1.
64. Wintringham, *With the Lincolnshire Yeomanry in Egypt and Palestine, 1914–1918*, p. 58.
65. When I, the author, child-like said I would have liked to have been a sniper, he replied that I wouldn't have because "they'd soon bring a mortar to bear on you."
66. Pierre van Paasen, *The Days of Our Years* (New York: Dial Press, 1940), p. 197.
67. Private Mortlock. Interview, 12 December 1971.
68. Sand-fly fever is spread by any of the small biting two-winged insects (families *Psychodidae*, *Simuliidae*, and *Ceratopogonidae*).
69. *The Times* (London) Tuesday, November 6, 1917, p. 2b.
70. Ibid., Thursday, November 8, 1917, p. 7.
71. Ibid., November 12, 1917, p. 6.
72. MacMunn and Falls, *The Official History of the War: Military Operations; Egypt and Palestine*, Vol. II, Part 2, p. 65.
73. Blackwell and Axe, *Romford to Beirut, via France, Egypt and Jericho*, pp. 109–110.
74. Mills, *Great Uncle Fred's War*, p. 43.
75. Frank D. Davison, *The Wells of Beersheba: An Epic of the Australian Light Horse, 1914–1918* (Sydney: Longmans, 1933; revised edition 1947), p. 57–58.
76. *Everyman at War: Sixty Personal Narratives of the War*, edited by C. B. Purdom (London: J. M. Dent and Sons, 1930), pp. 319–325.
77. Pvt. Jake Mortlock. Interview, 20 April 1967.
78. Fair and Wolton, *The History of the 1/5th Battalion: "The Suffolk Regiment,"* pp. 82–83.
79. Blackwell and Axe, *Romford to Beirut, via France, Egypt and Jericho*, p. 110.
80. Teichman, *The Diary of a Yeomanry M.O.*, p. 217.
81. Halidè Edib, *Memoirs of Halidè Edib* (New York: Century Company, 1923), pp. 459–460.
82. Teichman, *The Diary of a Yeomanry M.O.*, p. 195.

Chapter Four

1. H.A.L. Fisher, *A History of Europe: Vol. III, The Liberal Experiment* (Cambridge, Mass.: Riverside Press), p. 1179.
2. Carlton J. H. Hayes, *Contemporary Europe Since 1870* (New York: Macmillan, 1953), p. 407.
3. Churchill, *The World Crisis, 1916–1918*, Vol. II, p. 47.
4. Gilbert, *The Romance of the Last Crusade: With Allenby to Jerusalem*, 154–170.
5. May, *Signal Corporal: The Story of the 2nd London Irish Rifles*, 110–111.
6. Badcock, *The History of the Transport Services of the Egyptian Expeditionary Force*, p. 814.
7. *The Holy Bible* (King James Version), The Book of Daniel, 12: 12.
8. Gilbert, *The Romance of the Last Crusade: With Allenby to Jerusalem*, pp. 174–76, 177–79.
9. Ibid., p. 180.
10. Halsey, *The Literary Digest History of the World War*, Vol. 8, p. 216.
11. Ibid.
12. Van Paasen, *The Days of Our Years*, p. 379.
13. Squires, *Peregrine Papers*, pp. 163–166. On the occasion of his visit in 1898 the Kaiser presented the city with a clock, set on a tower above the Jaffa Gate. Two of its faces are in Latin and two in Arabic.
14. Sapper Harry P. Bonser, in *Everyman at War: Sixty Personal Narratives of the War*, p. 315.
15. Halsey, *The Literary Digest History of the World War*, Vol. VIII, p. 219. "When the late Kaiser made his memorable tour of the East (1898), the Sultan, as a courtesy between excellent, good friends, had a wide gap made in the

wall beside the Jaffa Gate for his entry. It proved such a convenience that it has never been closed" (Squires, *Peregrine Papers*, p. 163).

16. *The Story of the Great War*, Vol. VII, ed. Frederick Palmer (New York: P. F. Collier and Son, 1917), pp. 273–274.

17. Ibid., and Halsey, *The Literary Digest History of the World War*, Vol. 8, p. 219.

18. Gilbert, *The Romance of the Last Crusade: With Allenby to Jerusalem*, pp. 174–76.

19. T. E. Lawrence, *Seven Pillars of Wisdom* (Garden City, N.Y.: Doubleday, Doran and Company,, 1936), p. 453.

20. Murphy, *The History of the Suffolk Regiment*, p. 311.

21. "We were early astir next morning—November 13th—and started on the march again at 6.15, our destination being Julis, some five miles N.E. of Mejdel, where we arrived at 8 o'clock. I understood the brigade was to be in reserve to the 75th Division, which was a few miles ahead, pressing hard upon the retreating Turks. We spent some hours resting in a delightful hollow, wondering what our part in the day's work was likely to be. It was evident that a brisk action was in progress, and from a vantage point above our hollow the Turkish shrapnel could be seen bursting in white puffs high above what were evidently the attacking troops of the 75th Division. I understood the objective to be 'Junction Station,' the junction with the Jerusalem railway at the foot of the hills about 15 miles away. Some miles to the west the 52nd Division was also seen to be engaged." Gibbons, *With the 1/5th Essex in the East*, pp. 106–107.

22. MacMunn and Falls, *The Official History of the War: Military Operations; Egypt and Palestine*, Vol. II, Part 2, p. 265–267.

23. Mills, *Great Uncle Fred's War*, pp. 25–26.

Chapter Five

1. Blackwell and Axe, *Romford to Beirut, via France, Egypt and Jericho*, p. 125.

2. Personnel of the 1/5th Suffolks were billeted in a large white building which dominated the skyline on a postcard-photograph Private Mortlock sent his mother, dated January 15, 1918. Mortlock Family Papers.

3. Gurney, *History of the Northamptonshire Regiment, Vol. I, 1742–1934*, p. 327.

4. Teichman, *The Diary of a Yeomanry M.O.*, pp. 202–206.

5. Fair and Wolton, *The History of the 1/5th Battalion*, pp. 91–92.

6. Stoddard, *John L. Stoddard's Lectures*, Vol. II, pp. 115–116.

7. Blackwell and Axe, *Romford to Beirut via France, Egypt and Jericho*, p. 147.

8. Sapper H. P. Bonser, Detached Duty, U.U. Cable Section, Royal Engineers, Palestine and Syria, 1917–1918, personal narrative in *Everyman at War: Sixty Personal Narratives of the War*, pp. 315–316.

9. Private Mortlock. Letter to his cousin Jack Parker dated March 1, 1918.

10. Blackwell and Axe, *Romford to Beirut, via France, Egypt and Jericho*, p. 129.

11. S. Ilan Troen, *Imagining Zion: Dreams, Designs and Realities in a Century of Jewish Settlement* (New Haven and London: Yale University Press, 2003), p. 33. "The prosperity of the Templers, German religious societies that had settled in Palestine in the latter half of the nineteenth century, was persuasive evidence in support of private ownership of land: 'These (Templer settlements) are not merely self self-sustaining, they are decidedly prosperous. The neat two-story stone houses, their large barns usually of stone, and their plantations, livestock and equipment make a pleasing rural picture which is enhanced by close examination.'"

The Encyclopædia Judaica, Vol. 15 (Jerusalem: Keter Publishing House Jerusalem, 1978), p. 6757, is more explicit: "Individual Templers also settled in Jerusalem and in 1878 founded a residential quarter (the German Colony) in the Emek Refaim district; others settled in Jaffa and Haifa. In 1875, according to figures given by the founders of the sect, there were 750 Templers living in Erez Israel, who maintained two schools and a hospital. In 1902 they founded a settlement in the Lydda plain, naming it Wilhelma (after the Kaiser), and in 1906 two small villages, Bethlehem and Waldheim, were established in Lower Galilee by Templers who had rejoined the Lutheran Church. In the towns, Templers and ex-Templers (who had returned to Lutheranism) owned hotels, stores, and workshops. By 1914 their number had risen to 1,200. When the British conquered Palestine in 1917–1918, the German settlers were deported as enemy aliens, but were allowed to return after the war. In the summer of 1938 there were 1,500 Germans of Templer origin living in the country, owning 6,700 acres of land. When World War II broke out, they were interned and by 1943 they were repatriated to Germany—in exchange for Palestinians who had fallen into German hands—or deported to Australia. Their property was taken over by the Israel government in 1948, and was taken into account in the Reparations Agreement concluded with the German Federal Republic."

Via Internet searches I discovered several things. The original aim of the Templers was to rebuild the Temple at Jerusalem in anticipation of Christ's Second Coming. The original trademark of two Templer settlements' orange groves included a large orange with "Jaffa Oranges" across the equator with "Sarona" in an arc above and "Wilhelma" likewise below. The site of the Sarona community is where some government offices in Tel Aviv are located. A *moshav* is a communal enterprise very much similar in conception to a *kibbutz*.

12. Now (2006) known as "Bene Atarot" *moshav* in Sharon, just over four miles north of Ben Gurion Airport (Tel Aviv). It was founded 1948 on lands of former German colony, Wilhelma, pop. 350. Memorial to former *moshav* Atarot and its members who died in the War of Independence. Wilhelma-Hamidya is a German colony named after Kaiser Wilhelm II and Turkish Sultan Abdul Hamid II, founded in 1903. During World War II it served as an internment camp for German citizens who were later deported to Australia. *Gazetteer of Israel*, 5th Edition, 141: 59; p. 101.

13. Murphy, *The History of the Suffolk Regiment, 1914–1927*, p. 312. Private Mortlock sent his mother a postcard of Wilhelma, dated January 1918, indicating a large white building atop a hill in the center of village, possibly a school, where he and others were billeted. Interview, January 1968.

14. Fair and Wolton, *The History of the 1/5th Battalion*, pp. 89–91.

15. Blackwell and Axe, *Romford to Beirut, via France, Egypt and Jericho*, p. 129.

16. Bonser, in *Everyman at War: Sixty Personal Narratives of the War*, p. 315.

17. Candler, *The Long Road to Baghdad*, Vol. II, p. 198.

18. Fair and Wolton, *The History of the 1/5th Battalion*, p. 93.

19. Blackwell and Axe, *Romford to Beirut, via France, Egypt and Jericho*, p. 136.

20. Sassoon, *Sherston's Progress*, pp. 136–137.

21. Albert Hourani, *A History of the Arab Peoples* (Cambridge, Mass.: Belknap Press of Harvard University Press, 1991), p. 289.

22. A Siegfried Sassoon concert party, Wilson, *Siegfried Sassoon: The Making of a War Poet*, pp. 456–457. Also Sassoon, *Sherston's Progress*, pp. 156–157.

23. This was not *The Rose of Gaza* production which the men were compelled (marched) to attend, occasioning much cursing at the time, but eventually enjoyed immensely by all, as recounted by Private Jake Mortlock (interview), unless an encore. Upon checking I have discovered that the performance occurred prior to Gaza III.

24. Hankey, *The Supreme Command 1914–1918*, Vol. II, p. 760.

25. MacMunn and Falls, *The Official History of the War: Military Operations; Egypt and Palestine*. Vol. II, Part 2, p. 411.

26. Fair and Wolton, *The History of the 1/5th Battalion: "The Suffolk Regiment,"* p. 94.

27. Ibid., 94–95.
28. Ibid., 95–96.
29. Teichman, *The Diary of a Yeomanry M.O.*, p. 223.
30. Badcock, *History of the Transport Services of the Egyptian Expeditionary Force*, p. 319.
31. Ibid., pp. 320–321.
32. Ibid., p. 412.
33. Martin Gilbert, *Winston S. Churchill: Vol. IV; The Stricken World, 1916–1922* (Boston: Houghton Mifflin, 1975), p. 84.
34. Gibbons, *With the 1/5th Essex in the East*, pp. 125–130.
35. MacMunn and Falls, *The Official History of the War: Military Operations Egypt and Palestine*, p. 418.
36. Blackwell and Axe, *Romford to Beirut, via France, Egypt and Jericho*, Vol. II, Part 2, pp. 137–138.
37. Hankey, *The Supreme Command 1914–1918*, Vol. II, p. 817.
38. Ibid., p. 818.
39. Private Jake Mortlock (the author's father). Interview, June 18, 1968.
40. Petrie, *The History of the Norfolk Regiment, 1685–1918: Vol. II*, pp. 157–158.
41. David R. Woodward, *Field Marshal Sir William Robertson: Chief of the Imperial General Staff in the Great War* (Westport, Conn.: Praeger, 1998), p. 211.
42. Sassoon, *Sherston's Progress*, pp. 148–149.
43. Ibid., p. 152.
44. Gibbons, *With the 1/5th Essex in the East*, p. 124.
45. Teichman, *The Diary of a Yeomanry M.O.*, p. 252.
46. Blackwell and Axe, *Romford to Beirut via France, Egypt and Jericho*, p. 147.
47. Wilson (ed. Millgate), *Palestine 1917*, p. 112.
48. Leslie Stein, *The Hope Fulfilled: The Rise of Modern Israel* (Westport, Conn., and London: Praeger, 2003), p. 138.
49. *Letters from Fallen Englishmen*, pp. 38–39.
50. Victor H. Rothwell, *British War Aims and Peace Diplomacy, 1914–1918* (Oxford: Clarendon, 1971), pp. 189–190.
51. Gibbons, *With the 1/5th Essex in the East*, pp. 134–135.
52. Ibid., pp. 134–136.

Chapter Six

1. Wavell, *The Campaigns in Palestine*, p. 195.
2. Sanders, *Five Years in Turkey*, p. 254.
3. Ibid., pp. 256–261.
4. Ibid., p. 259.
5. Ibid., 260.
6. John Patrick Douglas, Baron Kinross,

Ataturk: A Biography of Mustafa Kemal, Father of Modern Turkey (New York: William Morrow, 1965), p. 138.
   7. Badcock, *A History of the Transport Services of the Egyptian Expeditionary Force*, pp. 9–10, 158.
   8. Liddell Hart, *The Real War, 1914–1918*, p. 439.
   9. Halsey, *The Literary Digest History of the World War*, Vol. 8, p. 226.
   10. Ibid., p. 206.
   11. Blackwell and Axe, *Romford to Beirut, via France, Egypt and Jericho*, pp. 149–150.
   12. Gilbert, *The Romance of the Last Crusade: With Allenby to Jerusalem*, pp. 220–224.
   13. Ibid., p. 224.
   14. Massey, *Allenby's Final Triumph*, p. 127.
   15. Ibid., pp. 126–127.
   16. *Evangelical Dictionary of Biblical Theology*, ed. Walter A. Elwell (Grand Rapids, Mich.: Baker Book House Company, 1996), p. 38. "A name occurring only once in the Bible and designating the place where the last great battle of the ages will take place."
   17. Chaim Herzog and Mordechai Gichon, *Battles of the Bible* (London: Greenhill Books, Lionel Leventhal, Ltd., 1997, pp. 66–67.
   18. Gibbons, *With the 1/5th Essex in the East*, p. 224.
   19. Ibid., pp. 139–140.
   20. MacMunn and Falls, *The Official History of the War: Operations Egypt and Palestine*, Vol. II, Part II, pp. 472–473.
   21. Wavell, *Allenby: A Study in Greatness*, pp. 272–273.
   22. Ibid., p. 273.
   23. Ibid.
   24. Gibbons, *With the 1/5th Essex in the East*, pp. 144–145.
   25. MacMunn and Falls, *The Official History of the War: Military Operations; Egypt and Palestine*, Vol. II, Part 2, pp. 469–476.
   26. Ibid., pp. 506–507.
   27. Massey, *Allenby's Final Triumph*, p. 174.
   28. Ibid., pp. 153–154.
   29. Moir, *The History of the Suffolk Regiment*, pp. 104–105.
   30. Murphy, *The History of the Suffolk Regiment, 1914–1927*, pp. 315–16.
   31. Ibid., 317.
   32. Lloyd George, *War Memoirs of David Lloyd George: Vol. VI, 1918*, p. 206.
   33. Neiberg, *Fighting the Great War: A Global History*, p.148.
   34. Sanders, *Five Years in Turkey*, pp. 273–274.
   35. Ibid., pp. 275–277.
   36. Hankey, *The Supreme Command, 1914–1918*, Vol. II, p. 839.
   37. *Source Records of the Great War*, Vol. VI, pp. 340–341.
   38. Squires, *Peregrine Papers*, pp. 88–89.
   39. Ibid., pp. 88–89.
   40. Grigg, *Lloyd George: War Leader, 1916–1918*, p. 606.
   41. Ibid.
   42. Mills, *Great Uncle Fred's War*, p. 39.
   43. *Ground Warfare: An International Encyclopedia*, Vol. 2, edited by Stanley Sandler (Santa Barbara, Calif.: ABC-Clio, 2002), p. 560.
   44. *Paris 1918: The War Diary of the British Ambassador, the 17th Earl of Derby*, edited by David Dutton (Liverpool: Liverpool University Press, 2001), p. 215.
   45. *The Times* (London), Monday, September 23, 1918, p. 8b.
   46. MacMunn and Falls, *The Official History of the War: Military Operations; Egypt and Palestine*, Vol. II, Part 2, pp. 509–510.
   47. Private Jake Mortlock was a Lewis machine-gunner with No. 13 Section, 'D' Company, 1/5th Battalion, the Suffolk Regiment. Interview and Mortlock Family Papers.
   48. Gibbons, *With the 1/5th Essex in the East*, pp. 146–147.
   49. Massey, *Allenby's Final Triumph*, pp. 251–253.
   50. Ibid., pp. 252–253.
   51. Ibid., p. 253.
   52. Ibid., Appendix D, pp. 342–343.
   53. Wilson, *Palestine, 1917*, p. 114.
   54. *The Times*, Monday, 7 October 1918, p. 11b.
   55. Wavell, *The Campaigns in Palestine*, p. 230.
   56. Wavell, *Allenby: A Study in Greatness*, p. 282.
   57. MacMunn and Falls, *The Official History of the War: Military Operations; Egypt and Palestine*, Vol. II, Part 2, pp. 596–597.
   58. Squires, *Peregrine Papers*, pp. 43–44.
   59. Gibbons, *With the 1/5th Essex in the East*, p. 148–150.
   60. *The Times* (London), Friday, October 11, 1918, p. 7b.
   61. Gibbons, *With the 1/5th Essex in the East*, pp. 154–155.
   62. Ibid., pp. 156–157.
   63. Squires, *Peregrine Papers*, pp. 28–29.
   64. Wavell, *The Campaigns in Palestine*, p. 230.
   65. Woodward, *Field Marshal Sir William Robertson: Chief of the Imperial General Staff in the Great War*, p. 211.
   66. Arthur Banks, *A Military Atlas of the First World War*, commentary by Alan Palmer (New York: Taplinger, 1975), p. 199.
   67. Harry R. Rudin, *Armistice 1918* (New Haven, Conn.: Yale University Press, 1944), pp. 191–192.
   68. Lloyd George, *War Memoirs of David Lloyd George, Vol. VI, 1918*, pp. 207–208.

69. Hankey, *The Supreme Command, 1914–1918*, Vol. II, p. 839.
70. Blackwell and Axe, *Romford to Beirut, via France, Egypt and Jericho*, pp. 164–164.
71. Ibid., 152–153.
72. MacMunn and Falls, *The Official History of the War: Military Operations; Egypt and Palestine*, Vol. II, Part 2, pp. 510–511.
73. Halsey, *The Literary Digest History of the World War*, Vol. VIII, p. 230.
74. Gilbert, *The Romance of the Last Crusade: With Allenby to Jerusalem*, p. 226.
75. Gibbons, *With the 1/5th Essex in the East*, p. 158.
76. Ibid.
77. From mid mid-1917 until November 1918, South African artillery and infantry units fought under British command in operations against the Turkish forces in Palestine (now Israel). They earned eight battle honors: Gaza; El Mughar; Nebi Samwil; Tel Asur; Megiddo; Sharon; Nablus; and the more comprehensive Palestine, 1917–1918.
78. One squadron of Egyptian Army cavalry, one company and one machine-gun section of Egyptian Army infantry were deployed.
79. Peter Young, "Modern Warfare," pp. 174–175, in *Dictionary of Battles: The World's Key Battles from 405 B.C. to Today* [1987], editor David Chandler (New York: Henry Holt and Company, 1987).
80. Halsey, *The Literary Digest History of the World War*, Vol. 8, p. 230–231.
81. Plevna or Pleven, Russo-Turkish War of 1877–1878, a North Bulgarian town held by Turks and scene of three battles, a two-and-a-half month siege (September 20–December 10, 1877.) Russian forces thrusting south were three times repulsed by this formidable fortification, whereupon they elected to besiege it. When eventually the Turks attempted to break out they were defeated in the Fourth Battle of Plevna. Apparently Churchill considered it to be a by-word for fortification.
82. Churchill, *The World Crisis, 1916–1918*, Vol. II, pp. 47–48.
83. Frances Stevenson, *Lloyd George: A Diary by Frances Stevenson*, edited by A.P.J. Taylor (London: Hutchinson and Company, 1971), p. 174.
84. *Paris 1918: The War Diary of the British Ambassador, the 17th Earl of Derby*, ed. David Dutton, pp. 245–246.
85. Edmund Candler, *The Long Road to Baghdad*, Vol. II, p. 295.
86. Gibbons, *With the 1/5th Essex in the East*, p. 158.
87. Blackwell and Axe, *Romford to Beirut, via France, Egypt and Jericho*, pp. 167–168.
88. Gibbons, *With the 1/5th Essex in the East*, p. 161.
89. Private Jake Mortlock. Interview, October 31, 1968.
90. Badcock, *The History of the Transport Services of the Egyptian Expeditionary Force*, p. 327.
91. Ambara Salam al-Khalidi (1897–1986), in *Lines of Fire: Women Writers of World War I*, edited by Margaret R. Higgonet (New York: Plume Books/Penguin Putnam, 1999), pp. 330–331.
92. Gibbons, *With the 1/5th Essex in the East*, p. 163.
93. These two belligerents signed armistice agreements on October 30, 1918.
94. *The Daily Telegraph* (London), November 11–14, 1918, p. 1, column 1.

Chapter Seven

1. Petrie, *The History of the Norfolk Regiment, 1685–1918: Vol. II*, p. 596.
2. Mills, *Great Uncle Fred's War*, pp. 41–42.
3. Gibbons, *With the 1/5th Essex in the East*, pp. 164–165.
4. Mills, *Great Uncle Fred's War*, p. 43.
5. Private Jake Mortlock maintained that replacement drafts sustained a much higher percentage of casualties in battle than seasoned troops. Interview, 12 January 1965.
6. MacMunn and Falls, *The Official History of the War: Military Operations; Egypt and Palestine*, Vol. II, Part 2, p. 644.
7. Murphy, *The History of the Suffolk Regiment, 1914–1927*, p. 350.
8. Gibbons, *With the 1/5th Essex in the East*, p. 166.
9. Murphy, *The History of the Suffolk Regiment*, p. 350.
10. *The Cambridge History of Egypt*, Vol. 2, edited by M. W. Daly (Cambridge: Cambridge University Press, 1998), p. 249.
11. Gibbons, *With the 1/5th Essex in the East*, p. 167.
12. Mansfield, *The British in Egypt*, pp. 223–225.Only a prostitute (or 'public woman,' as Lord Wavell charmingly describes her) showed pity in trying to protect the bodies. Later the British community in Egypt considered offering her a piece of land in recognition of her action but she preferred jewelry and was presented with an inscribed gold bracelet and signet ring (Mansfield's footnote, p. 225).
13. *The Times*, 17 March 1919, p. 12b.
14. Hayes, *Contemporary Europe Since 1870*, pp. 496–497.
15. Murphy, *History of the Suffolk Regiment*, pp. 350–351.
16. Gibbons, *With the 1/5th Essex in the East*, p. 171.
17. Petrie, *The History of the Norfolk Regiment, 1685–1918: Vol. II*, pp. 159–160.

18. Gilbert, *The Romance of the Last Crusade: With Allenby to Jerusalem*, pp. 232–235.

Postscript

1. Patricia Anne Cobbold (*née* Mortlock), letter recalling her late father, 12 April 1995.

2. Private Jake Mortlock. Interview, March 8, 1969.

3. Murphy, *The History of the Suffolk Regiment*, p. 351.

Bibliography

Primary Sources—Books

Aaronsohn, Alexander. *With the Turks in Palestine*. London: Constable, 1917. Account of a Jew who was pressed into service by the Turkish military authorities. Conditions in barracks and in the cities of Jerusalem and Jaffa described; also treatment of native population by Turkish army personnel and military governors.

Adivar, Halidé Edib. *Memoirs of Halidé Edib*. New York: Century, circa 1926. By one of the daughters of a high official in the sultan's service; gives insight into civilian life in Turkey, Palestine and Syria during the Great War.

Aitken, Alexander. *Gallipoli to the Somme: Recollections of a New Zealand Infantryman*. London: Oxford University Press, 1963. Relates army life in Egypt.

Anonymous. *The Northamptonshire Regiment, 1914–1918*. Aldershot, England: Gale and Polden, 1932.

Armitage, Flora. *The Desert and the Stars: A Portrait of T. E. Lawrence*. London: Faber and Faber, 1956. Gives insight into the Egyptian, Palestinian, and Syrian aspects of the campaign.

Armstrong, H. C. *Gray Wolf: The Life of Kemal Ataturk*. New York: Capricorn Books, 1961.

Arthur, Sir George. *Life of Lord Kitchener*. 3 Vols. New York: Macmillan, 1920. Vol. III substantiates the Russian promise "of an Army Corps" to back the Dardanelles venture.

Ashwell, Lena. *Myself a Player*. London: Michael Joseph, 1936. This actress took it upon herself to organize concerts for the fighting men both on the Western Front and in Egypt.

Asquith, Herbert Henry. *Memories and Reflections, 1852–1928, by the Earl of Oxford and Asquith, K.B.* Boston: Little, Brown, 1928.

Attlee, Clement. *As It Happened*. New York: Viking Press, 1954. Egypt and Gallipoli addressed in Chapter 5; also relates being at Alexandria 1915–1916.

Austin, Walter F., and Charles F. Horne, eds. *Source Records of the Great War*. Seven Vols. Washington, D.C.: National Alumni, 1923. Contemporary commentaries, assessments, and firsthand accounts.

Badcock, Brevet Lt. Colonel G. E. *A History of the Transport Services of the Egyptian Expeditionary Force, 1916–1918*. London: Hugh Rees, 1925.

Baedeker, Karl. *Egypt and The Sudan: Handbook for Travelers*. Leipzig: Karl Baedeker; London: T. Fisher Unwin; New York: Scribner's, 1914.

Bell, Gertrude. *The Arabian Diaries, 1913–1914*. Edited by Rosemary O'Brien. Syracuse, N.Y.: Syracuse University Press, 2000. Contains a useful glossary.

Bidwell, Robin. *British Documents on Foreign Affairs: Reports and Papers from the Foreign Office Confidential Print: Part II; From the First to the Second World War. Series B: Turkey, Iran, and the Middle East, 1918–1939; Vol. 1: The End of the War, 1918–1920*. Cambridge: U.P.A., 1985.

Blackwell, Edwin, and Edwin C. Axe. *Romford to Beirut, via France, Egypt and Jericho: An Outline of the War Record of "B" Battery, 271st Brigade, R.F.A. (1/2nd Essex Battery, R.F.A), with Many Digressions*. Clacton-on-Sea, Essex, U.K.: R. W. Humphris, 1926. Compiled in narrative from diaries, etc., with illustrations by Gordon Jackson and twenty photographs.

Brittain, Vera. *The Chronicle of Youth: The War Diaries of Vera Brittain, 1913–1917.* New York: William Morrow, 1982. Nurse Vera Brittain paints vivid contemporary pictures of military hospitals, hospital ships, the personnel and the patients.

_____. *Testament of Youth.* New York: Seaview Books, 1980.

Brown, Malcolm, ed. *T. E. Lawrence: The Selected Letters.* New York: W.W. Norton, 1989.

Burrows, John William. *The Essex Regiment — Essex Units in the War, 1914–1919.* 6 Vols. Southend-on-Sea, Essex, U.K.: J. W. Burrows, 1923–1935.

Candler, Edmund. *The Long Road to Baghdad.* 2 Vols. Boston: Houghton Mifflin, 1919.

Churchill, Winston S. *The World Crisis. Vols. II, III, and IV, 1914–1918.* New York: Scribner's, 1923–1927.

Clark, Andrew. *Echoes of the Great War: The Diary of the Reverend Andrew Clark, 1914–1919.* Oxford: Oxford University Press, 1985.

Cooper, Duff. *Old Men Forget: The Autobiography of Duff Cooper (Viscount Norwich).* London: Rupert Hart-Davis, 1954.

Creighton, O. [Oswin] C.F. *With the Twenty-Ninth Division in Gallipoli: A Chaplain's Experiences.* London: Longmans, Green, 1916.

Davison, Frank D. *The Wells of Beersheba: An Epic of the Australian Light Horse.* Sydney: Angus and Robertson, 1933. Revised edition, 1947.

Dutton, David, ed. *Paris 1918: The War Diary of the British Ambassador, the 17th Earl of Derby.* Liverpool: Liverpool University Press, 2001.

Elgood, Brig. General Percival George. *Egypt and the Army.* London: Oxford University Press, H. Milford, 1924.

Ellis, John, and Michael Cox. *The World War I Databook: The Essential Facts and Figures for All the Combatants.* London: Aurum Press, 2001.

Facey, A. B. *A Fortunate Life.* Ringwood, Victoria: Penguin Books Australia, 1981.

Fair, Captain A., and Captain E. D. Wolton. *The History of the 1/5th Battalion: "The Suffolk Regiment."* London: Eyre and Spottiswoode, 1923.

Frederick the Second, King of Prussia. *Mémoires de Frédéric II, Roi de Prusse.* 2 Vols. Paris: Henri Blon, 1866. Vol. 2 has detailed account of the Battle of Minden with Frederick's assessment.

Garnett, David. *The Essential T. E. Lawrence.* New York: E. P. Dutton, 1951.

_____, ed. *The Letters of T. E. Lawrence.* New York: Doubleday, Doran, 1939. Sheds light on many aspects and personages connected with the Egyptian, Palestinian, Syrian, and Arabian regions during the war.

Gibbons, Lt. Col. Thomas. *With the 1/5th Essex in the East.* Colchester: Benham, 1921. Excellent material of some 211 pages, plus 25 illustration and six first-rate maps. Published within two years of the author's return to England, it contains informative digressions connecting locations with their Biblical and Crusader counterparts.

Gilbert, Major Vivian. *The Romance of the Last Crusade: With Allenby to Jerusalem.* New York: D. Appleton, 1925. This work deals with the author's war service with the 60th (London) Division in France, Salonika, Egypt, Sinai, Palestine, and Syria.

Gorman, E. *With the Twenty-Second: A History of the Twenty-Second Battalion, A.I.F.* Melbourne: H. H. Champion, 1919.

Graves, Robert. *Goodbye to All That.* New York: Doubleday, 1929.

Grey, Edward. *Twenty-Five Years, 1892–1916,* Vol. II. New York: Frederick A. Stokes, 1925.

Gurney, Lt. Colonel Russell. *History of the Northamptonshire Regiment, Vol. I, 1742–1934.* Aldershot, U.K.: Gale and Polden, 1935.

Halsey, Francis Whiting. *The Literary Digest History of the World War: Compiled from Original and Contemporary Sources; American, British, French, German, and Other. Vol. 8: August 1, 1914–October 1918.* New York and London: Funk and Wagnalls, 1920. Scholarly and thorough; a veritable mine of information.

Hamilton, Lt. General Ian. *Gallipoli Diary, Vol. II.* New York: George H. Doran, 1920. Contains a fascinating and informative comparison between artillery ammunition supply on Gallipoli and the Third Battle of Gaza, which in artillery preponderance per yard of frontage compared favorably with the Western Front.

Hankey, Maurice, Lord. *The Supreme Command, 1914–1918.* 2 Vols. London: George Allen and Unwin, 1961. Details the War Cabinet's decision to relieve Sir Archibald Murray; Smuts was first choice as his successor. Gives comparative strengths in Gaza-Beersheba sector, and relates the capture of Jerusalem.

Hanssen, Hans Peter. *Diary of a Dying Empire.* Trans. by Oscar Osburn Winther. Ed. by Ralph H. Lutz, Mary Schofield, and O. O. Winther. Bloomington: Indiana University Press, 1955. First published in Copenhagen in 1924, these illuminating insights into the deliberations of the German Reichstag and its various committees come from the pen of a member of those inner circles.

Horne, Charles F., and Walter F. Austin, eds. *The Great Events of the Great War.* Vol. V. Washington, D.C.: National Alumni, 1923.

Housman, Laurence, ed. *War Letters of Fallen Englishmen.* Philadelphia: Pine Street Books/University of Pennsylvania Press, 2002. (Originally published in 1930 by E. P. Dutton, New York.)

Hynes, Samuel. *The Soldiers' Tale: Bearing Witness to Modern War.* New York: Penguin Books, 1997.

Jones, Thomas. *Whitehall Diary.* Ed. Keith Middlemas. London: Oxford University Press, 1969. Contains some interesting behind-the-scenes insights.

Kearsey, Lt. Colonel A. *The Operations in Egypt and Palestine, 1914 to June 1917: Illustrating the Field Service Regulations.* Aldershot: Gale and Polden, 1919. All battles, including 2nd Gaza, covered.

The King of Hedjaz and Arab Independence: With a Facsimile of the Proclamation of June 27, 1916. Together with the Proclamation issued at Baghdad by Lieut. General Sir Stanley Maude, after the occupation of That City by the British Forces. (Pamphlet.) London: Hayman, Christy and Lilly, 1917.

Kipling, Arthur L., and Hugh L. King. *Head-Dress Badges of the British Army.* London: Frederick Muller, 1966.

Knyvett, Captain R. Hugh. *"Over There" With the Australians.* New York: Scribner's, 1918. Good section on the Ferry Post and the Suez Canal Defenses. Before the war Captain Knyvett had had some experience with camels in Western Queensland. He was killed on the Western Front in 1918.

Kress von Kressenstein, General Friedrich F. *Mit den Türken zum Suezkanal.* Berlin: Vorhut-verlag Otto Schlegel, 1938.

_____. *Zwischen Kaukasus und Sinai.* Vol. 1. Berlin: Mulzer and Cleeman, 1921.

Lawrence, M. R., ed. *The Home Letters of T. E. Lawrence and His Brothers.* New York: Macmillan, 1954.

Lawrence, T. E. *The Seven Pillars of Wisdom.* London: Jonathan Cape, 1973.

_____. *The Seven Pillars of Wisdom: The Complete 1922 'Oxford' Text.* London: J. & N. Wilson, 2004.

Letters from a Lost Generation: The First World War Letters of Vera Brittain and Four Friends; Roland Leighton, Edward Brittain, Victor Richardson, Geoffrey Thurlow. Ed. by Alan Bishop and Mark Bostridge. Boston: Northeastern University Press, 1999. Brittain served as a nurse throughout the war; the volume contains much about military hospitals, hospital ships, personnel and patients.

Lengel, Edward G. *World War I Memories: An Annotated Bibliography of Personal Accounts Published in English Since 1919.* Lanham, Md.: Scarecrow Press, 2004.

Liman von Sanders, Otto. *Five Years in Turkey.* Annapolis, Md.: U.S. Naval Institute Press, 1927.

Lloyd George, David. *War Memoirs of David Lloyd George.* 6 Vols. Boston: Little, Brown, 1933–1937. In particular Vols. III, IV, and V.

MacMunn, Lt. General George F., and Captain Cyril Falls. *Official History of the War: Military Operations: Egypt and Palestine.* 2 Vols. London: H.M.S.O., 1928–1930.

Massey, W. T. *Allenby's Final Triumph.* London: Constable, 1920. Massey was the war correspondent for *The Times* (London) newspaper.

May, Ernest. *Signal Corporal: The Story of the 2nd London Irish Rifles (2/18th Battalion), The London Regiment, 1914–1918.* London: Johnson, 1972.

Memoirs of Frederick, King of Prussia. Translated by E. Boutaric and E. Campardon. 2 Vols. Paris: Henri Blon, 1898. Vol. 2 has detailed account of the Battle of Minden with Frederick's assessment.

Mills, Sapper Frederick T. *Great Uncle Fred's War: An Illustrated Diary, 1917–1920.* Researched and edited by Alan Pryor and Jenifer K. Woods. Whitstable, Kent: Pryor, 1985.

Murphy, Lt. Colonel Charles C. R. *The History of the Suffolk Regiment, 1914–1927.* London: Hutchinson, 1928.

Murray, Lt. General Archibald. *Sir Archibald Murray's Despatches, June 1916–June 1917.* London: J. M. Dent and Sons, 1920.

Nicolson, Harold. *Some People.* London: Constable, 1927. His post-war journey from Alexandria, via Cairo, El Kantara, and Jerusalem to Baghdad is humorously recounted.

Nogales, Rafael de. *Four Years Beneath the Crescent.* London: Cassell, 1922.

Official German Documents Relating to the World War. Vol. I. New York: Oxford University Press, 1923.

Papen, Franz von. *Memoirs.* Trans. Brian Wilson. London: André Deutsch, 1952.

Parker, Gilbert. *The World in the Crucible: An Account of the Origins and Conduct of the Great War.* New York: Dodd, Mead, 1915.

Parliament's Vote of Thanks to the Forces: Speeches Delivered in the Houses of Parliament, Westminster, on October 29, 1917. London: H.M.S.O., 1917. Includes a verbatim a speech made to the House of Lords by Earl Curzon of Kedleston on the Territorial Army, Gallipoli, Salonika, Egypt and Palestine, and Mesopotamia.

Part, L/Cpl. Thomas. *The War Diary of Thomas Reginald Part.* Digital reproduction of actual diary by Pauline Carter and David Jones. Sydney: Jones Digital, 1997. L/Cpl. Part was a signaler with the Australian Imperial Force. He was stationed in Egypt, recording his impressions and activities in his diary. He served a couple of months on the Gallipoli Peninsula and after the evacuation went back to Egypt for a short time before being shipped to the Western Front, where he was killed in 1918.

Petrie, F. Loraine. *The History of the Norfolk Regiment, 1685–1918: Vol. II, 4 August 1914 to 31 December 1918.* Norwich: Empire Press/Jarrold and Sons, 1953.

Purdom, Charles B., ed. *Everyman at War: Sixty Personal Narratives of the War.* London: J. M. Dent and Sons, 1930.

Rawlinson, Lt. Colonel Anthony. *Adventures in the Near East, 1918–1922.* New York: Dodd, Mead, 1924. Describes a train ride from Alexandria to Suez via Ismailia in August 1918, including Australian cavalry training and details of the Suez Canal environs.

Researching World War I: A Handbook. Westport, Conn.: Greenwood Press, 2003.

Sassoon, Siegfried. *Collected Poems.* New York: Viking Press, 1949.

_____. *Sherston's Progress.* Boston: Little, Brown, 1938. Gives a detailed account of journeys to and from Egypt, Palestine and Syria and vivid descriptions of flora and fauna. Rather unrealistic comparison to Western Front made — by the time S. arrived, the battle lines had flowed northwards from the entrenchments in front of Gaza.

Smith, George Adam. *Syria and the Holy Land.* New York: George H. Doran, 1919.

Smollett, Tobias. *The History of England, Vol. III: From the Revolution of 1688 to the Death of George the Second.* Philadelphia: M'Carty and Davis, 1839.

Squires, W.H.T. *Peregrine Papers: A Tale of Travel in the Orient.* Norfolk, Va.: W.H.T. Squires, 1923. The author contributes some rather unique personal accounts by native occupants of areas involved in the hostilities.

Stallings, Laurence, ed. *The First World War: A Photographic History.* New York: Simon & Schuster, 1933.

Stevenson, Frances. *Lloyd George: A Diary by Frances Stevenson.* Ed. A.J.P. Taylor. New York: Harper and Row, 1971. Intriguing insights into the inner workings of cabinet government by David Lloyd George's former secretary and second wife.

Storrs, Sir Ronald. *The Memoirs of Sir Ronald Storrs.* New York: Putnam's, 1937.

Taft, William Howard, Frederick Harris, Frederick Houston Kent, and William J. Newlin, eds. *Service With Fighting Men: An Account of the Work of the American Young Men's Christian Associations in the World War.* Vol. II. New York: Association Press, 1922.

Teichman, Captain Oskar. *The Diary of a Yeomanry M.O.: Egypt, Gallipoli, Palestine, and Italy.* London: T. Fisher Unwin, 1921.

A detailed and fascinating war record, completely devoid of hyperbole.

Thomas, Lowell. *With Lawrence in Arabia*. New York: Century, 1924. Details Lawrence's meeting with Allenby.

Toynbee, A. J. *Turkey: A Past and a Future*. New York: George H. Doran, 1917.

Turkish Prisoners in Egypt: A Report by the Delegates of the International Committee of the Red Cross. London: Official Reports of the Red Cross Society, 1917.

The War Cabinet: Report for the Year 1917. London: H.M.S.O., 1918.

Wavell, Colonel A. P. *The Palestine Campaigns*. London: Constable, 1928.

Wavell, General Archibald. *Allenby, A Study in Greatness: The Biography of Field-Marshal Viscount Allenby of Megiddo and Felixstowe, G.C.B., G.C.M.G.* New York: Oxford University Press, 1941.

Wiener, Joel H., ed. *Great Britain: Foreign Policy and the Span of Empire, 1689–1971*. Vol. I. New York: Chelsea House/McGraw-Hill, 1972.

Wilson, Robert Henry, ed., Helen D. Millgate. *Palestine 1917*. Tunbridge Wells, Kent: Costello, 1987.

Wintringham, Colonel J. W. *With the Lincolnshire Yeomanry in Egypt and Palestine, 1914–1918*. Grimsby, Humberside: Lincolnshire Life, 1979.

The World's Work: A History of Our Time. Vols. 29 (November 1914 to April 1915); 30 (May 1915 to October 1915); 31 (November 1915 to April 1916) ff. Ed. Arthur W. Page. Garden City, N.Y.: Doubleday, Page, 1915–1919. Many firsthand accounts of military, naval, economic, political and diplomatic affairs and events.

Primary Sources— Newspapers

Bury Free Press (Bury St. Edmunds, Suffolk). Article about Minden Day, 27 July 2001.

The Daily Telegraph (London). Special 4 page section featuring reports and photographs associated with the Armistice, which appeared in various editions of the paper between November 11 and November 14, 1918. *The New York Times*. Most reports and *communiqués* published emanated from identical sources to this and other newspapers. Editions quoted from specifically are: Tuesday, April 3, 1917, and Sunday, April 15, 1917; both refer to the reports on the First Battle of Gaza.

The New York Times Index, Vols. III, No. 1–4; IV, No. 1–4; and V, No. 1–4 (1914–1918.) New York: Reprinted for the New York Times Company by R. R. Bowker Company, 1965.

Palestine News. October 10, 1918. Contains Lawrence's unsigned letter claiming that Feisal's Arab irregulars captured Damascus. Closely matches that in *The Times* of October 17, 1918. Lt. General Sir Henry Chauvel, commander-in-chief of the Desert Mounted Corps, and Brig. General Wilson, commanding officer the Third Australian Light Horse Brigade, both utterly refuted this claim.

The Times (London). Various editions 1916–1920. In particular January 3, 4, and 12; April 2, 7, 10, and 12; July 9, 16, 26, and 30; August 8; September 1, 3, 7, 10, 13, and 21; and December 10, 1917; April 1, 1918; October 9, 11, 15, 17, 1918; November 5, 6, 7, 8, 10, 7, 12, and 14.

The Times (London) *Official Index*. Vols. III, IV, V, and VI, for years 1914–1919. London: John Parkinson Bland, at *The Times*, 1968.

Primary Sources—Periodicals

Apperly, Dr. Frank L. "The Young Medical Officer goes to War," *Journal of the American Medical Association, Medicine and War Section* Vol. 119 (May 1942), pp. 349–351.

Darrah, Thomas W. "The Palestine Campaign," *Infantry Journal*, Vol. 25 (1924), pp. 649–667.

The Great War: The Standard History of the World-Wide Conflict. Eds., J. A. Hammerton and H. W. Wilson. Vol. 13, Pt. 250, May 31, 1919, p. 161.

"I Was There": *A Pictorial History of the Great War*. Edited by John Hammerton. Monthly. Various Nos. of Vols. from 1919 to 1922. Eventually published as a bound volume under the same title.

Palestine: The Organ of the British Palestine Committee. Vol. II, No. 16 (November 24, 1917).

Wykes, Alan. "The Battle of Minden," *British History Illustrated*. Vol. I, No. 4 (October 1974), pp. 54–62.

Primary Sources—Interviews, Personal Accounts, Letters

Bolton, Charles, Private, L/Corporal, ? Coy., 2/5th Battalion, the Suffolk Regiment, and 'D' Coy., 1/5th Battalion, the Suffolk Regiment, 1914–1919; also Trooper, Corporal-Farrier, Royal Horse Artillery, India, 1920–1927. Reminiscences—recorded Christmas 1956, and his letter prior to his coming to stay at Manor Farm.

Bonser, Sapper Harry P., 74th Divisional Signals Coy., Royal Engineers, Egypt and Southern Palestine; Detached Duty, Fayoum Area; U. U. Cable Section, Royal Engineers, Egypt, Palestine and Syria, 1916–1919.

Burlham, Private Timothy, 'D' Coy., 5th and 1/5th Battalions, the Suffolk Regiment, 1913–1919.

Cobbold, P. Anne, *née* Mortlock. Daughter of Pvt. J. Mortlock. Letter, dated 3 October, 1993, setting out her memories of his accounts of his experiences.

Drackett-Case, Frederick Charles. Son of Madge Drackett-Case. Shared commemorative brass plaque awarded to a dead soldier's next of kin, in this case Pvt. William Rumbelow's. Also a letter written January 11, 1917, by Rumbelow prior to returning to Middle East.

Drackett-Case, Frederick Philip ("Uncle Fred"), Pvt., L/Cpl., Cpl., & Sgt., 'A' Company, 1st King's (Liverpool) Regiment, Western Front, 1916–1919.

Drackett-Case, Madge. Recollections. Her brother, Pvt. W. ("Billy") Vincent Rumbelow, D Coy., 5th, & 1/5th Battalion, the Suffolk Regiment, 1913–1917, served at Gallipoli; thereafter served in Egypt and the Sinai, and died of wounds sustained on Mansura Ridge opposite Gaza, in the Egypt/Palestine theatre of war.

Fair, Capt. A., M.C., 1/5th Battalion, the Suffolk Regiment. Co-author of the Battalion's *History*.

How, George, Pvt., L/Corpl., Corpl. and Sgt., 'D' Coy., 5th and 1/5th Battalions, the Suffolk Regiment, 1913–1919. Recollections.

Jaggard, Pvt. Robert ("Bob"), 'D' Coy., 5th and 1/5th Battalion, the Suffolk Regiment, 1913–1919. Letters, 1916–18.

Johnson, Pvt. William E., 2nd Battalion, the 23rd London Regiment, 181st Brigade, 60th (London) Division. France, Salonika, Palestine and Syria, 1915–1918.

Kent, Trooper Harold, 'Q' Squadron, the Suffolk Yeomanry. South Africa, 1899–1901. Personal experiences recounted.

Lane, Capt. Reginald E. S., Pvt., 1st Battalion, the Cambridgeshire Regiment, 1914, Pvt., 'D' Coy., 5th Battalion, the Suffolk Regiment, and L/Corpl., and Corpl., 'D' Coy, 1/5th Battalion, the Suffolk Regiment, 1914–1916, 2nd Lieut., Lieut., and Captain, Egyptian Labour Corps, 1917–1919.

May, Signal-Corpl. Ernest, 2/18th Battalion, the London Regiment (2nd London Irish Rifles), 60th (London) Division, France, Salonika, Egypt, and Palestine, 1914–1918.

Mortlock, Mrs. Chrissie (*née* Ward), sister-in-law of Private Jake. Reminiscences over an extended period.

Mortlock, Desmond Peter, Officer-Cadet, 2nd Lieut., and Lieut., Punjabi Light Infantry, Indian Army, 1945–1947, and Sgt., 'Q' Battery, 358 Medium (The Suffolk Yeomanry) Regiment, Royal Artillery, Territorial Army, 1948–1953. Memories of his uncle Private Jake's recounting his war experiences, letter 1996.

Mortlock, Gwendoline May. Sister of Pvt. Jake. Memories. Her *fiancée*, Pvt. W. Vincent ("Billy") Rumbelow, died on May 1, 1917, of wounds sustained in battle.

Mortlock, Richard Joseph. Second son of Pvt. Jake. Letters, 1994 and 1997, spelling out his recollections of his father's anecdotes of war service. Provided wartime letter of his father's, and autograph album that covered the period 1913–1918.

Mortlock, Pvt. S. Jacob ("Jake") P., of 'D' Coy., 1/5th Battalion, the Suffolk Regiment, 1913–1919. Reminiscences. Letters, 1916–18. Correspondence with his cousin, Jack Parker, of Beck House Farm, Beck Row, Mildenhall, West Suffolk.

Neve, Arthur, 2nd Lieut., Lieut., ? Battalion, the Suffolk Regiment, and Capt., Major, Egyptian Labour Corps, 1914–1920.

Parker, Jacob "Jack." Private Jake Mortlock's cousin with whom he corresponded throughout the war.

Phillips, Aircraftsman Frank, Royal Flying Corps/Royal Air Force, Western Front,

1915–1919. Related rigid standards enforced on leave-bound personnel.

Rolfe, Sapper Frank, Royal Engineers. Western Front. Told of rats gnawing sleeping soldiers' fingernails.

Uttridge, Private Harry, Coy. and Battalion unknown, Suffolk Regiment. France and Salonika, 1915–1919.

Walters, Herman Edwin, Private First Class, Corporal, 133rd Infantry Regiment, 34th Division, U.S. Army, North Africa & Italy 1943–1945. First-hand information re: Gurkhas and their enemies' ears' trophies.

Wavell, Lt.-Colonel Archibald Percival, M.C., France. Military *Attaché* with the Russian Army in the Caucasus, 1916–1917; Egypt, Palestine and Syria with XXth Army Corps (G.S. Officer 1918–1919).

Williams, Pvt., L/Corpl., and Sgt., 'D' Coy., 5th, and 1/5th Battalions, the Suffolk Regiment, and 2nd. Lieut. Maurice, 15th (Suffolk Yeomanry) Battalion, the Suffolk Regiment, 1913–1917; also Lieut. and Capt., the South Staffordshire Regiment 1917–1919.

Wilson, Lieut. Robert Henry, 'D' Squadron, the Royal Gloucester Hussars, Egypt, Palestine and Syria, 1916–1919.

Wolton, Capt. E. D., 5th Battalion, the Suffolk Regiment. Co-author of the Battalion's *History*.

Wolton, Coeur de, Lieut. H., 'D' Coy., the 1/5th Battalion, the Suffolk Regiment.

Secondary Sources—Books

Adelson, Roger. *London and the Invention of the Middle East: Money, Power, and War, 1902–1922*. New Haven: Yale University Press, 1995. Sound scholarship; many new viewpoints.

Ahmad, Feroz. *Turkey: The Quest for Identity*. Oxford: One World, 2003. Concise summary of the Great War, before, during and after. Foreign policy analyzed.

Alexander, Bevin. *How Great Generals Win*. New York: W. W. Norton, 1993.

Allen, George H. *The Great War: Vol. IV, The Wavering Balance of Forces*, and *Vol. V, The Triumph of Democracy*. Philadelphia: George Barrie's Sons, 1919.

Andrews, E. M. *The Anzac Illusion: Anglo-Australian Relations During World War I*. Cambridge: Cambridge University Press, 1993.

Aramco and Its World: Arabia and the Middle East. Edited by Ismail I. Nawwab, Peter C. Speers, and Paul F. Hoye. Washington, D.C.: Arabian American Oil Company, 1980.

Armenian Activities in the Archive Documents, 1914–1918. Vols. I and II. Ankara: Genelkurmay Basim Evi, 2005.

Bambrick, Susan, ed. *The Cambridge Encyclopedia of Australia*. Cambridge: Cambridge University Press, 1994.

Banks, Arthur. *A Military Atlas of the First World War*. New York: Taplinger, 1975.

Barker, Lt. Colonel A. J. *Famous Military Battles*. London: Hamlyn Publishing, 1974.

Barnett, Correlli. *The Great War*. New York: Putnam's, 1980.

_____. *The Sword Bearers: Supreme Command in the First World War*. New York: William Morrow, 1964.

Barthorp, Michael. *British Infantry Uniforms Since 1660*. Poole, Dorset: Blandford Press, 1982.

Bayly, Christopher, ed. *Atlas of the British Empire*. New York: Facts on File, 1989.

Becker, Carl L. *Modern History*. New York: Silver Burdett, 1939.

Becket, Ian F. W., and Keith Simpson, eds. *A Nation in Arms: A Social Study of the British Army in the First World War*. Manchester: Manchester University Press, 1985.

Benns, F. Lee. *Europe Since 1914*. 4th ed. New York: F. S. Crofts, 1939.

Bibliography of British History, 1789–1851. Eds. Lucy M. Brown and Ian R. Christie. Oxford: Clarendon Press, 1977.

Bidwell, Robin. *Dictionary of Modern Arab History: An A to Z of Over 2,000 Entries from 1798 to the Present Day*. London: Kegan Paul International, 1998.

Black, Jeremy. *The Cambridge Illustrated Atlas of Warfare*. Cambridge: Cambridge University Press, 1996.

_____. *The Making of Modern Britain: The Age of Empire to the New Millennium*. Thrupp, Gloucestershire: Sutton, 2001.

_____. *War and the World: Military Power and the Fate of Continents, 1450–2000*. New Haven, Conn.: Yale University Press, 1998.

Bogle, Emory C. *The Modern Middle East: From Imperialism to Freedom, 1800–1958.* Austin: University of Texas Press, 1995.
Bond, Brian. *The Unquiet Western Front: Britain in Literature and History.* Cambridge: Cambridge University Press, 2002.
Bourne, J. M. *Britain and the Great War, 1914–1918.* London: Edward Arnold, 1989.
Boyle, Susan Silsby. *Betrayal of Palestine: The Story of George Antonius.* Boulder, Colo.: Westview Press, 2001.
Brassey's Encyclopedia of Military History and Biography. Col. Franklin D. Margiotta, ed. Washington D.C.: Brassey's, 1994.
Brent, Peter. *T. E. Lawrence.* New York: Putnam's, 1975.
British Military History: A Supplement to Robin Higham's Guide to the Sources. Gerald Jordan, ed. Chapter 11, "First World War on Land," by Dominick Graham. New York: Garland, 1988.
Brook-Shepherd, Gordon. *November 1918.* Boston: Little, Brown, 1981.
Burg, David F., and L. Edward Purcell. *Almanac of World War I.* Louisville, Ky.: University of Kentucky Press, 1998.
Busch, Briton Cooper. *Britain, India, and the Arabs, 1914–1921.* Berkeley: University of California Press, 1971.
Butt, Gerald. *The Arabs: Myth and Reality.* London: I. B. Tauris, 1997.
Callard, Ernest. *The Manor of Freckenham: An Ancient Corner of East Anglia.* London: John Lane, 1924.
Cardwell, M. John. *Arts and Arms: Literature, Politics and Patriotism during the Seven Years' War.* Manchester: Manchester University Press, 2004.
Carlyle, Thomas. *History of Friedrich the Second, Called Frederick the Great.* Six Vols. New York: Harper and Brothers, 1874. Vol. 5 gives a lengthy account of the Battle of Minden.
Carman, W. Y. *A Dictionary of Military Uniforms.* London: B. T. Batsford, 1977.
Carmichael, Joel. *The Shaping of the Arabs: A Study in Ethnic Identification.* New York: Macmillan, 1967.
Carver, Field Marshal Michael. *The Seven Ages of the British Army.* New York: Beaufort Books, 1984.
Cassar, George H. *The Tragedy of Sir John French.* Newark: University of Delaware Press. London and Toronto: Associated University Presses, 1985.
Catchpole, Brian, with Edward Barratt. *The Complete Atlas of World History, Vol. III: The Modern World, 1783–Present.* Armonk, N.Y.: Sharpe Reference, 1997.
Cattan, Henry. *The Palestine Question.* London: Saqi Books, 2000.
Churchill, Winston S. *The Island Race.* New York: Dodd, Mead, 1964.
Clark, Alan. *The Donkeys.* New York: William Morrow, 1962.
Clayton, Major G. J. *The New Zealand Army: A History from the 1840s to the 1990s.* Wellington: New Zealand Army, 1990.
Cline, Eric H. *The Battles of Armageddon: Megiddo and the Jezreel Valley from the Bronze Age to the Nuclear Age.* Ann Arbor: University of Michigan Press, 2000. Chapter 1, "History Repeats Itself," replete with maps and photographs, compares Ancient Egyptian campaigns with Allenby's triumphant finale. Other pages deal with Allenby's tactics and battles through history at this location.
Clodfelter, Micheal. *Warfare and Armed Conflicts: A Statistical Reference to Casualty and Other Figures, 1618–1991.* 2 Vols. Jefferson, N.C.: McFarland, 1992.
Cohen, Ethel, and Frank Cohen, eds. *Palestine: A Study of Jewish, Arab, and British Policies.* Vol. I. New Haven, Conn.: Yale University Press, 1947.
Cook, Chris, and John Stevenson. *British Historical Facts 1760–1830.* Macmillan, 1980.
Corvisier, André. *A Dictionary of Military History.* Trans. from the French by Chris Turner. English edition edited by John Childs. Oxford: Blackwell, 1994.
Cottrell, Leonard. *Egypt.* New York: Oxford University Press, 1966.
Crowley, F.K., ed. *A New History of Australia.* Melbourne: William Heinemann Australia, 1974.
Daly, M.W., ed. *The Cambridge History of Egypt.* Vol. 2. Cambridge: Cambridge University Press, 1998.
d'Artagnan, Jack (pseud.). *Sentimental Journey.* Bury St. Edmunds: Ulysses Press, 1973.
Davis, Paul K. *100 Decisive Battles: From Ancient Times to the Present.* Santa Barbara, Calif.: ABC-CLIO, 1999.
DeGroot, Gerard J. *Blighty: British Society in*

the Era of the Great War. London: Longman, 1996.
A Dictionary of Military History and the Art of War. Ed. André Corvisier. English edition revised, expanded and edited by John Childs. Translated from the French by Chris Turner. Oxford: Blackwell, 1994.
The Dictionary of National Biography. Vol. 26: 1931–1940. L.G. Wickham Legg, ed. London: Oxford University Press/Geoffrey Cumberlege, 1949. The entry for Field Marshal Edmund Henry Hynman Allenby, First Viscount Allenby of Megiddo (1861–1936), was compiled by the eminent military historian Cyril Falls.
Dixson, Miriam. The Imaginary Australian: Anglo-Celts and Identity, 1788 to the Present. Sydney: University of New South Wales Press, 1999.
Dodwell, H.H., ed. The Cambridge History of the British Empire, Vol. V: The Indian Empire, 1858–1918. Cambridge: Cambridge University Press, 1932.
Dover, Lord. The Life of Frederic the Second, King of Prussia. Two Vols. New York: Harper and Brothers, 1844. Vol. 2 contains an account of Battle of Minden.
Dugdale, Blanche E. C. Arthur James Balfour. New York: Putnam's, 1937.
Dupuy, R. Ernest, and Trevor N. The Encyclopedia of Military History. New York: Harper and Row, 1977.
Earle, Edward Mead. Turkey, the Great Powers, and the Baghdad Railway. New York: Macmillan, 1923. Includes Djemal Pasha's attempt on the Suez Canal and Allenby's triumphant advance from Sinai to Syria.
Edwards, Major Thomas Joseph, Regimental Badges. Revised by Arthur L. Kipling. 4th edition. Aldershot: Gale and Polden, 1966.
Eggenberger, David. A Dictionary of Battles. New York: Thomas Y. Crowell, 1967.
Ellis, John. Cavalry: The History of Mounted Warfare. New York: Putnam's, 1978.
Ellis, John, and Michael Cox. The World War I Databook: The Essential Facts and Figures for All the Combatants. London: Aurum Press, 2001.
Enser, A.G.S. A Subject Bibliography of the First World War: Books in English 1914–1987. Aldershot: Gower Publishing, 1990.
Esposito, Brig. General Vincent J. A Concise History of World War I. New York: Praeger, 1964.
European History Since 1900. Edited by Hans Hoch. Heidelberg: Heidelberg University Press, 2000.
The European Powers in the First World War: An Encyclopedia. Edited by Spencer C. Tucker. New York: Garland, 1996.
Evangelical Dictionary of Biblical Theology. Edited by Walter A. Elwell. Grand Rapids, Mich.: Baker House, 1996. Entry on Armageddon.
Everett, Suzanne. World War I: An Illustrated History. Chicago: Rand McNally, 1980.
Falls, Cyril. The Great War. New York: Putnam's, 1959.
Farago, Ladislas. Palestine on the Eve. London: Putnam, 1936.
Farwell, Byron. The Gurkhas. New York: W. W. Norton, 1984.
Feiler, Bruce. Walking the Bible: A Journey by Land through the Five Books of Moses. New York: William Morrow, 2001.
Ferguson, Niall. The Pity of War: Explaining World War I. New York: Basic Books, 1999.
Ferro, Marc. The Great War, 1914–1918. Translated by Nicole Stone. London: Routledge and Kegan Paul, 1973.
Fighting With Figures: A Statistical Digest of the Second World War. Prepared by the Central Statistical Office. Text by Peter Howlett. London: Her Majesty's Stationery Office, 1995. Gives comparative figures for First World War casualties.
Fisher, H.A.L. A History of Europe. Vol. III: The Liberal Experiment. Cambridge, Mass.: Riverside Press, 1936.
Fraser, George MacDonald. The General Danced at Dawn, and Other Stories. First American edition. New York: Alfred A. Knopf, 1973. Rail journey from Egypt to Palestine described in "Night Run to Palestine." Also Suez Canal garrison life humorously depicted.
French, David. Raising Churchill's Army: The British Army and the War against Germany, 1919–1945. Oxford: Oxford University Press, 2000.
Friedman, Isaiah. Germany, Turkey, and Zionism, 1897–1918. New Brunswick, N.J.: Transaction Publishers, Rutgers, 1998.
_____. Palestine: A Twice-Promised Land, Vol. 1: The British, the Arabs, and Zionism,

1915–1920. New Brunswick, N.J.: Transaction Publishers, Rutgers, 2000.
Fromkin, David. *A Peace to End All Peace: Creating the Modern Middle East, 1914–1922.* New York: Henry Holt, 1989.
Fussell, Peter. *The War in Modern Memory.* New York: Oxford University Press, 1975.
Garnett, David. *The Essential T. E. Lawrence.* New York: E. P. Dutton, 1951. Murray, Allenby, and Gaza battles are included.
Gartner, Lloyd P. *History of the Jews in Modern Times.* Oxford: Oxford University Press, 2001.
Gelvin, James L. *The Modern Middle East: A History.* Oxford: Oxford University Press, 2005.
Gilbert, Martin. *The First World War: A Complete History.* New York: Henry Holt, 1994.
_____. *First World War Atlas.* New York: Macmillan, 1970.
_____. *Winston S. Churchill: Volume III, The Challenge of War, 1914–1916.* Boston: Houghton Mifflin, 1971.
_____. *Winston S. Churchill: Volume IV, The Stricken World 1916–1922.* London and Chicago: Houghton Mifflin, 1971.
Glenny, Misha. *The Balkans: Nationalism, War and the Great Powers, 1804–1999.* New York: Viking Penguin, 2000.
Goldshmidt, Arthur, Jr. *Modern Egypt: The Foundation of a Nation State.* Boulder, Colo.: Westview Press, 2004.
Goldstein, Erik. *The First World War Peace Settlements, 1919–1925.* London: Longman, 2002.
Goodspeed, Lt. Colonel D. J. *The German Wars, 1914–1945.* Boston: Houghton Mifflin, 1977.
Graves, Richard Perceval. *Lawrence of Arabia and His World.* New York: Scribner's, 1976.
Graves, Robert. *Lawrence and the Arabian Adventure.* New York: Doubleday, Doran, 1928. Contains a great deal about Allenby and Gaza.
Gray, Randal, with Christopher Argyle. *Chronicle of the First World War: Vol. I, 1914–1916;* and *Vol. II, 1917–1921.* New York: Facts on File, 1990 and 1991.
Green, Andrew. *Writing the Great War: Sir James Edmonds and the Official Histories 1915–1948.* London: Frank Cass, 2003.
Green, Lt. Colonel Howard, *The British Army in the First World War: The Regulars, the Territorials and Kitchener's Army—With Some of the Campaigns Into Which They Fitted.* London: J. Trehern, 1968.
Grigg, John. *Lloyd George: War Leader 1916–1918.* London: Penguin Books, 2003. Much about Gaza, Megiddo, Allenby and Murray.
Ground Warfare: An International Encyclopedia. 3 Vols. Stanley Sandler, ed. Santa Barbara, Calif.: ABC-CLIO, 2002.
Hall, Walter Phelps. *Wars and Revolutions: The Course of Europe Since 1900.* New York: D. Appleton-Century, 1943.
Halsey, Francis Whiting. *A Literary Digest History of the World War: Compiled from Original and Contemporary Sources; American, British, French, German, and Other, Vols. 8 and 10; Turkey and the Balkans.* New York: Funk and Wagnalls, 1920.
Hayes, Carlton J. H. *Contemporary Europe Since 1870.* New York: Macmillan, 1953.
Haythornthwaite, Philip J. *An Illustrated History of the First World War.* London: Arms and Armour Press, 1995. Several good photographs.
_____. *The World War One Source Book.* London: Arms and Armour Press, 1996.
Heinl, Colonel Robert Debs, Jr. *Dictionary of Military and Naval Quotations.* Annapolis, Md.: U.S. Naval Institute, 1966.
Herman, Arthur. *To Rule the Waves: How the British Navy Shaped the Modern World.* New York: HarperCollins, 2004.
Herwig, Holger H., and Neil M. Heyman. *Biographical Dictionary of World War I.* Westport, Conn.: Greenwood Press, 1982.
Herzog, Chaim, and Mordechai Gichon. *Battles of the Bible.* London: Greenhill Books, 1997.
Heyman, Neil M. *World War I.* Guides to Historic Events of the Twentieth Century Series. Westport, Conn.: Greenwood Press, 1997.
Higgonet, Margaret R., ed. *Lines of Fire: Women Writers of World War I.* New York: Plume Books/Penguin Putnam, 1999.
Higham, Robin, ed. *A Guide to the Sources of British Military History.* Berkeley and Los Angeles: University of California Press, 1971.
_____, ed. *The Writing of Official Military History.* Westport, Conn.: Greenwood Press, 1999.
The History Today Companion to British History. Edited by Juliet Gardiner and Neil

Wendon. London: Collins and Brown, 1995.
Hogg, Ian V. *Battles: A Concise Dictionary.* San Diego, New York, and London: Harcourt Brace, 1995.
_____. *Historical Dictionary of World War I.* Lanham, Md., and London: Scarecrow Press, 1998.
Hollywood's World War I: Motion Picture Images. Edited by Peter C. Rollins and John E. O'Connor. Bowling Green, Ohio: Bowling Green State University Popular Press, 1997.
Horne, Charles F. *The Great Events of the Great War.* Vol. V. New York: National Alumni, 1923.
Hough, Richard. *The Great War at Sea, 1914–1918.* Oxford: Oxford University Press, 1983.
Hourani, Albert H. *A History of the Arab Peoples.* Cambridge, Mass.: Belknap Press, 1991.
_____. *Minorities in the Arab World.* London: Oxford University Press, 1947.
Howard, Harry N. *Turkey, the Straits, and U.S. Policy.* Baltimore: John Hopkins University Press, 1974.
Howard, Major James. *The History of the Royal Norfolk Regiment.* Norwich: Jarrold and Sons, 1995.
James, Lawrence. *The Golden Warrior: The Life and Legend of Lawrence of Arabia.* New York: Paragon House, 1993.
Jankowski, James. *A Short History of Egypt.* Oxford: Oneworld, 2000.
Johnston, Mark. *At the Front Line: Experiences of Australian Soldiers in World War II.* Cambridge: Cambridge University Press, 1996. Some retrospective anecdotes of World War I.
King, Joan Wucher. *Historical Dictionary of Egypt (African Historical Dictionaries, No. 36).* Metuchen, N.J. and London: Scarecrow Press, 1984.
Kirk-Greene, Anthony. *On Crown Service: A History of H.M. Colonial and Overseas Civil Services, 1837–1997.* London: I. B. Taurus, 1999.
Knaplund, Paul. *The British Empire, 1815–1939.* New York: Harper and Brothers, 1941.
Langsam, Walter C. *The World Since 1914.* Fifth ed. New York: Macmillan, 1943.
Latham, Bryan. *A Territorial Soldier's War.* Aldershot: Gale and Polden, 1967.

Leed, Eric J. *No Man's Land: Combat and Identity in World War I.* Cambridge: Cambridge University Press, 1979.
Lengel, Edward G. *World War I Memories: An Annotated Bibliography of Personal Accounts Published in English Since 1919.* Lanham, Md.: Scarecrow Press, 2004.
Lewis, Bernard. *From Babel to Dragomans: Interpreting the Middle East.* Oxford: Oxford University Press, 2004.
Liddell Hart, Captain Basil H. *Colonel Lawrence: The Man Behind the Legend.* New York: Dodd, Mead, 1934.
_____. *History of the First World War.* London: Cassell, 1970. One comes to expect good solid stuff of this expert, and this particular piece is no exception.
_____. *The Real War 1914–1918.* Boston: Little, Brown, 1930.
_____. *The War in Outline, 1914–1918.* New York: Random House, 1936.
Lucas, James. *Experiences of War: The British Soldier.* London: Arms and Armour, 1989.
Macintyre, Stuart. *A Concise History of Australia.* Cambridge: Cambridge University Press, 1999.
Mackenzie, S. P. *The Home Guard: A Military and Political History.* Oxford: Oxford University Press, 1995.
MacMillan, Margaret. *Paris 1919: Six Months that Changed the World.* New York: Random House, 2001.
Manchester, William. *The Last Lion: Winston Spencer Churchill, 1874–1932.* Boston: Little, Brown, 1983.
Mansfield, Peter. *The British in Egypt.* New York: Holt, Rinehart and Winston, 1971.
March, Francis A. *History of the World War: An Authentic Narrative of the World's Greatest War.* Vols. II and V. New York: Leslie-Judge, 1919.
The Marshall Cavendish Illustrated Encyclopedia of World War I, Vols. 8 and 9 (1917–1918). Editor-in-chief, Brigadier Peter Young. New York: Marshall Cavendish, 1984.
Marshall, P. J., ed. *The Cambridge Illustrated History of the British Empire.* Cambridge: Cambridge University Press, 1996.
Marshall, S.L.A. *World War I.* New York: American Heritage Library, 1985.
The Middle East. Ninth ed. Edited by Robin Surratt and Jerry Orvedahl. Washington, D.C.: CQ Press, 2000.

Millar, T. B. *Australia in Peace and War: External Relations 1788–1977.* New York: St. Martin's Press, 1978.

Moir, Guthrie. *The Suffolk Regiment.* Famous Regiments Series, ed. Lt. General Brian Horrocks. London: Lee Cooper, 1969.

Mollo, Boris. *The Indian Army.* Poole, Dorset, England: Blandford Press, 1981.

Monroe, Elizabeth. *Britain's Moment in the Middle East.* Baltimore: John Hopkins University Press, 1981. Montgomery, Bernard Law. *Memoirs.* London: Collins, 1958. By the field marshal and viscount of Alamein.

Moorhouse, Geoffrey. *Hell's Foundations: A Social History of the Town of Bury in the Aftermath of the Gallipoli Campaign.* New York: Henry Holt, 1992. Some interesting observations of, and reactions to, Egypt.

Morris, James. *Farewell the Trumpets: An Imperial Retreat.* San Diego: Harcourt Brace Jovanovich, 1978.

Mortlock, M.J. "Suvla Bay 1915: The Lost Chance to Change the Course of the Great War." Doctoral Dissertation, University of Richmond, Va., 1999.

_____. "Suvla Bay: The Golden Opportunity Let Slip." Master's Thesis, University of Richmond, Va. 1994.

Mosley, Leonard. *Curzon: The End of an Epoch.* London: Longmans, Green, 1960.

Mullett, Charles F. *The British Empire.* New York: Henry Holt, 1938.

Murray, Anne. *The United States, Great Britain and the Middle East: Discourse and Dissidents.* Boulder, Colo.: Social Science Monographs, 1999.

Nasir, Sari J. *The Arabs and the English.* Second ed. London: Longman Group, 1979.

Neiberg, Michael S. *Fighting the Great War: A Global History.* Cambridge, Mass.: Harvard University Press, 2005. A great deal of modern scholarship and perspective, well-researched.

The New Cambridge Modern History, Vol. 12: The Shifting Balance of World Forces 1898–1945. Revised ed. Edited by C. L. Mowat. Cambridge: Cambridge University Press, 1968.

_____. *Vol. 13: Atlas.* Edited by H. C. Darby and Harold Fullard. Cambridge: Cambridge University Press, 1970.

Newton, Arthur P. *A Hundred Years of the British Empire.* London: Duckworth, 1940.

Nicholson, Harold. *Some People.* London: Constable and Constable, 1927. Humorous anecdotes on traveling in Middle East.

Nutting, Anthony. *The Arabs.* New York: Clarkson N. Potter, 1964.

Official Histories: Essays and Bibliographies from Around the World. Edited by Robin Higham. Manhattan, Kan.: Kansas State University Library, 1970.

Orlans, Harold. *T. E. Lawrence: A Biography of a Broken Hero.* Jefferson, N.C.: McFarland, 2002.

Oxford Atlas of World History. General editor, Patrick K. O'Brien. New York: Oxford University Press, 1999.

The Oxford Companion to Australian History. Edited by Graeme Davison, John Hirst and Stuart MacIntyre, with Helen Doyle and Kim Torney. Melbourne: Oxford University Press Australia, 1998.

The Oxford Companion to Military History. Edited by Richard Holmes. Oxford: Oxford University Press, 2001.

Oxford History of the British Empire, Vol. 3: The Twentieth Century. Edited by Judith M. Brown and William Roger Louis. Oxford: Oxford University Press, 1999.

The Oxford History of the Crusades. Edited by Jonathan Riley-Smith. Oxford: Oxford University Press, 2000.

The Oxford Illustrated History of Modern Europe. Edited by T.C.W. Blanning. Oxford: Oxford University Press, 1996.

Oxford Illustrated History of the British Army. Edited by David Chandler and Ian Beckett. Oxford: Oxford University Press, 1994.

Palmer, A. W. *A Dictionary of Modern History: 1789–1945.* Baltimore: Penguin Books, 1962.

Palmer, Alan. *Victory 1918.* New York: Atlantic Monthly Press, 1998.

Panton, Kenneth J., and Keith A. Cowlard. *Historical Dictionary of the United Kingdom. Vol. I: England and the United Kingdom.* Lanham, Md., and London: Scarecrow Press, 1997.

Paris, Michael. *Warrior Nation: Images of War in British Popular Culture, 1850–2000.* London: Reaktion Books, 2000.

Parsons, Timothy H. *The British Imperial Century, 1815–1914: A World History Perspective.* Lanham, Md.: Rowman and Littlefield, 1999.

Permanent Book of the 20th Century: Eye-wit-

ness Accounts of the Moments that Shaped Our Century. Ed. Jon E. Lewis. New York: Carroll and Graf, 1994.

Perrett, Bryan. *A History of Blitzkrieg.* New York: Stein and Day, 1983.

Pope, Stephen, and Elizabeth-Anne Wheal. *The Dictionary of the First World War.* New York: St. Martin's Press, 1995.

Preston, Richard A., and Sydney F. Wise. *Men in Arms: A History of Warfare and Its Interrelationship with Western Society.* New York: Praeger, 1970.

Quataert, Donald. *The Ottoman Empire, 1700–1922.* New Approaches to European History Series. Eds. William Beik and T.C.W. Blanning. Cambridge: Cambridge University Press, 2000.

Quinn, Patrick J. *The Great War and the Missing Muse: The Early Writings of Robert Graves and Siegfried Sassoon.* Selinsgrove: Susquehanna University Press. London and Toronto: Associated University Presses, 1994.

Raymond, André. *Cairo.* Translated by Willard Wood. Cambridge, Mass.: Harvard University Press, 2000.

Reader's Guide to Military History. Ed. by Charles Messenger. London and Chicago: Fitzroy Dearborn, 2001.

Reynolds, Francis J., et al. *The Story of the Great War.* Vol. VII. P. F. Collier and Son, 1920.

Ridpath, John Clark. *History of the World.* 10 Vols., Vols. 8 and 9 consulted. Cincinnati: Ridpath Historical Society, 1936.

Robins, Keith, ed. and comp. *A Bibliography of British History 1914–1989.* Oxford: Clarendon Press, 1996.

Rogan, Eugene L. *Frontiers of State in the Late Ottoman Empire.* Cambridge: Cambridge University Press, 1999.

Rogers, Colonel H.C.B. *Mounted Troops of the British Army, 1066–1945.* Imperial Services Library, Vol. III. London: Seeley Service, 1959.

Ropp, Theodore. *War in the Modern World.* New York: Collier Books, 1962.

Rosignoli, Guido. *World Army Badges and Insignia.* Poole, Dorset: Blandford Press, 1983.

Ross, Stewart. *Causes and Consequences of World War I.* Austin, Texas: Steck-Vaughn, 1998.

Rothwell, Victor H. *British War Aims and Peace Diplomacy 1914–1918.* Oxford: Clarendon Press, 1971.

Royal Historical Society. *Writings on British History, 1901–1933.* Vol. V, Part 2. Ed. Prof. H. Hale Bellot. New York: Barnes and Noble, 1970.

Royle, Trevor, comp. *A Dictionary of Military Quotations.* New York: Simon & Schuster, 1989.

Roze, Ann. *Fields of Memory: A Testimony to the Great War.* London: Cassell, 1999.

Rudin, Harry R. *Armistice 1918.* New Haven, Conn.: Yale University Press, 1944.

Ruether, Rosemary Radford, and Herman J. Ruether. *The Wrath of Jonah: The Crisis of Religious Nationalism in the Israeli-Palestinian Conflict.* San Francisco: Harper and Row, 1989.

Schmitt, Bernadotte E., and Harold C. Vedeler. *The World in the Crucible, 1914–1918.* New York: Harper and Row, 1984.

Segev, Tom. *One Palestine, Complete: Jews and Arabs Under the British Mandate.* Trans. Haim Watzman. New York: Metropolitan Books, 1999. Huge amount of factual information about Allenby; great detail regarding surrender of Jerusalem.

Sellwood, A. V. *The Saturday Night Soldiers: The Stirring Story of the Territorial Army.* London: Wolfe Publishing, 1966.

Seymour, William. *Yours to Reason Why: Decisions in Battle.* New York: St. Martin's Press, 1982. Chapter 13 deals with the three Gaza battles, outlining the options open to the commanders on both sides.

Sherrow, Victoria. *Encyclopedia of Youth and War: Young People as Participants and Victims.* Phoenix: Oryx Press, 2000.

Shotwell, James T., ed. *Economic and Social History of the World War (British Series): War Governments of the British Dominions,* by Arthur Berriedale Keith. Oxford: Clarendon Press, 1921.

Siberry, Elizabeth. *The New Crusaders: Images of the Crusades in the Nineteenth and Early Twentieth Centuries.* Aldershot: Ashgate, 2000. Chapter Five is devoted to the First World War.

Simonds, Frank H. *History of the World War.* Vols. 2, 3, and 4. Garden City, N.Y.: Review of Reviews Company/Doubleday, Page, 1918–1919. Vol. 3 has "My Visit to the Dardanelles" by American Ambassador to

Turkey Henry Morgenthau. Good photographs in Vol. 4.

Stansky, Peter. *Sassoon: The Worlds of Philip and Sybil*. New Haven, Conn., and London: Yale University Press, 2003.

Steel, Linda. *Veils and Daggers: A Century of National Geographic's Representation of the Arab World*. Philadelphia: Temple University Press, 2000.

Stewart, John D. *Gibraltar: The Keystone*. Boston: Houghton Mifflin, 1967.

Stein, Leslie. *The Hope Fulfilled: The Rise of Modern Israel*. Westport, Conn., and London: Praeger, 2003.

Stoddard, John L. *John L. Stoddard's Lectures. Vol. II: Constantinople, Jerusalem, and Egypt*. 10 Vols. Boston: Balch Brothers, 1905.

The Story of the Great War, Vol. VII. New York: P. F. Collier and Son, 1917.

Strachan, Hugh. *The First World War, Vol. I: To Arms*. Oxford: Oxford University Press, 2001.

Stubbs, Kevin D. *Race to the Front: The Materiel Foundations of Coalition Strategy in the Great War*. Westport, Conn.: Praeger, 2002.

Tabachnick, Stephen Ely. *T. E. Lawrence*. Twaynes English Authors Series, Kinley Roby, ed. New York: Twaynes, 1997.

Taylor, A.J.P. *English History, 1914–1945*. New York: Oxford University Press, 1965.

Terraine, John. *The First World War, 1914–1918*. London: Hutchinson, 1965.

_____. *The Great War: 1914–1918; A Pictorial History*. New York: Macmillan, 1965.

_____. *To Win a War: 1918, The Year of Victory*. New York: Doubleday, 1981.

Thomson, Alistair. *Anzac Memories: Living with the Legend*. Melbourne: Oxford University Press, 1994.

The Timechart of Military History: 3000 B.C. to the Present. New York: Timechart, 1999.

Troen, S. Ilan. *Imagining Zion: Dreams, Designs and Realities in a Century of Jewish Settlement*. New Haven and London: Yale University Press, 2003. Contains aerial photographs of Jerusalem, Haifa, Jaffa, Tel Aviv and Rehovoth taken during the Great War.

Trumpener, Ulrich. *Germany and the Ottoman Empire, 1914–1918*. Princeton, N.J.: Princeton University Press, 1968.

Tuchman, Barbara W. *Bible and Sword: England and Palestine from the Bronze Age to Balfour*. New York: Ballantine Books, 1984.

Turner, John, ed. *Britain and the First World War*. London: Unwin Hyman, 1988.

_____. *British Politics and the Great War: Coalition and Conflict 1915–1918*. New Haven, Conn.: Yale University Press, 1992.

Van der Kiste, John. *Kaiser Wilhelm II: Germany's Last Emperor*. Stroud, Gloucestershire: Sutton, 1999.

Van Paasen, Pierre. *Days of Our Years*. New York: Dial Press, 1940. Some vivid descriptions of Egypt and Palestine, also many jaundiced pronouncements on the Arab-Israeli problems.

Vance, Jonathan F. *Death So Noble: Memory, Meaning, and the First World War*. Vancouver: University of British Columbia Press, 1997.

The Virago Book of Women and the Great War, 1914–1918. Ed. Joyce Marlow. London: Virago Press, 1998.

Wallace, Edgar. *Kitchener's Army and the Territorial Forces: The Full Story of a Great Achievement*. London: George Newnes, 1916.

War Poetry. London: Pocket Books, 2001.

Wawro, Geoffrey. *Warfare and Society in Europe, 1792–1914*. London: Routledge, 2000.

Wayne, Scott, and Damien Simonis. *Egypt and the Sudan: A Travel Survival Guide*. Hawthorn, Victoria, Australia: Lonely Planet, 1994.

Webster, Frederick A. M. *The History of the Fifth Battalion, The Bedfordshire and Hertfordshire Regiment (T.A.)*. Bedford: Old Comrades' Association Committee, 1930.

Whitton, Frederick E. *The Northamptonshire Regiment, 1914–1918*. Aldershot, U.K.: Regimental History Committee, 1932.

Who Was Who: A Set of Volumes Containing the Biographies Removed From Who's Who on Account of Death, With Final Details and Date of Death Added. London: Adam and Charles Black. New York: Macmillan. Various year volumes consulted.

Who's Who: An Annual Biographical Dictionary With Which is Incorporated "Men and Women of the Time." London: Adam and Charles Black. New York: Macmillan. Various year volumes consulted.

Wilkinson, Frederick. *Militaria*. New York: Hawthorn Books, 1969.

Williams, John F. *Anzacs: The Media and the*

Great War. Sydney: University of New South Wales Press, 1999.
Wilson, Jean Moorcroft. *Siegfried Sassoon: The Making of a War Poet; A Biography 1886–1918*. New York: Routledge, 1999.
Wilson, Jeremy. *Lawrence of Arabia: The Authorized Biography of T. E. Lawrence*. New York: Atheneum, 1990. Contains some previously unpublished material.
Wilson, Trevor. *The Myriad Faces of War: Britain and the Great War, 1914–1918*. Cambridge: Polity Press, 1986. Chapters 13 and 35 deal in depth with Gallipoli. Chapters 35 and 45 deal with Egypt, Palestine, and Syria.
Winter, J. M. *The Experience of World War I*. New York: Oxford University Press, 1989.
Winter, Jay, and Blaine Baggett. *The Great War and the Shaping of the 20th Century*. New York: Penguin Studio, 1996.
Woodward, David R. *Field Marshal Sir William Robertson: Chief of the Imperial General Staff in the Great War*. Westport, Conn.: Praeger, 1998.
____. *Lloyd George and the Generals*. Newark: University of Delaware Press, 1983.
Woodward, Llewellyn. *Great Britain and the War of 1914–1918*. London: Methuen, 1967.
The World Atlas of Warfare: Military Innovations that Changed the Course of History. Lt. Colonel Richard Holmes, ed. New York: Viking Studio Books, 1988.
World War I: A History. Ed. Hew Strachan. Oxford: Oxford University Press, 1998.
World War I: A Visual Encyclopedia. General editor, Simon Forty. London: PRC Publishing, 2002.
Yardley, Michael. *A Biography: T. E. Lawrence*. New York: Stein and Day, 1987.
Younger, R. M. *Australia and the Australians: A New Concise History*. Adelaide: Rigby, 1974.
Zürcher, Erik J. *Turkey: A Modern History*. London: I. B. Tauris, 1997.

Secondary Soures— Periodicals

Austrian History Yearbook, Vol. 36, 2005. Center for Austrian Studies, University of Minnesota. New York: Berghahn Books, 2005.
History Today, countless issues, dating from 1965.
Infantry: A Professional Journal for the Combined Arms Team, Vol. 70, Nos. 5 and 6 (September–October, November–December 1980).
Malvern, Sue. "War, Memory and Museums: Art and Artefact in the Imperial War Museum," *History Journal Workshop* Issue 49 (Spring 2000), pp. 177–203.
Military Review: The Professional Journal of the U.S. Army, Vol. 65, No. 1 (January 1985). Book review by Major Charles McFetridge.
Naval History. Published by the Naval Institute Press, Annapolis, Md. Various issues over a lengthy period—naval gunnery one area of interest.

Secondary Sources— Background Information

Agnew, Major. Commanded 'Q' Battery, 358 (Suffolk Yeomanry) Medium Regiment, Royal Artillery, T.A., 1956–1958.
Alexander, "Alec," Sapper, L/Corpl., Corpl., and Sgt., Royal Engineers. North Africa, Italy and Austria, 1942–1946.
Aves, Arthur, Trooper, Lance-Bombardier, Mercer's Troop, Waterloo Battery, 2nd Regiment, Royal Horse Artillery, 1951–1953. Suez Canal zone, and Cyprus.
Barton, Ronald "Butch," Gunner though Battery-Sergeant-Major, 202 (Norfolk & Suffolk Yeomanry) Battery, 100 Medium (and subsequently 100 Field) Regiment, Royal Artillery, T.A. England, Wales, and West Germany (Rhine Army). 1972–1985.
Bowman, Derek, Gunner through MT/Sergeant, 202 (Norfolk & Suffolk Yeomanry) Battery, 100 Medium (and subsequently 100 Field) Regiment, Royal Artillery, T.A. England, Wales, and West Germany (Rhine Army). 1970?–1985.
Brown, Aircraftsman Arthur "Sonny," Royal Air Force. Egypt 1942–43; Italy.
Brown, Gunner Gordon, GHQ Rhine Army Royal Artillery, Düsseldorf, 1951–1953, and 'Q' Battery, 358 (Suffolk Yeomanry) Medium Regiment, R.A., T.A., 1953–1956.
Carter, John, Gunner, Lance-Bombardier, Bombardier, Sergeant, 58th Medium (latterly Suffolk Yeomanry) Regiment, Royal Artillery, T.A., 1937–1957. North Africa, Italy.

288 Bibliography / Secondary Sources—Background

Carter, Thomas, Gunner, Lance-Bombardier, 25th Field Regiment, Royal Artillery. Malaya, 1953–1955. Supplied information on shrapnel fuse-setting technique. Related the incidence of a 'premature'—a shell which exploded shortly after leaving the muzzle of a twenty-five-pounder.

Champness, Lt.-Colonel Peter, T.D., 'Q' Battery, 358 (Suffolk Yeomanry) Medium Regiment, Royal Artillery, T.A., 1953–1956.

Clarke, Trooper Nigel "Nobby," 2nd Regiment, Royal Horse Artillery, Suez Canal Zone, 1952–1953. 'Q' Battery, 358 Medium (Suffolk Yeomanry) Regiment, Royal Artillery, T.A., 1954–1956.

Cockerton, Gunner Leslie, 46 Niagara Battery, 18th Medium Regiment, Royal Artillery, and 'Q' (Suffolk Yeomanry) Battery, 358 Medium Regiment, Royal Artillery, T.A., England, Scotland, and Wales, 1951–1956.

Collen, Anthony, Rating, Ordinary-, Able-Bodied-, and Leading-Seaman, Royal Navy, 1946–1953; Reserve, 1953–1958.

Cook, Brian, Gunner through Battery Quartermaster Sergeant (Permanent Staff), 'Q' (Suffolk Yeomanry) Battery, 358 Medium Regiment, Royal Artillery, T.A., and 202 (Norfolk & Suffolk Yeomanry) Battery, 100 Medium and 100 Field Regiments, R.A., T.A., England, Wales, Scotland and West Germany (Rhine Army), 1951–1985.

Cudmore, Gunner Derek, 46 Niagara Battery, 18th Medium Regiment, Royal Artillery, 'Q' (Suffolk Yeomanry) Battery, 358 Medium Regiment, Royal Artillery, T.A., and 202 (Norfolk & Suffolk Yeomanry) Battery, 100 Medium and 100 Field Regiments, R.A., T.A., England, Wales, Scotland and West Germany (Rhine Army), 1951–1985.

Darling, Clifford, Gunner, Lance-Bombardier, Bombardier, Sergeant, 305 (Suffolk Yeomanry) Battery, 100 Medium Regiment, Royal Artillery, T.A., and 202 (Norfolk & Suffolk Yeomanry) Battery, 100 Medium Regiment (subsequently 100 Field Regiment), Royal Artillery, T.A., England, Wales and West Germany (Rhine Army), 1969–1983.

Eley, Gunner Anthony, 202 (Norfolk & Suffolk Yeomanry) Battery, 100 Medium Regiment and 100 Field Regiment, Royal Artillery, T.A., 1978–1985.

Eck, Barbara-Jean Walters, daughter of Private First Class, later Corporal, Herman E. Walters, 133rd Infantry Regiment, 34th Infantry Division, U.S. Army. North Africa and Italy, 1943–1945. Gurkha anecdotes.

Francis, Major O. D., P.S.O. (Permanent Staff Officer), 202 (Suffolk & Norfolk Yeomanry) Battery, 100 Medium Regiment, Royal Artillery (V), King's Road Barracks, and latterly the TAVR Centre, Suffolk. Circa 1973–1983.

Fuller, Aircraftsman Jack, Bomber Command, Royal Air Force, 1939–1946. South Africa, training, Della Sieger, North Africa and Italy.

Halls, Gunner Walter ("Hot Legs"), 17th Training Regiment, Royal Artillery (Oswestry), 45 Colenso Battery, 20th Field Regiment, Royal Artillery, and 'Q' (Suffolk Yeomanry) Battery, 358 Medium Regiment, Royal Artillery, T.A. Korea, 1952–1953. All service, 1952–1957.

Hobbis, Alfred Private through Company-Sergeant-Major, other information unknown. North Africa, Italy and India (Military Academy, Quetta), 1938–1947.

Houghton, Private Vivian, 'D' Coy, 1st Battalion, the Suffolk Regiment, 1939–1947. Egypt, Palestine, Low Countries and Germany.

Hubbard, Rifleman Arthur, ?? Company, 2nd Battalion, the Somerset Light Infantry, North Africa and Italy, 1944–1945.

Hubbard, John, Gunner, Lance-Bombardier, Bombardier, 171 (Broken Wheel) Battery, 37th Heavy Ack Ack Regiment, Royal Artillery, England and Wales 1950–1952. Army Emergency Reserve 1952–1956.

Jakes, George N., Aircraftsman, Leading-Aircraftsman, and W.O.II (?), Royal Air Force Regiment, England, Cyprus, and Iraq, 1953–1960.

Jenkinson, Major Nicholas C., T.D., Battery Commander, 202 (Norfolk & Suffolk Yeomanry) Battery, 100 Medium Regiment, Royal Artillery, T.A., England Wales and West Germany (Rhine Army) 1977–1980.

Johnson, Bombardier Derek, 202 (Norfolk & Suffolk Yeomanry) Battery, 100 Medium Regiment, Royal Artillery, T.A., Cyprus, England, Wales, and West Germany (Rhine Army) 1970–1987.

Kennedy, Captain Quintin B., Royal Field Artillery, Western Front and India, 1914–1937.

Bibliography / Secondary Sources — Background

Kill, Samuel, Lance/Corporal (Acting/Unpaid) to Sergeant, Royal Corps of Military Police. Provost Sergeant, Suez Canal Zone, Egypt 1950–52; Inkerman Barracks Corps Depot, Woking, Surrey, 1952–1953.

Lawley-Yorke, William Lanchester, Gunner, Lance/Bombardier, and 2nd Lieutenant, 'D' Troop, 22 Gibraltar Battery, 52nd Location Regiment, and Dettingen Battery, 87th Heavy Ack Ack Regiment, Royal Artillery, England and Wales, 1952–1954, plus T.A. and Army Emergency Reserve service.

Leadbetter, Albert, Lance-Corporal (Acting/Unpaid), Corporal, Royal Corps of Military Police, 1941–1955. Egypt, Suez Canal zone.

Locksmith, Brian, Private, Lance-Corporal, Corporal, Sergeant, Royal Army Medical Corps (attached 202 [Norfolk & Suffolk Yeomanry] Battery, 100 Medium — subsequently 100 Field — Regiment Royal Artillery, T.A.). England, Scotland, Wales, and West Germany, 1973–1988.

Lucas, Raymond, Rating, Ordinary-and Able-bodied-Seaman, Royal Navy, 1950–1957 — plus five years Reserve.

Midgeley, Ernest, Gunner, Lance/Bombardier, 'D' Troop, 22 Gibraltar Battery, 52nd Locating Regiment, Royal Artillery, and West Yorks Hussars, R.A., T.A., 1951–1957. England, Scotland, and Wales.

Moore, Anthony E., Lance-Corporal (Acting/Unpaid) through Company Quartermaster Sergeant, Royal Corps of Military Police, 1933–1955 (seconded to the Palestine Police 1946–1948). North Africa, and Italy with 55th (London) Division. Palestine with the Palestine Police. Last posting, Gibraltar, 1954.

Morton, Richard ("Dick"), Gunner, Lance-Bombardier, Bombardier, and Acting Sergeant, Royal Artillery, 1940–1946. North Africa, Italy, and Austria.

Neve, Major Arthur, served with the Suffolk Regiment and Egyptian Labour Corps.

Orchard-Lisle, Brigadier-General Paul.

Parker, Flying Officer Ronald Rhodes, Bomber Command, Royal Air Force, 1939–1946.

Parker, Flying Officer Spencer Furlong. Royal Flying Corps, 1915–1918.

Phillips, Victor C., Private, Lance-Corporal, 'A' Coy., 5th Battalion, the Suffolk Regiment, 1938–1946. Fall of Singapore — P.O.W. 1943–1945.

Rice, Richard ("Dick"), Gunner, Lance-Bombardier, Bombardier, and Sergeant, ? Battery, 58th Medium Regiment, Royal Artillery. North Africa, Italy, and Western Europe, 1941–1944.

Rochester, Gunner Nigel "Rocky," storeman, B.Q.M.S. stores, 202 (Norfolk & Suffolk Yeomanry) Battery, 100 Medium Regiment, Royal Artillery, T.A.

Rose, Rifleman Stanley B. S., "Tall Story Stan," 'C' Coy., 2nd Battalion, The Green Jackets, 1953–1955. Suez Canal zone.

Rudd-Clarke, Lt.-Colonel Lionel Le Mesurier, C.O., 52nd Locating Regiment, Royal Artillery, Larkhill, 1951–1953. Commandant, Shepton Mallet Military Prison, Somerset, 1953–1957.

Setchell, Trooper Vincent, ?? Troop, ?? Squadron, 3rd King's Royal Hussars, 1940–1946. North Africa, Italy, 1942–1945.

Seton, Lt.-Colonel Ronald, Royal Artillery & the Royal Artillery Association. India, North Africa, and Italy, 1933–1946. Personal reminiscences.

Sheridan, Widnes, Private, Acting/Unpaid Lance-Corporal, Lance-Corporal, Provost-Corporal, Royal Corps of Military Police. Trieste 1950–1951. Inkerman Barracks, Woking, 1953. Served in British Zone, Austria, 1953–1955.

Smith, Donald, 2nd Lieutenant, Lieutenant, ? Company, 1st Battalion, the Seaforth Highlanders, United Kingdom, North Africa, and Italy, 1940–1946.

Smith, Rifleman Frederick B. S., Kings Royal Rifle Corps, United Kingdom, North Africa, Italy and Austria, 1939–1946.

Smith, Terence E. M., Gunner/TARA through Battery Sergeant-Major, TEM, Royal Artillery, 1954–1982. Suez Canal zone 1953–1954. Served with the Norfolk Yeomanry, and 202 (Suffolk & Norfolk Yeomanry) Battery, 100 Medium and 100 Field Regiments, Royal Artillery, T.A., England, Scotland, Wales, and with the Rhine Army in West Germany, 1953–1983 (not continuous service).

Thompson, Trooper Arthur Copsey, Royal Tank Regiment, Normandy, Belgium, and Germany, 1944–1946.

Thornalley, Trooper George A., 2nd Royal Tank Regiment, North Africa and Italy, 1943–1945.

Treble, Staff Captain Herbert Livingstone, ?? Company, 1st Battalion, the Somerset Light

Infantry. India. Various World War II theaters; Staff Officer G,H.Q., British Commonwealth Division, Korea, 1951–1953.

Turner, Guardsman Reginald, 2nd Battalion, the Grenadier Guards, Guards' Armoured Brigade, North Africa and Italy, 1942–1945.

Walters, Herman E., Private First Class, Corporal, Company C, 133rd Infantry Regiment, 34th Infantry Division, United States Army, North Africa and Italy, 1943–1945.

Woods, Charles Gunner, Limber-Gunner, and Lance-Bombardier, Permanent Staff, 202 (Norfolk & Suffolk Yeomanry) Battery, 100 Medium and 100 Field Regiments, Royal Artillery, T.A., England, Scotland, Wales, and with the Rhine Army in West Germany, 1973–1990.

Wrigley, Walter, Private through Sergeant, the Parachute Regiment, World War II; Gunner through Sergeant, 'Q' Battery, 358 (Suffolk Yeomanry) Regiment & 202 (Norfolk & Suffolk Yeomanry) Battery, 100 Medium Regiment, Royal Artillery, T.A. Served from 1942 until 1990.

Other Sources

Communiqué read in House of Commons, March 29, 1917, re: successes in the Sinai Peninsula.

Imperial War Museum, Duxford, Cambridgeshire.

Imperial War Museum, London.

Public Records Office (National Archives), London.

Suffolk Regimental Museum, Gibraltar Barracks, Bury St. Edmunds, Suffolk.

Suffolk Yeomanry Museum, King's Road, Bury St. Edmunds, Suffolk.

Index

Entries in **_bold italics_** indicate photographs or illustrations.

Abbas Helmieh (Abbassia) 227
Abbassia Helmieh (Cairo) 227–228
Abu Hareira, Beersheba (Gaza III) 105
advanced dressing stations 48, 82
aeroplane 106–108, 115, 133
Afuleh (Megiddo/Sharon theater) 197, 207
airmen 75; brandy drinker 95
Aitken, Private Alexander 38, 262, 273
Ajlin 80, 94, 97, 115, 120; Ajlin Mosque 127
Al Muqattam (Anglophile Cairo newspaper): offices sacked 230
Aleppo 104, 200, 206, 211; advance to 219–220; captured 223
Alexander the Great 17, 218
Alexandria 7–8, 10, 12, 20–21, 25–26, 29, 32, 34, 37, 98, 102, 107, 136, 178; quayside scenes 10; restored order in 229, 260, 273, 276
The Alexandria Club (Y.M.C.A.) 37, 136
Ali el Muntar: attacked on 65–67, 80, 137, 143; capture of defensive position 69, 79–81
Allenby, General Sir Edmund 1; appointed to succeed General Murray 98, 101–102; arrival in Egypt 75, 101; biography of 103; Gaza III success 116–133; great victory 192–200; "Jerusalem by Christmas" directive 102; made C. in C. of E.E.F. 103; moved G.H.Q. 103; personality 104; plan of attack 188–189; prior career 75; report of 203; seen by Sassoon 177; 181, 184; stated requirements 113–114, 106, 110, 116; Turkey out of war 206–207, 240, 245
"Allenby's pets" (nickname given to 54th Division) 1, 177
Alloway, Sergeant C.T. 127
almonds 163
Altham, General G.O.C. 32, 34
Althaus, Captain F.R. 156
Ambrose, Sergeant N. 127
ambulances 97, 170
American Oil Company 279; pipes commandeered from 106
American Y.M.C.A.: operating at Alexandria 37
Anderson, Corporal P. 127

Andrews, Private Harold 127
ANZAC 4, 12, 65, 72–73; entered Gaza 77, 103, 114, 240
Anzac Hostel (Cairo): opened 37
Anzac Ridge (Gaza II) 81
Apperly, Lieutenant Frank L., R.A.M.C. 21–**_22_**, 261, 277
apricots 174
Apsley House **_103_**
Arab Bureau 34
Arab Irregulars 205, 210, 212, 277
Arab Revolt 34
Archer, 2nd Lieutenant 126, 182
Armageddon 1, 185–186, 188, 196–197, 203, 240, 242, 249, 280
Armageddon, Plain of 196
Armenian M.O. deserter 79, 99, 155
Armenian troops: participating in action at Battle of Sharon 197
armistice 219–220, 223, 225, 228, 233, 258, 270
armored cars 11, 24, 69, 218; breakout by at Gaza I 73–74
armored trains 11, 14, 24
Armstrong, Brigadier General St. G.B. 247
Army Corps: XXth, 11–12, 42, 51, 62, 106, 118, 245, 248; XXIth 106, 114, 116, 118–119, 146, 158–159, 173, 185, 187, 192–193, 196, 207, 224, 239, 247
Army Service Corps: "Ally Sloper's Cavalry" 255–256
Ashwell, Lena 15, 17, 260
Askelon 133
Asquith, the Right Honourable Herbert Henry 273
Aswan (Upper Egypt) 231
Atawine Redoubt (Gaza) 80, 105, 115, 120
Athanasian Creed 32
Attawineh Redoubt *see* Atawine Redoubt
Auja River 176
Australia Hill (Gaza II) 80
Australian Infantry Brigades: 244–245
Australian Light Horse 1, 117, 266–267, 274; brigades 3, 109; 1st A.L.H. captured 165; 2nd A.L.H. 244; 3rd A.L.H. 162, 245, 277,

314; 4th A.L.H. 213, 229, 245; 10th A.L.H. 245; dead trooper 108–138
Australian Red Cross 37
Australian troops 176; *see also* Australian Infantry Brigades; Australian Light Horse
Austrian gunners 67, 72, 74, 78, 143, 153, 218, 222, 260, 265
Avery, Captain 127
A.W.O.L. (Absent without leave) 52
'Azzum Ibn 'Atme (Battle of Sharon) 201

Bacon, Lieutenant Frank 123, 125, 126
Badcock, Brevét Lieutenant Colonel G.E. 62–63, 102, 152, 174, 185, 224
badges of rank 127
Baghdad 63
Bagot-Chester, Captain W.G. 120
Bahr Jusef 43
Bailkie, Brigadier General H.A.D. Simpson, C.B., C.M.G., G.O.C. 130, 247
Baka (Megiddo) 203, 249
Baker, Private, Lieutenant 174
Baker, "Scrounger" 140–141, 143
Balaam, Private A. 310
Balah Trench (Gaza III) 114–115
Balfour, A.J. 281
The Balfour Declaration 281, 286
balloons 138, 172
bands 161st Brigade Band 216, 219, 224
Barak, Israelitish 186
barbed wire 46, 72, 85, 88–89, 98, 104–107, 114, 121–122, 124, 129–130, 141–142, 143, 165, 182–183, 192, 198
Barnard, 2nd Lieutenant 182
"The Barnstormers" 17
Barrow, Major General C. de S., C.B. 245
Barz ed Din (Judæan Hills) 170
bash raises (Egyptian C.T.C.) 63
Battle of Blenheim *see* Blenheim, Battle of
Battle of Magdhaba *see* Magdhaba, Battle of
Battle of Marathon *see* Marathon, Battle of
Battle of Minden *see* Minden, Battle of
Battle of Romani *see* Romani, Battle of
Battle of Sharon *see* Sharon, Battle of
Battles of the Bible 141, 270
Bayonets: bullet-bent 97
bazaars: of Damascus 216, 253
Beach Post (Gaza III) 115, 123, 125, 128, 133
Bean, Captain C.E.W. 42, 262*n*11
Beck Row (Suffolk) 264*n*48
Bedfordshire Regiment 175, 232, 247
Bedouins 95
Beersheba 12, 55–56, 62, 69, 76–77, 79, 82, 85–88, 91–93, 102, 104, 110, 116–120, 133–134, 136, 140
Beirut 200, 206, 214, 217–225, 249
Beisan (Battle of Sharon) 190, 203, 207, 249
Beit Lit 221
Beit Nebala (Judæan Hills) 156, 159, 181
Bell, Lieutenant Edward W. 8–9, 73
belt 265*n*83

Bene 'Atarot (Israeli *Moshav*) 269*n*48
Benha (Kalioubieh Province) 230–232
Berkshire Yeomanry 245
Bible 112, 153, 169, 264*n* 216; references 134, 137, 154, 189, 219, 264*n*22, 266*n*7; Daniel 153; Exodus 266*n*15; Ezekiel 168, 188–189, 218; Genesis 216, 219; Jonah 165, 219; Judges 188; Kings I 219; Numbers 266*n*15; Old Testament 196, 218–219; Psalms 154; Revelation 188; Zechariah 185–186
Bidya (Megiddo) 193–194
bilharzia 43
"Bill Harris" *see* bilharzia
billets 232; at Wilhelma 167
Birkbeck, Captain G.W. 82, 86, 254, 265
Birsalem (Mulebbis) 165
Black Ace Gang 31
Blazed Hill (Gaza II) 90, 93, 97–98
Blenheim, Battle of 202
Boer Wars 278
Bols, Major General Sir L.J., K.C.M.G., C.B., D.S.O. 244
Bolton, Private, Lance Corporal Corporal Farrier Charles 59–60, **162**, 172, 278
"Bombay bowlers" **119**
Bonar Law, the Right Honourable Andrew 74
Bonser, Sapper Harry P. 41, 154, 165, 169
Bornat Hill (Judæa) 156
Borton, Lieutenant Colonel Arthur, V.C., D.S.O. 141–143
Boundary Wadi 172–**173**
Bourchier, Brigadier General M.W.J. 214
Bourchier's Force: at Damascus 214
bread 167
H.M.S. *Bristol* 102
British Divisions: 52nd (Scottish) 55, 62, 64, 80–82, 85–86, 88–90, 97, 103, 106, 114, 119, 121, 123, 159, 175, 247, 268*n*21; 53rd (Welsh) 6, 10, 55, 62, 64, 76, 78, 80–81, 86, 90, 103, 106, 165, 191, 245; 54th (East Anglian) 6, 10–12, 55, 62, 64, 80–89, 103,106, 114, 116, 121–122, 127–128, 134, 147, 152, 165, 177, 185–186, 188, 190–192, 194–197, 203, 207, 214, 219, 221, 227–229, 232, 237, 239, 247, 253–255, 258, 264*n*43; 60th (London) 104, 106, 139, 149, 152, 165, 177, 186–187, 246; 74th 80–82, 89–90, 103, 106, 176, 186, 191, 221, 247; 75th 104, 115, 119–120, 159, 170, 186, 191, 247–248
British Legion 235
British Red Cross **8**, 37
British West India Regiment 205
The Brook Kishon 217
brothels 41
Brown, Aircraftsman Arthur (Sonny 287
Brown, Ordinary Telegrapher Albert J. **13–14**
Bruce, Sergeant N. 127
Buckinghamshire Yeomanry 245
Budrus (near Lydda) 159
Bulfin, Lieutenant General Sir Edward S., K.C.B., C.V.O. 106, 119, 158, 160, 182, 224, 230, 239, 247

Index

"Bully beef" 42, 69, 167
Bureid Ridge (Battle of Sharon) 181–183, 190, 194–195
Burj Trench (Gaza III) 124, 128
Burjabye Ridge 120
Burlham, Private Timothy 31, 172, 278; see also Black Ace Gang
Burma Infantry: 93rd battalion at Megiddo 195
Burtenshaw, Corporal 86
Bury St. Edmunds (Suffolk) 48, 237, 277
Byford, L/Corporal P.E. 209
Byles, Sergeant H. 127

cacolets (Egyptian C.T.C.) 63, 257
cactus: gardens 190; hedges 56, 67, 79, 73, 143, 177
Cæsarea 217
Cairo 7–8, 10, 12–13, 20, 29–30, 33, 34, 36–38, 41–43, 49–50, 55, 70, 75, 79, 93, 98–99, 102–104, 138, 145, 227–233, 261n5, 262n40, 267
Cambridgeshire Regiment 278
Camel Brigade 62, 64, 85–86, 88, 90, 245
Camel Corps 74, 77, 88, 103
Camel Transport Corps 17, 62–63, 128, 184, 221
Camelry 78, 117, 213
camels 17, 20, 24, 26, 34, 35, 36, 44–45, 48, 57, 62–65, 72, 74, 77–78, 80, 85–88, 90, 93, 103, 117, 121, 128, 138, 153, 162, 169, 172, 179, 184–185, 205, 213, 215, 219, 221, 242, 245; and Captain R. Hugh Knyvett 44
Cameronians (Scottish rifles) 120, 122, 247
Campbell, Lieutenant General Walter 62, 103, 244
Cana of Galilee 154, 204–205
canteens 37, 59
Carnarvon Sector (Gaza) 115
Carr, Captain 85
Castle Hill (Mulebbis/Mirr) 172
Casualty Clearing Stations 82
caterpillar tractors 45
cavalry 56, 65, 69, 72–74, 78–79, 100, 115, 117–118, 129, 136, 171, 187, 190, 192–193, 196–197, 202–204, 207, 211–214, 217–218, 220–222, 241, 249, 271n78; 14th Cavalry Brigade 212
The Central Powers 177, 220, 249
Chapman, Sergeant 50; accidentally shot by sentry 98
Chasseurs d'Afrique (French) 245
Chauvel, Lieutenant General Sir H.G., K.C.B., K.C.M.G., G.O.C. 92, 106, 118, 158, 210, 239, 244, 266n33
Chaytor, Brigadier General Sir Harry G. (later Lieutenant General) 92, 244
Cheetham, 240
Chetwode, Lieutenant General Sir Philip W. 51, 64, 69, 75, 90; 92–93, 239, 245
Churchill, the Right Honourable Winston Spencer 117, 149, 175, 222
cigarettes 31, 56, 143, 153

The Citadel (Cairo) 30, 37
Citroën 45
Clayton, Brigadier General Gilbert 156
clippers (Egyptian C.T.C.) 63
coal boxes (German 5.9" shells) 79; see also "Jack Johnson's
Cobbold, P. Anne (neé Mortlock) 272, 278
Cœur de Lyon, Richard 181, 233
Colchester (Essex) 52
Cole, Lieutenant F.J. 272
Colston, Brigadier General, the Hon. E.M., C.M.G., D.S.O. 248
Colvin, Lieutenant 21; Gaza battles 123, 126–127
Commonwealth War Graves Commission 95
Connaught Rangers 246
Constantinople (Istanbul) 104, 146, 204, 259n22, 286
Cooke, Private T.F. 70–*71*
Cooper, Sergeant, D.C.M. 125
Copinger-Hill, Major 156
The Corn Exchange 237
Corn Hill 237
corned beef see "bully beef"
Cox, Private A.E. 210
Cox, Brigadier General C., D.S.O. 244
Creighton, Padré Oswin, C.F. 274
Crested Rock (Gaza) 115, 128, 131
cricket 107; match at Ludd 174
Cricket Redoubt (Gaza) 115, 123, 126; seized 128–129
"Crocodile River" (northern Palestine) 217
Crown Hill (Battle of Sharon) 193–195
crusaders 180, 217, 233, 285
The Crusades 284
Curzon, Lord 175, 276

Da Costa, Brigadier General E.C., C.M.G., D.S.O. 246
Dahabiehs 6
The Daily Telegraph 225–226
Dallas, General, C.O. 65, 69
Damascus 34, 146, 191, 200, 204–207, 253; capture of 206, 210, 227; disputed Allied first entry of 210, 215; ladies' welcome 213
Daniel see Bible
The Dardanelles 3, 10, 13, 63, 133, 253, 273, 285
dates 86, 107
David (King) 152, 154–155, 252; see also Bible
Dawnay, Brigadier General G.P. 82, 244
Dead Sea 165, 178, 180
Deakin, Lieutenant 123, 125
Deir el Balah (Gaza) 62; station 82
Deir Tureif 1917, 159
Deiran 162–163
Demimondaines: of Alexandra and Cairo 12
De Piépape, Colonel P., O.C 188, 193
Desert Mounted Corps 51, 106, 210, 212, 214, 239, 244, 248

desertion 99, 182, 201
Détachement Français de Palestine et Syrie (D.F.P.S.) 193
Deversoir (Suez Canal defenses) 51
The Diary of a Yeomanry Medical Officer 276–277
Dikerin 172
discipline 3, 37, 50, 70, 104, 107
disorderly conduct 41
The Dispatches of Sir Archibald Murray 276
Divisional Train (54th) 155–156
Dobell, Lieutenant General Sir Charles 51, 64, 74–75, 79, 90; relieved of command 92–93
The Donga (Gaza III) 115
donkey transport 7, 20, 26, 62, 170–171, 184–185, 242
Dorsetshire Yeomanry 247
Double Hill (Mulebbis/Mirr) 172
Drackett-Case, Frederick Charles 278
Drackett-Case, Sgt Frederick P. 278
Drackett-Case, Marjorie neé Rumbelow 268n107, 278
drivers (Egyptian C.T.C.) 63
drunkenness 41–42, 224
druses 212
Duke of Lancaster's Yeomanry 248
dust 42, 51, 71–72, 98, 104–105, 124, 128, 130, 139, 141–142, 165, 173, 177–178, 187, 192, 216–217, 219
Duxworth (Cambridgeshire): Imperial War Museum 290

Eames, Lieutenant 194
East Mirr (Mulebbis District) 163
Eastern Force 50–51, 55, 64–65, 79–82, 86, 92–93, 103–106
Edib, Halidé 145–146, 267n80, 275
Edinburgh Sector (Gaza III) 115
Egypt 1, 3, 5–7, 10–12, 14, 19–22, 25–26, 29, 32, 34, 36–38, 41–46, 49–50, 55, 57, 74, 76, 78, 91, 100, 102, 104, 113–114, 149, 152–153, 165, 171, 176, 179, 184–185, 186, 197, 220, 227–233, 237, 239–240, 250, 254, 258; unrest 229–231, 239; Upper Egypt 231
Egyptian Expeditionary Force 11, 17, 34, 41–42, 62, 71, 100, 118, 185, 218, 231, 240, 244
Egyptian Labour Corps 5, 10, 62, 95, 239, 264n40
Ekaterinoslav 227
El Arish 12, 17, 55, 57–**59**, 60, 93, 107; military cemetery 95
El Arish Redoubt 79, 108–**109**, 110, 112, 114, 115, 119–121, 123=124, 128, **133**, 134–135, 136
Elgood, Colonel Percival G. 38, 274
El Hammam 21, 24–25
Elijah 219; *see also* Bible
El Mendur(Gaza II) 80
El Mughar 271n77
Encyclopædia Judaica 268n11
Enver Pasha 104, 184

Esani (Gaza) 56
Esdraelon, Plain of (Megiddo/Sharon) 185–186, 190, 203–204, 216, 233
Es Salt 203
Essex Regiment 7, 15, 21, 30, 67, 97, 146, 161, 222, 227, 247; 1/4th battalion 69, 123, 161, 172, 183, 190–191, 193–195, 216, 233, 247; 1/5th battalion 7, 15, 21, 30, 48, 67, 69, 97, 123–126, 131, 161, 175, 178, 181–183, 190–191, 193–195, 207–210, 216, 222, 224, 227, 232–233, 247; 1/6th battalion 69, 87, 123, 125–126, 128, 161, 183, 190–191, 193–195, 207, 216, 224, 247; 1/7th battalion 69, 123, 126, 161, 182, 191–193, 207, 216, 224, 247
Et Tire (Megiddo, Plain of Sharon) 159, 202, 258
Evans, Lieutenant 124, 179–180
Eversden, Captain Robert, R.F.C./R.A.F. 179–180
Exodus *see* Bible
Ezbekiah Gardens (Cairo) 36, 261n37
Ezekiel *see* Bible

Facey, Private/Trooper Albert B. 38
Fair, Captain A., M.C. 44, 88–89, 105, 143, 167, 171–173, 199, 228
fanatis 82, 153, 265n71
Fawley, Captain, A.I.F. 42
Feisal, Emir 149, 210, 277n16
Fenn, Lieutenant 194
Ferdinand, Prince, Duke of Brunswick 48
54th Division, artillery brigades: 270th Essex, R.F.A. 247; 271st Essex, R.F.A. 15, 52, 57, 60, 65, 67, 83, 138, 179, 247; 272nd Norfolk, R.F.A. 81, 247
54th Division, infantry brigades: 161st 21, 50, 65, 67, 78, 86–87, 97, 120–121, 161, 182–183, 193–194, 209–210, 215, 247; 162nd 65, 86–89, 120, 122–123, 126, 129, 170, 175, 190, 192–193, 195–196, 217, 232, 247; 163rd 64, 82–83, 85–86, 88, 102, 108, 116, 120–121, 128, 156, 159–160, 169, 175, 192–193, 197, 217, 247
figs 174
fish 176, 218–219; fishing with firearms 176
Fisher's Orchard (Gaza III) 122
flash-spotting 159
Fletcher, Lieutenant Horace 11, 259n25
flies 46, 98, 181, 217; fly-sprayers 98
Foley-Whaling 182
food parcels 56
football 7, 21, 51, 141, 181, 227
France 1, 5, 14, 17, 29, 45, 51, 53, 92, 95, 104, 107–108, 166, 171–172, 175–178, 190, 194, 220, 222–223, 239, 259n20; French troops 98, 190
Franklin, Lieutenant 123–126
Freckenham (Suffolk) 94, 280
Frederick the Great 280
French, L/Corporal F.L. 210
French, R.S.M.J.J., D.C.M 228
French, Sergeant R.T. 182

French Foreign Legion 193
From Gallipoli to the Somme 278
Fryer Hill (Gaza) 79, 114
Fuller, Aircraftsman Jack 288
Fusilier Ridge 94–95

Galilee: Cana 186, 204; Sea of 186
Gallipoli 1, 3, 5–8, 11–12, 20–22, 26, 29, 32, 34, 41–42, 55–56, 104, 116, 120, 141, 172, 190, 240, 258
Garnett's Wood (Mulebbis/Mirr) 171–172
Garsia, Lieutenant Colonel 127
gas: drill at Wilhelma 167; gas shells 90, 114, 117; use of 86, 133
Gates of Gaza 17, 134, 137
Gaza 17, 41, 51, 55–56, 62, 67, 70–75, 76–96, 102–105, 108, 110, 115–125, 130, 132–139, 143–145, 153, 159, 169–170, 190–194, 210, 216, 224, 228, 239–240, 243–244, 254, 258; gates of 17, 137, 137; "Gateway to Palestine" 55; Gaza I 64–79; Gaza II 79–91; Gaza III 108–138; *see also* Gates of Gaza
Genesis *see* Bible
Gezira 102
Gibbons, Lieutenant Colonel Thomas 7, 15, 21, 25, 30, 48–50, 67–69, 97–99, 123–124, 127, 175–178, 181–183, 190, 194, 207, 209–210, 216–219, 222–226, 229–230, 232–233
Gibraltar 114, 128–129, 131; barracks 278
Gideon, Israelitish General 186
Gilbert, Major Vivian 36, 112, 117, 149, 151–156, 175, 186–187, 221, 232–234
Gilead 216
Gilgal 216
Giza (Gizeh) 30
Gloucester Hussars 19, 46, 107, 176, 213, 245
Good Samaritan's Inn 165
The Governorate (Cairo) 231
H.M.S. *Grafton* 116–117
Grant, Brigadier General 245
grapes 174
Green Hill (Gaza) 65, 69, 80, 172; *see also* Green Mound
Green Mound (Gaza) 67; *see also* Green Hill
Greer, Brigadier General F.A., C.M.G., D.S.O. 247
Gregory, Brigadier General 212
Grey, Sir Edward 274
Gun Hill (Gaza) 115, 120, 129
Gurkha Rifles *see* Gurkhas
Gurkhas 120, 158; collecting dead enemies' ears 279; reputation of 120; 2/3rd Gurkha Rifles 34, 159; 3/3rd Gurkha Rifles 34, Gurkhas under Captain Bagot-Chester in

Habieta (Suez Canal defenses) 46, 51
Hableh (Battle of Sharon) 187
Hableh-Tul Keram line 187
Hadra 160; Hadra bridge 160
Haifa **217**; 54th Division arrived at 217; 54th Division departed 217

Haig, Field Marshal Sir Douglas 5, 17, 177
halfway house 130
Hampshire Regiment: 1/8th Battalion, 163rd Brigade 8, 19, 82–83, 85, 87–88, 91, 108, 128, 193, 196, 228, 247, 253; 2/4th Battalion, 233rd Brigade (not 54th Division) 158, 248; 2/5th Battalion, 233rd Brigade (not 54th Division) 159, 248
Hankey, Colonel Maurice 171, 176, 203, 221, 266*n*10
Happy Valley (Gaza III) 97, 120
Harbord, Brigadier General 115
Hare, Major General S.W. Hare, C.B., O.C. 12, 65, 87–89, 114, 119–121, 123, 130, 188, 191, 193–195, 197, 207, 209, 247
Harrington, Private F.J. 129
Harrington, L/Corporal K.T. 210
Harris, Sergeant 219
haversacks 120, 140
hawking 95
Heart Hill (Gaza II) 94
Hebron 114, 118, 152, 204, 264*n*22
Hedjaz 34, 212; King of 203, 249; railway 205
Helen of Troy 7
Helmieh 227
Herefordshire Regiment: 1st battalion 67, **69**, 245
Herod 175, 217
Hertfordshire Yeomanry 248
Highland Light Infantry 247
The History of the 1st/5th Battalion: "The Suffolk Regiment" 274
The History of the Hampshire Regiment 259*n*9, 277
The History of the Norfolk Regiment 276
The History of the Suffolk Regiment 276
The History of the Transport Services of the Egyptian Expeditionary Force, 1916–1919 276–277
Hodgson, Major General H.W., C.B. 245
Holt caterpillar tractors 45
Homs (Syria) 206, 214, 221
Horsford, Private William 26, 27, **28**, **29**
Hoskins, Major General A.R., C.M.G., D.S.O. 188
How, George **162**, **229**
Howard-Vyse, Brigadier General 244
Howitzers 70, 73–74, 80, 86, 106, 121, 123, 125, 159, 190, 195–196, 223, 248
Huddleston, Brigadier General H.J., C.M.G., D.S.O., M.C. 115, 248
Hudeira (Battle of Sharon) 196
Huj (Gaza) 55, 72–73, 76, 145
Humphreys, Brigadier General E.T., D.S.O. 247
hunting 174
Hurcomb, Sergeant 149, **151**
Hureira 55–56, 80
Hussars 19, 46, 167, 179, 213, 245

Ibanne Ridge (Kh. Ibanne) 159

Imbros (Ægean island) 5, 245
Imperial Service Cavalry Brigade: at Gaza 129-130
Imperial War Museum (Duxford, Cambridgeshire) 290
Imperial War Museum (London) 290
Imperial Yeomanry Brigade 10; Lincolnshire 42, 277; Middlesex 245; Sherwood Rangers 245; Suffolk 246, 278-279; Worcestershire 51, 145, 240, 245; *see also* Yeomanry Regiments
Imtarfa Isolation Hospital (Malta) **26-27**
Indian (Imperial Service) Infantry Brigade: 20th 129
Indian troops 98; replace British infantry 175, 177
indiscipline: of Australian troops 37-38, 41
insects 175, 267n67; insect sprays 98
H.M.S. *Irresistible* **14**
Islam 3, 250-251
Island Wood (Gaza) 114-115, 126, 131
Ismailia 12, 20, 43, 48-51, 99-100, 160, 259n26
Israelites 104
Italian contingent 106; at Jerusalem triumphal entry 155, 222, 252; gallantry of at Gaza III 134, 153

Jabin, King of Canaan 186
"Jack and Jill" 88
"Jack Johnson's" (German 5.9" shells) 79, 127; *see also* coal boxes
Jackal Tepe (Sharon) 190
jackals 162, 174; substituting for a fox 174
Jaffa 55-56, 76, 79, 117, 119, 149, 155-156, 160-161, 163, 165, 167, 173-174, 178-179, 181, 214, 233, 258; oranges 163, 169, 174
Jaggard, Private Bob 137, **162**, 172, 278
Jarrold, Corporal A.R. 125
Jebaliye (Gaza) 81
Jemal Pasha 76, 146, 210-212
Jericho 55, 174, 179, 187, 260n37; capture of 165
Jerishe 160
Jerusalem 55, 63, 76-79, 100, 113-114, 117, 146, 149, **151**, 157, 161-163, 165, 169-170, 179, 181, 184, 187, 203-204, 207, 216, 233, 249, 258; Allenby's entry into 154-155; mayor of 151; military governor of 151; official surrender accepted 152-154
Jessop, Mr. William 37, 262n42
Jesus 11, 204; *see also* Bible
Jevis Tepe (Battle of Sharon) 190; is taken 194
Jewish Battalions (Jewish Legion) 179; *see also* Royal Fusiliers
Jewish Legion *see* Jewish Battalions
Jezreel Valley **186**
Jijulia (northern Palestine) 194
Jlil (northern Palestine) 221
John Trench (Gaza III) 115
Johnson, Private William G. 139-143

Jonah *see* Bible
Jonathan (son of King Saul) 181, 203-204; *see also* Bible
Jordan River 161, 179, 203, 205-207, 249; *see also* Jordan Valley
Jordan Valley 174, 179, 187; heat and unhealthiness of 179; *see also* Jordan River
Judæa 78; Judæan Hills 55-56, 72, 113, 138, 161, 162, 163
Judges *see* Bible
Junie Bay (north of Beirut) 225
Jupiter 25

Kafr Kasim 173, 182, 190, 199
Kaiser Wilhelm II 154
Kaiser's Clock 154-156
Kakon 216
Kamoan Rifles 232
Kantara (also rendered Qantara) 12, 14, 37, 45, 51, 57, 98, 153; base depôt 12, 14-15, 36, 106, 118, 132, 138, 146, 148, 160, 179, 205, 227; war memorial cemetery 95, 278
H.M.T. *Kashmir* 10
Kasim Wood 190, 194
Kasr el Nil barracks (Cairo) 233
Kate, Aunt Booty (*née* Parker) 56
Katoomba Post (Suez Canal defenses) 49
Kearsey, Lieutenant Colonel A., D.S.O., O.B.E. 55, 62, 94, 262n59
Kefar Bara (Battle of Sharon) 194
Kemal, General Mustapha 104, **185**, 205, 239
Kemp, Sergeant G.J. 125
Kent, Trooper Harold 278
Kh. Deir el Qassis (Battle of Sharon), 193
Kh. El Bir (Gaza II) 80-81, 85
Kh. Es Sumra (Battle of Sharon) 195
Kh. Hadra 160
Kh. Ibanne 159
Kh. Kufiye (Gaza) 81
Kh. Sirisia (Battle of Sharon) 194
Kh. Zeifizfiye, Beit Nebala 159
Khalasa (Gaza) 56
Khamsin 32, 45, 130
Khan en Nebi Younes 219
Khan Yunis 12, 62, 89, 114-115, 130
Khirbet Sihan (Gaza battles) 77, 80, 82, 86-88, 90, 105
Khuweilteh (Gaza III) 137
Kibbia 159; *see also* Qibye
King George V 44, 225
King Saul 186; *see also* Bible
Kings *see* Bible
King's Own Scottish Borderers (25th of Foot) 172, 247
Kirbet 82, 218; *see also* Khirbet Sihan
Kishon 217
Kitchener, Lord Horatio 3, 5
Kitchener's Army 241
Kliwitsky 163
knife-rests 72
Knyvett, Captain R. Hugh 36-**37**, 44-45

Kress von Kressenstein, General Friedrich F. 45, 74–76, 118, 128–*129*, 239
Kufr Qasim 193–195
Kukris *120*
Kurd Hill (Gaza II and III) 56, 106
Kurkur 217

The Labyrinth (Gaza II) 79–80
Ladell, Lieutenant E.E. 232
Lahore: 3rd (Lahore) Division 188, 190–192, 193–194, 221
Lancers (Indian 2nd Regiment) 98, 197, 217
Lane, Corporal, 2nd Lieutenant *70*, 94–96, 239, 278
Langdon Wood (Mirr) 163
Lawrence, Lieutenant Colonel T.E. (Lawrence of Arabia) 1, 10, 33–34, 149, 156, 205, 210, 212–214
Lebanon 219–220, 223–224, 233
Lee's Hill (Gaza III) 120
Leggett, Brigadier General A.H. 119, 247
Légion d'Orient *193*
Leinster Regiment 246
Lemnos (Ægean island) 5, 7, 20; armistice signed at 220, 259*n*3
lemon groves 173
Lemon Wood (Mulebbis/Mirr) 163
Lena Ashwell 15, 17, 260*n*35
Levant 259*n*3; Levant base 32, 34
Lewis guns 86–87, 108, 126, 140, 142, *162*, 196, 209, 220
lice 122
Light Armoured Motor Battery: 11th 197, 214
Lincolnshire Yeomanry 42–43, 262*n*64
Lion trench (Gaza III) 129–130
Litani (Kasimiyeh) River 218
Little Gleaner 56
Little Waltham 50
Lloyd George, David 63, 75, 78; on replacing Murray 100; view of conduct of Palestine campaign 110–112; summary of Allenby's successful strategy 222–225, 226, 265*n*21
Lockwood, Private R. 210
Lockwood, 2nd Lieutenant 181, 209
Lofts, L/ Corporal E.A. 209–210
London 17, 22, 26, 29, 77–78, 92–93, 132, 137, 155, 207, 210, 212, 217, 225, 231, 237, 240; Lieutenant Colonel Woolaston killed in air raid in 49, 171
London Division: 60th 104, 136, 139, 149, 246
London Infantry Brigade 10
London Regiment: 1/10th battalion 87–88, 108, 126, 129, 170, 193, 195–196; 1/11th battalion 87, 193, 195; 2/18th battalion 152; 2/19th battalion 149, 151; 2/20th battalion 112, 149; 2/22nd battalion 139
Lone Hill (Mulebbis/Mirr) 160–161
Long, Private F. 125
Long Wood (Mulebbis/Mirr) 163
Longley, Major General J.R., K.C.M.G., C.B. 246

Loyal North Lancashire Regiment: 2nd Battalion 172
Lucas, 2nd Lieutenant 182
Ludd 156, 161–162, 170, 178, 273
Ludendorff, General 171, 184
Lutheran Church 268*n*11
Luxor 230
Lydda 146, 158–159

Maadan (Sinai) 58
MacAndrew, Major General H.J.M., C.B., D.S.O. 214
Magdhaba, Battle of 17; *see also* Magdhaba Trench
Magdhaba Trench (Gaza II and III) 80–81, 114–115; *see also* Magdhaba, Battle of
Majdal Yaba (Battle of Sharon) 178
malaria 176, 179, influenza confused with 214
Malta *26*, 120, 229, 231–232
Manor Farm (Worlington, Suffolk) 235, 278; *see also* Warren Farm
Manor of Freckenham: An Ancient Corner of East Anglia 94, 280
Mansura Bluff (Gaza II) 86
Mansura Ridge 56, 65, 67, 82, 86, 93–*95*, 115, 278
H.M.T *Marathon* (Gaza III) 115–116
Marathon, Battle of 202–203
Maris, Captain A.A. 156
Maronites 219
Marriott-Dodington, Brigadier General, C.O. 87, 120, 247
Marseilles 29, 42, 235
Massey, W.T. 71–72, 132–134, 136–138, 151, 188, 197, 210–213, 270*n*14
Maxwell, Lieutenant General Sir John 5, 10, 20, 32, 34, 42, 240
May, Signal Corporal Ernest 107, 152, 266*n*13
Mazar 80–81
McMahon, Sir Henry 3
McNeil, Brigadier General A.J., D.S.O. 169, 172
medical officers (Egyptian C.T.C.) 63
medical officers (M.O.s) 21, 51, 79, 127, 136, 161, 167, 276–277
medical orderlies (Egyptian C.T.C.) 63
medical services 26, 63, 176
Mediterranean Expeditionary Force 4–5, 10, 32, 34, 42
Mediterranean Sea 93, 104, 114, 187, 220, 233
Medjel Yaba *see* Majdal Yaba
Meerut Division (Indian Army) 221
Megiddo 188–189, actions at 185, 188–189, 197, 200–205, 222, 239
Meinertzhagen, Lieutenant Colonel Richard 109–110, 112
Meldrum, Brigadier General 244
Mena Camp 7, *9*, 12, 30
Mesha (Battle of Sharon) 193–194
Meshahera (Gaza) 81

Index

Mesopotamia 11, 34, 51, 64, 81, 171, 177, 179, 185, 223, 261*n*17
Mesopotamian Expeditionary Force 169
Messudiyeh Junction (Megiddo) 203, 249
meteors 25
Mezeireh (Battle of Sharon) 172, 190
Middlesex Hill (Gaza II and III) 80, 88, 114
Midie 158–159
Mildenhall (Suffolk) 235, 264*n*44
Mills, Sapper Frederick T. 15, 17, 36, 106, 114, 116, 118, 132, 138, 146, 148, 160, 179, 205, 227, 260*n*39
Minden, Battle of **48**, 202, 277
Minden Day 48–49
Minden Regiments 277
Minden Rose 48
Minenwerfers **99**, 125–126
Minieh (Egypt) 230
Minnewaska 20
Mirr *see* Castle Hill; Double Hill; East Mirr; Garnett's Wood; Langdon Wood; Lemon Wood; Lone Hill; Long Wood; Mulebbis; Rouge Farm; Ruin Hill; temple; Wadi Ballut; West Mirr
"Moaning Minnies" 99
Moascar (Suez Canal zone) 49, 51, 58
Moncera 204–205
Money, Brigadier General N., D.S.O. 246; Money's detachment (Gaza I) 69
monitors 116–117, 130, 134
Monro, Lieutenant General Charles Carmichael 4–6
Mortlock, Gwendoline May 93, 95, 278
Mortlock, Private S. Jacob P. **26**, **27**, **35**, **52**, **53**, 56, 59–60, 70–71, 88, 90–91, 93–95, 106, 108, **119**, 120–122, 134, 136–137, **162**, 167, 170–172, 176, 224, 234–236, 240, 261*n*25
Moscow (Musk), Corporal 26
Moslems 78, 155, 230, 233, 250–251
mosques 20, 31, 58–59, 72, 127, 143–**145**, 155
mosquitoes 51, 175, 179, 218
Mott, Major General S.F., C.B. 245
Mount Carmel 186, 216–217
Mount Lofty (Suez Canal defenses) 51
Mounted Divisions 244–245
Mousky 31
mud huts **59**, 160
Mudge, Brigadier General A., C.M.G. 87, 120, 195, 247
Mudros 7, 220, 254, 259*n*3
muezzins 58
mulberries 174
Mulebbis 160–161, 169, 173, 175; *see also* Castle Hill; Double Hill; East Mirr; Garnett's Wood; Langdon Wood; Lemon Wood; Lone Hill; Long Wood; Rouge Farm; Ruin Hill; temple; Wadi Ballut; West Mirr
mules 69, 139–140, 184
Murch, Private 149, 151–152
Murray, Lieutenant General Sir Archibald 5–6, 10–11, 17, 32, 34, 42, 50, 64–78, 79–91, 93–98, 100, 102–103, 113–114, 240
museums 290
Musk, Private 26
Muslims 31–32, 58
Musmus Pass (Battle of Sharon) **196**
Mysore Lancers 1918, 98, 215

Nabala (Beit) 156
Nablus 184, 190, 202, 205, 271*n*77
Nahr el 'Auja 156, 160
Napoleon 17, 59, defeated Turks 186, 204, 217, 233
Nashui Bey 184
Nasrieh School (Cairo) 233
native batmen (Egyptian C.T.C.) 63
Nazareth 186, 192, 197, 200, 202–207, **209**, 249
Nebi Kasim (Megiddo) 221
Neve, Major Arthur 278
The New York Times 74–75, 78, 277
Newcombe, Lieutenant Colonel 118
Nile River 6, 10, 20, 30, 43, 114, 186, 230, 251; delta **17**, 19, 26, 43, 114, 153, 230, 251, 260*n*4; water piped to front line 62, 113, 153
Norfolk Post 156
Norfolk Regiment battalions: 1/4th 7, 82–83, 85–87, 102, 105, 107–108, 128, 130–131, 159, 169, 192–194, 227; 1/5th 7, 82–83, 85–87, 88–90, **91**, 102, 107–108, 128, 131, 172, 175, 177, 192–194, 127
North Belah 108
Northamptonshire Regiment battalions: 1/4th 7, 43, 88, 129–130, 161, 163, 181, 193, 247, 259
nose-bags 257
Numbers *see* Bible
nurses 10, 132, 154

Observation Hill 197, **198**, **199**
Oglu Tepe (Battle of Sharon) 190
oil company 106, 279
Old Comrades' Associations 235
Old Testament *see* Bible
Olden, Major, Lieutenant Colonel A.C.N., C.O. 211–212
Oldham Post (Suez Canal defenses) 45, 50
olive groves: at Gaza 72; at Jaffa 163; at Ramleh 233
Oliver, Major B.E. 237
Oliver, Lieutenant G.G. 48, 198
One Tree Hill 163
Opera House Square (Cairo) 228
Oppen, Colonel von. German officer 201–202
oranges 162–163, 169, 174, 268*n*1; groves at Mulebbis 163
Orpen-Palmer, Brigadier General H.B.H., D.S.O. 209
Ottoman Empire 41, 285

Index

Outpost Hill (Gaza) 80, 88–90, 97, 99, 106, 114–115, 117, 120
The Oxford Illustrated History of the British Army 284

Palestine 1, 34, 62, 51, 55, 57, 70, 72, 74, 76–78, 93, 100–101, 103–104, 113–114, 116–117, 124, 132, 137–139, 145, 148–149, 153, 155–156, 163, 165–166, 170–171, 175–177, 179–181, 184–187, 193, 200–203, 210, 212–214, 218, 220–224, 227–228, 232–233, 239–240, 252, 254; Palestinians 205, 268n11
Palestine Tank Detachment (Gaza III) 120
Palmer, John 224
pamphlets/leaflets 182, 185
Papen, Major Franz von 108–109, 276
Parker, Jack 90, 136–**137**, 170, 224, 264n44, 278
Parker, Lieutenant Spencer F. 289
Part, L Corporal Thomas 7, 20, 41, 44, 259n12
Pearson, Brigadier General V.L.N. 246
Peregrine Papers: A Tale of Travel in the Orient 261n27
Pfeiffer, Major 202
Philistia 55, 127
Philistine Hill (Gaza III) 115
Philistines 186, 203–204
Phillips, Victor 289
pipelines 6, 62, 240
Plain of Armageddon *see* Armageddon, Plain of
Plain of Esdraelon *see* Esdraelon, Plain of
Plain of Sharon *see* Sharon, Plain of
pomegranates 165, 263n13
Port Said 6, 10, 12, 117, 165
Port Tewfik 46
Portway, Lieutenant 194; *see also* Portway Hill
Portway Hill 194
Powers, Lieutenant Bernard Alexander **53**, 136
Prince of Wales 44–45, 143
propaganda 3, 182, 185
Psalms *see* Bible
Ptolemaic forces 219
"Public woman" 271n12
pyramids 30, **35**, 36

Qantara *see* Kantara
Qibye 159
quail 107–108
Queen Adelaide 278
Queen's Hill (Gaza II) 97
Quilter, L/Corporal H. 127

rabbits 31, 170
Rafa **61**
Rafah 55, 62, 119, 122; Rafah Junior (Gaza III) 115; Rafah Redoubt (Gaza Battles) 80–81, 114–115, 123, 126–129
Ra-fat salient (Battle of Sharon), 193

H.M.S. *Raglan* (monitor) 116–117
railways 6, 12, 20–21, 24, 29, 42–44, 59, 62–63, 74, 79, 93, 100, 105, 113, 136, 138, 146, 148, 158–159, 166, 169, 175, 179, 187, 203, 205, 207, 212, 220, 222, 227, 230–231, 240, 249; from Suez Canal to Gaza 63; *see also* armored trains
raises (certain Egyptian C.T.C. personnel) 63
Ramallah 177
Rantieh 169
Ras el Ain 195, 199
Ras el Tin 173
Raspberry Hill (Gaza III) 116
rats 279
Reconnaisance Corps **28**
Red Cross 37, 153–154, 277
Red House Wood (Sharon) 182
Red Sea 2
Regent's Park (Gaza III) 115
Regimental Reunion Dinners 235
Rennison, Padré the Rev. E.D., C.F. 39, 167
Requin, French 80, 116–117
Revelation *see* Bible
Revolt in the Desert 275
Richmond 2nd Lieutenant 126
riots 229–230, 231, 239
Robertson, General Sir William 5, 42, 100, 203, 221
Rolfe, Sapper Frank 279
Rolph, Sergeant 182
Roman temple 172
Romans 12, 57
Romani, Battle of 49–**50**
Romford, Essex 223, 259n20
Romford to Beirut, via France, Egypt and Jericho 259n20, 273–274
H.M.T. *Rose* 178
Rose of Gaza 108, 269n23
Rouge Farm, Red House Wood (Mulebbis/Mirr) 182
Round Hill (Suez Canal defenses) **25**, **43**, 49, 51
Royal Air Force (R.A.F.) 179, 278
Royal Army Medical Corps (R.A.M.C.) 21, 51, 65, 75, 145, 240
Royal Artillery 116, 244–245, 247; heavy batteries 79, 246, 248; siege batteries 80, 246, 248;
Royal Engineers 36, 41, 65, 121, 152, 169, 246, 248
Royal Field Artillery 246–248
Royal Flying Corps 46, 53, 81, 95, 179, 248
Royal Fusiliers 179
Royal Garrison Artillery 248
Royal Gloucester Hussars 19, 46, 179, 213, 278
Royal Horse Artillery 245–246
Royal Irish Rifles 246–247
Royal Navy 3, 13–**14**, 79, 102, 114
Royal Scots 123, 128; Fusiliers 246–247
Royal Welch Fusiliers 11, 245–246

Index

Ruin Hill (Mulebbis/Mirr) 172
rum ration 139–140
Rumbelow, Private W. Vincent 93–*95*, 278

saddlers (Egyptian C.T.C. personnel) 63
"Said" 31
Said, Emir 210–212
St. Mary's Church 237
Saki Bey 211
Saladin 72, 181, 233
Salford Post (Suez Canal defenses) 45
Salonika (Greece) 5–6, 11–12, 32, 34, 50, 98, 106, 179, 203, 207, 221, 223
Samaria 187, 208
Samson and the Gates of Gaza 63, 72, 134, 137, 264*n*22; *see also* Bible
Samson Ridge (Gaza) 56, 80, 90, 94, 108, 132
Samson's Necklace 105
sand bags 46, 48, 105, 121, 127, 129, 257
sand dunes 69, 80, 122–123, 132–133
sand fly fever 136, 176, 267*n*67
sand storms 25, 32, 42, 45–46
sangars 172, 182–183
sanitary squads (Egyptian C.T.C.) 63
sanitation 41, 98
Sarepta *see* Surafend
Sarona 174, 268*n*11
Sassoon, Lieutenant Siegfried 12–15, 20, 45, 170, 177
Saul, King 186
Savoy Hotel (Cairo) 34, 43
Schwarz, Captain Marek 153
Scottish Rifles 120, 122, 247
Scurry Hill (Sharon) 193
Sea of Galilee 186
Sea of Tiberias 201
Seaforth Highlanders 289
Sedgewick, Sergeant 149, *151*
Seirat (Sinai) 56–*57*, 62, 65, 69, 82, 93
Senussi 21, *23–24*, 262*n*42
Serapeum 46, 48, 51
Seven Pillars of Wisdom 268*n*19
Sharon 140, 203
Sharon, Battle of 191–196; *see also* 'Azzum Ibn 'Atme; Beisan; Bureid Ridge; Crown Hill; Hableh; Hudeira; Jevis Tepe; Kefar Bara; Kh. Der el Qassia; Kh. Es Sumra; Kh. Sirisia; Majdal Yaba; Mesha; Mezeireh; Musmus Pass; Oglu Tepe; Ra-fat salient; Sivri Tepe; Sivri Wood; Three Bushes Hill; Tul Keram
Sharon, Plain of 140, 163, 172, 190, 203, 217, 240
Shea, Major General J.S.M., C.B., C.M.G., D.S.O., G.O.C. 152, 154, 231, 246
Sheikh Abbas Ridge (Gaza I, II, and III) 56, 65, 76, 80–82, *83*, 86–88, 90–*91*, 94, 115, 143, 264*n*43; 54th Division's role in seizure of 64–65, 79–80, 108; first occupied 64; relinquished 79; retaken 108
Sheikh Aijin (Gaza) 80, *84*, 94, 97, 115, 120
Sheikh Gharbawi 159

Sheikh Hasan (Gaza III) 114–115, 119, 121, 123, 129–130
Sheikh Muwannis 160
Sheikh Redwan (Gaza II and III) 82
Sheikh Zowaid 12; Sheikh Zowaid Redoubt (Gaza I, II, and III) 62, 128, 131
Shellal (Gaza) 12, 51, 76, 80
Shepherd's Hotel (Cairo) 36, 261*n*36
Sheria 55–56, 118, 127, 137–139; wells of 138–139
Sherif Nasir 212
Sherif of Mecca 210
Sherwood Rangers 245
Short Wood (Mulebbis) 169
sickness 6, 179, 200, 214
Sidi Bisr 8, 19, 25
Sidon 219
Sikhs 11
Sinai Peninsula 45, 50–51, 55, 59, 62–63, 75, 102, 104, 107, 114, 121, 133, 149, 153, 155
"Sir Archibald Murray" [a tank] 88
Sirius 25
Sisera 188
Sivri Tepe (Battle of Sharon) 190, 194–195
Sivri Wood (Battle of Sharon) 194–195
Smith, Brigadier General C.L., V.C., M.C. 245
Smith, Private H.H. 210
Solomon's Pools 152, 218
Sore, Sapper 87
sound-ranging 159
South Africa: Field Artillery Brigade; 159 participation 111, 159, 205, 248, 271*n*77
South African Wars 258
Spaull, L/Corporal John 210
Sphinx Post (Suez Canal defenses) 49, 51
Squires, Dr. W.H.T. 276
star shells 25, 179
Station Post (Mulebbis) 169
Stokes' mortars 123
Stone, Gunner 123
storemen (Egyptian C.T.C.) 63
Storrs, Sir Ronald 38, 276
stretcher-bearers 142, 210
Sublime Porte (Constantinople) 184
Suez 10, 37, 52, 99; Suez Canal 3, 5–6, 12, 19, 42–43, 45–46, 49, 55, 57, 105, 113–114, 116, 160
Sufa (Judæan Hills) 177
Suffolk, County of 235–*236*; West Suffolk 278
Suffolk Regiment, battalions: 1/5th 30–*31*, 39–40, 48–49, 58–59, 70, 82–83, 85–88, 102, 108, 128, 131, **152**, 156, 166, 171–*173*, 176–177, 192–193, 197–199, 228–229, 232, 239–240, 247, 253, 258, 278
Suffolk Regimental Museum 290
Suffolk Regiment's Old Comrades' Association 235
Suffolk Yeomanry (15th battalion) 246, 287–288, 290; barracks 299
Sukri Pasha Ayoubi 210, 212

Surafend 161–162
Susan Trench (Gaza III) 130–131
Sweet Water Canal 12
Syria 133, 146, 181, 185, 204, 213–214, 218–220, 222, 224–225, 232, 239

H.M.S. *Tagus* 227
Tank Redoubt (Gaza battles) 85, 88–89, 265n84
Tank Ridge (Gaza) 88
tanks: detachment (Gaza III) 115–116, 120; employment of 83, 85–89, 224, 265n84; Private Mortlock's opinion of 170
Taranto 20, 178, 235
Tasker, L/Corporal 127
Teichman *see* Teichmann
Teichmann 51, 65, 75, 77, 90, 145–146, 161–163, 173, 240, 276–277
Tel Jemmi (Gaza) 94
Tell el Ahmar (Gaza) 82
Tell el Sheria (Beersheba/Gaza) 137
temple (Mulebbis/Mirr) 172
Templers 166–167, 268n11
Tewfik, Port 46
Thaxted (Essex) 50, 99
Thetford (Norfolk) 232
Three Bushes Hill (Battle of Sharon) 193
Thutmose III 17, 188
Tibbs, Lieutenant 123
Tiberias, Sea of 201
tibn 43
Tiller, Major 75–76, 202
The Times (London) 71–72, 78, 92–93, 132–134, 136–138, 207, 210, 212–213, 217–218, 231–232, 277
Timsah, Lake 48, 259n26
Tirailleurs Algeriéns 193
Tireh (Philistia) 258
Tortoise Hill (Gaza III) 123
Toussum (Suez Canal defenses) 51
trench mortar battery 97
trench warfare training 98
Triangle Trench (Gaza III) 128, 131
Tul Keram (Battle of Sharon) 187, 202
Turkish Divisions/Regiments: 3rd 121; 4th 75–76; 7th 121, 185, 202; 11th 76, 202; 16th 76, 201; 20th 202; 46th 202; 53rd 121; 79th 75; 125th 75
Turner, Private Freddie **35**, 112–114, **119**, 136, 172
Turtle Hill (Gaza III) 120
Tyler, Sergeant 209
Tyre 218–219

umbrella: inside out one adopted by 54th Division 136–137
Umbrella Hill (Gaza) 56, 105, 114–115, 119–124, 133–134
Umm el Bureid 182
University of El Azhar (Cairo) 230
Uttridge, Private Harry 279

venereal disease 37–38, 41
Verminous 139
Vernon, Brigadier General H.A., D.S.O. 245
Véry Lights 182, 213, 223
Vester, Mrs. Fred 153–154
veterinary orderlies (Egyptian C.T.C.) 63
Viney, Major H.B., M.C. 174
Von Falkenhayn, General Erich 104, **105**, 117, 146, 239
Von Sanders, General Otto Liman 184, 192, 200–203, 222, 239, 275

Wadi Ayun 193, 198–199
Wadi Ballut (Mulebbis/Mirr) 172
Wadi Boundary 172–**173**
Wadi Deben 192
Wadi el Arish (River of Egypt) 55
Wadi Ghuzzie 56, 62, 64–65, **66**, 69, 72, 74–75, 77–80, 92, 94, 97
Wadi Hesi 134, 138
Wadi Ikbar 192
Wadi Ishkar 175
Wadi Jofet Zeben 165
Wadi Kumran 165
Wadi Maraba 211
Wadi Mukaddeme 86–87
Wadi Nukhabir 69, 80
Wadi Orwell 192
Wadi Raba 182, 190, 194
Wadi Simeon 115
Wadir 41
Wafd 232
Walker, Captain 25, 192
Walters, Corporal Herman Edwin 266n37
War Cabinet 78, 93, 100, 174–175, 177, 221, 277
War Council 74, 176, 203
War Graves Commission (Commonwealth) 95
War Memoirs of David Lloyd George 266
War Memorial (Australian) 213
Ward, Brigadier General T., C.M.G., C.O. 64, 86, 120, 156, 172, 247
Warley Wood (Mulebbis) 163
Warnes, Captain G.G. 156
The Warren 79
water 12, 20, 42, 44–45, 48, 50, 56–58, 62–65, 70, 74, 82–83, 92, 97, 105–107, 113, 117–118, 121, 128, 139–140, 149, 152–153, 187, 199, 216–218, 221, 234, 265n71; dumps 97; filtration of 12; pipelines 6, 12, 106, 152; supply 12, 92, 121, 152, 161, 163, 221; transport of 187, 265n71; wells 187; *see also fanatis*
watermelon 141
Watford 253
"Watling Street" (Gaza III) 120
Watsham, Sergeant Harold 125
Watson, Brigadier General C.F., D.S.O. 152, 246
Watts, Trooper Walter 279

Wavell, Colonel Archibald Percival (later Field Marshal Sir 34, 76, 184, 192, 213–214, 220, 277
wells: of Sheria 138–139
Welsh infantry 72–73
West Mirr 163
western front 1, 5, 14,17, 29, 45, 51, 53, 92, 104, 116–117, 133, 171, 175, 177, 203, 220–222, 228, 273
Whitehall 275
Wigan, Brigadier General 245
Wigh el-Birka 41
Wilhelma 161, 166–*167*, 268*n*11
Williams, Private Maurice *32*, 279
Willmer, Major Fritz 202
Wilson, Brigadier General, C.O. 210, 245
Wilson, General Sir Henry, C.I.G.S. 203, 222
Wilson, Lieutenant Robert Henry 19, 46, 107, 179, 213
Wilson, Major W.E., D.S.O. 127–128, 131, 161
Wilson, Sergeant Major Coy 126
wine 163, 166, 170
Wingate, General Sir Reginald 229
Wintringham, Lieutenant Colonel 42–43, 277
wire-netting roads 57–*58*, 121
With the 1st/5th Essex in the East 274
With the Lincolnshire Yeomanry in Egypt and Palestine
Wollaston, Lieutenant Colonel, C.O. 48–*49*, 156, 171

Wolton, Captain Eric Donald, D Company 44, 88–89, 105, 113, 156, 167, 171–172
Wolton, Lieutenant H.C. 156, 172, 235–237
The World Crisis 274
Worlington (Suffolk) 235
Wray, Lieutenant, A/Captain 125, 182

Yehudieh 156
Yeomanry Mounted Division 103, 106, 245
Yeomanry Regiments: Berkshire 245; Buckinghamshire 245; City of London 245; County of London 246; Gloucestershire 245; Hertfordshire 248; *see also* Imperial Yeomanry Brigade
Young Men's Christian Association (Y.M.C.A.) 37–38, 146, 227, 260; American involvement with 37, 262*n*42
Youngs, Sergeant G., 13 Platoon 193
Yunis Trench (Gaza III) 130

Zaghlul, Saad 250
Zecheriah *see* Bible
Zeifizfiyeh Hill 156
Zeitoun (Egypt) 232
Zero Hour 79–80, 120, 191
Zimmarin 217
Zionism 281
zoo 31
Zowaid Trench (Gaza III) 123–125, 127, 267*n*53

www.ingramcontent.com/pod-product-compliance
Ingram Content Group UK Ltd.
Pitfield, Milton Keynes, MK11 3LW, UK
UKHW041925140426
5217IPUK00014B/319